The Music Makers

The Music Makers

Deena Rosenberg Bernard Rosenberg

Foreword by Barry S. Brook

1979

Columbia University Press

New York

Deena Rosenberg is a musicologist and a writer on music.

Bernard Rosenberg is Professor of Sociology at the City College of the City University of New York.

Portions of the Gregor Piatigorsky interview appeared in The New York *Times*, September 19, 1976, and in *Musical America*, November 1976. Used by permission, all rights reserved.

The Michael Steinberg interview appeared in *The Musical Newsletter* vol. 6, no. 4 (Fall 1976). Used by permission.

Library of Congress Cataloging in Publication Data

Rosenberg, Deena, 1951–
   The music makers.

   Includes index.
   1. Musicians—Interviews. I. Rosenberg,
Bernard, 1925–   joint author. II. Title.
ML385.R8   780'.92'2 [B]   78–15564
ISBN 0–231–03953–0

Columbia University Press
New York Guildford, Surrey

To Sarah, Daniel, and Rebecca—
without whom nothing would be possible

Contents

Foreword   ix
Overview   1

Part I. Composers

1. Aaron Copland   31
2. Milton Babbitt   39
3. Miriam Gideon   61
4. Theodore Antoniou   71
5. Earle Brown   79

Part II. Scholars and Teachers

6. Edward Downes, Musical Man of Letters   95
7. Leonard Stein, Music Educator   115
8. Carl Schachter, Music Theorist   129
9. Frank Hubbard, Harpsicord Maker   143

Part III. Conductors

10. Eugene Ormandy   155
11. Margaret Hillis   161
12. Neville Marriner   171
13. Michael Tilson Thomas   185

Part IV. Performers

14. Gregor Piatigorsky, Cellist   205
15. Claudio Arrau, Pianist   217
16. Lydia Artymiw, Pianist   229
17. Doriot Anthony Dwyer, Flutist   237
18. Kurt Loebel, Violinist   251
19. Julius Levine, Free-Lance Bass Player   263
20. Kermit Moore, Free-Lance Cellist   277

21. Eileen Farrell, Singer 289
22. Larry Adler, Harmonica Player 297

Part V. Music in the Inner City

23. Dorothy Maynor, Singer 313
24. Henry Mazer, Conductor 325
25. Natalie Limonick, Opera Coach and
  Music Educator 331

Part VI. Managers, Patrons, Impresarios

26. Harry Zelzer, Impresario 343
27. Rudolph Bing, Opera Manager 353
28. John Edwards, Orchestra Manager 363
29. Paul Fromm, Music Patron 377
30. Lawrence Morton, Concert Manager 393

Part VII. Critics

31. Thomas Willis 411
32. Michael Steinberg 433

Index (compiled by Donna Whiteman) 455

Foreword

This book was created by a sociologist and his musicologist daughter who have sought to document the patterns and panorama of contemporary musical life exclusively through the techniques of oral history.

The traditional historian usually writes history long after the fact. In most cases, when he begins his work, all but the merest fraction of the significant evidence has been dispersed or has disappeared altogether. The measure of his effectiveness lies first in his skill in unearthing whatever evidence has survived, second, in the degree to which his explanation fits the evidence, and third, in the extent to which his intuition and imagination succeed in weaving evidence, hypothesis, and conclusion into a convincing chronicle.

The oral historian functions differently. To begin with, he is not writing history; he is employing a method of gathering contemporary historical data. His method provides the traditional historian and the historical disciplines with an added dimension, for he sets out deliberately to create a body of significant evidence. The measure of his effectiveness lies first in the extent of his preparation and planning before interviewing, so that he knows what evidence to seek; second, in his skill in selecting the most appropriate respondents and his sensitivity to them before, during, and after interviewing so that the significant evidence is accumulated; and third, in the accuracy, objectivity, and usability of his presentation of that evidence. Strictly speaking, his work as an oral historian stops there. He may then, of course, transform himself into a traditional historian, by weighing, evaluating, and sifting the oral evidence against hypotheses and conclusions—in precisely the same way the scholar deals with evidence of any other kind—and by using it in conjunction with such evidence.

An advantage of his oral evidence is that he himself has planned its creation. He is thus better able to assess its truthfulness than is the traditional historian, who must deal with literary sources with which he has had no prior connection. Furthermore, after studying all available evidence (written and oral) he can often resolve contradictions therein by further interviewing. To give some idea of oral history's importance at present, it should be noted that in the fifth supplement of the *Dictionary of American Biography* "sixty percent of the entries had to be produced without collections of letters or papers." As this ratio increases, so will the significance of oral history.

The Rosenbergs have demonstrated splendidly that there are other advantages to oral history. I am referring to the nature and breadth of the evidence that oral history is ideally suited to produce: the intimacies, the subtleties, the inflections—the sound and sense of a life history. It is not that written sources, such as letters and memoirs, are totally lacking in this type of evidence. The point is that in an age in which letter writing has been so extensively replaced by telephoning, few people write anything but lists, checks, and postcards. Indeed, several of the lesser known music makers whose words and views are recorded in this volume might otherwise have remained "unheard" altogether—and forever—were it not for the availability of oral history procedure. This is why old people carrying dying traditions are prime subjects for oral history. The more famous music makers can be too busy selling themselves to the public to provide the real answers. And the interviewing journalist is often so bent on extracting a hot story that he ignores vital, long-range questions with which the historian or sociologist would be concerned.

As an historical musicologist who has specialized in eighteenth-century music, I have studied and written about countless musicians—including many *illustres inconnus*—about whom information could hardly have been more meager. This had led me, naturally, to libraries, archives, memoirs, newspapers, and quite often frustration. It led me to a concern for the means and methods of gathering evidence—in all periods. It has led to an interest in oral history, to discussions with successful practitioners of it in music such as Thomas Willis and Vivian Perlis, to consultation with Louis M. Starr and Elizabeth B. Mason, director and co-director of the Oral History Office of Columbia University, which concentrates on statesmen and writers, and to the establishment at the City University of New York of the Project for the Oral History of Music in

America, or POHMA, of which the present volume is the first published product.

There are interesting distinctions—as well as similarities—between the nature of traditional documentation and that created by oral history. This can be demonstrated by looking at the case of Mozart, about whom promoters of oral history often say: "How wonderful it would be if we could talk to Mozart via time machine and tape recorder!" This despite the fact that Mozart is probably the best documented composer before the nineteenth century. (Whenever possible, his doting father preserved every note and word his son put down on paper.) The letters, as will be seen in a moment, are of particular importance to history—and to our discussion. First, an outline of what we do know about Mozart and his music in Paris of 1778: (1) the musical documents; the works of art themselves; (2) the literary sources—his letters of course, other people's letters and memoirs, newspapers, archives, and the like; (3) the iconographical sources, here unfortunately all too few. Using these documents we can create, to a limited extent, a portrait of Parisian musical culture at the precise period when it was intersected by Mozart's presence and music.

We do indeed know a lot about Mozart, and yet so little; so many unanswered questions remain. Were oral history available two hundred years ago, we could learn, for example, what Mozart thought of Parisian musical life and culture in 1778 when, at the age of 22, accompanied by his mother, he visited the French capital in pursuit of fame and fortune. We could also learn what his fellow composers thought of him; what the conductor, the bassoonist, and the concert master of the Concert Spiritual, as well as the nobleman, the burgher, and the student in the audience had to say; what his then dying mother could tell us, and why he left Paris so precipitously. Above all, we could learn *why* he made many of his artistic choices and career decisions.

Wolfgang's many letters are prized among literary sources of any place and time. Why are they so treasured? First, they are informative and accurate, as only first-hand observations can be. There is no intervention or interpretation by another; since he was communicating mainly with people he loved and trusted, they are written in the most personal mode, with the fewest motives to distort the truth. Second, they are spontaneous: they were written when he had something he wished to say: they communicated wit, word, a stream of consciousness, which almost projects Mozart into the present. Third, they are revelatory: they provide insight into Mozart's mind, creative process, and perception of self. At best the letters conjure up the private, unconscious, and metaphysical realm.

His letters, in short, represent an intimate self-portrait, a personal chronicle of his life and work, and a kind of inner gyroscope. These are also the special qualities—in task and promise—of oral history. Thus, when thinking of what the letters offer and what one would like to know in addition about Mozart and his music, about his lesser contemporaries and the social, political, and cultural milieu in which they lived, one recognizes more easily the kinds of questions the oral historian should ask today.

The rich potentials of oral history in music are illustrated by the variety of studies initiated or sponsored by POHMA and carried out by students, faculty, and associates. Among the specific projects now under way are monographs about Roger Sessions, Nadia Boulanger, and Yip Harburg; retrospective studies (through students and colleagues) of Edgard Varèse and Stefan Volpe; a discussion of women composers in America; and works on jazz in our time, the American musical theater, the urban free-lance musician, audience response to serious concert music, and of course *The Music Makers.*

The mode of interviewing and the presentation of the results may vary widely. The Rosenbergs preferred to work together during the interview. This usually resulted in a relaxed three-way conversation with each interviewer, operating from different vantage points, checking and supplementing the other. This method has been highly successful in other projects and will often avoid the necessity of retakes. In their preparation of the spoken material for publication they have chosen to incorporate their questions within the subjects' narrative, thereby seeming to remove themselves completely from the finished product. Having heard and seen the raw tapes and transcripts, I can attest to the skill and integrity with which they have been edited. This is not a matter of authentic source versus freewheeling interpretation. Transcribed raw oral data do not always make for easy reading. As long as the sources themselves can be consulted when desired, the type of presentation Denna and Bernard Rosenberg have chosen is eminently valid, and it is preferable to finding the interviewer's own questions and lengthy statements forever intruding upon the continuity of the subject's words.

The Music Makers demonstrates another and powerful oral history function, the kaleidoscopic portrait of serious musical life of our time as seen through the articulate voices of 32 key individuals. Their words are lightly distilled from their responses to a carefully orchestrated series of questions—questions designed to reveal basic patterns, divergences, and developments.

No musician—be he singer, scholar, or harpsichord maker —can be isolated in any one area of music, nor within his own area of technical expertise. The countless makers of music functioning today are all pushing in many contradictory directions. They operate on many levels and as members of many different pressure groups. And the actions of any one music maker will affect the lives of many individuals and institutions. Thus the decisions of a Michael Tilson Thomas, who must face orchestra, board of directors, critics, management, soloists, radio and television moguls, and audiences, are crucial for thousands; the appointment of a Michael Steinberg to a powerful critic's post in Boston caused widespread reactions and crosscurrents. His resignation to work for the Boston Symphony Orchestra set a whole new series of ripples into motion.

As Adam Smith might have viewed it, what seems like organized chaos, with thousands of individual musical entrepreneurs and institutions working at cross purposes, causes musical life today—and the economy and culture as a whole—to move forward. No one person can grasp it all, no one can really do much to hold it back or move it ahead. Yet we must strive to grasp how all the parts of the musical firmament fit together, for unless we understand something of the whole, we can never really comprehend any of its parts. It was the objective of the Rosenbergs in this study, to provide the materials that will help us understand the whole, an objective they have realized brilliantly.

Barry S. Brook
Director, Project for the
Oral History of Music in America
City University of New York
June 1978

Overview

Human culture taken as a whole may be described as the process of man's progressive self-liberation. Language, art, religion, science, are various phases in this process. In all of them man discovers and proves a new power—the power to build up a world of his own, an "ideal" world. Philosophy cannot give up its search for a fundamental unity in this ideal world. But it does not confound this unity with simplicity. It does not overlook the tensions and frictions, the strong contrasts and deep conflicts between the various powers of man. These cannot be reduced to a common denominator. They tend in different directions and obey different principles. But this multiplicity and disparateness do not denote discord or disharmony. All these functions complete and complement one another. Each one opens a new horizon and shows us a new aspect of humanity. The dissonant is in harmony with itself; the contraries are not mutually exclusive, but interdependent: "Harmony in contrariety, as in the case of the bow and the lyre."—from *An Essay on Man* by Ernst Cassirer

The Music Makers

This book is about the social substance of music making. That substance is to be found in the patterns of perception which music makers themselves reveal. The floor will be theirs in a moment—after we strike a note or two in defense of the sociological approach that underlies our inquiry.

Music and Civilization

To be human is to endow objects with meaning and value. When men and women evolved from an arboreal past, they became decisively differentiated from all other animals, most distinctively as a species that communicates with symbols. With their erect posture, plus their highly developed nervous systems, human beings created a culture and thereby re-created the physical environment that enveloped them. Each of many little bands evolved a dynamic "universe of discourse" by which their members were not only able to beget but also to transmit and perpetuate culture.

Any discussion of human affairs must begin with the culture concept—anthropologically defined to include everything made by man. Within this culture concept one can distinguish (analytically if not otherwise) between material and nonmaterial culture, between our tools and our rules, or between technology and conventions, ideas, folkways, and mores. Together they constitute human culture, which is divided into very many separate cultures. Upon close examination each of the separate cultures turns out to be a mosaic of small units, sometimes called subcultures. If we believe in "the psychic unity of mankind," as the authors do, it is worth our while to postulate a common human nature and therefore to join the quest for generalizations that fit every member of our species. Without that quest, social science or philosophical anthropology has little to offer those who contemplate the human condition. But just as a grain of sand may contain the whole universe, so the study of one subculture can lead us to a deeper understanding of the symbolic forest through which we all wander.

With time, and most especially since industrial civilization, that forest has grown thicker and denser, so that today we can seldom make our way through the cultural maze that confronts us. To disentangle the complexities of language, age, and sex has never been easy. It is necessary to cope with them at every level of social organization—and industrial civilization remorselessly piles one level upon another. The rudimentary division of labor with which we began now yields to a steadily more complex division of labor. Then the age of super-specialization descends upon us. With it comes more sub-cultural segmentation. Whole groups, no matter how close or far apart physically, occupy worlds of their own, each encapsulated in its own special sphere.

All this has a direct bearing on our subject matter. So too does that short list of "universals" you will find in almost any textbook devoted to the human enterprise. Such a list is short because it rarely goes beyond "the family" and "religion," for no known culture is devoid of either. But the list is scandalously incomplete if it omits a major universal which sociologists, but not anthropologists or historians, do tend to omit—that universal which we call art.

The universality of art is—or should be—a starting point for further inquiry. Evidence abounds that art is an integral part of every culture. To the ancient thinkers who invented philosophy this fact was self-evident. When they came to reflect upon art, men like Plato decided that it was basically an act of reproduction or imitation. Despite constant criticism, the Platonic theory persists in many quarters. That it has enjoyed so long a vogue is testimony, in John Dewey's opinion, of a close connection between the fine arts and daily life. Had the idea of art as imitation (Mimesis) been remote from our everyday experience, it would never have occurred to anyone. As Dewey notes, "the doctrine did not signify that art was a literal copying of objects, but that it reflected the emotions and ideas that are associated with the chief institutions of social life." Plato felt the connection so strongly (just as tyrants today feel it) that he came to favor censorship of poets, dramatists, and musicians. Dewey writes that Plato may have exaggerated in saying that a change from the Dorian to the Lydian mode in music would be the sure precursor of civic degeneration, but no contemporary of the Athenian philosopher would have doubted that music was an integral part of the ethos and the institutions of the community. Whoever doubts it today is lacking in Plato's elementary insight.

If art is an integral part of human culture, then the esthetic impulse is quite possibly an integral part of human nature. Art is about as necessary to us as love or sex: without them, we can go on living, but with considerable diminution of our well-being.

Small children spontaneously express themselves with whatever art materials they find. They react to art and to music with a measure of authenticity few of them attain later on in their lives. What happens is like what has happened to American taste buds in this era of frozen and packaged foods. Bread, once the staff of life, is now a compost of air and glue; oats, which once only horses ate, are sold as dry cereal. A diet like this can deaden anyone's palate. With gruel today and gruel tomorrow, who can savor gourmet meals? Similarly, prolonged pseudosexual behavior produces fixation at that level, all but barring real erotic fulfillment.

In precisely the same way, kitsch and instant education, if ingested long enough, lead to intellectual dyspepsia or anesthesia. This circumstance is a direct threat to the public; to audiences; to "culture consumers," as one pop sociologist has barbarously and in some perverse sense accurately dubbed them. For people may be robbed of an essential esthetic experience that unimpeded would only add to their humanity. Without that esthetic experience, they will turn to lifeless and perpetually unsatisfying substitutes.

Yet art has survived all attempts to squelch it. And artists, whether ignored or oppressed, persevere and sometimes flourish against all odds. Like every one of us, they suffer even in the best of times. And these are scarcely the best of times. What is it about these times in this country that differentially impinges on those artists, and certain of their auxiliaries, who make music for us? Not all music, but the kind generally called "classical." Finicky scholars point out that much "Classical" music is actually "Romantic." Their point is well taken. But so far they have achieved no consensus about an alternative term. Experts, when not themselves lapsing into the old nomenclature, offer the layman a choice among "art music," "concert music," and "serious music." Each term has its shortcomings. We will settle for any of them so long as they are understood to represent an art form significantly different from, although sometimes blended with, "popular music" and "folk music"—related fields to which rough-and-ready meanings are also attached. If we consider all of human history, the distinction between one kind of music and another is fairly recent, but for some time and with no necessarily pejorative intention, it has been worth making.

We turn then to the world of "classical" music making, a small but extraordinarily diverse occupational subculture, encompassing many professions: composers, teachers and scholars, a wide variety of practitioners (including conductors, instrumentalists of all kinds, and singers), managers and patrons, and critics. Thus the musical world is inhabited by individuals with varied perspectives; they compose in a profusion of styles, teach many different aspects of music, play one or more among numerous instruments, make music alone or in groups, and hope to reach elite or mass audiences. By presenting the views of men and women who make music happen in vastly varied ways, we hope to convey many if not all of the layers and dimensions of a rich and complex little universe.

Thirty-two people speak to us in these pages, and each one has an intrinsically interesting story to tell. All of them deserve the full-scale treatment very few are likely to receive. Indeed, after repeated contact, we were sorely tempted to think of the life of any one of our cast of characters as the basis for a whole book. Such literature does exist. Some technical studies and even some metaphysical disquisitions in this field are superb. Diaries, letters, biographies, and very occasionally autobiographies, brilliantly illuminate what might otherwise have remained forever obscure. There are also *Talks With . . . Composers* or *Conductors* or *Performers*.

These uneven compendia have their uses. We do not intend to belittle them by taking a related but basically different tack. It is not exactly the tack of academic musicology, which deals overwhelmingly with the inner history and formal development of music. Rather, our concern is to supplement all other musicological sources with documents such as those that follow, which taken together provide a more complete picture of American musical society.

These documents are painstakingly assembled out of taped and transcribed, three-way, open-ended interviews. Rapport—but not so much of it as to preclude a measure of detachment—was absolutely essential in these exchanges. Experience has taught us that the presence of a second interviewer facilitates the necessary rapport. Furthermore, in this case, for reasons of affinity and consanguinity, the interviewers (one a musicologist, the other a sociologist) understand their joint purpose rather well. Finally, they have edited themselves out of each conversation and rearranged responses only for the sake of coherence.

All along, the basic idea was to present a kaleidoscopic view of serious music makers, to clarify how they got where they are and what makes them tick. To that end, we set out four years ago equipped with certain preconceptions drawn from our respective areas of competence. These preconceptions were sometimes confirmed, at other times not, and frequently so modified that by now it may be fair to call them only researchable hypotheses. Ours is an effort for which we make no greater claim than that it seems to us to be richly suggestive.

Since our chosen area of study is so vast, we could scarcely dream of covering every function, the total process, or the entire structure of classical music in this country. On the periphery of the musical subculture and in its interstices may be located several more types than are found in this book (yes, we should hear from the record manufacturer, the music publisher, and so on). We have had to pick and choose, sacrificing some scope for depth where, for one reason or another, it seemed wise to do so. Though all-inclusiveness was out of the question, our book *does* cover a range of types and themes seldom before attempted within this context.

Socialization

How does one get to be a composer in the first place? Or a conductor? A musician of any kind? Or for that matter, an opera coach, a free-lance rather than a steadily employed performer, a manager, a patron? With any such question we plunge into all the issues surrounding socialization—that process through which culture, in this instance musical culture, is transmitted by its bearers to those who will soon be its bearers.

For psychologists, socialization pertains to the early years of life, and nowhere are those years slighted in this book. We accept the proposition that, apart from genius—where genetic endowment might well be operative—to a great extent environment determines whether people are musical or not. The Suzuki method, by which very young children—irrespective of their ancestry—are quickly transformed into proficient performers is only the most recent evidence in support of that proposition. Dorothy Maynor, famous as a singer, returned to teaching, her first love, some years ago. She presides over the Harlem School of the Arts, where it is a daily delight to her that the Suzuki method continuously vindicates her faith in it.

Schools count, but there are very few like the Harlem School.

Even the sparse fare of traditional public schools exercised a positive effect on the musical development of our American-educated respondents. Some have fond recollections of their early schooling, and others shudder at the mention of it; but all somehow profited from that modicum of curricular and extracurricular music that was once taken for granted. Only in the past few years have music and art come to be defined by some administrators as totally expendable frills. As public schools are eroded by austerity, these "frills" are being eliminated. Musical entrepreneurs not only deplore the spread of this misfortune, but they also worry about who in a culturally starved generation will grow up to fill their halls. Consequently, symphony managers and musical directors foster youth concerts. Henry Mazer, assistant conductor of the Chicago Symphony, found himself in charge of such concerts. He discovered that his job consisted of busing unprepared ghetto children to concerts that had no meaning for them. Convinced that "you can't just take kids off the streets, put them in a hall and expect them to know how to react," Mazer began bringing music to the schools. He shows sensitivity and enthusiasm in the performance of this task—which is nevertheless Sysyphean even in his own eyes.

School was once a major agency of musical socialization. For the present, it has very largely ceased to be that. More important is the church whose choral liturgy, hymnody, and psalmody have much to do with the origin of Western music and almost everything to do with the origin of American music. By their own attestation, sacred music helped, in varying measure, to shape the musical sensibilities of Earle Brown, Lawrence Morton, Eileen Farrell, Dorothy Maynor, Thomas Willis, Aaron Copland, Miriam Gideon, Julius Levine, Larry Adler, and Michael Tilson Thomas (on some of whom, notably the last two, Yiddish folk and theatrical music made a greater impact than cantorial or other synagogue music). Evidently the church has purveyed some kind of musical inspiration throughout this secular century. Since church attendance waxes as much as it wanes, institutionalized religion may continue to have this effect.

We cannot ignore radio as an impersonal agency of socialization. The New York Philharmonic under Walter Damrosch and the NBC Symphony under Arturo Toscanini, like the Metropolitan Opera Saturday matinee performances, boradcast live, left a lasting impression on children who later became singers, players, composers, and critics. They were, however, children of the 1930s and 1940s, a pre-TV era the young nowadays have trouble even imagining. Milton Babbitt's description of a cross-country drive in which his car radio picked up nothing but rock, or country and western music dramatizes the change in that medium. With the advent of FM, radio was polarized: as AM preserved mass culture, medium-and-highbrow culture, including recorded "serious" music with its special problems, was consigned to FM. It was a fateful split similar to that which obtains today between commercial and public television. For the last thirty years radio has been of relatively minor importance in igniting the musical imagination of Americans.

Be that as it may, the principal theorists of socialization (Jean Piaget, Sigmund Freud, George Herbert Mead, Émile Durkheim and Charles Horton Cooley) all emphasized direct, intimate, face-to-face or "primary group" association. That the enormous plasticity of one's earliest years can never be recaptured is incontrovertible. And these are the years in which socialization, chiefly by parents but also by age-mates, is generally thought to take place. Of late, however, it has occurred to more and more observers that socialization is a life-long process. Quite often the individual is socialized into a spineless state so flexible that rapid, if not effortless, changes of personality can take place. While far from rigid, our subjects differ markedly from the norm, exhibiting strongly formed "inner-directed" rather than "other-directed" personalities; they are not given to shifting with the winds of doctrine that sway most of us. And much of this is no doubt due to the nature of their childhood socialization.

On that score we learn, for instance, that the mothers of Doriot Dwyer, Margaret Hillis, and Eileen Farrell took them out of their provincial settings to big-city concerts, and in general supervised their exposure to "good" music. Dwyer's first teacher was her mother, and so was Hillis'. Neville Marriner, from a small English town, and Philadelphia-bred Lydia Artymiw (still in her early twenties) stress the significance of having had fathers who practiced with them. To Claudio Arrau and Michael Steinberg it is important that their mothers were pianists. Milton Babbitt and Michael Tilson Thomas speak of two musically oriented parents. The grandmothers of Margaret Hillis and John Edwards, played a role in eliciting their musicality. Earle Brown's father sang, as Aaron Copland's sister played the piano to accompany an older brother's violin. Miriam Gideon was "adopted" in her adolescence by an uncle who became her mentor.

Gregor Piatigorsky insists that, as a little boy, he was "neither encouraged nor discouraged" by his family, but that he himself "felt absolutely determined to become a musician." Nevertheless, his parents "played without really being musicians" and he "heard music at home all the time." So it goes. Obviously, we cannot come too early to music. And those who come too late suffer the same fate as adults who struggle to learn a second language, and who are forever uncomfortable with its pronunciation, grammar, syntax, rhythm, and idiom.

In early childhood, the family circle—or its functional equivalent—can be decisive. Even the precociously gifted, who remain a mystery, are affected by their immediate social surroundings. To say that genius is God-given is to admit that the mystery abides, that within it an irreducible "x factor" is at work. Hence, Larry Adler, the consummate mouth-organist for whom many classical composers have written special works, is simply *sui generis*. Lacking formal instruction—which however he gives to others—Adler practices very little on his chosen instrument. From early adolescence to middle age, his career has led him into nightclubs and concert halls. As a boy he did play the piano. Beyond that, the musical genesis of this unique performer is as inexplicable to himself as to us. On the other hand, once he began his career and was accepted as a remarkable mouth-organist, his history, however peculiar to himself, is intelligible to anyone familiar with music-making in our day.

But most musicians, including prodigies, need teachers who are second in salience only to parents and who actually may turn into father, and mother, substitutes. Consequently, we hear over and over of a teacher, or the restless quest for one—somebody who will act as a guide through the thorny paths of professional socialization.

The relative lack of such role-models may account in part for the dearth of notable American composers until this century. Until about 1900, American music was almost wholly derivative. Charles Ives (1874–1954) is widely regarded as the first native composer of impressive stature; if so, Aaron Copland may have been the second. Copland was acutely aware of the absence of a substantial American musical heritage on which he could build. As he recently wrote:

In the mid-nineteenth century, when our literature could boast such writers as Whitman and Thoreau, Emerson and Emily Dickinson, we had no comparable figure in the field of serious music. . . . Not until the advent of this greatly gifted New Englander [Ives] were we able to point to a comparable figure in the world of symphonic literature.

Though Ives had few predecessors he did have a parent and a teacher who played important roles in his musical development. Vivian Perlis tells us in her oral history of Ives, that the composer "had a solid academic musical education from his father, combined with firsthand daily experience in almost every aspect of practical music making." Charles Ives also had the example of his father—a cornetist, bandleader, and choral conductor—who, for all his musical gifts, subsisted as an assistant bookkeeper in Danbury, Connecticut. At Yale, Horatio Parker—himself a composer, organist, and teacher—showed no enthusiasm for Ives' music. Neither did any other professor. But just after the death of Ives' father, a surrogate materialized in the person of John Cornelius Griggs, described by Perlis as choirmaster and baritone soloist at Cenet Church on the Green in New Haven, where Ives got a job as organist while still a freshman at Yale. In 1930 he wrote to Griggs: ". . . You didn't try to superimpose any law on me, or admonish me, or advise me, or boss me, or say very much—but there you were and there you are now."

Griggs was evidently the kind of supportive father figure whose unobtrusive presence was enough to ratify a young experimental composer's sense of his own worth.

While compositions poured out of him, Charles Ives led a double life. Like Wallace Stevens, a seminal American poet, he prospered in the insurance business. Ives was not in touch with other composers of his time and he rarely heard his pieces performed. Ives' basic tragedy always preoccupied and puzzled Copland: "How, I wondered, does a man of such gifts manage to go on creating in a vacuum?" Here Copland forgets three of his four previously cited literary examples. Whitman was not so highly regarded as half a dozen of his contemporaries who have gone into well-deserved eclipse; Thoreau died with more copies of *Walden* in his own possession than had ever been sold on the marketplace; and Dickinson, arguably our greatest poet, was a woman who, much more than Ives, went on creating in a vacuum with no audience at all. Among Copland's literary quartet, only Emerson was highly esteemed in his own time—as he was to be neglected or steeply downgraded in our day—from which we may learn once again not to make premature judgments of any artist who has not passed the test of time. But this is an issue to which we shall return.

What of the mystery? Will the enormous drive that has sustained so many American artists persist? So long as they feel a compulsion to create, there is no reason to suspect that public indifference or outright hostility can stop them. But those who followed Ives deplored the isolation in which they found themselves, and sought teachers and peers to ease and enhance the transition from primary to professional socialization.

Europe and America

Aaron Copland realized early on that the kind of instruction in composition he sought was not available in this country, so he went abroad to perfect his craft. His destination was France rather than the Germany of his elder compatriots. In Paris he found the soon-to-be-fabled teacher of composition, Nadia Boulanger, herself a performer and intimate of Igor Stravinsky. Ever since the early twenties, a procession of Americans has followed Copland's example.

European study used to be *de rigueur* for all kinds of musicians, not only composers. Alternatively, study with Europeans in the United States was acceptable; Milton Babbitt, for example, studied with Italian teachers in his native Jackson, Mississippi, as Miriam Gideon worked with Soviet-born Lazare Saminsky in New York. After their educations are completed here, most musicians spend a considerable amount of time on the other side of the Atlantic. Motives vary but the result is a kind of international hopscotch. A few cases in point drawn from our interviews make this dramatically clear.

According to Natalie Limonick, a veteran West Coast opera coach, singers are frequently invited to perform at New York City's Metropolitan Opera House only if they first succeed in Europe. Earle Brown feels that he scored points here because his works were applauded in Germany, where they are still more frequently performed and appreciated than in this country. Julius Levine exclaims, "Musi-

cally, I was born at my first Pablo Casals Festival in Prades, France!"
To hear that is nearly to understand the nature of a revelation. Furthermore, Levine clarifies the master-student relationship, and he
does it with remarkable lucidity. Several others take note of why it is
advisable for would-be conductors to go abroad, especially to Germany and Italy where "every town has a subsidized opera house" and
every opera house is in need of conductors. Seasoning there may lead
to an opening here. If their goal is New York, still the Big Apple for
music makers (who sometimes speak of the "Eastern Establishment,"
presumably to encompass Boston as well), they find themselves taking
a circuitous route to England, France, Italy, or Germany—and then,
with good notices and good fortune, storming the American culture
capital. And a precisionist like the harpsichord-maker Frank Hubbard
had to spend years in Europe examining old instruments before he
could try to duplicate them at home.

All of this is perhaps to say no more than that American culture
is and always has been a part of Western civilization, which those
who reached these shores sought only to maintain. In all the arts, a
steady influx of immigrants linked Europe to America. Ironically, the
last massive infusion of European culture contributed to a general
emancipation of American artists from the inferiority complex that
had previously plagued so many of them. When Hitler conquered
most of Europe, a large number of artists, denounced as Jews and
degenerates, found refuge in the United States. Here some of them
languished. For instance, much discussed in these pages is Béla
Bartók, an internationally renowned composer, gravely neglected as
an émigré. Kurt Loebel, a first violinist of the Cleveland Orchestra,
vividly describes his own struggle in New York as a cultivated refugee
from Hitler's Austrian *Anschluss*. Arrau and Piatigorsky abandoned
Berlin which, under National Socialism, became as loathsome to
them as it had once been beloved. Uprooted and transplanted, these
cosmopolites made their presence felt on the American musical scene
which they greatly enriched. Multiplied manyfold—in every domain
of music from esoteric theory to performance practice—theirs is a
paradigmatic story of acculturation.

But that story is so endlessly complex that it too deserves independent study. Let us settle for one point, and briefly explore its
implications. Artistic as well as intellectual life in North America was
transformed by brilliant Europeans who came here as involuntary ex-
iles—and they in turn were transformed by it. Too often forgotten is

that acculturation has a bilateral nature. A host culture absorbs elements of a foreign culture or its carriers, while the latter accommodates itself to and alters the former.

When Copland went to France in the 1920s he joined a dazzling contingent of expatriate American artists. Roger Sessions chose Germany and Austria; still others, Italy or England. Musicians, poets, dramatists, choreographers, painters, and sculptors often lived a bohemian life. Seldom have all the arts been more richly cross-fertilized than in Europe between the two world wars. Despite economic instability and political rot, and in a sense because of the ethos they partly engendered, a cultural efflorescence took place during the 1920s which has not been surpassed in this century. How good it was for a man like Copland to be "twenty in the twenties." That decade looms now as it did then to Copland from his vantage point on the Left Bank: stimulating and interesting in its openness to new art forms. He remembers the period of his return at age twenty-four as one in which American composers took steps to reduce their isolation, formed societies such as the League of American Composers, and organized concerts "to focus attention on American works." In 1928 the Copland-Sessions concerts were specifically designed for that purpose—with Sessions back from ten years abroad. By the 1930s, after sustained exposure to the ferment of European culture, a generation of creative artists who had come home seemed determined to work in a characteristically American idiom. It was as if they could find their native ground only by leaving and ultimately coming back to it.

By then, however, more eruptive social forces were at work. Europe ceased to be habitable for a great many scientists, intellectuals, and artists. When a significant number came to America, the tides of exile and expatriation were reversed. A sizable part of the European mind was transferred to this hemisphere, with consequences we cannot begin to measure. A few scholars have attempted to assess the qualitative impact of this migration on American science and American painting. No one as yet has systematically studied its impact on American music. The task is a worthy one, or so it strikes us more than ever as we ponder the meaning of our data. Clues are scattered throughout this book; they appear in one life history after another.

Let us examine in a little detail an important instance of European influence on American musical life. Chance brought a small

concentration of European luminaries to California. There the composers Arnold Schönberg and Igor Stravinsky, among others, took up
residence. Of these, the first in particular left an unmistakable mark
on that state. Regional variations, as perceived by those who experience them, are very real. None is more striking than Schönberg's effect as a teacher in Los Angeles. Leonard Stein, a prominent
Schönbergian and life-long Angeleno, began playing the piano at age
five-and-a-half as a student of "Richard Buhlig, who studied with the
great Theodor Leschetisky around the same time Artur Schnabel did.
Buhlig was among the first to play for Schönberg in Berlin. He came
to L.A. from Chicago, bringing contemporary music in his fingers.
. . . I became increasingly interested in the *avant garde* under the
influence of Buhlig, . . . and Roy Harris, the composer who was
one of Schönberg's first pupils in L.A."

Stein, who was more sophisticated in music than most of
Schönberg's American students at USC and UCLA, became his
teaching assistant and collaborator in completing textbooks on harmony, counterpoint, and composition. A peak experience occurred
when he watched Schönberg conduct the Los Angeles Philharmonic
in a concert of his own music. Along with Peter Yates and others,
Stein founded a regular series of chamber music concerts originally
called "Evenings on the Roof," thereafter, "The Monday Evening
Concerts." Stein reminisces: "One of our earliest concerts was an all-
Schönberg evening." Although this series never attracted more than a
few hundred listeners, it profoundly affected almost all the creative
Southern Californians we happened to interview.

Doriot Dwyer declares, "You might say I've been well posi-
tioned for comparisons." And why not? "I'm now on the East Coast,
I spent time on the West Coast, and I come from the middle [of
America]." Moreover:

> . . . we had a wonderful music series in L.A., "Evenings on the
> Roof," . . . It was a musician's paradise, a place where music was
> made by musicians for musicians; musicians made up a large part of
> the audience; our purpose was to play for each other. . . . The Eve-
> nings introduced a lot of important twentieth-century music to this
> country.

Or take young Michael Tilson Thomas, born and bred in Los
Angeles. Upon graduation from high school, he "wound up" at

USC, because his piano teacher and "other teachers who accepted me like a member of their families" were on the staff. Thomas benefited from the milieu not least on account of "a very interesting circle of people around the university" who were connected with the Monday Evening Concerts . . . "where Igor Stravinsky, Aldous Huxley, and the manager, a man named Lawrence Morton, were the prime movers. As a result of contact with that group, I was exposed to and learned to play much more contemporary music than I would have on the East Coast."

Lawrence Morton, the highly sophisticated concert manager to whom Thomas alludes, ran the Monday Evening series for over thirty years, for six of them at the Los Angeles County Museum as its Curator of Music. He had come to Los Angeles from Minnesota in 1939 and was soon acquainted with the celebrated composers of his adopted city, more so with Stravinsky than with Schönberg, but of the latter he says: "Schönberg taught at UCLA, and from that position exerted a big influence on music education in L.A." Morton reminds us that Schönberg's textbooks "focus on the classics; he never taught people the twelve-tone technique. Stravinsky didn't teach. And somehow, "though each had a faithful following, there were no big activities centering around either composer. But they certainly influenced the few of us who stood in awe of them and for whom contact with them was terribly important. . . ."

A final voice may be added to this little West Coast chorus. It is that of Natalie Limonick, who never planned to specialize in opera, but "just sort of fell into it" with no retrospective regrets. "But I had plenty of interesting musical experiences even before I knew a single aria." In her own words:

I arrived at UCLA from New York in 1944, the semester Arnold Schönberg was retiring, just in time for one stupendous class with him. I felt cheated when he was forcibly retired at age sixty-five. A few years later the thought hit me: shouldn't a bunch of us ask him to conduct a private seminar? . . . Yes, he would be delighted. And as soon as one seminar was completed we'd start another.

. . . His purpose was to unfold a total theoretical background. He tried out his well-known counterpoint text . . . on us. . . . Schönberg took his educational responsibilities very seriously; like many great composers of the past, he felt it was his duty to pass on the basics of the musical language to the next generation.

The pedagogic impulse is extremely potent. Men like Copland, Bartók, and Stravinsky who did not act upon it are the exception to a rule that fits not only eminent composers but those who make music at every level.

Such is the overall reality. We have chosen for illustrative purposes to use a microscope rather than a telescope to examine the special case of Los Angeles. Similarly close inspection of Chicago or Cleveland or even less populous cities would divulge comparable peculiarities, particularly "the Second City" syndrome that seems to afflict all of them. (Thus Stein cannot refrain from musing on how much better off Schönberg might have been had he settled in New York instead of California. Zubin Mehta leaped at the chance to leave the Los Angeles Symphony in order to become musical director of the New York Philharmonic. Chicagoans blinked with disbelief when their symphony orchestra was wildly applauded in New York: only then could it proceed on a triumphal tour of Europe with local supporters half-believing that Chicago had "the best orchestra in the world.") Despite this syndrome, important music may be incubating in relatively small, not necessarily academic, centers. And still, arrival means acceptance by the "Eastern Establishment." Inside and outside that Establishment, the two-way contact of Europe and America will have been decisive. Those who sat at the feet of the last wave of European masters now teach others, and in so doing carry on as they modify a specific tradition. Start with Arrau and you go back through Liszt and Czerny to Beethoven; follow Piatigorsky and you reach Tchaikovsky by way of Davidov; Levine leads straight to Casals, Gideon to Bartók, Berg, and Schönberg; Morton traces his orientation mainly to Stravinsky while Stein and Limonick look more emphatically to Schönberg. Every such sequence is a living tradition, of which there are many more in our midst. Their coexistence goes far toward explaining the inordinate eclecticism of the contemporary musical scene.

Mobility: Horizontal and Vertical

Until recently, European-American cross-fertilization seems to have produced largely positive results. But ever since the advent of travel by jet, performers, for reasons inherent in the internationalization of

the work they do, have experienced more than their share of move-ment from place to place—and not all of them are sure they like it.

Among our respondents, the most positive voice on this issue is Claudio Arrau's; although he has his misgivings, he still takes pleasure in breathless travel. "I enjoy seeing different countries, although there certainly isn't enough time in any one place," says the seventy-five-year-old master who recalls "having been everywhere" (except China—a prospective destination).

His near contemporary, the great cellist Gregor Piatigorsky, held an opposite view. Like Arrau, he spent his formative musical years in Weimar Germany, and concertized at a hectic pace before more or less anchoring himself on the same college faculty (USC) that wel-comed his friend Jascha Heifetz:

> I'd rather not travel like a madman, as I used to do. Sometimes I didn't know where I was. Once I played in London, I think on Monday, and on Tuesday I had a rehearsal in Missouri with the St. Louis Sym-phony. Imagine the time difference, jet lag and all that. For me, it's—shall we say—less than ideal to live this way.

Piatigorsky gave vent to these feelings shortly before his untimely death (of whose imminence he must have been aware, as we were not). Evidently it had never pleased him to rush about as an itinerant star.

Michael Tilson Thomas, a conductor several decades Pia-tigorsky's junior, already looks back unhappily on his "jet-set years" when the "record and concert business" were too much with him. He echoes Piatigorsky: "I discovered that they can put you in London today, in Paris tomorrow, three days later in Berlin and three days after that in New York. . . . This frantic activity does not contribute to music or even to the places where you make music." This from a conductor in his early thirties who takes pleasure in his present posi-tion as conductor of the Buffalo Philharmonic—and looks forward to relinquishing it. Thomas, like many conductors before him, hopes to achieve greater fulfillment as a composer.

Finally, a septuagenarian, Rudolph Bing, contrasting today's frenzy with the relative tranquility that prevailed in 1930 when he first came to manage the Metropolitan Opera House: "Today you have people singing on Monday in Hamburg, on Wednesday in Vienna, on Friday in London, and on the next Monday in New

York—which is crazy. It ruins their voices. In the past that madness was impossible. . . ."

Spontaneous expressions of this kind, as well as answers to pointed questions, suggest that whereas mobility is not peculiar to music makers, there is more of it in their lives than in most of ours and that many of them view it with great distaste.

Musicians also experience their share of movement up and down the social scale. Even the greatest of singers, like the best of dancers, have an unusually limited occupational life-span. They go through years of professional preparation to become performers for a limited stretch of years, a period that can be prolonged only by those few in possession of extraordinary stamina. Sooner or later their physical equipment breaks down and then they resemble athletes who are over the hill. At that point, a large proportion of them become full-time teachers, and as such some discover their true passion. On the other hand, orchestral musicians, most of whom set out to be soloists (especially, as Kurt Loebel points out, if they are string players) may suffer from a certain sort of immobility. Sheer boredom, occasioned by the seemingly endless and merely mechanical repetition of "old war horses" is their occupational hazard. Industrial and office workers are beset with this hazard. So are many players (and no one has yet thought to relieve the monotony of their operations with an industrial wonder like Muzak). But once in a while it is possible to rise out of the pit after a long period of anonymity in it. The accomplished violinist Sanford Allen (not interviewed here) is a spectacular case in point, which recently received prominent attention from an influential journalist in a widely discussed article. For many years the only black player in the New York Philharmonic, Allen recently resigned from that organization to pursue a solo career. He will henceforth perform as a free-lance musician. Kermit Moore, the well-known cellist, chose to free-lance almost from the start of his professional career, because that way "you can choose exactly what you want to do. You're master of your own fate." On the other hand, Julius Levine, one of the world's best known bass players, who also prefers to be his own boss, finds that "when you come right down to it, a free-lance player is someone who wants no master and finds out that he has many masters."

Doriot Dwyer's upward mobility is remarkable not so much because she was the first woman to hold a first flute position in a major American orchestra or even because she moved from the Los Angeles Philharmonic to the Boston Symphony but because she also moved from second to first flute. Symphony orchestras have a notoriously rigid internal hierarchy. To penetrate that hierarchy on any level is far less difficult for white males than for blacks and women. Women are making more dramatic inroads than blacks. But people "in the know" believe that, in many cases, members of both groups must be twice as good as white men to secure jobs by auditions that are "objectively" evaluated. Prejudice and discrimination still weigh heavily on these oppressed groups.

Accordingly, no major orchestra in the United States has a female conductor. Margaret Hillis admits to having opted for the position of choral director when it was borne in upon her that she could not realistically aspire to be an important orchestral conductor. But recently, at the height of her career, a chance factor asserted itself. Between the time of our conversation and the writing of these notes, Margaret Hillis got her opportunity to conduct a symphony orchestra at Carnegie Hall. In October of 1977, Sir Georg Solti, premier conductor of the Chicago Symphony, sustained an injury that, while minor, nevertheless required that someone substitute for him at a long-scheduled engagement in New York. Hillis stepped into the Maestro's shoes. So newsworthy was her appearance that the New York *Times* reported it on the front page. In the orchestral world, apparently, feminism has done more for women than the civil rights movement has done for blacks. Both are inching their way upward, one a little more rapidly than the other, but it will still take some time (and it is now only a question of time) for them to gain equal admission into the major orchestras.

Meanwhile, on another front, the battle for minority rights is being waged somewhat more vigorously. This is the composers' front. Recently, whole evenings in New York have been devoted to works by women or black composers. It is arguable that concerts organized around sex and race are an objectionable form of artistic segregation. But beyond much cavil those concerts point toward recognition for creative artists of whose existence the public scarcely knew or even now knows. We have no doubt that dissertations will soon be written or already exist on the rise of black and women composers. At this moment an ambitious oral historical study of women as composers in the United States is underway under the direction of two musicologists, Elizabeth Wood and Ruth Julius. The time is ripe for a complementary study of black composers. And yet, if the prevailing bigotry could be documented and dispelled tomorrow, so that women and blacks achieved equal standing with white male composers, a host of bigger problems would remain. They are the problems faced by every contemporary composer, even one who is "established." On these problems each of our five composers casts a good deal of light.

Contemporary Music

The music of our century, particularly of its last several decades—or rather its reception—constitutes a vexatious problem. Why the obdurate resistance to it—especially now, when resistance to equally "obscure," "difficult," or "abstract" literary and visual art has dwindled? Long is the list of answers. We can do no more than offer a sampling.

Milton Babbitt, who is most eloquent on the contemporary composer's plight, holds that most educated people are less prepared to cope with music *per se* than with any of the other arts. He adjures us to look at the number of serious art and literary magazines compared with those about music. "Well, you might say . . . that's the trouble, they're *about* music whereas the literary magazines are literary and the art magazines carry reproductions. . . . You can look at a picture but you can't read a sound. . . . How can students possibly come to my music when their musical awareness stops with the beginning of the twentieth century?"

Lawrence Morton looks back to a time when people interested in the arts fought to see exhibitions of Klee or Mondrian and lesser painters. The same people would not and will not accept Schönberg. "These people read James Joyce and even Mallarmé. But somehow they won't accept any new music." Why? Morton speculates along these lines: "Anything that appeals to the eye comes closer to the center of one's being than anything you hear. I think the eye is closer to . . . the consciousness of man."

He also quotes Stravinsky's comment on the bromide that people know what they like. "No," said Stravinsky, "people like what they know"—a sentiment shared by the manager Bing and the impresario Zelzer. But Bing adds: "Since visual art can be displayed, perhaps it conveys a sort of snob chic to own modern paintings whether you like them or not. Contemporary music doesn't have the same kind of snob appeal."

And Arrau feels that "Audiences have trouble with contemporary music because it doesn't give them what they expect. . . . I'm afraid what they expect is to be put into a certain mood. *The mood is that of daydreaming, of romantic feelings unavailable at home.*" (Our emphasis.)

As these greatly different men of music see them, modern audiences respond to music for its narcotic, hypnotic, or soporific effect. "But," adds Arrau, "emotion in contemporary music means something else. It is like the music of other planets—vastly different from earlier music. It's not what commercial audiences have been trained to like and enjoy. Modern music asks for a lot of effort from listeners to open up, listen again and again until they get the meaning. . . ."

Dorothy Maynor, like Arrau widely associated with the interpretation of familiar music, is prepared to champion unfamiliar modern music and to think aloud about why it is resisted: "It's like the refusal to taste certain foods which children won't try because they're not accustomed to them. You have to enter another world with an open ear, listen repeatedly, work at it, and eventually you'll understand."

Thomas takes a long historical view, and *embourgeoisement* is at its center. Consequently:

> *As the middle class became stronger and stronger economically, it was on its way to becoming the new proprietary class. They were most impressed with the conditions they were creating and the music they were commissioning. The interest in more and more new music couldn't last. . . . The composers' output for the most part got smaller and smaller partly because the new ruling class was more interested in preserving the past than in fostering change. So we behold a musical society memorializing itself.*

A pivotal figure in this controversy is another of Hitler's refugees, the seventy-year-old patron Paul Fromm, to whom American composers are profoundly indebted:

> *People obviously are afraid to face the unknown. . . . Music is up against greater odds than the other arts; ours is a verbal-visual culture; our intelligentsia doesn't take music seriously. It is considered entertainment more than serious art.*
> *On the basis of limited experience, audiences develop limited ex-*

*pectations. . . . Most listeners continue to project expectations gained
from Brahms'* Haydn Variations *onto Carter's* Variations for Orchestra.

The range of attitudes toward contemporary music extends from
tolerance to enthusiasm. No one, not even respondents we expected
to be hidebound in this area, flatly denounced contemporary music
as such. Even Eugene Ormandy, a conductor of the old school who,
in the statement we have included, elucidates his craft wonderfully
well, concedes a slight shift away from the "standards" that a well-
conditioned public has demanded throughout this century. Eileen
Farrell, who says, "Give me Verdi, good old grand opera—cornball
opera, that's for me," also sang Alban Berg's *Wozzeck*, conducted by
Dmitri Mitropoulos—her favorite. To Harry Zelzer, "the last of the
impresarios," as to Ormandy and everyone else who takes a pragmatic
view, nineteenth-century classics still fill the hall. But the slight shift
that Ormandy spots seems somewhat greater to Michael Steinberg:
"Fortunately, I think the fixation in the concert hall on the eight-
eenth- and nineteenth-century German-Viennese music is beginning
to break down a bit. To be interested in music on either side of that
narrow segment no longer seems as eccentric as it did maybe twenty
or thirty years ago."

Steinberg's opinion rings true for practically everyone. Not only
composers, with their vested interest in new music, but performers,
teachers, and all the rest refrain from blanket indictments—or auto-
matic approval. They discriminate, preferring this twentieth-century
piece to that, one body of work as against another. We venture to
guess that it is no longer professionally "proper" to declare oneself in
favor of or against every genre and every style except that one which
has been dinned into our ears for more than a century. Older, newer,
stranger music is no longer automatically ruled out of order by these
professionals. They even offer some evidence that audiences have
started to be more receptive than they were only a decade or two ago.
Miriam Gideon, musically formed by the vanguard of her youth,
chiefly through the direct influence of Roger Sessions, cannot go
unheeded when she confidently asserts that ". . . contemporary
music is increasingly acceptable to music students, musicians and
even the public." How so? They get it into their ears more or less
unconsciously. It reaches them in legitimate theaters, in movie
houses, on television. Background music is frequently quite ad-

vanced. Then, the admonition that you should listen closely to the background sound on a TV show; you'll find that extreme, dissonant music may be used most effectively. This extreme, dissonant, "far-out" contemporary music, reflexively dismissed as noise by a multitude of concert-goers, is subtly insinuating itself into the public consciousness.

More than one belated revolution in the arts has proceeded by such indirection. We need only remember the sudden acceptance of abstract expressionism. This movement evoked prolonged derision until those who jeered suddenly started to applaud. Pictures that had been scorned began to command huge sums of money, and those pictures, aped everywhere—even illicitly in Eastern Europe—made New York City the world art capital. What happened between the time Jackson Pollock was contemptuously dismissed as "Jack the Dripper" and that moment when he became "Pollock the Genius"? Cultural historians will not fail to record that abstract design was first accepted as interior decoration. What draperies or sofas did for Pollock, de Kooning and their confrères, TV may be doing for experimental composers.

Estrangement

Meanwhile, whatever happens, we are still left with the composer's predicament. To Milton Babbitt, things are only superficially better at present than they were three or four decades ago. Composers do get more performances, along with some recording and occasional publication. "That situation has improved, but we have no larger or more knowing an audience." Babbitt goes to "the best concerts" of contemporary music in New York and sees "the same hundred or so people there week after week." (This hard core has its parallel in other sections of the country.) He excoriates his generation of composers because so few "colleagues who grew up on the streets of New York fighting the composer's battle," show up to hear a young composer's music. "As a result, many young composers are, I hate to use the word, 'alienated' even within their own profession." To Babbitt this is "a sad and symptomatic state of affairs" that prevails at a time "when the very survival of serious musical activity" is threatened.

Babbitt's position is the grimmest; it goes farther even than that of other composers who predictably voice their discontent. The discontent stems directly from a long-standing estrangement between modern composers and the public. And if Babbitt is right (we think he is), then age differences have produced some generational estrangement. In that frame of reference, yesterday's vanguard is dated, and so Babbitt's electronic music is not as advanced as that of composers who use more sophisticated technology. To them, his music is old-hat. Meanwhile, most concert-goers have yet to catch up with turn-of-the-century music.

Maybe the best of twentieth-century music is inherently inferior to 150 classics of the past. About this no one can ever make a final judgment. If insiders already introduce a new note of interest, they also hedge their bets. Even the most ardent promoters of new music have reservations about it. Thus Morton admits, "There is no individual on the scene now for whom I would go all out and say, as Schumann did of Chopin, 'Hats off, gentlemen, a genius.' This appears to be a transition period following a period of several great composers." Stein speaks subtly, reasonably, and knowledgeably in the same vein. So, too, with their own insights, do such protagonists of new music as Fromm and Willis.

But the problem of estrangement remains. Practically all our contributors come to grips with it, none more provocatively than Carl Schachter, who teaches music theory at the Mannes College of Music and at Queens College in New York City. Schachter, who believes strongly that music, apart from its internal dynamic, is very much connected with society at large, takes us back to where we began this essay—to the relentless atomization and disintegration of community life, a process that perhaps began with the Industrial Revolution but that has accelerated alarmingly throughout this century. Schachter holds that the estrangement we have been discussing is partly traceable to a general fragmentation or superspecialization, which has been tearing our culture apart for some time. Hence, "the marked separation of theory, composition and performance into different disciplines has become a key feature of modern musical life . . . ," certainly to the detriment of that music. In the past, he continues, "most of the great performers were also composers. . . . There was a close relationship between what was composed and what was performed; there was continuity between what one played, what one listened to, and what one wrote oneself."

Today, "in contrast to the past, people in different walks of musical life often have very little to do with each other." He ruefully adds, "I find this 'development' rather sad." Many of our respondents express similar sentiments. Michael Steinberg graphically describes his student days at Princeton where "the graduate program was sharply split into composers and musicologists. . . . Not only were the two halves of the academic world cut off from one another; both were cut off from the performing world. And of course that's still true. . . . It's a bunch of nonsense because really we are all under one great musical umbrella." Paul Fromm also finds the situation most distressing:

> *What troubles me is that at most concerts of contemporary music—at least in Chicago—I almost never see composers, performers, musicologists, music historians and teachers of music in the audience. . . . I appeal to composers to join together in a community of musicians who will recognize their interdependence on each other and further each other's professional interests.*

Fromm and others who are interested in creating—or re-creating—a strong, broad-based musical community are more or less aware that they are bucking a strong tide, one that is affecting every aspect of civilization. Yet they persist in trying, and we can only applaud their earnest and sustained attempts. Fromm told us, "I have devoted my life to building a living musical culture, one in which there is a sympathetic interaction among composer, performer, and audience." And indeed, he has taken many practical steps to create this culture—from bringing composers and performers together for summers at Tanglewood to organizing a contemporary music festival with the New York Philharmonic and Juilliard.

Thomas Willis and Carl Schachter work in the classroom to bring about similar ends. In his general music classes at Northwestern University, open to music majors and nonmajors alike, Willis shows his students that

> *Anyone can make music and enjoy it. . . . I show kids how to teach music to themselves and their friends. . . . We should encourage people to adopt the composer's outlook. . . . So one student (or several) makes up a piece, learns to play it, figures out how to write it down, and hands the composition to a classmate who then has to play it. Afterward, they engage in a dialogue about the new piece, which we usually record when performed. . . .*

Schachter in turn deals almost exclusively with music students, both performers and musicologists. He spends a lot of time showing them that theory and practice are intimately related, and that one is really meaningless without the other.

Conclusion

This, then, is a sampling of the rich and complex story our thirty-two respondents have told us. Given our interest in the themes discussed above, we deliberately did not strive for statistically impeccable representativeness. Composers and critics—both in need of demystification—are deliberately overrepresented; the first because when not wholly neglected they are egregiously misunderstood, the second because they are so generally and deeply maligned. These two groups are, accordingly, given ample opportunity to elaborate upon the nature of their activities. When interviewed, Thomas Willis of the Chicago *Tribune* and Michael Steinberg of the Boston *Globe* were two of the best reviewers in this country. Few could match their erudition, their grasp of old and new music, or their skill at writing for a mass of urban readers. We thought the inclusion of two such men writing regularly for the daily press would serve to explode a common stereotype shared by some of our respondents and much of the musically sophisticated public: that daily reviewers, who wield great power, do not know their business. Clearly, Willis and Steinberg knew theirs. And, as this is written, both have withdrawn from that business. Yet, fortunately, they are not lost to music. They are merely operating through different channels.

We had intended to argue that with men of such stature in the field, its level was palpably rising. Their departure weakens a point that may still be defensible. For editors are probably no longer so cavalier about selecting music and art critics from their general pool of reporters as they once were. Poorly prepared hacks remain, but reviewers who perform a difficult task with great skill come readily to mind. That their profession continues to arouse strong, mostly negative, feelings among music makers, the reader cannot fail to notice.

A word about the categories into which we have placed our respondents. Where does a harpsichord maker who was also an active scholar belong? The reference is to Frank Hubbard, a brilliant and amiable man, who died prematurely some months after a lively discussion we had with him in his Cambridge workshop. His name appears in the table of contents under "Teachers, Scholars and Educators." So does that of Edward Downes. It fits. But Professor Downes' activities, ranging from those of radio commentator and opera explicator to critic and program note writer, are so diverse that it would be misleading to pigeonhole him. Musicians are classifiable, but they seldom do only one thing at a time; and over the course of long years most of them typically do many things. "Managers, Patrons and Impresarios" can most easily be identified with limited and specific roles, but labeling them also makes us uneasy. Consider that Sir Rudolph Bing, long associated with the New York Metropolitan Opera, upon his "retirement," spent five years as Professor Bing of Brooklyn College, and now occupies himself with other musical matters.

That academia looms large for creative artists in the United States—and therefore in this book—should surprise no one at all acquainted with their social situation. Take a miscellaneous handful of composers like the four men and one woman with whose narratives we begin and you will find that, continuously or sporadically, their attachment to institutions of higher learning is close and vital. This is perhaps least true of one of America's most renowned composers, Aaron Copland, who did teach in his youth at the New School for Social Research (giving talks that were later to be published) and used a series of lectures at Harvard as the text for another of his books. At present Copland zestfully conducts symphony orchestras here and abroad. Milton Babbitt has long been a fixture at Princeton where he followed his mentor, Roger Sessions, the distinguished composer who now teaches at Juilliard. Miriam Gideon belongs to the professoriat in a branch of the City University of New York. And Earle Brown has for some time been a peripatetic academician.

Perhaps the most interesting example is that of Theodore Antoniou, a young Greek composer, deeply involved in the American musical scene, who also teaches in various American universities. Antoniou, opposed to the military despots who temporarily ruled in his homeland, secured a foundation grant for work in this country. We spoke to him at the Tanglewood Music Festival—an enduring musical institution, founded by Serge Koussevitzky—in which Antoniou is an active participant. For all its particularity, his experience illustrates the kind of academic connection and institutional affiliation toward which composers, as well as other music makers, are drawn in our society. It reveals something about private patronage and the inevitability of political entanglement; and perhaps most tellingly, Antoniou's account reflects the cosmopolitanism of artists—comparable to that of scientists—in an age of rampant nationalism.

It was a pleasant surprise to us that almost everyone we talked to had formulated a cogent assessment of what was going on in American musical life, and we are glad to be able to present such well-reasoned and many-sided responses. It pleases us even more to include the remarks of many of our respondents because our book gives them a forum to explain some of the fine points within their particular bailiwick. Carl Schachter, for example, told us that "marvelous classes with Felix Salzer" marked the turning point in his life. For Salzer, in turn, had been a student of "the brilliant Heinrich Schenker [who] everyone now agrees was the greatest music theorist of the twentieth century." Schachter is one of the foremost theorists in America; nowhere will laymen find a clearer presentation, in nontechnical language, of how Schenker analysis, a difficult but deeply penetrating approach to music, relates to the broader musical scene.

It is similarly gratifying to us that Earle Brown feels he has never before had a better chance to explain the influence of poetry and visual art on his supposedly inaccessible work. It is important to know that, for him, science and philosophy were also active elements within his musical imagination—as they were, with such disparate consequences in the mind of Milton Babbitt. The selective interaction of artists, regardless of their specialities, their convergence and divergence, their responsiveness to the interdependence of human knowledge, and its musical expression, is repeatedly documented in the mini-biographies of these voluble men and women.

By triangulating past, present, and future, they present us with a multiplicity of social patterns. Contours and configurations come to the fore—with reference, say, to labor unions, government support, and the record industry—in ways that this overview has barely touched. The cross-references are instructive, and those who make them help us to understand an enterprise that is both solitary and communal. All, to some extent, are exemplary figures struggling to uphold a humanistic value system that we now desperately need in these distressing times.

Part One: Composers

1: Aaron Copland

Musically speaking, I think I was born into a fortunate generation. At the turn of this century America was very much under the influence of Europe; we had no composers whose music sounded specifically American. Even in the popular field, Irving Berlin and George Gershwin hadn't come along yet. I was lucky enough to be part of a new wave of serious composers in our country and that was a great advantage. It's very tough to have the sense that you are all alone when you're trying to create something new in an art form.

I knew I wanted to go into music when I was about fifteen. My parents, who weren't musical, couldn't have been more surprised, since we'd had no artists in the family (and it was a very large family). My father owned a neighborhood department store in Brooklyn. My oldest brother played the violin, to my sister's piano accompaniment, but neither of them had any intention of becoming a professional. One of the few serious pieces I heard around the house was the Mendelssohn violin concerto.

I recall hanging around my sister, who was seven or eight years older than I, when she practiced her scales. She'd say to me, "What are you standing there for? Why don't you go out and play?" Apparently, something fascinated me. There was scarcely anything else that mattered much musically in the milieu of my childhood. I don't remember being particularly affected by liturgical music. My family was conventionally religious, though not in any dedicated sense. Father was president of the local Conservative synagogue, but since it was not nearby we didn't go there every Saturday. So I only heard cantorial music on High Holidays. I suppose this rubbed off in one way or another; if you're a kid who's musically inclined, any kind of music you hear in a solemn setting is bound to have some effect on you.

I started studying piano at age 13; I was never good enough to give concerts, but I played O.K. Now, if you're sitting at the piano and find yourself inventing little tunes that you like, and then making up some more, eventually you start wondering how you put the tunes together. Suddenly you're involved. When I was about seventeen I began taking harmony lessons from Rubin Goldmark in New York. Four years after that, I was off to Paris.

Aaron Copland lives in Peekskill, New York, and was interviewed at the Tanglewood Music Festival, Lenox Massachusetts, in August 1975, and at his home in October 1977.

Like many others, I found it was important to go abroad to complete one's studies. Following Edward MacDowell's example, several composers from around Boston went to Europe before World War I, especially to Germany. The generation before mine hadn't thought much about France. But after the war, Germany had a rather poor reputation so we turned our eyes elsewhere. We knew of Debussy and Ravel, and that Stravinsky was living in Paris; the new music movement appeared to be centered there. So the thing for a young composer to do, it seemed, was to go to Paris rather than to Berlin or Munich. Also, if for no other reason, it struck us as a course different from that of our elders—and therefore attractive.

I'm still in touch with Nadia Boulanger, my old composition teacher. Unfortunately her eyes have gone bad. She doesn't see well any more, but other than that she's alive at 90 and still [in 1977] living in the same apartment where I studied with her in 1921. That's quite a record.

Though she had been teaching for a number of years before I arrived, I believe I was Mlle. Boulanger's first American composition student. Many of the books that have biographical information about me say that I went to Paris to study with Nadia Boulanger, but that's not true. Before I reached France, I had never heard of her. I went over to attend the newly established Fontainebleau School of Music, a summer school for Americans. It's still functioning; they celebrated their fiftieth anniversary in 1971. When I got there I was told about a gifted harmony teacher, Mlle. Boulanger. After seeing her function in a classroom, I suspected she was right for me. What knowledge that woman possesses! And she has a special gift for bringing out each student's musical potential.

That early dose of Parisian musical life meant that Stravinsky loomed large in my musical background. All of us who studied with Mlle. Boulanger felt his presence very strongly. We often saw him at her Wednesday five o'clock teas. Every time a new Stravinsky work was premiered there was lots of excitement—everybody went to hear it. It was a very lively creative atmosphere.

I knew Ravel, but only slightly. I got better acquainted with the group known as Les Six [Auric, Durey, Honegger, Germaine Tailleferre, and] especially Darius Milhaud and Francis Poulenc, who became good friends. Though Gershwin was in Paris in the twenties, I met him only later in New York; I was at his apartment once or

twice. People often talk about Gershwin and myself in the same
breath, as leading American composers. But apart from a few fine
concert works like his piano concerto [*Concerto in F*], he was basically in a different field. His was essentially the world of popular
music, and I didn't have anything to do with that.

Virgil Thomson was a fellow Boulanger student in Paris. I also
met Gertrude Stein; I went to some parties at her apartment in Paris,
and spent a weekend one summer at her home down in the south of
France. She and Virgil did some fine work together. Gertrude was
very literary, but I don't think she had much feeling for music.

In Paris it was delightful to associate with a variety of artists
other than musicians. I lived in the Quartier near the corner of
Boulevards Montparnasse and Raspail, right where everything was
happening. We were very aware of Ernest Hemingway and James
Joyce, as well as André Gide and many of the other French writers. I didn't know them well, but used to see them occasionally at the
next table in cafés, and also at a bookstore called Shakespeare and
Company, run by Sylvia Beach, an American from New Jersey who
had been brave enough to publish James Joyce's *Ulysses*. Her shop
was a literary meeting place. She ran a lending library; we went there
to borrow and return books, and talk with each other. She created a
kind of modest cultural center for us on the Left Bank.

My first published piece was a little piano work I had written in
Brooklyn and played at a concert in Fontainebleau called *The Cat
and the Mouse*. It was meant to be a light, cute, somewhat Debus-
syesque piece, and that's how it still strikes me. Until I finished my
studies in Paris, my family supported me. When I got back to New
York I was almost 24 years old. It was time to make some dough on
my own. Naturally I could never have earned a living as an unknown
composer. But I was extremely lucky: The Guggenheim Foundation
was established in 1925 and I was awarded the first Guggenheim, and
then it was renewed. So I had a two-year reprieve. After that, starting
in 1927, I fell into lecturing at the New School for Social Research. I
used to give a course called "What to Listen for in Music." I later
made a book of the same title based on those lectures. I discovered it
was easier to earn a living by talking to 200 students for an hour than
by teaching them one at a time. It drew an interested audience, and I
enjoyed the experience. I used to go down to Twelfth Street one

night a week for an hour, give my talk, and leave. Though I wasn't too closely associated with the people there, I'm very grateful to the New School for supplying that audience and that source of income.

The twenties were a very lively period—very lively indeed. I wouldn't have wanted to miss them. And I was very lucky to be twenty in the twenties. Stimulating, interesting things were going on. Everything had slowed down culturally during the first world war; afterward, there was a renewed spurt of interest and excitement in new ideas and new art forms. I'd have to be twenty all over again to be able to tell whether any other decade has been as exciting.

It was in the twenties that American composers began to take steps to get to know each other, rather than continuing to work in isolation. Societies of all sorts were formed. Though never part of any specific circle, I was musically closest to the League of Composers, which had been organized while I was in Paris. When I came back I became active in that group for more than ten years. The League did valuable work with their concerts and magazine, introducing new music from both Europe and America. A little later, in 1928, Roger Sessions and I organized the Copland-Sessions concerts, in order to focus attention on American works. Such activities certainly helped to give composers a sense that somebody cared, which was very important at that time to all of us.

New York was and is the pivotal place for contemporary music in this country. More people make for more possibilities—more concerts, more audiences, more everything. The liveliness of the city is a creative stimulus in and of itself; you have your peers, your friends, other people doing similar things. There's always somebody to talk to. It must be rather discouraging to be the only composer in Squeedonk, U.S.A.

For American composers to think in terms of a national musical tradition is a relatively recent development. When I began, I didn't sense much of a tradition behind me. My colleagues and I were more aware of the whole Western musical heritage than of a specifically American one. I would agree with Paul Fromm that by and large American music has come into its own in the last thirty or forty years. Time marches on, and our musical life in general has become much more independent of Europe. That fact works toward a freer musical atmosphere, and one in which the European experience is less preponderant.

You see, by the thirties it became a preoccupation for many of us to write a music that could be recognized as specifically American. The Depression contributed to that impulse. I became more politically conscious and rather anxious to reach a larger public. Actually, I'd already been interested in creating an American musical idiom in the twenties. My piano concerto which dates from 1927 was based on jazz materials, though I didn't do much with American folk-like material until later, in ballets like *Billy the Kid* (1938), *Rodeo*(1942), and *Appalachian Spring* (1944).

Some people persist in saying that my output seems too diversified to be the work of one person. It may seem that way to them, but it doesn't to me. Different situations and tasks lead you to explore different aspects of yourself. If you're devising a very simple piece for kids who are learning to play the piano, you write one way; if you're doing a work for the Boston Symphony, you write another way; if you're composing a ballet it's another story again. It's been very challenging to put myself into assorted musical contexts. Not all composers have the temperament to write comfortably for varied purposes. But I've always enjoyed it.

I've found it's rather a help to know in advance, as far as possible, whom you're writing for, and the quality of the performers involved. This knowledge influences what you write because naturally you might wish to tailor the work to a particular talent or group. Martha Graham, for example, has a very personal way of choreographing which I very much took into account when I wrote *Appalachian Spring* for her company. Writing for a certain choreographer is something like writing a concerto for a specific instrumentalist whose style you know. On the other hand, when you write a symphony you're freer—you're simply writing what comes out of your head and not filtering the composition through the needs and skills of one performer or another.

Whether or not you write for a specified individual or group, it always helps to hear your music performed well, simply in order to know what's there. You *think* you have a sense of how the notes you put on paper will sound—but then the test is actually to hear what you wrote.

When thinking about musicians who do my music especially well, Leonard Bernstein comes immediately to mind. Then there's Leo Smit, a fine pianist who's touring about now doing concerts of

all my piano works. In the past, of course, I was close to Serge Koussevitzky; he helped me and many other American composers a great
deal. Every one of us has had the feeling that our music isn't getting
enough exposure, especially at the beginnings of our careers. It's
always an uphill fight to establish oneself. Koussevitzky provided
tremendous support. I think he was a frustrated composer who took
this out by interesting himself in young creators, encouraging them,
setting up prizes, playing their music when they were completely unknown, doing pieces he knew the public wouldn't accept easily. He
gave my music a big boost. I can't imagine my career without him.
No conductor has come along since who's done as much for young
American composers as Koussevitzky.

I think the position of the composer in our society has improved
over my lifetime, probably because there are many more of us writing
now than fifty years ago. Proportionately there may not be more attention or performances, but the mere fact that there are more of us
means that more performances of new music take place and more
people become aware of our presence on the scene. Where there
were ten composers then, one got performed; now if there are one
hundred, ten get played. The increase in numbers has another advantage: Among ten composers there might be one good one; among
fifty, chances are better for finding talent.

The situation in publishing and recording new music has improved somewhat, though I can't say it's sensationally better. As with
performances, there's still a big lag in keeping up with production.

Something that *has* changed a lot is the fact that now more and
more young composers find themselves in universities. This state of
affairs has its pros and cons. On the one hand, academia provides a
regular income and a built-in audience, and the atmosphere is often
very lively; on the other hand, it may be stultifying to be in such an
environment all the time. I've very much enjoyed teaching at various
universities—as a visitor. I don't know how I would have liked an
academic lifestyle. When I started out, of course, not as many big
universities had music departments to hand out jobs. That's new.
Along with the increase in composers has come an increase in music
departments. At least now many young composers have found steady
jobs.

Like many of my colleagues, I've been conducting my own
music for some time now, all over the country and the world. For

myself and others, the urge to conduct our own music began to grow when we watched other people leading it. You gradually find yourself thinking, "I want to get up there and do it myself—the way I really feel it." It starts there. Then you need an orchestra to practice on. After you've developed enough technique to get your ideas across adequately, why, you're on your way.

I never really took any conducting lessons except perhaps one or two at Fontainebleau long ago. I learned mostly by watching other conductors and being present at rehearsals of my own and other people's music. I got a lot out of my close alliance with Koussevitzky and the Boston Symphony; after all, we were at Tanglewood together for some 25 summers, between 1940–65, when I headed the composition department of the Berkshire Music Center, the wonderful summer school Koussevitzky founded for young musicians. That experience had the greatest influence on me as a conductor.

The first time I conducted a series of concerts was in South America in 1947. That was a very good experience and led to many more. It's hard to summarize what I do differently from other conductors with my own music. Somehow, since I write it, I'm in the best possible position to know how I think it should sound. Another conductor might give your work a somewhat different interpretation, that you may like as well or better. But if you're technically able to manage it, it's always a profound pleasure to get up there and conduct your piece in exactly the way you dreamed it when you were writing it. It's really an enormous satisfaction.

2:   *Milton Babbitt*

I was a southern boy, who grew up in great comfort in Jackson, Mississippi. My family was lower upper class, economically well off. There was an enormous amount of music in my life, to go along with that literary tradition which has always been the cultural core of the South. I grew up, for example, arm in arm with Eudora Welty, not only in the same town and virtually on the same street, but with our fathers working for the same insurance company.

Everyone in my family played a musical instrument. I began with the violin when I was four years old but quickly switched to wind instruments because they were more useful for social events. I played in orchestras and bands from the age of eight or nine. My father was familiar with a great deal of music, and especially liked Italian opera, because of his European upbringing. My mother had also heard a lot of music at home. She came from a sophisticated bourgeois Philadelphia family. I have a brother who's still an excellent flutist and double bassist. He's now with the Department of Defense and listens to much more music than most musicians I know. That fact has to do with an aspect of the South that one must never discount. If you were fortunate enough to be in an upper economic bracket, you took the idea of the cultivated gentleman very seriously. You behaved like a gentleman, and you read and thought and talked and listened to music like a gentleman.

My first music teachers were all Italian; that's the tradition that has prevaded the South since the nineteenth century. Typically, an Italian flute player or cellist who couldn't make a living in Italy would be imported by a small Southern city like Jackson to take charge of musical activity. Our Italian could hardly speak English, and never quite got adjusted, though he married a Mississippi girl. The director of the orchestra in Jackson was a French violinist. What made Europeans so attractive? Well, foreign musicians were, even as now, glamorous, and the growing audiences took strongly to Italian and French opera. I didn't encounter a single German musician in Jackson; that tradition was much less important. Except for one American violin teacher, I got all my early training from Italians and Frenchmen. This continued until I went to college.

The Italian flutist was not a highly sophisticated musician, just routinely competent. He had to teach nearly every instrument and

Milton Babbit lives in New York City and was interviewed there in May 1976.

knew a little bit about every one, but his heart was with Italian opera. He regarded himself as being fairly special because he had heard some early Sibelius. That's as far into modern music as he went. Luckily I had an uncle who opened up the worlds of Stravinsky and Schönberg for me. Such are the accidents of family that count.

My aunt was a concert pianist; my uncle was less of a pianist and more of a composer and very much interested in contemporary music. When I was about ten, he played the Opus 11 and Opus 19 Schönberg pieces for me, and then later the Stravinsky piano sonatas. When you're only ten years old, you're interested in anything or nothing. The music didn't make a great deal of sense to me but I was intrigued nonetheless.

Another uncle was a celebrated music critic, and he had traveled to Europe. When he came back from Paris he brought some scores—a Honegger symphony and some others—just for fun for me. I still have them. That was it! Curiosity turned to a serious and what would be lifelong interest in new music. I owe my uncles an eternal debt of gratitude.

I went off to college at the age of fifteen which is one of the greater mistakes of the many I have made. But I graduated from high school at that age and wanted to matriculate at Tulane because it was in New Orleans, a city that I loved and still love. But they wouldn't accept me because I was too young. So I was sent to the University of Pennsylvania, since I had relatives in Philadelphia who could presumably look after me.

Well, off I went to Penn, where I was supremely unhappy. Knowing that the musician's life was a hard one, I thought I would major in mathematics or logic and if Penn had been a better institution in those fields then I probably would have done that. But I had one good man in logic and couldn't take much of the rest. I spent most of my time playing in bands, orchestras and with various other groups.

Since Penn had no music department then, I transferred to the University of North Carolina which had a good, but I assure you unwarranted, reputation. The following February I transferred to Washington Square College, New York University (N.Y.U.) because there was a wonderful woman there named Marion Bauer who had just written a book called *Twentieth Century Music*. It was the first American book in which there were actually musical examples from

Schönberg's and Stravinsky's works. I said, "That's for me!" This time, of course, my major was music. When I graduated at nineteen, I went to study privately with Roger Sessions. The year was 1935.

We were in a deep Depression, which didn't affect me at all. I lived on Washington Square, went to school there, took in every-thing and everybody and attended concerts galore. There was *much* more musical activity then than now, and I reveled in it. Marion Bauer asked me to do music criticism for a magazine called *Musical Leader*, which is long since defunct, I'm happy to announce. It was routine writing, often rewritten, and I did it only for free concert tickets. There were sometimes four or five concerts a night to be cov-ered at four or five different halls. Performers were making debuts every night. Heaven knows why the musical scene was so active. Perhaps because the Depression brought deflation and things were terribly cheap, even the presenting of concerts. Somehow or other, there was a colossal amount of music, but mainly of the past.

So there I was, living independently and studying privately. It was marvelous. Naturally, I couldn't have survived this way without my father's help. But few of my friends, no matter how poor, seemed very hard up. When I began studying with Sessions—David Dia-mond and I started together—we were not aware of the Depression as such. Nobody had much money, not even I, and I was the rich man of the gang. But we could eat and buy some scores and study with Roger. At that time Roger had no official teaching position. He was living off fees from private students, not particularly well, but pass-ably, until he secured a teaching job at Princeton.

The WPA [Works Progress Administration] did not support com-posers. It was chiefly for performers. And yet there was a great deal of contemporary musical activity thanks to the WPA. I can re-member walking out on a Sunday afternoon and wondering, "Should we go to the Brooklyn Museum to hear a work by Sessions like the *Black Maskers* or should we go up to the Museum of Natural History to hear an orchestra play a piece of . . . you name it?" There were some second rate or worse orchestras doing the playing but at least they were playing and giving festivals of contemporary music thanks to the WPA. Also, the Composers Forum began on the WPA. The 1930s was a period in which most artists tried to reach out to mass audiences. But most composers still didn't expect and never obtained a mass audience. Aaron Copland is an exception, one of, say, two contemporary American composers who were renowned in the 1930s. I knew of Copland's music by 1930 or 1931. He had written *Music for the Theater*, which got more publicity than performance. Aaron was the first living American composer of serious music I did not know personally of whom I became aware because I heard his music and heard him talked about. Then came Roy Harris. In the thirties only those two could be characterized as widely known. Sessions was known only to a small group of professionals. Beyond them, the names came and went.

If many composers at that time paid lip service to the notion of "music for the masses," few actually attempted to realize it compositionally, and fewer still even approximately succeeded, for it was mainly an ideological consequence of their real or imagined political attitudes. Roger, perhaps as a result of a decade spent in Europe— mainly in Italy and Germany—showed little interest in such activities, politically or musically, and consequently he felt and actually was isolated from most of his fellow American composers, particularly musically.

My own extramusical interests derived from a vastly different kind of ideological source, and were represented by the first American textbook which reflected what then was termed "logical positivism": *Philosophical Analysis*, by James Burnham and Philip Wheelwright, both of whom taught at Washington Square College in my time there. I already had been aware of the writings of the Vienna Circle from which the book manifestly derived, and from that time forward the philosophers of logical empiricism, and more recent logical and analytical philosophers, have been central to my thinking, including my musical thinking. They have suggested how I might talk and think about music, and therefore how I might think in music itself. The vast and exciting literature of such philosophy has been a potent intellectual force in what I like to regard as "our musical circle," and it has been particularly influential on such younger musical thinkers and writers about music as Benjamin Boretz, John Rahn, and many—if not enough—others.

On the other hand, most of my closest composing colleagues appear to have little interest in or relation to the "visual" or "plastic" arts, its creators, and its spokesmen. To be sure, there are composers (I think immediately of Earle Brown and Morton Feldman) who seem to feel close and attracted to that world, and this in turn may reflect the extent to which our educational backgrounds and current professional milieus are so dissimilar as to be nearly disjoint. I must confess that it is not just general intellectual disposition, but voracious and selfish pofessional taste and appetite that leads me to read *The Journal of Philosophy* rather than to visit art galleries.

Of all my colleagues, close and distant, I am perhaps the one who feels least uncomfortable about regarding himself as an academic. I seem to be more at home in the university than are many of my colleagues not only because the most informedly problematical and responsibly advanced thinking and creation can be done, if at all, mainly in the academy, but also perhaps because I grew up in an informally academic environment, thoroughly enjoyed the role of student (particularly at NYU, where my life was "turned around," as one would not have said then), and feel strongly that the academic, as our last and only hope, must be our best hope. But even so, when I graduated from college I swore I'd never enter another academic institution. I had delusions of compositional independence, but after a few months of mere observation of the great commercial, public music scene, I learned, almost forever, a nonacademic lesson.

Besides philosophy, other academic disciplines, particularly those associated with literature and its exegesis, have been and still are important to me. For me and for many of my contemporaries Joyce was enormously influential, while Proust—during my undergraduate years—was still the most widely read writer, which was understandable at a time when the question of the treatment of "time in the novel" was an issue of crucial interest, particularly for creators of time in and with sound. Faulkner was becoming celebrated and even read, and he fascinated me for a variety of reasons: I had met him in Mississippi when friends of mine had been in his classes; the contrast between the apparent man and the elaborately fashioned fiction; the structural suggestiveness of such books as *Absalom, Absalom*; and, eventually, the Oxford, Mississippi–Hollywood contradiction or compound. After that student period I came to read less and less fiction, an abandonment probably hastened by the likes of Mann's *Dr. Faustus*, which I found silly, pretentious and offensive, as apparently also did Schönberg.

If I now read little fiction, as compared with technical literature in my own and a host of related disciplines, I still read a considerable amount of poetry. I have set much verse, having started when I was quite young. At the age of eight, I began to write "popular" songs, with lyrics by others and by me. My first "serious" attempts at text setting—of some haiku—came when I was about fifteen, but—as far as I can recall—the first contemporary poet I set was William Carlos Williams, and if I haven't set many contemporary poets, it's not only because I find few current poems in English susceptible to my kind of musical setting, but also—to be candid—because they are not in the public domain.

Still, my two large works for soprano and synthesized sound are settings of Dylan Thomas' *Vision and Prayer* and John Hollander's *Philomel*; the latter poem was written for me for the particular medium of "live" soprano, recorded soprano, and electronically synthesized sound. But I have just completed A *Solo Requiem*, employing poems by Shakespeare, Hopkins, George Meredith, and Stramm. August Stramm was a still relatively little-known German expressionist poet whose poems I used, in German, in my cycle, *Du*. I confess to being intrigued by the German language, its poetry, and its susceptibility to musical exploitation. In my tiny *Four Canons* for two voice parts on a fragment of a German text by Schönberg, I tried to turn natural language into a kind of synthetic speech by various and varying distributions of verbal and vocal emphases without destroying intelligibility.

There is a profusion of demanding compositional issues attending the setting of poetry to music, for one must consider an enormous number of multiple relations between the multidimensional musical and the multidimensional verbal. When just the "musical" aspects of the texts—the sonic, durational, accentual rhythms and their progressive successions—become part of a total musical structure, those attributes of poetic coherence are so reoriented as to be attenuated and even obscured as characteristics in themselves; but their structural functions can be restored and reinforced in the new amalgam by the associative means of the correlated musical materials. It is with such considerations that my settings begin. On the "semantic" side I often then read critical commentary and exegesis which can help to shape one's attitude toward the musical treatment of anything from a single word to the whole poem.

I wish I could explain my corresponding musical techniques simply, but of course I am reassured that I can explain them only with complexity—and then only incompletely, and then only as of

the moment. And the whole question of text setting is further aug-
mented by the availability of electronic means of specification and
control of every aspect of musical sound, so that the acoustical components which determine, for instance, the structure of a vowel
sound can be produced and mutated, and the characteristic noise
spectra of particular consonants similarly can be produced and modified—all as constituents of the purely musical "accompaniment."

To return to chronology: I studied with Roger Sessions privately
from 1935 to 1938 and we became very close. We reached the point
where my lessons became much more like professional discussions; in
any case, he was much less interested in scrutinizing the music I
wrote than in looking at and analyzing other music, from Bach
chorales and Beethoven sonatas to the Stravinsky Piano Concerto
and Berg's *Der Wein*. I did mountains of exercises, and we even sang
solfège together. Roger had begun teaching at Princeton University,
where Roy Dickinson Welch was Chairman of what wasn't even a
music department, but rather merely a section of the Art and Arche-
ology Department.

At first Roger felt a little isolated and lonely; Roy Welch had
hired a musicologist, Oliver Strunk, and a composer, Sessions, as
departmental mainstays. In 1937, when Roger was 40 years old and
still an instructor, he asked me if I would be interested in teaching at
Princeton, since Welch had been authorized to hire a young assistant
for the Department. In those days of Nazi Germany and similar phenomena, I was aware that there was a problem with the "Jewish
issue" in Ivy League music (and other) departments. So I simply
asked Roger: "Do the powers that be know that I regard myself as
Jewish?" Roger himself was surprised by the disclosure only because
he knew me to be from Mississippi and thought of me as a "Southern
boy," and because the name Babbitt wasn't normally taken to be
"Jewish." Roger himself comes from an old New England family,
genuine seventeenth-century American stock, and I knew the "racial"
question didn't concern him; he was devoted to his teacher, Ernest
Bloch, the well-known Swiss-Jewish composer, and he would not
then or since have been concerned with matters of ethnicity. He simply said that he had not known that I regarded myself as Jewish, but
neither could he imagine that it would make any difference. Soon
after, we learned that it did make a difference. Apparently, it was felt

by someone that perhaps the first junior appointment in the Music Section should not be Jewish, even if that prospective appointee, regarded himself as Jewish, did not wish to be in any way evasive about being Jewish by any then-applicable criteria, but claimed no particular adherence to the religion. I was not hired then. But the following year another opening arose and I was hired. That was in 1938, and I have stayed on to this very day. The only break in my connection with the Princeton Music Department came during and after World War II, which created a considerable chasm in my musical life and development. I was involved with military matters for seven years, from before the war until well after it ended. Part of that time I taught in the Princeton Mathematics Department while commuting to Washington constantly. During that extended and exhausting period, music all but went out of my life; creatively, it was an enforced dry spell. I did have bits of time to think about musical issues, but writing music was completely out of the question.

That requires uninterrupted concentration, and I had to work on nonmusical matters about twenty-eight hours a day. Directly after the war I went back to Jackson to rest up for six or seven months. I just sat in the good old family home and began writing out ideas I had thought about during the war. I wrote a monograph that George Perle has cited, but almost nobody else has seen. I was very very tired. I really didn't know what to do next. I had been offered a position in the Princeton Mathematics Department and could have taken it. But I was a professional musician, surely not a professional mathematician.

So, my wife and I returned to New York, partly to have our child in that city. I decided to try to be a full-time composer. I had had only one consequential New York performance before the war. My first important New York performance after the war was *Three Compositions for Piano*, which I wrote in 1947, played by the now celebrated pianist Robert Helps. In the late 1940s I also wrote a film score for *Into the Good Ground*, a picture nobody remembers. It used to be played on television, but they cut out most of the credits, for which I'm grateful. It was an extremely pretentious film full of Broadway actors with fourteen flashbacks within flashbacks, the kind of movie they made in the late forties.

I went back to teaching—music—at Princeton, though we continued to live in New York. And I became reinvolved in an area that

had intrigued me in the 1930s—electronics and music. When I first
went to teach at Princeton in 1938 I was already aware of a development called the handwritten soundtrack. You won't find many references to it any more. In those days, if you read a book on film music
you would find references to two people, Pfenninger and Fischinger.
Pfenninger worked in Munich, Fischinger worked in Berlin; and independently they had produced samples of writing directly on soundtrack to produce sound. A number of composers, if not well-known
ones, made use of the handwritten soundtrack. They realized that everything they wanted to record for sound film—a genre in the early
stages of development in the 1920s—could be recorded as a single
signal on the side of the film track, either as variable area or variable
density sound representations. Clearly, this discovery was attractive.
It made possible the direct manual representation of complex sound,
including wild sound, speech, instrumental sound. I was intrigued by
it all.

    After the war no one was interested in a handwritten soundtrack
any more; by then it seemed clumsy. The tape machine and the synthesizer made it obsolete. I was not interested in working with tape
mutation, and tape modification, however, though I did become a
close colleague of Vladimir Ussachevsky and Otto Luening at Columbia. They were working very seriously on the synthesis of sound,
entirely with tape, through methods which were simply not for me.

    Then RCA invented the synthesizer. RCA had some superb en-
gineers, who said, in effect. "Look at those stupid musicians, splicing
tape together to produce a single spectrum. If they had any brains
and a few million dollars they could avoid all that dirty work." And
for General Sarnoff's seventieth birthday they unveiled the first RCA
synthesizer. Now these engineers were not musicians at all. They
produced a record labeled "The Sounds of the RCA Synthesizer."
Musically it was unsophisticated but, with some sophistication on the
listener's part, its extraordinary capabilities could be inferred. Once
RCA discovered there were composers of whom even they had heard
who were fascinated by this development, they brought in other engineers on the project and built the Mark II Synthesizer. It was much
larger and infinitely more flexible. That was the synthesizer with
which I began to work in 1957, largely because it was housed at
Princeton, not at the University but at the Sarnoff labs. Ussachevsky
and I went to those labs to acquaint ourselves with the machine and

found that the technicians apparently had no idea of what to do with it musically. We secured Rockefeller Foundation money to set up the Columbia-Princeton Electronic Music Center, but there were not sufficient funds to buy the synthesizer; it probably cost at least a quarter of a million dollars to build. So the RCA people told us, in effect: "You seem to know what you want to do with the machine; we don't. What about our moving it to New York, putting it in your studio and maintaining it at a certain cost?" Finally they just turned the machine over to us. It has remained my favorite instrument, though nowadays most of my young colleagues have turned to the computer for sound production.

Somehow, I have never become a computer nut. I have never used one, although I think I understand the techniques and I try to keep closely in touch with developments at Princeton and elsewhere. It was probably a great mistake not to have become more active, but other commitments were more pressing. As a composer becomes older, and thus more "established," he is likely to receive more commissions than he can fulfill or afford, particularly if he composes slowly and in time stolen from other professional obligations. And over so many of those commissions hovers the spectre of performance. For so often the economically most feasible commissions are those for the richest performing groups, the groups least prepared for and least genuinely interested in the suitable performance of demanding contemporary music. There are a few groups of relatively young and ill-rewarded performers, and a larger group of individual performers who have established and adhered to extraordinary standards of performance, but the problem is so serious, and even they are so threatened, that I, like many other composers of my generation and even more of the later generation, have turned to the electronic medium at least partly for that reason. With the electronic medium the roles of performance and composition are joined. The composer can walk into the electronic studio with his composition in his head and eventually walk out of the studio with a tape of his performed work in his hand. This is not to contend that as yet one can do everything with electronics, but many things already can be done very well indeed, and many important musical things are now possible which never could have been done before.

The composer of fairly complex music is faced with immense problems from the outset, even before the actual performance stage is

reached. In an ensemble work, after you have prepared a full score
and have the individual parts expensively reproduced by a professional, there's the proofreading—and errors are guaranteed. I'll give
you one case in point: I wrote a piece commissioned by the New
York Philharmonic for its 125th anniversary—a very prestigious commission. Sessions received one too, as did several other composers.
At the time I had a respected publisher, but not the one I have now.
They took this work of mine, which was paid for by the Philharmonic, and had the parts reproduced by a similarly respected copyist.
I did not see those parts before they were sent over to the orchestra.
The publisher told me not to bother checking them: "We'll take care
of everything, we'll check everything." I arrived for the first rehearsal
on a Monday morning; Leonard Bernstein was conducting. Lenny
began, and from the first downbeat it was obvious that the instrumental parts were in terrible shape. Measures on end had been copied in-
correctly; the flute part had become the oboe part and so on. Neither
the copyist nor a representative of the publishing house was there.
After half an hour, a violinist screamed, "What's happening? What
measure are we in?" I had to say, and Lenny had to agree, that we
couldn't go on. We canceled the performance. I spent the next six
months checking those parts so the piece could be performed, as it finally was later in the season. And this is just one instance of the practical and humiliating problems we encounter all the time.

As for the "subtler" issues, like adequate rehearsal time, and appropriate performers, consider the case of an orchestral piece the
Koussevitzky Foundation commissioned me to write. Gunther
Schuller asked to do the first performance. He had his choice of either the Chicago Symphony or the Cleveland Orchestra—and perhaps mistakenly chose Cleveland. In those days it was reputed to be a
better disciplined orchestra. Gunther is a most remarkable conductor,
particularly under conditions that afford minimal rehearsal time,
which was definitely the case. My piece is about 450 measures long;
it lasts about eighteen minutes. It is intricate but it can and has been
performed. But it was to be played on a program of premieres (for the
Cleveland orchestra) by Webern, Messiaen, Schuller and me, for
which only *four* rehearsals had been allocated—that is, ten hours rehearsal time for the whole program of five complex contemporary
scores. In other words, each composer got two or two and a half
hours. Now compute the arithmetic of the dilemma. If a pianist were

going to learn a new Chopin etude, how long would he or she work on it? Quite a few weeks at least—and it's idiomatically familiar music with no ensemble problems. My piece has no literal repetitions as far as I know; each measure has to be worked out individually. If you spent, let's say, only five minutes on a measure, you'd need around forty hours of rehearsal time. It received two and a half hours at the very most. And my experience is a commonplace. I don't want to say anything about the performance—but there certainly was not enough preparation time for anyone involved.

Neither composers nor performers are villains. We're simply [co-]victims of an impossible situation. I don't want to have to put my music in front of people and say, "Now look, you have exactly two hours to try to learn this extremely intricate and unfamiliar piece." It's ridiculous. And yet I've been more fortunate than most. Since the late 1940s a few performers have been devoted to my music and they've given extraordinary performances of it. Bethany Beardslee the singer, Robert Helps and Robert Miller, the pianists, Paul Zukofsky, Gunther Schuller (in his role as conductor). But on the other hand I have had many very poor performances and not because the performers were poor or because they were ill-willed. No one has ever played a piece of mine who didn't want to or for lack of any option (except orchestras like the Philharmonic or the Cleveland). When people play my string quartets, for instance, it's not because they're obliged to. It's just the terrible economic time that undoes us all.

The record situation is even worse. First of all, recording time is dreadfully expensive. So usually performers are told "We've got to do it all in this one session. C'mon, we'll put things together somehow. Let's do this snippet of the piece and splice that snappet from the end," and so on. I don't care how well each snippet of the piece sounds—that's not a musical performance. A work proceeds from beginning to end and performers and listeners must have some sense that it does. On records, too often, one doesn't—because different parts of the piece are recorded separately, instead of the whole piece straight through. In many cases when records have been made of my pieces I haven't even been consulted.

Performance problems are endless. I constantly come across a major one, since I teach composition at Juilliard one day a week. I learned very quickly that young composers and young performers are going along largely dissimilar paths. Their teachers are consciously or

unconsciously training them for very different goals and they have
very different musical dispositions. Even if a young performer is interested in performing contemporary music, or is just interested in
finding out whether he is interested, his teacher is likely to advise:
"Why spend weeks learning some difficult new work you are likely to
play only once or twice, when—in the same time—you could learn a
repertory work which, if you are lucky, you'll play in twenty places,
and for the rest of your life?" By contrast, the young composer says:
"Here is a young performer who could play my music expertly, but
begs off for lack of time or money, and therefore he can afford to
learn only the music of the past. What if I were to say that only the
performers of the past are worthy of being listened to?" If the conflict
begins there, it blossoms into ultimate antagonism and a complete
divergence of life and musical styles. It's compounded by the condition that, again, most American composers are university trained
and/or university teachers. Even in his generation, Aaron Copland is
the notable exception. So, composers and performers either attend
different institutions or lead different lives in the same institutions.
Schools like Princeton and Juilliard equally represent this critical
misunderstanding between "academically minded" composers and
"public minded" performers. Simply trying to get the two groups to
understand each other's plight, concerns, and language is an enormously difficult task.

And while there are those comparatively few exceptional performers of contemporary music, there are more who play it on occasion because they believe they can get away with playing it less
consideredly, or even less accurately, or play an occasional work
chosen as if to discredit all contemporary music, as if that body of
music were a monolithic, undifferentiated collection of compositions. Thus does the "fallacy of composition" invade our lives. Surely
the unprecedented range of musics of our time and place requires particular care, skill, and comprehension for their suitable performance.
You recall that Schönberg said: "My music isn't dissonant; it's just
badly performed." And even his still often is. The performers simply
do not know the works, even though they may think they know how
to play them. We still hear wretched performances not only of the
large ensemble pieces, but of—say—the *Phantasy*, a work violinists
play these days if they feel obliged to include a contemporary work on
their programs. And this, first of all, because they haven't even both-

ered to check the printed score for typographical errors. I have to assume they do not care because I dare not assume they do not know that all of Schönberg's very late works were printed with such errors because of the condition of his manuscripts, due to his desperately failing sight.

Brahms said something interesting about all this; he said that the best performance of *Don Giovanni* he ever heard was while sitting in his study with the score. We all know what he meant. I too hear a performance in my head, but there's a great difference between that and a finally externalized performance. When you mentally imagine a performance you use a lot of energy re-creating the music for yourself. That kind of energy doesn't have to be expended when someone presents the music to you. Experienced performers won't allow a composer to attend the first or second rehearsal of a work of his. And they're right, because you'll be listening from the start for wonderful little details that you so treasure. And they'll just be trying to get the notes sorted out, not even to grasp the dynamics and the rhythms. Then, if you go hear a later rehearsal when they have shaped a performance, you forget your own mental performance. You don't try to match theirs against yours any more. But you can still make suggestions on specific passages, on nuances and details. The trouble is, you very seldom have a chance to hear your pieces at an in-between stage; you usually go to a last run-through where the performers ask, "Do you want this faster? Do you want that louder? Is this an E-flat or an E?" I didn't write an orchestral piece for substantially this reason until the 1960s. I do not yet know whether many of the mistakes I heard in the performance of that piece were mistakes of performance or mistakes in the printed music. If I had tried to stop the Philharmonic or the Cleveland Orchestra over each mistake they made, they would never have gotten through the piece. And they would never have allowed so many interruptions. Why, I've seen Hindemith with Mitropoulos, the conductor saying to the composer, "Now don't bother me with details. We don't have time." *None* of us was ever treated any differently. I've seen the great names of our time, including Stravinsky, having exactly the same problem with Fritz Reiner doing *Rake's Progress* at the Metropolitan. There's never any time! It costs $1000 a second or whatever.

I think composers may be the worst off among creative artists in our time. My friends the poets say they have an analogously difficult situation, that they must teach in universities in order to write, that the "educated public" doesn't read their poetry as it doesn't listen to our music. But the analogy stops there. Poets are not dependent upon performers, the trappings of performance, or the expensive, refractory electronic alternatives. The printing of poetry is far less expensive and complicated.

A number of years ago, Arthur Berger showed me a column in the New York *Times* in which the journalist included us in a reference to "established composers." Arthur asked me if I felt "established." I knew well why he asked, and I could answer only, "It depends." Certainly I had and have little relation to the establishments of public music, or the world of public musicians. Not just the singers at the Met, but the celebrated and powerful conductors of our time, who control the repertory of our most competent orchestras, even some of our best student orchestras, or those journalists, executives, and executants, who largely determine what can be widely heard, and eventually what will therefore be composed.

I know of no conductor now, surely not one who conducts an orchestra of such ability and prestige as the Boston Symphony possessed in the thirties, who plays the role in American music that Koussevitzky did then. I do, however, have a rather different view of him from that of some of my colleagues. It is a relatively impersonal one; his years of power came before I could have been considered "on the scene." He obviously did wonderful things for Copland, Harris, Schuman, and even such younger composers as David Diamond. But I was a Roger Sessions student and adherent, and he and Roger broke in the thirties. As I understood it, Roger's Violin Concerto was commissioned to be played by Albert Spalding with the Boston Symphony under Koussevitzky. Spalding demanded that Roger change the violin part of the last movement, and Koussevitzky supported this demand. Roger, who had spent years composing the work, refused. The work was not done by Koussevitzky, with Spalding or any other violinist. (The work has been recorded as Roger wrote it by Paul Zukofsky.) Hence my limited picture of Koussevitzky, who nevertheless had a permanent effect upon the course and development of American composition.

But it is not only performers who shun many of us composers; composers are not so wonderfully concerned with each other. I am saddened, if not angered, when I attend a concert such as the one I heard last night, an ISCM [International Society for Contemporary Music] concert in which an extraordinary young pianist, Robert Black, played five new works by young or younger composers which had been selected in the ISCM international piano competition. The sole reward was to be a public performance in New York by Black, a pianist of whom probably most of the entrants had not then even heard. But there were 260 submissions, some from celebrated composers. It would appear that even celebrated composers have to seek these means of getting their music played. There were so many worthy works that the three fine judges, Beveridge Webster, Robert Helps, and Seymour Shifrin, selected ten for two concerts rather than five for one. At the first concert, what made me sad was that I was the only composer of my generation who was present.

If there were 100 people in the hall I'd be surprised; there were a few young composers, a number of people I couldn't identify (probably friends of the pianist's and the composers' families)—and that was it. The sense of colleagueship has been lost, totally lost. And to that extent that's new.

I think *I* know by name almost every functioning American composer from Aaron's and Roger's generation on. Some of them I know extremely well; I have known all of them well at one time or another and some of us were intimates—people like Arthur Berger, Irving Fine, George Perle, Ben Weber. Now the composer's world is fragmented, but, to be sure, it has vastly expanded. How many young composers were there in New York in 1935? A very small number. There are many, many more now. That alone could explain part of the change, but not why there is no more interest than was demonstrated at the concert. That concerns me very much.

Composers are often asked for whom they write. I write for anyone who's genuinely interested. I once wrote an article entitled "Who Cares if You Listen?" That article has haunted me much of my life because of the title, which I didn't write. It made me notorious and celebrated in circles where not a note of my music has ever been heard. It has been reprinted in at least three anthologies. The title embarrasses me because "Who Cares . . . ?" reflects very little of the letter and nothing of the spirit of the article. This is what happened. While teaching at Tanglewood in 1957, I gave a public lecture about contemporary music. Aaron was there with me, so were

Irving Fine and Karl Kohn. We presented a series of lectures and I gave one about the state of contemporary music. It was purely expository. The then editor of *High Fidelity* asked me to write it up for that magazine. So I did, only *my* pretty prosaic title was "The Composer as Specialist." I grant that's not very provocative, but it was accurate. The article, you see, did not remotely suggest indifference to listeners. I was trying to face the fact that very few people are even aware of the existence of most contemporary music. Even fewer people listen to it with the kind of interest some of us have in fields outside our own specialities. Therefore, the composer has perforce become a specialist, writing for other professionals, mostly for other composers. What are the implications of this situation? How do you live with it? I simply described how we do live. We live in universities; we cannot support ourselves by our music; it is a product with very little commodity value. Then I tried to ascribe this condition to certain purely musical and some social causes. Music *did* change overwhelmingly within the past half century. Don't tell me that there wasn't *that* much of a break, that we're just too close to it, that great historical perspective is needed. That's just not so. The most influential composers of our time, like Schönberg, are still not in any standard repertory; works he wrote fifty years ago are still little known to the concert public. Yet *we* composers know them as thoroughly as we know Beethoven's *Eroica* Symphony, and young composers already think they are as much of the past as the *Eroica*. I meant to indicate that this condition creates difficulties for all of us, not only for listeners but also for composers and for performers too. It's not a question of who cares if you listen; the point is that very few people *do* listen and we're concerned not only *that* they listen, but about *how* they listen. All this was misconstrued to mean that I really didn't care if anybody listened. How absurd! I'd love to have our music widely heard, widely understood, widely sold, and widely published. My two large orchestra works continue to go unpublished. No one can afford to publish them. They would cost $15,000 to publish in any form whatsoever. They're available as manuscripts and parts from publishers. My work for string orchestra and tape, which has been done many times by Boulez, by Schuller, by James Levine, is not published. Those works have never been recorded—again, much too expensive. As a matter of principle I have never personally subsidized anything—couldn't really afford it anyway. And who am I? Why, one of "the established American composers!"

Sure, go to the National Institute of Arts and Letters, or the American Academy of Arts and Sciences and there I'm part of the establishment—for one day at a time. And when I'm there I usually feel that talking to my colleagues in other fields is as hopeless as would be talking with people I've seen on the subway on the way to the meeting. Not just as a composer, but altogether, I'm enormously discouraged about the situation of intellectuals in contemporary society. I feel much more of a threat now than I did in 1939 when I was worried to death about Hitler—and was personally terrified and screaming bloody murder. I feel that way today in many respects, personally and professionally. If few composers today speak of reaching out to the masses with their music, it is because they are not provided even with the means of reaching their interested colleagues, and because we are increasingly deluged by the products of a people's cultural democracy. The masses have their music, and if anyone doubts it or doubts how they revel in it, he need merely, as I have, be driven by car across or up and down this country and listen to the radio. The continuous, and continuously the same, country and western and rock music is interrupted only when one approaches a metropolis which identifies its cultural resources by the presence of what is proudly termed a "beautiful music" station, which plays Muzak. It is not that I never hear the music of Schönberg or Donald Martino, but that I can't hear Brahms or Mozart, or even jazz.

And I fear that music, being still the most expensive of noises, is being more deeply affected by such homogenization than are other areas. For instance, we receive brilliant, privileged freshmen at Princeton, who in their first year of college are likely to take a philosophy of science course with Carl Hempel, and then return to their dormitories to play the same records that the least literate members of our society embrace as the only relevant music. When such students take a contemporary music course in which we try seriously to approach them, justifiably or not, as young intellectuals, they are found to suffer from irreparable musical illiteracy and early miseducation. These young people seem less prepared to take music seriously or cope with music than with any of the other arts. And so too with most relatively educated people, even in the universities. I have found few nonmusician academics who are acquainted even with the names, not to say the music, of my most influential colleagues. The best performed concerts of the most carefully selected contemporary music are matters of no interest to my fellow noncomposer faculty members at Princeton and, to a slightly lesser extent only, at Juilliard. The intersection of awareness and concern is so slight among fields that few of my Princeton faculty friends are even aware of the presence of composers on university faculties, and—therefore—of the complex cultural conditions that cause their presence there.

One needn't go beyond the nearest public newsstand to discover the differences in the states of the arts. There are, for all of their methodological naïveté, a large number of elaborate and relatively serious periodicals devoted to the literary and visual arts, as opposed to those concerned with serious contemporary music. Well, you may say, that is the considerable difference. The literary magazines have literature to be read; the art magazines have art objects to be seen as well as talked about. Many can read their native language, and many can look at a reproduction of a picture, but relatively few nonprofessionals can read a score mentally and accurately. It is words without musical reference that make the words we encounter "about music" the thoughtless, dangerous objects that they so often are. And the most considered, coherent, and correspondent words about music can aid only the most concentrated listening, not the passive, casual listening that easy access to phonograph records has encouraged. It is that short-term hearing which such listening seems to encourage that makes listeners to, for instance, my electronic works conclude that either it doesn't sound like music at all or that it is "interesting" because of its "new sounds." To the first response, I can reply only that such a listener probably would have the same reaction to my nonelectronic compositions, for the issue is not that of the medium, but of that enormous gap between their listening repertory and mine, my musical internalizations and theirs. A listener can't jump into our music without the conditioning of the intermediary stages: the Schönberg Violin Concerto must be as familiar as Beethoven's Opus 130. Such a condition is not reached by descriptive acquaintance with a theory of music any more than proper preparation for the reading of a serious contemporary novelist would be the reading of a volume on English phrase structure and grammar without any considered experience of literature itself.

I'm afraid that, if anything, the musical audience is less sophisticated than it was when I was younger. Somehow there are far fewer individuals who have really come to grips with music by listening hard or performing. We used to have a lot of amateur musicians. They would go to music shops regularly and inquire, "What music was published this week? Let me take some miniature scores home to read and play on the piano." Who does that now? My impression is, very few indeed.

Superficially things might have seemed worse in the 1930s and 1940s. The audience seemed more sophisticated then, but there were not as many opportunities for composers. We do get our music performed now, we do get some recordings, we do occasionally get published. Back then Sessions was getting one or two performances a year in small rooms. That situation has improved, but we have no larger or more knowing an audience. I go to the best concerts of contemporary music and see the same hundred or so people there week after week. I repeat, because it concerns me so, very few of my colleagues, who grew up on the streets of New York fighting the composer's battle, turn up to hear a young composer's music. As a result many young composers are, I hate to use this word, "alienated" even within their own profession. This is indeed a sad and symptomatic state of affairs, when the very survival of serious musical activity is so seriously threatened, by those within and outside the profession.

Photo by Judith Liegner

When I was very young, I wanted to be a pianist, and had childhood fantasies of playing at Carnegie Hall. And then—I can't remember why, maybe I never knew—when I was about eleven I wanted to compose. And I did; but my first attempts, mostly for piano, were completely uninteresting even to me. In my late teens I began writing songs, setting poems that really moved me. The first one I wrote meant more to me than anything else I had done before. From then on, which was a long time ago, I've been obsessed with composing. Not twenty-four hours a day by any means, and I don't keep little notebooks in my pockets to jot down ideas, but it's my main interest, my basic drive.

I was born in Colorado, where I lived until the age of six. My father taught at a university there, and after that we moved eastward, finally reaching New York, where I grew up. My parents liked music, but in those days not every family had a phonograph, let alone a hi-fi. We didn't even have a piano. But my father's brother, Henry Gideon, who was a very fine musician—he was music director of Temple Israel in Boston—visited us and discovered that I was musical, so he took me under his wing and unofficially adopted me. Through high school and college I lived with him in Boston. There I studied piano with Felix Fox, a fine pianist, and went to Boston University, where I took all the music courses they gave. That was long before Boston University had a separate school of music, as it has now.

After I graduated from Boston University I came back to New York and went to New York University for some graduate courses, thinking I'd ultimately get a teacher's license. I got acquainted with the music faculty and played them some of the pieces I had written. I'll always be grateful to Martin Bernstein, one of the professors. He said, "Why, you're a composer!" That meant a lot to me at the time because he could just as well have said, "Oh, you need an awful lot of study," or, "What do you mean, you want to compose, you're a woman . . ."

After that I studied with Lazare Saminsky, a distinguished Russian composer. He was very helpful in consolidating my previous knowledge and allowing me to discover my own voice as a composer. After a couple of years he suggested that I work with somebody else.

Miriam Gideon was interviewed at her home in New York City in April 1976.

At that moment, in the mid-thirties, two noted composers had just arrived in this country. One was Arnold Schönberg and the other was Roger Sessions, who had been in Europe for so many years that he was practically an expatriate. I didn't know which one to choose and let Saminsky be the judge. He decided the matter on a very practical basis. It seemed that Schönberg would not be on the East Coast very long and that Sessions would. Since I wanted to stay in the East, that settled the issue. Now, Schönberg was a marvelous teacher and I'm sure it would have been a great experience to have studied with him, but Sessions, with whom I worked for many years, was also wonderful. He taught privately, as well as in a group, which was more practical as far as his time went and beneficial to everybody involved. My first contact with him was as part of a group of composers that included David Diamond, Milton Babbitt, Leon Kirschner, Hugo Weisgall, Vivian Fine, Edward T. Cone, and quite a few others.

We used to meet at the Dalcroze School for three or four hours in the morning, and later at a studio Sessions had in New York. We all brought our recent work and played for one another. It was a great experience. There was a lot of give and take between teacher and pupils and among the students themselves. Afterward, we would go out for coffee and talk some more. Sessions put most of us through a pretty rigorous study of strict counterpoint. He had studied with Ernest Bloch, who as a sixteenth-century specialist felt that that discipline was most important. I got a tremendous amount from Sessions' approach, which combined the study of basic music theory with assessment of our latest compositions. At that time he was in his late thirties, and was well known for his brilliant youthful compositions, like *The Black Maskers,* as well as for his more complex works.

This century has produced several very gifted composition teachers. Students of Schönberg say that he, like Sessions, and Nadia Boulanger, another extremely influential teacher, stressed fundamentals. Very few of Schönberg's students ever studied twelve-tone writing with him; he thought a lot of preparation was required before young composers were ready to use tone-rows. Most never got to that stage. I feel the same way in dealing with young composers, who often want to get started immediately with avant-garde techniques.

In those years I was able to hear a great deal of contemporary music in New York. There were the Copland-Sessions concerts, a vigorous League of Composers, the Pan-American Society, and other

groups whose activities I attended. I heard works by Stravinsky and
Schönberg as well as by my American colleagues. The creative scene
was lively. Many European composers visited or emigrated to the
United States, and we met them at concerts and receptions. I remember especially Béla Bartók. I didn't do any more than say, "How
do you do, Mr. Bartók?" but I was struck by his beautiful bright blue
eyes. I must add that Bartók influenced a great many composers,
myself included. There's hardly one of us who hasn't gone through a
Bartók stage, especially when it comes to string quartets.

In the 1940s I went to Columbia University and received a Master's Degree in musicology. Some years later I was granted a Doctor
of Sacred Music in Composition from the Jewish Theological Seminary of America, on the basis of a number of works I wrote—a
Sacred Service, a cantata based on the Book of Proverbs, and a set of
Spiritual Madrigals.

How did I get interested in Jewish music? Well, during my
teens, when I lived with my uncle in Boston, I attended many services and heard very fine choral singing. All that stayed somewhere
in my consciousness. I didn't actually do any composing or thinking
about Jewish music until Dr. Hugo Weisgall, the chairman of the
faculty of the Cantors Institute at the Jewish Theological Seminary,
asked me if I would teach there. That was more than twenty years
ago. I've been there ever since.

In the last few years I've had two commissions for services, one
in 1971 from David Gooding, the music director of The Temple in
Cleveland, who suggested that I write in any style I wished and for
any instruments. I set the traditional Hebrew service in terms of what
it meant to me, in my own somewhat complex musical language,
and employed, besides the organ, a small chamber group of winds
and strings. The Psalms especially have quite an emotional impact
on me and I tried to reflect this impact in my setting of them. In
1974 Cantor David Putterman, of the Park Avenue Synagogue in
New York City, approached me about another service. If I wished it
to become part of the repertoire, he suggested that I make this service
simpler and that I use some traditional elements. Trying to preserve
my own integrity while drawing on tradition was a challenge I wel-
comed.

It's only since the 1940s that I can speak of my own style. So
many early songs of mine were in the tradition of German romantic

lieder, except for the very first song I set, which was by an American poet whose name I've forgotten. My parents were born in this country, but their parents were German. My father got his degree in philosophy at the University of Marburg. German was spoken at home, more or less as a secret language. Through my husband, Frederic Ewen—who has written a book on Bertolt Brecht, and has translated Heine and other German poets—the German influence continues. I've recently set quite a bit of German poetry as well as poetry in other languages, such as French, Spanish, Latin, Hebrew, and even Japanese. I'm particularly fascinated by setting the same poem in the original language and also in translation. The challenge of finding a different musical garment for the same poetic idea, with all the subtleties of color and connotation that each language presents, is a never-ending source of creative interest to me.

Setting *The Hound of Heaven,* or lines from it, by Francis Thompson, was a turning point for me. Now, that's a poem of religious conversion. Strangely enough, it was commissioned by Lazare Saminsky for the 100th anniversary of the founding of Temple Emanuel. I used only a few lines, concentrating on the aspects of life experience so graphically expressed in the poem. That was probably the first piece written in what I would call my own style. It's been well received, recorded, and published. I can't help feeling that if Saminsky were alive he would be very happy about it.

Everything I write has to surprise me—otherwise I can't get excited about it. Most of my works seem to me to be fresh, original statements. I haven't made basic or radical changes in my musical vocabulary. I have been called a vanguard composer. Whether that term is valid depends on what you mean by it. In relation to much recent music, for example, mine would probably seem rather conservative.

How do I feel about current trends in music? Most composers these days are curious about electronic music, if only because they want to understand it better. I've never felt drawn to this medium because I've never been able to relate to it enough as music. To me it's a fascinating experiment in sound—a totally different mode of experience. I think, however, that the words "music" and "concert" as applied to electronic music are misleading. I don't know what other words to substitute, but I'd try to find other ones if I thought anyone would use them. As for aleatoric music, it seems to me that composing is a serious and highly responsible art that cannot be relegated to chance, or to performers under the illusion that they are participating in the "creative process." It's interesting to see that there is a tendency now for some of our most advanced composers to go back to using very traditional language, and even to quote classical compositions in their works. I wonder if this is not an evasion, to escape from coming to grips with what they really want to say in music.

To some extent, I need to hear my works played in order to feel that they have come alive. I sometimes make changes after a first performance, not so much in basic structure as in details of instrumentation, dynamics, or tempo.

Looking back over my composing career, I started out with songs and went on to chamber music, mostly string quartets, which were always a great love of mine. Then I wrote orchestral pieces, among them a *Sinfonia Brevis*, requested by Professor Fritz Jahoda of the music department of City College for the City College orchestra. I asked him whether I should temper my style, and he said "No, you can write anything you want and we'll play it!" So I wrote a really difficult piece for large orchestra, and they played it remarkably well. Since then it has been recorded by a professional orchestra in Europe, and is a revealing example of the vehement style of my "middle period." After that, and for some years now my interest has veered in the direction of chamber ensembles of various combinations, many with solo voice.

I think my first commission came from Temple Emanuel, back in the 1940s. Since then, besides the two Sacred Services, I've received a number of commissions from private sources, including one for a piano suite, *Of Shadows Numberless*, and another for a work for voice and chamber group, *Nocturnes*—both from a parent who preferred to commission a composer than to spend money on parties for his children's important birthdays. Another commission has come from the New York State Music Teachers Association, for a chamber work, *Fantasy on Irish Folk Motives*; and most recently there was a grant from the National Endowment for the Arts for a work for solo voice and orchestra, *Songs of Youth and Madness*, on poems of Friedrich Hölderlin.

Most of my commissions have come in the last few years, but earlier I had requests for works for performance from the League of Composers, the International Society for Contemporary Music, and similar groups, and from soloists or chamber groups planning a concert. It's many years since I've composed a piece without knowing who would perform it, except for a short opera I wrote just because I felt like it. That was a reckless sparring with Fate. It hasn't as yet been produced.

Like most composers, I couldn't earn a living solely from my compositions. I do get a yearly stipend from Broadcast Music, Incorporated; then there are small royalties from my published works; most of the royalties from recordings go back into repressings. Many composers subsist mainly by teaching, as I have done at Brooklyn College, City College, and the Jewish Theological Seminary.

When I step back and look at the academic situation, I feel that many young composers have been taught wrong musical values. Often they've been well schooled in sophisticated compositional devices—so well schooled that they've sacrificed spontaneity. I may sound a bit stuffy about this, but I've come to believe that it's very important at a certain stage in a young composer's development for him to write the way he really feels. He has to trust himself. Otherwise he's likely to flounder in a sea of persuasive techniques and never know who he is.

There are other aspects of the music scene that trouble me. For instance, the entire music world is competitive. You can't blame composers for seeking prizes, but you can be sorry about it when they are driven to pursue the very attention-getting techniques that keep them from realizing themselves as composers. Still, the performing situation is better than ever. There are a number of excellent groups around the country playing primarily contemporary music. Concerts by these fine groups are even more important to the composer than prizes, because they give him a chance to be heard under optimum circumstances. The growth of these organizations is encouraging. A very useful and recent catalog of these groups is available from the American Music Center, 250 West 57th Street, New York City, N.Y. 10019.

There is no doubt that contemporary music is becoming increasingly acceptable to music students, musicians, and even the public, who hear it more or less unconsciously in theaters, movie houses, and on television. Background music is frequently quite advanced. Resistance to new music is on the decline, especially in the big cities, because there it's constantly recorded and broadcast. The situation has dramatically improved over the years of my teaching career. I remember the day Bartók's death was reported in the press. I was teaching at Brooklyn College, and I said to the class, "Today I read about the death of an eminent composer. Did anybody notice the obituary?" Nobody had. When I told them that it was Béla Bartók, not one person in the room even knew the name. I don't think the same thing could happen today.

There's one question about composers I'm frequently asked that is as self-defeating as it is impossible to answer: "Why are there no great women composers?" I can repeat some of the obvious reasons: women came much later to all the professions, including the arts, and of the arts they probably came last to composing, as a career. We don't actually know yet if the past was as barren as it seems, and we can't judge the present with any great clarity. However, in the last few years there has been a tremendous upsurge of women composers. Much of their music is very fine, but it will take a long time before we really know their stature.

There were women composers in the sixteenth century and earlier, and scholars have just begun to do studies of them. To be sure, there have been fewer women composers in the past than women writers or painters, probably because it takes very special technical training to compose, and it hasn't been easy for women to get that. Admission to musical academies in the past has been difficult for women, and in their role as wives, mothers, and homemakers they have been hindered in sustaining an art that is so involved in technical complexities. In spite of these handicaps there are many works by women that compare with the best by their male contemporaries.

It can't be denied, however, that women have suffered from less attention and recognition as composers. I never thought so in the past. For years people would ask me about the hardships of being a woman composer, and I'd tell them, "*I've* never suffered from that. *I've* always had my fair share of recognition." Now I realize that the kind of recognition we don't get is something we very often don't know about. And since serving on many committees and juries, I've come to sense that there *is* a subtle discrimination against women. It's almost unconscious, but I've recognized it even in myself. When I'm being very honest, trying to nab my prejudices as I come across them, I'm aware of a tendency to be more sceptical about a woman composer than about a man. Now if *I* feel that way, surely my male colleagues do, too. Sometimes they bend over backward in their acceptance of women, and I find that most unfortunate. On this matter there's one other point that's very important: I feel that it is a mistake to isolate women on concert programs or broadcasts or recordings. Integrate women composers on an equal footing with men, but don't segregate them.

4: Theodore Antoniou

I have done a lot of traveling in my life. My birthplace was Athens, where I completed most of my musical studies some twenty years ago. I took a lot of music in high school, and later graduated from the National Conservatory of Music with diplomas and special projects in violin, composition, harmony, and fugue. In 1961 I received a German scholarship and then went to Munich, where I studied composition and conducting until 1966. I returned to Greece at that time. I was artistic director of the orchestra of the city of Athens. I wrote music for theater and conducted a good deal. It looked as if I would be spending most of my time in my native land.

Then in 1967 the Greek military junta came to power, and I had to interrupt all my activities. In 1968 I accepted an invitation from the city of Berlin, in conjunction with the Ford Foundation. Musicians were invited from all over the world—along with painters, architects, and other artists—to spend one year in Berlin.

I had visited America for the first time in 1966, on an invitation from the State Department, and lectured at various universities. I couldn't exactly return to Athens after my year in Berlin; I wasn't, shall we say, enthusiastic about the Colonels' regime. Also, what I did was too "radical" for a military dictatorship. So I accepted an invitation from Stanford University to teach there for a semester. That year, 1969, I was also commissioned by the Fromm Foundation to compose an orchestral work which Gunther Schuller conducted at Tanglewood. Apparently the performance was successful; from then on, these people followed my development wherever I went. In 1974 they asked me to come back to Tanglewood, this time as assistant director of contemporary composing and conducting activities. So for the past seven or eight years, I have taught in the U.S. part of every year; the rest of the time I spend in different parts of Europe. I certainly do a lot of traveling, which I never dreamed of when I was growing up.

My family was not musical, and my schoolteachers were very surprised that I turned out to be a musician. Thinking I was rather a good student, they had wanted me to become an engineer. My father had been a printer, but he was killed during World War II when I was two years old. I started working when I was six. I taught at the

Theodore Antoniou lives in Philadelphia and was interviewed at Tanglewood in August 1975.

National Conservatory from the time I was seventeen. From then on I knew I wanted to dedicate myself totally to music. I was always involved in much more than my studies. For example, I organized groups that were somehow oriented to the promotion of music, especially new music.

I helped organize the Hellenic Group of Contemporary Music in Athens; at Stanford I was involved in the Alea II New Music Group; and at the University of Utah, where I worked for a quarter, I started another group which even now I occasionally conduct. I have been working in Philadelphia since 1970, spending at least 20 or 22 weeks of the year there. I teach composition and head the symphony orchestra at the Philadelphia Musical Academy and also run another professional new music group, outside the school but in Philadelphia.

And fortunately, the junta is gone and I can spend time in Greece again. I'm very active in writing music for the theater there, for such plays as Sophocles' *Oedipus Rex*. What I write is not background music, but rather musical commentary or interpretation on the text.

At present, whatever part of the world I'm in, my life consists of teaching, conducting, and above all composing because I have many commissions. As long as I have the strength I will probably split my life in this way. Sometimes I think I may have to stop teaching and be only a composer. At another moment I say, well, I have taken on some educational responsibilities—and it is hard to withdraw from them.

I have composed maybe sixty or seventy works and they have all been performed. That's most unusual, very gratifying, and exceedingly helpful. Every composer's development is advanced if he can hear his music, so that he does not repeat the same problems or make the same mistakes. Unfortunately, many composers today don't get to hear their works played.

On the other hand, even if your works are done, they're not very often done well. The performances of my music at Tanglewood this summer were very good. Likewise the composers whose work I conducted—Shulamit Ran (an Israeli), Messiaen, and Berlioz. Messiaen was there and was most impressed. Perfection is impossible, particularly within the domain of new music; it's a question of coming close to the truth or straying far from it. I try to understand each contemporary composer I conduct on his own terms, and do right by his particular kind of music.

In my own pieces, I was influenced in the beginning by Greek traditional and folk music, and at the same time adapted new techniques, like Schönberg's twelve-tone system. My compositions of seventeen or eighteen years ago are full of those combinations. In the last eight years, I have been immersed in the more universal and humanitarian aspects of music. Today I address problems that are very strongly related to human beings—for example, in a recent series of pieces meant to question our technological achievements. Of course it is difficult to do this musically, but I try to communicate my ideas, to question, to take positions. I don't believe in art as a decorative type of expression. I believe it is a necessary form of communication.

And, as a composer, I think you should know what's happening around you, and not be apathetic or isolated. By being aware you probably incorporate more about society into your music than you realize. Then in expressing yourself you encompass much more than yourself. In composing, my aim is not just esthetic or social or political. It is all of them. By the time you are a genuine artist you have become a symbol in your society. You cannot be isolated from its problems; you cannot be oblivious to what is happening. I react as a human being; sometimes my sentiments are expressible in music.

Of course, I want to be recognized for my music, not for my political views. But I have the right to be inspired by anything, and if political conviction, such as opposition to militarism, makes me compose good music, I think that's wonderful.

I have composed two pieces which I call *Protest I* and *Protest II*. One of those was performed in Greece during the military regime, on one of my trips home. The police came. I had to escape to the U.S. the next morning. The piece was an obvious reaction against, let's say, certain surroundings that were not correct. I have another series of pieces called *Events—Events I, II* and *III*. My commission from the Fromm Foundation in 1969 resulted in *Events II*, in which I took important events around the world and tried to incorporate them—in an abstract way, of course.

I'm not an author, but sometimes one can be very provocative, radical or what-have-you in a nonverbal art form. Even without program notes or knowledge of what prompted me, I think that any sophisticated audience can understand a musical message of this kind. I'm sure an aggressive sound is an aggressive sound; the emotion carries beyond the sound itself. You will know that I want to provoke you by directing a very loud sound at you; that's clearly intended to be shocking. Ultimately my hope is that you will say, "Yes, that means something to me," or if I fail, "It does not mean anything at all." My musical statements are very personal. Nothing would make me happier than that all my worries, thoughts, and emotions would come through my music to everyone.

But I realize how diverse people are. I understand that they come from different backgrounds, each with a different education. What reaches one audience is unintelligible to another. Sometimes pieces that would be really revolutionary in a place like Darmstadt might seem crazy and unmusical in a place like Salt Lake City. I do my best to understand my surroundings wherever I am, to be part of them. But you never know exactly how your emotions will strike others.

Take a simple example. When I was in military service, the cook was illiterate, so he used to bring me his girlfriend's loveletters to read to him. They were so funny to me, I could hardly keep myself from laughing. And he was crying because they conveyed something entirely different to him. A sensitive person walking on the street sees a thousand details someone else fails to see at all.

I admire many composers, and in a very abstract or filtered way, I carry many with me. But I cannot point to passages in my music and say, "That was Bartók's, or this was Schönberg's influence." A newspaper critic has spoken about my gaining eclecticism without losing originality. I hope he means that my work has many elements but it's still my own, which would be very high praise. I don't believe you can find a single example in the arts which does not show traces of a tradition. The question is, how obvious is that tradition?

In my role as a performer, I choose to be very involved in whatever piece I'm doing. Even if the music makes little sense to me, I try to put something creative across. If pieces are well or seriously worked out, I don't have the right to stop and say, "Well, so-and-so is a bad composer. I'm not going to play his music." That's not fair at all. I respect people who approach their material seriously, and I struggle to make sense of things that do not personally appeal to me. You see, musical creativity for me is not just having music in my head and writing it down. The act of performance is also creative—

who's playing, who's listening, what changes are made from one rehearsal to the next? I enjoy the process of bringing music to life—especially recent music.

Unfortunately, in America and to some extent around the world, the repertory is mostly nineteenth-century German music. The main problem is that we educate people to like Beethoven and Brahms—and then, although audiences are totally unprepared for it, we throw in a new piece on a concert program and of course it's rejected. We have had, as we shall continue to have, good and bad music of all periods, but I think it is incumbent upon us to educate correctly, starting not from superficial things, but from those that go much deeper. Once, when I was conducting a large symphony orchestra, the ladies' committee wanted only Mozart and I intended to play Ligeti and do improvisation with the orchestra. I said to the women, "Don't expect me and my contemporaries to write music for your relaxation." For them, you see, music was a sophisticated drug. They forgot that the creator is no longer a court composer whom you pay to make you laugh and relax. My reminder shocked them. I asked them further, "What do you expect? I'm no different from Beethoven. He expressed his sound experiences with the media at his disposal. I do exactly the same thing. Of course, I am a nobody in comparison to a giant like that, but the relationship between the composer and his materials has not changed so much.

Of course, as a twentieth-century man, I have experiences that Beethoven never thought or dreamt about. Go to 42nd Street and Broadway in New York and just stand on the corner and listen. Well, you might say that what you hear is not music. But no sound in itself is music. When you start selecting and shaping sound sensations from the world around you, you start creating art.

In our time, news travels very fast. I know what Mr. Takemitsu is doing in Japan right now. I know all about the performance of Boulez's pieces in Darmstadt yesterday and that Shostakovitch died the day before yesterday. I cannot be isolated any more; no one can. Just for contrast, consider Bach. He had to travel I don't know how many days to hear a famous organist (Buxtehude), and we can just get on a plane and be places in hours. Half-centuries have now been collapsed into ten or fifteen years. Everything moves at a vastly accelerated pace for us, and for audiences, this is sometimes confusing to follow. But I think the big mistake is that they never start with the right question which is this: What music should we expect to be written today? Why is it absurd for contemporary composers to compose music in the style of Brahms? Sympathizing with a period which I didn't live through has its merits, but imitating the music of that period would get to be an inauthentic exercise after a while. I cannot be Brahms. Reincarnation is not a very common occurrence, you know.

One should try to make society more and more aware of the validity of contemporary artistic expression. I attempt to do this with my students and friends, explaining to them that I'm not generically different from all those other composers of the past. In every period, it's essential for composers to convey their own musical expressions— that's what Beethoven, Brahms, and Stravinsky did. But today there are new and different questions for composers to deal with. This must be impressed on people who hold strong philosophical positions concerning what art "should" be, and who feel all great music has already been written. You try to prepare them for the performance of your music. You can't be snobbish. You don't shout at them, "You are idiots and should know better." You say, "Let's discuss why I'm not supposed to be like the composers of the past and why it is unreasonable to expect me to speak in an archaic language."

I personally feel very close to Oriental music. And I discover music in unlikely surroundings and places. For instance, seeing a flower can be music for me. Thinking silently could be a musical experience. Music is not only something played by instruments. I have done a lot of mixed media compositions, in addition to the music for the Greek tragedies I mentioned. One is a mixed media piece for planetarium. I'm even using a miniature planetarium machine as an instrument.

Getting my own works performed has not been much of a problem, as I said. More frustrating is trying to introduce pieces by other persons whom I highly respect. I see many uninterested performers around, who don't like playing music of their own time, a sight I don't relish. Apathy breaks the great chain of music. Links disappear. Connections are lost. I know quite a few composers who are unknown and should be known. Some of them powerfully challenge musical understanding. It makes me unhappy they are slighted. I wish we were more open-minded as a society. I feel obliged to be involved, to know what is happening around me. Our musical tradition may have started some thousand years ago but it keeps growing. It does not end.

In some ways contemporary composers are better off than their predecessors. Nowadays there are many institutions that give commissions. And there's the whole university structure in which composers can at least orient themselves. As to government sponsorship, it all depends on the government. In Germany they spend lots of money on music, either because they believe in helping the arts or in reaction against other periods when the government treated the arts badly. The radio orchestras in Germany help us a lot. I'm very disappointed in the American star conductor who doesn't want to risk his big reputation and sticks to the hundred standard pieces. He's too lazy to learn new music. I'm convinced that fear of audience reaction is just an excuse. These conductors want to be loved, adored, so they make programs very carefully to satisfy almost everyone and provide easy gratification. I don't like the way they view their function. It's narrow and self-serving.

As an analogy, take the magazine business. Why has it turned increasingly to pornography? Because by doing that, magazines are guaranteed to make money. Readers do indeed buy pornography—but the whole premise is, of course, a very big lie. It is like giving more and more drugs to somebody, so that he does not react to anything, like Muzak in the supermarket. Music directors learn statistically what music they should play so that the public will buy more and more. They are cheating us in a very sophisticated and organized way. And a society that does not bother about our education, about making us more aware, is our enemy. In reality, the audience is very flexible; it is potentially interested in new music. You have to approach people slowly and really spend time educating them. Then they'll be willing to learn.

Now, what is our collective responsibility? It's a question that concerns me. If I had the power I would ask a team of people whose concerns and ideas I respect to work on an agenda for broadening people's horizons. We could not expect any great change today or tomorrow; it would probably take one or two generations. But someone ought to start the wheels moving. You need time to correct things—and in the arts somebody should start right away!

I was always involved with music, though as a kid growing up in Lunenburg, Massachusetts, fifty miles from Boston, I had no idea I'd become a composer. My home was full of music. My mother used to play the piano, and my father, to this day, sings in church choirs. Also, I remember him listening to the New York Philharmonic broadcasts on Sundays. I started piano lessons early and hated them. Maybe it was the teacher. Later, when I was about ten, I began studying trumpet and loved it, so the trumpet became my "professional" instrument. In high school I organized my own little dance band, with kids from neighboring towns.

As a teenager, I remember haunting a record shop in Fitchburg—the only one near my home. I'd listen mainly to jazz records, and buy as many as I could afford. Oddly enough, this small-town store had the old 78 r.p.m. version of Charles Ives' *Concord Sonata*. That record made a profound impression on me. I would frequently take it into the listening booth, put it on and wonder, "My God, what is going on? What kind of music is this?" The piece sounded so wild at first that I said to myself, "How can anybody play this?" Even more puzzling, how could anybody write it? I hadn't heard any Ives before, but after listening to the sonata a few times, I was hooked. I kept going back to the shop to listen to it until the owner finally said, "Nobody else ever touches that album. Why don't you buy it?" My answer was simple: "$12 is more than I can pay." But when he offered it to me for half price, I couldn't resist and I still have that record.

The Ives sonata was the first piece of "new" music I knew well. I felt a special kinship with Ives, since we were exposed to many of the same musical influences. I heard the town band time and again, as Ives did, and I played trumpet in it for years. Naturally, some of the musicians weren't too competent. I became all too familiar with the out-of-tuneness and rhythmic unsettledness that Ives captured so effectively in his music.

Aside from Ives, my early influences came from the popular music world. I didn't grow up immersed in the classics. When a kid in Lunenberg, Mass., starts playing the trumpet, he idolizes people like Bunny Berrigan, the jazz trumpet player. After high school I studied mathematics and engineering at Northeastern University, and

Earle Brown lives in Rye, New York, and was interviewed at Tanglewood in August 1975.

thought I'd become an aeronautical engineer because of my passion for airplanes and flying, but no sooner did I enter the Air Force in 1945 than World War II ended and I gravitated toward the service's orchestras. I played mostly in Randolph Field, Texas, for two years. And I started studying music on my own; I began to study arranging and went through Hindemith's books on composition by myself. In the service we played everything from classical music to big band jazz to combos to marches. The experience meant deep absorption in the trumpet again and I loved it. When those two years were up, airplane flying seemed like bus driving, and I was converted to music as a profession. I remember sitting on my bunk in Texas, holding a trumpet in my hand and thinking, "Wouldn't it be great if I could make my entire life with just this?"

But my interests soon shifted from performing to composing. When I got out of the Air Force in 1946 I went to the Schillinger House School of Music in Boston, now called the Berklee School of Music. It's primarily jazz oriented today, but at that time I mainly studied the Schillinger theories and techniques of musical composition, which I still admire although I find them fraught with esthetic difficulties. They involve numerical and mathematical generation, construction, and distribution of materials; it's a highly "structuralist" approach.

Simultaneously, I studied composition privately with Roslyn Brogue Henning on the history of compositional forms—conductuses, motets, madrigals, fugues and so on. She is a twelve-tone composer, and also a terrific teacher of older polyphonic forms. While studying theory and composition, I also took trumpet lessons with a very good professional teacher in Boston named Fred Berman. He was famous and very influential as an exponent of the "no pressure" school of trumpet playing.

I was also very eager to catch up on recent musical developments. As yet, I'd barely heard any Schönberg or Webern and certainly no Varèse or Cage, though I did have a piano reduction of the Berg Violin Concerto and a Schönberg score, probably *Pierrot Lunaire*. But postwar Boston was boring musically; it was very hard to get new scores or to hear any recent music. I often think that this musical vacuum stimulated my curiosity in other arts. I spent a lot of time in a little poetry shop on Boylston Street, where I discovered Kenneth Patchen. His poems were a revelation to me, and became a very important influence on my music. I have a commission now to write a piece for orchestra and chorus, and I'm using Patchen texts. They are quite graphic, full of fantastic sonic potentials and relationships.

During this period in Boston (1945–50) I also discovered the abstract expressionist school of art. Much of my esthetic orientation comes from an early exposure to Jackson Pollock's techniques and paintings and Alexander Calder's mobiles. I clearly remember reading an article in *Life* magazine in 1949 on the abstract expressionists, in which Jackson Pollock's "spontaneous" technique was described. Of course *Life* put it down, calling Pollock "Jack the Dripper." The press was very nasty to poor old Jackson at first. Somehow Pollock's paintings reminded me of musical polyphony: the lines, textures, densities, and details were the kinds of things I heard in my head. I discovered I had quite a visual sonic imagination; I could almost see orchestral textures and colors. Pollock's spontaneity and immediacy (as in my experience with jazz) were tremendously influential; his direct confrontation with the canvas—what Harold Rosenberg calls "action painting"—led me to scoring a kind of "action music."

Calder's mobiles also directly affected my outlook. Calder, and other founders of the kinetic movement in the visual arts, held to the basic premise that a work of art need never look the same from moment to moment. When I first saw a slowly moving Calder mobile, I thought, "Whether I move or stand still, the relationships within the work, and between myself and the work, constantly shift. It is one work of art, yet an integrally modifiable one. It doesn't sit still like a Henry Moore sculpture." And even a Moore presents different aspects as you walk around it.

I had been thinking that in music, the concept of absolute fixity—that is, rigid adherence to a written score—was a comparatively recent development. From the thirteenth and fourteenth centuries, when Perotin and Machaut wrote, up until 200 years ago, the performance of Western music was more flexible and open. Improvisation and individual approach were a part of it and were encouraged. But the prevailing deterministic philosophy in the eighteenth and nineteenth centuries led to more precisely determined art. By the twentieth century we'd made a full circle. The indeterminacy principle in physics and various other relativistic points of view in science and philosophy led me to feel it was natural to create mobile, non-rigid works of art, to set musical materials in motion in such a

way as to allow for fluidity and flexibility in performance. Philosophy, science, and the visual arts all pointed the way; I felt it was time
that "classical" music followed suit.

As I began to hear more and more recent music, the works of
two very different composers, Edgard Varèse and Anton Webern,
stuck in my head. Varèse once made a valid distinction between his
kind of music and Webern's by dividing composers into two basic
categories—"note" composers and "sound" composers. For example,
a note composer may start with one note, then write a second, third,
fourth, and so on, in a horizontal progression or use a twelve-tone
row. Sound composers would tend to think more acoustically, in
terms of chordal blocks and textures. In the history of recent music,
Webern was a note composer and Varèse a sound composer. Ives was
a sound composer; Milton Babbitt is a note composer.

I had an early Varèse recording including *Intégrale, Ionisation*
and *Hyperprism;* although not much of my music sounds anything
like Varèse's, I suspect that his blocks of sound were an important influence on my own very intricate polyphonic webs. As for Webern, I
loved the transparency and delicacy of his musical textures, though
they seemed a little thin, and his manipulation of the twelve-tone
row a little obvious.

While these poetic, artistic, and musical strands floated around
in my mind, I finished my Schillinger studies and became an authorized teacher of the Schillinger system in 1950. I went West, looking
for a place to set up a studio or teach Schillinger techniques, perhaps
in university extension courses. I ended up in Denver; I liked the
climate and the people and I liked to ski. I lived in Denver two and a
half years, between 1950 and 1952. During this time I experimented
with many kinds of composition. I did three works in an extended
twelve-tone Schillinger serial mode, but then I began to move away
from structuralism. I did some painting, to learn what it felt like, and
to comprehend the control of colors, because in a way composing is
also the control of color. I also composed graphic scores—scores
which were themselves not only sets of musical instructions, but also
drawings. I did highly experimental things with improvisation and
spontaneity as part of the performance process. And in 1953 I composed what I consider, and I guess everybody now considers, the first
really mobile, open form composition, called *25 Pages.*

One of my key experiences in Denver was meeting John Cage.

Cage, who is fifteen years my senior, was already a "presence" in the musical world. He came to Denver to play his *Sonatas* and *Interludes* for prepared piano—not my kind of music at all. But for all our differences, we found we had much in common: Jackson Pollock intrigued us both, and we had an instant rapport on many questions of music and esthetics. I was lucky to meet Cage when I did. He buoyed my self-confidence, and gave me courage to carry on. At Cage's suggestion, I sent a score of *Three Pieces for Piano* to David Tudor in New York and he performed it, giving me my first New York performance. Later, Cage invited me to New York to work with him and Tudor on their electronic music project.

Those were exciting days. Cage and I worked together all day; then we'd have a beer at the Cedar Bar, where other regulars included Bill DeKooning, Mark Rothko, and Jackson Pollock. They all became great friends of ours and we had a lot to talk about.

Later, the painters were quite bewildered at their rather rapid rise from virtual anonymity to widespread acclaim, seemingly overnight. They were not sure that it was quite "proper." It raised real moral questions for these "rebellious" painters when their works suddenly became so bloody valuable. I remember back in the early 1950s, I used to help Bob Rauschenberg cart his paintings to and from his studio for an occasional show. For a long time nobody bought his paintings. He was giving them away—to me, to Cage, to his other friends, and it really surprised Bob when the value of his paintings went sky high.

I'll never have that problem. Composers and music can never be negotiable like visual artists and their work. We may be puzzled, all right, but not because our compositions are suddenly worth a fortune. Cage, for instance, is in a curious double bind: On the one hand, he is famous and notorious; on the other, many people who praise Cage's ideas and theories really don't like his music. He is a philosopher as well as a composer; sometimes his music doesn't sustain itself as "music." Being in the musical avant-garde presents contradictions to all of us sooner or later.

In the early 1950s, Cage, Morton Feldman, Christian Wolff, and I were the four oddballs in American music. If my music hadn't defined my esthetic position by itself, my association with Cage would have put me immediately outside the mainstream. Cage was considered a nut even among composers—admired at a distance by

nearly everybody and at the same time deemed a dangerous character. So working on the tape project with him, and writing graphic
improvisatory scores, tended to isolate me from my contemporaries.
Also, American composers usually studied at a conservatory or university with such as Roger Sessions, Aaron Copland or Milton Babbitt; but I went a different route.

I didn't mind being out on a limb, working in highly experimental ways, because I was clearly oriented about what I wanted to
do in music. I never wanted to write, say, six related string quartets
that added up to "Earle Brown's Quartet Literature." I don't write
music only for music's sake; I'm motivated by concerns with broader
artistic questions.

Many of my innovations have been in the area of performer involvement, of adding the performer's creativity to the composer's as
an integral part of a piece. In my *Folio* scores of 1952–53, for instance, I tried to find a notation that would give musicians a creative
role in the performance process. Whenever I talk or lecture about
this concept, I sound like an old-fashioned, nostalgic trumpet player:
I simply love the act of performing.

From the start, audiences and performers "understood" what I
was driving at more readily than critics. Critics worry about whether
what I do is valid as "ART." They get particularly confused when the
forms of some of my pieces are not clearly delineated until the works
are performed. Some critics react with, "It sounded terrific, but if it's
going to sound different the next time, how can I tell whether it's any
good?" That's not my worry, though I think only a good piece would
sound good at any given performance. And I've had enough experience—25 years worth—of writing open form and mobile improvisatory pieces to be able to judge—although by no means all of my
music is improvisatory or in open form.

The critic Nat Hentoff was one of the few to see immediately
what I was trying to do. It didn't worry him that I didn't write out
every detail and control every nuance; to Nat, a jazz expert, the act of
composition includes the performance as well as the score.

To continue with my life story—as a result of working on the
electronic music project between 1952 and 1954, I gained some experience using machines and tapes. So between 1955 and 1960 I supported myself as a recording engineer for Capitol Records. That job

involved recording everyone from Count Basie to Nathan Milstein. What a great experience for the ears! Every two years, while working at Capitol, I'd save enough money to take a leave of absence and go to Europe.

I have always had a very positive response to my music in Europe. I was able to break into the European musical scene in the 1950s largely because of Pierre Boulez. Boulez saw my *Perspectives* piece when he was visiting the U.S. in 1953 as conductor of the Jean Louis Barrault–Madelaine Renaud company. He was impressed by this work, though the "improvisatory" pieces of mine displeased him; he thought they were irresponsible, and left too much to the musicians' whims. Nonetheless, he asked me to come see him whenever I came to Paris. When I got there in 1956, Boulez wrote five important letters of introduction for me. One was to Otto Tomek of Universal Edition in Vienna, who soon after became music director of the Cologne Radio. Another was to Hans Rosbaud, one of the greatest conductors of Schönberg, Webern, and Berg. One was to Karl Amadeus Hartmann, the director of new music in Munich, and yet another was to William Glock, until recently the head of the BBC.

When I first got to Europe, my music was still too far out for Boulez and even for Luciano Berio. On the other hand, a musicologist named Heinz Klaus Metzger was very struck by it. Metzger was a student of Max Horkheimer and T. W. Adorno, the famous German philosophers from Frankfurt. Metzger's outlook was strongly anti-authoritarian. When he saw my scores and heard me describe them, he said, "Ah, finally someone has written music that does away with the conductor and the composer as authoritarian figures! You, Earle Brown, allow everyone to do what he wants."

"No," I responded, "There are rules, definite instructions to be followed." To this day, Metzger and I disagree on the implications of my scores. It can be said that I had a subliminal societal motive—to make the musician more autonomous. But Metzger considers my scores revolutionary, calculated to destoy the social "nonsense" of an orchestra and a conductor, while I just wanted to do something poetic with sound and give performers a chance to participate actively and spontaneously in the making of my music.

In a way, Metzger has misunderstood my graphic works. He recorded an entire set of pieces (*Folio*) in Germany, in a box set entitled "Music Before Revolution." Well, I thank him for bringing about some decent performances of the *Folio* pieces. Unfortunately, the playing in some cases was molded by Metzger's misunderstanding of my motives. His idea was to put 25 people in a room, let them start playing whenever they wanted, play as long as they cared to, and then stop, doing anything they chose along the way. At one of the recording sessions, I asked the musicians to listen to one another (which was always my intention). Metzger would reply, "No, you must let free individuals do their own thing." In the notes to the record, which is on the German Electrola label, Metzger criticizes me for giving the musicians such suggestions. My response is, "Fine—but if they ignore the score and each other, don't call the resulting piece an Earle Brown." Sure, I'm aware of the political and social ramifications of my musical tendencies but I never self-consciously seek to "liberate" people. It would be pretentious to think that by bringing musicians to my score I could "liberate" them. I believe in freedom, but there is no such thing as total freedom. Stravinsky's *Poetics of Music* made a strong impression on me long ago. In it, Stravinsky contended that having some restrictions, outlining your areas, made for the greatest freedom, because then you and others know where you are, and what is real and what is not.

Cage and I have long had a similar disagreement. I recall an early conversation after I looked at a new score of his. I didn't think musicians would respond too favorably to it because Cage went so far as to say, "Play the piece if you want to, and don't play it if you don't want to." In other words, the musicians, if so disposed, could sit and do nothing for the duration of the piece. Now, that is too ambiguous. It doesn't define the work or honor the musician, though Cage thinks it's a tremendous honor to free the performer to choose whether to do something or nothing. I told Cage, "You're really not interested in experimental music; you're creating eccentric social situations, not musical ones. You're more a musical sociologist than a composer." Bemusedly, he agreed with me.

I'm not willing to go as far as Cage does, though I believe that great art is subtly subversive. By quietly undermining artistic values that have gotten distorted or exploited, the best art makes a tacit, rather than a violent or aggressive, attack on social stagnation and corruption. Art is not the most effective weapon for revolution of any kind, but it can signify or encourage change. Art necessarily has varying and unpredictable effects on people. I'm convinced that in a healthy society, artistic norms should be constantly under question, which is not, of course, to deny the need for continuity. I feel that my *Folio* pieces are reasonably within a tradition. When writing them, I was influenced by Western and non-Western as well as jazz heritages; later I learned a lot by sitting in now and then on a course at the New School that Henry Cowell called "Music of the World's Peoples"—which covered Indonesian, Balinese, and Japanese music, among others.

Critics on both sides of the Atlantic sometimes find it hard to follow my musical influences from diverse cultural traditions, but I generally have a much easier time abroad. I am forever indebted to Boulez for introducing me to important musical figures throughout the Continent. Apparently, my scores made an impression on European composers in the 1950s, many of whom were still locked into writing tightly controlled twelve-tone music. They saw and appreciated that I could write their kind of music, *and* go off in new directions, asking my own poetic questions. My pieces intrigued—and frightened—some of them. I think that the open form and flexibility principles that I developed, and the notation that went with them, helped to loosen up the European musical status quo.

Since the 1950s, I've had many performances in Europe, and nearly all my commissions come from there. The city of Darmstadt commissioned *Available Forms I*; the Rome Radio Orchestra commissioned *Available Forms II*; Kiel commissioned a piece for large orchestra called *Time Spans*, which has never been played in the U.S.; and I had a lot of performances on German radio in the 1960s. I first conducted *Available Forms II*, a piece for large orchestra and two conductors, with Bruno Maderna in Venice in 1962. Bruno said I had a flair for conducting. Several people I know think I ought to become a full-time conductor, but I don't agree. It is important to me to be able to conduct my own works, but I don't have the energy or the time or the inclination to study all of the standard repertoire.

European invitations have never stopped coming. Two years ago I was guest composer and lecturer-in-residence at Rotterdam Conservatory. I conducted a piece of mine with Edo de Waart and the Rotterdam Philharmonic. Last year, I taught some special courses at the Basel Conservatory in Switzerland and altogether the European experience has been most fortunate. Besides Boulez and Maderna, Luciano Berio, Luigi Nono, and Karlheinz Stockhausen have been real friends. As an American, I'm in a neutral position vis-à-vis the inevitable factional fights; I am very friendly, say, with Nono *and* Stockhausen, who consider themselves in different camps and rarely speak.

I am still much closer to my European colleagues than my American. I know Copland quite well; I like him and his music and I think he likes mine, but I'm still an outsider to the American music "establishment." Some American composers are jealous of my European performances, but it's not as if I went over like a traveling salesman and demanded them. My music was performed abroad because key figures in European contemporary music respected it; over here my techniques and esthetics have been seen as a threat to the twelve-tone bastions at Princeton and Columbia—though someone like Shulamit Ran at the University of Chicago has her students compose in the manner of my *Available Forms I*, which was the first open form piece for orchestra. I've consciously remained independent of any permanent academic connection, with all the paperwork and bureaucracy it involves.

Nonetheless, I am very interested in teaching young American composers how to listen and how to think creatively. Most of them need help opening their minds after strong doses of narrow-minded teachers or restrictive schools. I don't care what style a composer works in, as long as he's serious and consistent. If a student wants to compose like Bartók, I'll help him do it successfully; at the same time I'll prod him a little: "You know, it's really not all that exciting to rewrite the music of Bartók or Hindemith. Have you heard anything by Ligeti, or Boulez, or me, and explored the possibilities we open up?" Naturally, I never push anyone into writing music my way.

I travel about the country as much as I can; I like to meet all kinds of composers and other artists. I was composer-in-residence at the Peabody Conservatory in Baltimore for five years; I often spend the fall semester at the California Institute of the Arts, near Los Angeles. During the spring, I do many three-day residencies at different campuses; I give a lecture, conduct a workshop, then go to classes and talk to students. I try very hard to break down the idea that composers are unapproachable. I work closely with students, both through talking and music making. In a three-hour workshop I can teach kids so much about one of my scores. They may not play it exactly right, or at concert level, but they'll get to understand a lot about my attitude, the notation, how to play flexibly, and how to feel a phrase.

Teaching music students is one thing; teaching audiences is something else again. To some extent, audiences need to be educated. There's a common complaint that if a person doesn't have much knowledge of contemporary music, it's very hard for him to tell whether something new is good or bad. My comment on that is, sure, it's also hard to understand Seiji Ozawa when he's speaking Japanese if you don't know the language. But education isn't everything. There are people who come up to me after a concert and say, "Gee, I liked your piece. It was really terrific. But I don't understand it." My response is, "Don't try to understand it. I'm not writing music for you to *understand*, but to listen to, as a sound event in time." It does my heart good to hear people say they enjoyed a piece of mine, whether or not they "understood" it. Concert audiences need more than familiarity with and exposure to new music. They need self-confidence when they listen. Ultimately, it is up to them whether they like or dislike what they hear.

Of course, judging the music of one's own time is no easy matter. After listening to a tremendous amount of recent music, I have found that one can ask essentially two questions: Is the compositional technique capable, and is the piece original—does it have poetic freshness? It's much easier to meet the first criterion than the second. It's not so difficult to write a well-structured piece. If this element works and that one fits, you have a "good piece" in some historical sense. But I'm more impressed when I hear something that gives me a fresh viewpoint, when I say to myself, "My God, listen to those unusual sonorities," or whatever. The form may or may not be conventional, but if the piece works poetically, it takes me down a new path from beginning to end. Each piece should be like a journey—and every journey is different.

The one thing I demand in a composer is some degree of poetic originality; I'm not so concerned about whether what he's written is a "masterpiece" or not. Somebody once asked Gertrude Stein what she thought about history. She said, "History takes time." Designating masterpieces also takes time. Stein wrote a fantastic little book, *What Are Masterpieces and Why Are There So Few of Them?* There aren't many in any period, though we've had a handful in recent years.

Often I would rather hear a piece that may not be great but that provides a fresh approach.

It's crucial that contemporary music of all sorts be integrated more systematically into institutionalized concert life. I'm for programs which include all kinds of music, from very conventional to very new—this is more common across the Atlantic than here. One of my favorite concerts took place in Munich a while back; *Available Forms II* was on the bill with Debussy's *Jeux*, Webern's *Six Pieces For Orchestra*, Ives' *Three Places in New England*, and a piece by Nono. Now there's an interesting mixture: Debussy, Ives, Webern, Nono, Brown. But if you zap listeners with five very new works at one shot, you're going to boggle their minds. I remember when *Available Forms II* was done—fantastically—by Lenny Bernstein in 1964 on an avant-garde series. He spread works by Xenakis, Babbitt, Wolpe, Feldman, Cage and me (among others) over several concerts. The concert which included my music and Cage's started with Vivaldi's "Winter" from *The Seasons*, was followed by Tchaikowsky's *Pathetique* Symphony, then intermission, and then the three new works. That's not integration—that's abrupt juxtaposition. I'm sure that this does not work as well as the Munich type of programming.

Boulez, with the New York Philharmonic and especially with his *Domaine Musicale* programs in France, tried to program more logically. Pierre is sensible. He's an avant-garde composer, but he doesn't overdo his bias. Pierre has a very good grasp of how to bring an audience into the twentieth century.

So did Bruno Maderna. He once did my *Available Forms I* on a program in Holland, along with works of Perotin (in Bruno's own arrangement), Beethoven, and Mozart. I said, "Bruno, you're going to get both of us hounded off the stage." Instead, everybody loved the concert. It was *very* gratifying.

Part Two: Scholars and Teachers

6: Edward Downes

Photo by Eugene Cook

I was born in Boston into a newspaperman's family. My father, Olin Downes, was music critic of the Boston *Post* at the time. He was also a pianist, but careers were no easier for pianists in those days than they are now and he had a family of six to support. When I was thirteen, he became the chief critic of the New York *Times*, in 1924.

Originally, I didn't aim to go into music at all. I wanted to be a civil or an electrical engineer. I always loved science and math. But between the end of high school and the beginning of college I decided to be a music critic. I must have been very naive; it never occurred to me that I was following in my father's footsteps. I just thought, "I like to write and I love music, and music criticism is a good combination of the two."

Anyway, I used to go regularly with my father to concerts and to the opera. In those days concerts didn't sell out as much as they do now. I got to know the doormen at Carnegie Hall and the Metropolitan Opera; often they just let me slip in to listen whenever I wanted. It was fabulous. Sometimes I went three, four, or five times a week to a concert or an opera. New York was livelier than Boston, and there was a great deal more new music played. In the early 1920s we were still getting first performances of pieces that had hit Europe before the war, such as Igor Stravinsky's *The Rite of Spring*. I didn't hear the New York premiere but I did see the first staged production here. Leopold Stokowski conducted. I forget who did the choreography, but I do remember the sacrificial virgin in the final dance was a very young lady, to me quite unknown, named Martha Graham. It was quite exciting.

By 1924 sophisticated music lovers knew they were supposed to like *The Rite of Spring* but many didn't. I remember one of the leading New York critics, it may even have been Lawrence Gilman of the *Herald Tribune,* leaving a concert at Carnegie Hall where the *Rite* had been played, referring to it as a "collapse into decadence." After all, the piece was still very new to us. My father loved it, though.

All this exposure to music had quite an effect on me; by the time I got to college I knew I would go into music. After a year at Columbia I was very impatient; the college required a certain number of math and science courses but I wanted to focus on music.

Edward Downes, a professor of music at Queens College, and a critic, program notes writer and radio commentator, was interviewed at his home in New York City in March, 1976.

I had loved physics, chemistry, and math in high school, but wasn't interested in broadening myself in those directions any more. So at the end of the year I switched to the Neighborhood Music School, which has since become the Manhattan College of Music. At the time it was a fine settlement school on the Upper East Side, with wonderful instruction in theory, piano, and counterpoint. Then I started to write a book and went abroad to do research. While working in the library in Munich I heard some fascinating summer lectures at the University. Astounded to find a university where they treated you like an adult and gave you real choices, I thought to myself, "This is for me." The year was 1930.

I went to Europe that summer not only for research, but mainly because Arturo Toscanini was to conduct at Bayreuth for the first time and I was a great Wagner fan. I spent my life savings to get to Bayreuth and then on to Munich. Two years later, after earning some money, I went back to Munich as a regular student at the University. I had always been more attracted to Germany than to France, which it took more maturity to appreciate. Somehow I didn't take to French manners or customs. And in music you almost have to go back to the Baroque to find a great age, a great constellation of French composers. I was unaware of French Baroque music at that time. So Germany was the place for me.

I saw no intimations of Hitler on my first visit in 1930. By 1932 there were plenty, though when I asked many Germans about Hitler they said, "That gangster will certainly not take power in this country." I still have friends there. Some of my oldest friends died in concentration camps, but some survived.

I found ordinary university education to be on a much higher level in Germany than college was in America. My fellow students had studied Latin for eight years, Greek for six, and calculus. They knew more American geography than I did. I was a complete ignoramus by comparison.

In the German university system, you had one major and two minors. Because of my interest in opera, I took theater history as a minor. That subject fell under the general heading of the history of literature. As a result one group of friends were majors in German literature and drama history. I got to know several young writers, and people who later became stage directors and actors. I lived right in the middle of Schwabing, Munich's famous Bohemian community, though its greatest days were then past. My friends were very nostalgic about the Schwabing of the 1920s.

Then, Stefan George, Thomas Mann, and even Wedekind had lived in Munich. We had one professor of theater history and literature who used to arrange marvelous gatherings: *Autorenabende*. He would invite various authors to meet with him and his students in a café and read from their works. Once the guest was Thomas Mann. To some extent, the early 1930s were a period of Expressionism in theater as well as in the visual arts—but the exciting days of the Brücke and the Blauer Reiter were past. Munich was still an artistic city, but no longer the vital creative center it had been.

My strong interest in literature has persisted. In Germany I read a lot and went to the theater frequently. I saw more Shakespeare in Munich than I ever managed in New York—plus all the German classics, lots of Grillparzer and Goethe and Schiller. My experiences abroad were rich, even if the book I intended to write never quite materialized. It was to be a history of opera focusing on premieres. I took twenty operas ranging from Gluck to Berg, and showed how they reflected the culture of their times. The subject still attracts me. I would rather like to finish the project someday.

My schooling took a long time; not only did I go to Paris as well as Munich, but I was working to earn my way all along. Matters got especially complicated when I worked in the U.S. and studied in Germany. One of my first jobs was in the publicity department of NBC in New York. Radio City was new then, and NBC was moving there from their old quarters. They needed somebody to help out for a little while in the press department. At the end of my two-week stint, they asked me to stay on. There I was, shuttling back and forth across the Atlantic, working here and studying there; I split my time evenly between the two continents. I'd finished my graduate course work and had started a dissertation when the war came along. I got back to the States at the last minute; in fact, I sailed after war was declared. I had a ticket on the Cunard Line but didn't dare sail on a Cunarder. My father managed to wangle me passage on the Dutch line; I served as a waiter and never worked so hard in my life.

I tried to volunteer for the Navy but I had bad eyes so they turned me down; then I was drafted. While in the Army, I hid my musical background as firmly as possible. I couldn't see myself playing a bass drum in the band. I ended up in the OSS in Washington, which was certainly an education all by itself. Many refugee German scholars were in the OSS. I was in "research and analysis." William Langer of Harvard headed that division; it was peopled largely with young professors and advanced graduate students, mainly in history and economics. As a musician. I was excited to be catapulted into such company. These were the first people to show me that American history could be interesting. I had hated it in school. We had had to make paper wigwams when I was in grade school and I didn't take to that version of history at all.

The OSS was a nerve center for information coming from diplomatic sources, Army and Navy intelligence, and other informants here and abroad. My job was to fit fragments of information together into a larger picture. I stayed on a bit after the war, while looking for a music critic's job. That was as hard a task then as now. The field is very small. It's spreading out in different ways, to include weekly and monthly as well as daily publications, but there are very few newspapers outside large metropolitan centers that care enough, or indeed, where there is enough musical activity to justify having a music critic. Often one cultural writer covers everything—movies, theater, music and art. I really don't know whether the situation is improving outside the big cities—where of course it's worse, for the simple reason that the number of newspapers has diminished radically. In 1924 there were many important daily papers in New York—maybe a dozen—and they all had men of stature as music critics. Nowadays, how many New York dailies are there? There are three. So I wrote to papers all over the country, to everybody I could think of. No one needed a music critic.

Now, in the Army it had been a distinct disadvantage not to have any academic degree. Also, my father always lamented his never having been able to finish his schooling; his family suddenly lost everything when he was quite young, and he had to go to work. He'd never been able to study music history systematically. It bothered him so much that I thought, "Well, by God, I'm going to plug along somehow and get whatever this background is that he considers so valuable." So I decided to resume my formal education. I had not taken my PhD in Munich, I had not taken a BA over here, and I was enough of a rebel to have refused to fulfill the conditions even for high school. I had no diploma at all, not even one from kindergarten. Meanwhile, my scholastic records had all gone up in smoke in

Germany. As I was casting around, a friend of my father's surprised me by saying "Harvard is a very liberal place. Why don't you apply there?" And I did. All they asked for was a description of my scholastic experience and took me at my word straight into the PhD program. At last I got a doctorate and I'm very glad that I did. Without it, I never would have gone into teaching.

Several professors at Harvard were enormously stimulating. Archibald Davison was one; he was very influential all over the country in the field of choral music in the schools. He gave a splendid "Music I" course for non-music majors. About seven hundred Harvard men plus a couple of hundred Radcliffe women registered for his course every year. Davison needed a flock of graduate assistants, and I was privileged to be one. He was a spellbinding lecturer and the sections I taught were thought-provoking. We graduate students got together regularly to plan our sections. We also made up, administered, and corrected exams.

When I finished coursework at Harvard, Professor Wallace Woodworth encouraged me to go into teaching. This was not at all what I had had in mind, but in looking around for jobs again, I discovered there were several teaching offers and nothing in criticism. I went into it almost *faute de mieux*. I *had* enjoyed the little bit of teaching I'd done at Harvard and Wellesley, but I still had criticism in my mind. Then gradually, as I got into teaching, I discovered I liked it just as much as writing.

My change in attitude was also due to the example of outstanding people at Harvard, such as Otto Kinkeldey, my first thesis advisor there. Most of my teachers had refreshingly unacademic points of view. Of the permanent music faculty, I believe only Davison had a PhD. Walter Piston had been a faculty member for years and years. I took his fugue class. I'm embarrassed to remember how little I then knew about counterpoint. My grounding at Manhattan was good, but hardly enough for Piston's class, where many of the students were already professional composers. Some were taking the class for the second or third time. For me, though, it meant learning fugue from the ground up, analyzing Bach's *Well-Tempered Clavier* and his *Art of the Fugue* and learning how to write a fugue of my own. This was part of the PhD requirement—you either wrote a fugue or did some orchestration. I chose fugue because I knew less about that.

The class was a fabulous experience, because Piston was an extraordinary teacher. We had two classes a week. In one we'd analyze a Bach fugue. For the other session we wrote a fugue exposition or episode. Piston would play our exercises at the piano and criticize them on the spot. This procedure explains in part why the composers felt they got something from taking the class time and again. Piston wasn't looking to correct obvious oversights, like parallel fifths, but rather for writing with shape and meaning. Since everybody in the class was working simultaneously on the same assignment, several solutions to one problem would be gone over in class every week. That was very helpful to the composers. The novices, like myself, had to keep to the style of the Bach model, which was best for us; the advanced ones could write in any style they chose.

I wrote my dissertation on the operas of Johann Christian Bach. My original topic, conceived during my Munich student days, was much too ambitious. It had been inspired by a wonderful professor, Rudolf von Ficker, the department head in Munich. He was a medieval and Renaissance man. It fascinated me that Ficker, a famous scholar, was a practical musician, a conductor, as well as a musicologist; so often scholars are not performers and vice versa. Ficker had delved seriously into performance practice, which was not as fashionable then as it is now. His area of specialization was roughly from Perotinus to Dufaÿ (from the late twelfth through the early fifteenth centuries.) I didn't even know the name of Perotinus when I went to Munich. Indeed, very little medieval music was in print and it was little studied in the U.S. in the early 1930s, though the field had opened up much earlier in Europe. Ficker was a pupil of Guido Adler, a pioneering scholar of early music, and even Adler was not the first.

So Ficker, working from the original manuscript, made a scholarly transcription of the music, and from that, a performance edition. Then he got a very good instrumental group together with the Vienna Sängerknaben and a male chorus, and they rehearsed the pieces and performed them under his direction at the Beethoven Centennial festivities of 1927 in Vienna. Later he performed more Perotinus, Machaut, and even Dufaÿ, in Vienna, and conducted some in Munich over the radio. He played some off-the-air recordings in class and I was bowled over by the Perotinus pieces. I thought, "Goodness, this is a great composer I'd never heard of!"—and I had enormous admiration for the scholar who could start with an original manuscript and end up conducting a performance. Ficker was a model to me.

Given such a stimulus, I wanted to do my dissertation in medieval music. All music students know about the style change around 1300 from the Ars Antiqua to the Ars Nova. I discovered there had been a similar "crisis" or shift of style in the visual arts, in architecture, and in literature. The relationship among the changes in the different arts looked like a perfect thesis topic. I went to Ficker and described my idea, after talking with the head of the art department. When I told Ficker my wide-eyed scheme for relating all these cultural developments he looked at me, smiled gently and said, "Well, when you are past sixty, if you're still interested you might start a book on that subject. In the meantime, choose something more manageable."

Ficker's sound advice coincided with an anniversary of Johann Christian Bach's birth, when a lot of his music was being performed. I heard a program of J. C. Bach arias and thought they were perfectly beautiful. I told this to a student friend who later became a very well known professor and he replied, "Oh, that's just conventional Neapolitan stuff." I thought to myself, "Maybe so, but it's beautiful music and I like it." I proposed a topic on J. C. Bach to Ficker and he was enthusiastic. So Christian Bach it was.

I've had a persistent interest in broad cultural interrelationships. God knows, we must have specialists to conduct sharply focused research. But I don't know that a specialist has to have a limited scope. In fact, context is necessary for perspective. In some lectures at the Metropolitan Museum of Art I was able to bring together my interests in art and music and show the related trends in various art forms. These were survey lectures on musical style in different epochs. I also stress context when I teach; I like to use slides of art and artifacts for clarifying the background and environment of the music, even though this requires hours of preparation. I always try to impress on my students that a general historical perspective on cultural matters is extremely important.

Fortunately, performers of early music are increasingly aware of this. One of the pioneers in suggesting total cultural environments at concerts was Noah Greenberg, with his Pro Musica ensemble for the performance of medieval and Renaissance music. I remember hearing of Greenberg and his involvement in the early music revival some time after World War II. I didn't know the man as well as I would have liked, but I remember being enchanted by his reenactment of the fourteenth-century liturgical drama *The Play of Daniel*. It was presented in a perfect setting, a Romanesque chapel at the Cloisters. The performance I attended took place in 1955 shortly after my father died, and I had joined the staff at the *Times*. I became low man on the totem pole of critics; one of my first assignments was to review the New York Pro Musica production.

After finishing at Harvard, I had taught at the University of Minnesota for five years as a member of the music department. Then my father died very suddenly of a heart attack, and my mother, who was ill, still lived in New York. At that juncture, Howard Taubman, my father's successor at the *Times*, invited me to join his staff. I was of two minds about it for a moment but couldn't resist the chance to come back home and back to music criticism. So I came—and stayed with the *Times* for three years.

It was a very exciting life, despite many routine concerts where people played the same old things that had been overplayed for fifty years—and didn't play them especially well. Taubman was very good about seeing that everybody in the department covered at least one really interesting event each week. It seemed that nobody else on the *Times* liked much recent music. That's my recollection, though I wouldn't want to malign anyone. Perhaps I took to new music more enthusiastically than some of my colleagues. Be that as it may, I was sent to a preponderance of the contemporary music concerts, which I enjoyed. Sure, some of the music was puzzling and didn't get through to me (or *I* didn't get through to *it*) but there was an awful lot that was rewarding. The variety of pieces I heard certainly stretched my mind; I had to make a serious effort to understand many kinds of musical expression.

As a newspaperman I avoided close contact with musicians. I was very much affected by my father's attitude on this which was, "Don't be influenced by personal friendships." Since he didn't trust himself to be totally objective, he tended to avoid such friendships. The danger in getting to know a musician, he felt, was that he would lean over backwards in criticizing and so perhaps be unfair to him. So I followed suit. Later I was sorry. I think that what you may lose in critical objectivity is more than outweighed by what you learn. It helps to know artists' problems and to join them in shop talk. And if you possibly can, you should go to rehearsals.

After I had been at the *Times* for two years I was offered a job teaching twentieth-century music at one of the Ivy League colleges. I was no specialist in this music at all; I had just written more columns on it than some of my colleagues. Honored but feeling ill-equipped, I turned the position down. Around the same time I was approached with a job proposal by Mrs. Souvaine, who runs the Metropolitan Opera intermission broadcasts. Robert Lawrence, the quizmaster for the programs, was off to Turkey as conductor of the national orchestra there, and suggested me as his successor. The *Times* said no. They didn't allow anybody to do anything regularly for pay outside the paper. The following year Mrs. Souvaine offered to equal my *Times* salary. This was tempting; the radio job was much less time-consuming and would allow time for research. After considerable thought, I resigned from the *Times* and went on the air.

After two years of the broadcasts, Queens College invited me to be a guest professor. I'd hardly accepted that when I was invited to write program notes for the New York Philharmonic. I was in a great quandary—there was too much to do. For a while, besides doing the opera quiz, I wrote opera résumés which Milton Cross read. For some time I wrote every word that Milton Cross spoke on the opera broadcasts (except his descriptions of curtain calls). I took on the program notes, but declined the teaching post right then. The radio job turned into a twenty-year stint—but I did start teaching at Queens full time in 1966.

The radio experience has been exhilarating and I'm still at it. The opera quiz is a light popular type of program in the second intermission of most Metropolitan Opera broadcasts; it's intended as sugar coated education. The questions sent in by the listening audience range from "Who stabs whom in the third act of what opera?" to "Who invented leitmotifs?" The quizzes draw a lot of mail. Every once in a while I receive some very appreciative remarks—or some kicks in the teeth. Mrs. Souvaine and I sometimes disagree about which questions to use, and our arguments often end with her bursting out: "Oh, Edward, you're just a professor! You don't understand the entertainment world." Once we conducted a poll asking people whether they preferred "quizzy" questions like 'Who stabbed whom?'

or discussion questions covering larger topics, with a little more perspective. I was sure people liked substance more than trivia. We got
tons of mail, and the result was exactly fifty-fifty. The poll resolved
absolutely nothing. So we keep on with the same mixture as before.

Occasionally I do an analytical broadcast in the first intermission, especially for less familiar operas. And for some time there were
the New York Philharmonic broadcasts, which went off the air for a
while, but happily have resumed. I did intermission comments and
interviews. That was fun. I also do take part in a radio program called
"First Hearing," where a panel of three critics comments on new
recordings.

In some ways, the program notes were the most challenging
among my varied activities. They often involved quite a bit of musical analysis, historical research, and constant scrutiny of different
scores. Both Leonard Bernstein and Pierre Boulez, the last two music
directors of the New York Philharmonic, put a strong emphasis on
contemporary music, so there was a plentiful supply of new scores for
me to keep up with. Often I tried to get the composer of a new work
to write about his own piece for the program booklet; his statement
becomes a historical document and is more important than anything
anybody else would have to say. Commentators and analysts can
always come along later, but the composer won't be around forever.
Not that he's necessarily good at writing about his own compositions.
I remember one very distinguished contemporary composer who
wrote about one of his symphonies in a way that was completely
unintelligible to me. I could not even understand the first sentence,
much less the first paragraph. I asked him about that opening line,
and he maintained that it was perfectly clear to *him*. I said, "I'm sure
it is, but I'm not as sophisticated as you are. Could you clarify it for
me?" He went on for a long time about fields of force and other
expressions that to me remain at best analogies, and at worst, rather
mystical stuff. I realized after two hours that he was not going to say
anything I could grasp—and he couldn't have cared less. By implica-
tion he didn't seem to care very much about whether the audience
understood him. I thought, well, I should not try to influence him;
this *is* what this composer *wants* to say to his listeners. So I printed it
unchanged.

At the other extreme there's Aaron Copland who is among the
most articulate of composers (and a master of lucid prose.) Aaron can

go to the heart of a subject and say something meaningful in words that are not too technical for a layman. Such verbal eloquence is rare among composers.

On the other hand, some composers object to the whole business—they just don't believe in program notes. I understand their attitude perfectly. They think (rightly) that too many people may read the notes and listen too carefully for whatever those notes mention, thereby missing a real listening experience, which happens (I think) on a more intuitive level. One time William Schuman was having a new piece done by the Philharmonic. I asked him, as I had in the past, if he would write something about it—and this time he refused. Schuman *did* give me some factual background on the piece and expressed interest in what *I* would have to say. "Happy sailing," he said. I took the liberty of printing his note in the program book, and did my best.

My own feeling about program notes is best described by comparing it to my early experiences with the visual arts. My second minor field in Munich had been art history. Although I had no wish to be an art historian, I got an enormous amount out of the lectures. Often, a professor would take a group of students to a museum. Munich had very fine modern museums as well as more traditional ones. Guidance through them left a big impression on me. I found that going to a museum with someone who knew or loved a certain picture, looking at it together, and having him tell me in any terms that were handy precisely what he admired made my own contact much faster. The friend didn't have to be a scholar—just somebody who really loved a particular work of art and who knew something about it.

He might say, "Look, here's Rubens' Battle of the Amazons. I'm crazy about the dynamic effect he gets here with a brushstroke and his spiral motion . . ." or whatever. I would look at the painting; first I would mumble, "Huh?" and then I would say, "Oh, I see what you mean." It's a matter of getting across a feeling for an art work's specialness, sometimes just by telling you in general what direction the work is aiming at. If you start to listen to Mozart and you want something like Tchaikowsky, you aren't going to like Mozart, and vice versa. Sometimes a friend—or a program annotator—can put you on the right track; you can find your own way after that.

So, in doing program notes, I see myself first as a purveyor of factual information which might enhance the musical experience—things like when a piece was written, where it was first performed, why it was written, how the composer felt about the piece.

Is there any danger that information might replace the esthetic experience? Not if a person is looking for an esthetic emotional experience. If people imagine that by learning a lot of dates, or by diagramming the geometry of a Raphael, they've got the point, they're hopeless anyway. I don't believe people like that are ever really going to grasp a composer or a painter's message. But if you're already curious, even if only by contagion, it's a different story. Say I have a friend who collects old cars. I couldn't care less about old cars but if I spent an evening with an enthusiast I might easily catch his enthusiasm.

What do I do when I dislike a work I have to write about? Donald Tovey, who wrote wonderful program notes a long time ago, said it well. He felt that the program annotator should be an attorney for the defense, pointing out the good things and passing in silence over the weak ones. Of course there are composers for whom I have blind spots and pieces that I dislike. These are relatively few but they exist. I simply try to be as objective as possible, noting the obvious strong points and what other informed people consider praiseworthy. A quotation from somebody else can be very handy in such situations.

Looking through all my program notes while preparing some of them for publication in book form, I found that I have come to love pieces of Stravinsky's that didn't make much sense to me twenty years ago. At another point in the musical spectrum, I have come to like Haydn more and more. I now feel that he's a *very* great composer; I blush to remember that I once thought of him as little more than an important contemporary of Mozart. The shift in Haydn's favor is pretty general, I think, as well as personal. As you look around, it's probably no accident that Bernstein is a fine Haydn conductor, and so is Boulez. Haydn is coming into his own. In his day he was rightly exalted, but since the early nineteenth century, he's been completely overshadowed. Not so anymore.

I'm glad to have done so many different things. It's hard to say which has given me the greatest satisfaction. I enjoyed writing for the *Times* but the paper's policy allowed me to do little else. On the whole it was good that I left because then I was able to branch out.

And one task richly fertilized the others. Maybe what pleases me most is when a student, or even a whole class, takes fire. It does happen. And sometimes ten years later, a student visits me or writes, fondly recalling a course that mattered to him. Or another brilliant student gets a job writing program notes for the Minnesota Symphony. That feels awfully good. Each job has special rewards.

*Two Program Notes by Edward Downes**

Wolfgang Amadeus Mozart.
Ein Musikalischer Spass (A Musical Joke), K. 522

Seldom has so much wit been lavished to produce an impression of witlessness—of helpless, bumbling incompetence. This delectable trifle, a masterpiece of satirical art, was tossed off in Vienna while Mozart's mind must have been occupied with the vaster project of his *Don Giovanni*. June 14, 1787, is the completion date inscribed on Mozart's autograph (which has been missing from the Prussian State Library in Berlin since the end of World War II).

For what occasion this featherweight score was composed, or who its fortunate first listeners were, we may never know. But since Mozart rarely composed anything without an immediate performance in view, the occasion probably followed completion of the score within a matter of days.

Mozart's *Musical Joke* had an ancient and honorable lineage. Parodies of bumbling performers had been cultivated by his father and by generations of composers before him. But Mozart's *Joke* differed from most of its predecessors in satirizing primarily the bumbling composer and only secondarily his unhappy performers. Thus the well-known alternative titles conferred on the score after Mozart's death: *Bauernsinfonie (Peasant Symphony)* and *Dorfmusikanten (Village Musicians)* completely obscure the point of the piece. The butt of Mozart's wit is the would-be composer who lacks both technique and imagination. (Possibly an aristocratic amateur or a desperately unfit pupil? Mozart had known plenty of both.)

* From *The New York Philharmonic Guide to the Symphony*. New York: Walker Publishing Company, Inc. 1976. Copyright © 1976 by the Philharmonic Symphony Society of New York, Inc. and Edward Downes. Used by permission.

Mozart did not classify his *Musical Joke*. But to label it a *divertimento*, as is often done, is misleading. For the imagined composer of this score is attempting nothing so modest as a *divertimento*; his object all sublime is a symphony.

I. *Allegro*. Our master knows, approximately, how a symphony goes. But even his first and most important theme struggles in vain to get off the ground. . . . Tradition tells him that his second principal theme should begin in the dominant key (C major). But how to get there? His first attempt at a transition or bridge is frustrated by the orchestra, which obstinately keeps reverting to the home key of F major. Since his bridge does not work, he simply jumps with both feet, as it were, into the key of C major. Somehow our hero manages to reach the end of his exposition, where he salutes his achievement with a vigorous fanfare. The graver problems of the so-called development section are met after a fashion, by making it short.

II. *Minuetto: Maestoso*. The minuet, normally far simpler than first-movement form, also presents its comic hurdles. The most obvious of these occurs in a passage for two horns marked "softly" (*dolce*). But with the modest talents of his horn players, what was to have been a poetic interlude turns out in [an] excruciating form. . . .

III. *Adagio cantabile*. In the traditionally songful slow movement our composer clearly has in mind the standard graces of eighteenth-century *style gallant*. In imitating the clichés of his betters he is awkward, but with a difference. He is an awkward composer being *portrayed* for us by one of the supreme masters of all time. The result is a paradox: an awkwardness with a certain grace, or at least charm. It is as if Don Giovanni were masquerading as Leporello. And we can not take it amiss when an ambitious cadenza leads the unhappy first violin into a desperate, stratospheric flight that sounds more and more like a twentieth-century whole-tone scale.

IV. *Presto*. But the best is yet to come. The *rondo finale* is full of pitfalls; even the opening refrain presents monstrous problems. The effort to force this basic recurrent refrain to end in the proper key (tonic F major) involves our master in a harmonic wrench that is almost Chaplinesque.

In the ensuing episode our master does battle with the problem of *fugato*. It is an unequal struggle which will be especially relished by any earnest novice who has tried to write a fugue. This entire *fi-*

nale is so rich in humor on every level from the subtleties of late-eighteenth-century *rondo* style to the slapstick final cadence, that there is almost too much to grasp in just one hearing.

The outwardly simple score calls for only 2 horns and strings. Scholars are not entirely agreed as to whether Mozart intended the score for 6 solo players or for horns and string orchestra, but the weight of opinion strongly favors the symphonic group.

Edgard Varèse. Arcana

When Varèse finished the first version of his *Arcana* in 1927, it was one of the boldest scores of its day and one of the most irritating to people of conservative taste. Today, by comparison, it seems positively tame: a far from arcane extension of attitudes and techniques which Stravinsky had brought to a preliminary climax in his 1913 *Rite of Spring* and then abandoned.

Although Varèse considered himself an American composer and was domiciled in New York City during all of his mature life, he was born in France and did not come to the United States until 1915, when he was thirty-two years old. Like several twentieth-century composers, he had studied mathematics and science before music. By the time he became one of the most brilliant pupils of D'Indy, Roussel and Busoni, he was already a rebel, ready to defend his own ideas and even to disregard, on occasion, the orders of his illustrious teachers.

Among Varèse's earliest and most prophetic convictions was that modern science should make possible the new acoustical effects which he was constantly imagining and which could be only approximated on the conventional instruments then available. He became "obsessed," as he himself said, with the concept of space in music. He once told me that this obsession came to him, neither from the Berlioz *Requiem* (of which he conducted a memorable performance soon after his arrival in New York) nor from the Venetian polychoral style of the sixteenth century (with which he was very familiar), but from claustrophobia, which had plagued him when he was a child.

Most music sounded to him terribly "corseted." "When you project a tone in an enclosed space," he said, "it is like an object attached to the end of an elastic. Before you know it, it comes back and hits you in the face. I like music that explodes into space. I like a nice rich sound." From the age of twenty he felt sure "that somehow I would someday realize a new kind of music that would be spatial— from then on I thought only of music as spatial. . . ."

Today, as we listen to such relatively early works of Varèse as *Arcana*, there is a temptation to hear them as preliminaries, as first steps toward his late electronic works—especially since we know that Varèse later went through a period of more than ten years of experimentation and searching for new sounds—a decade during which he completed no new works, but at the end of which he did find what he was searching for, namely the newly invented means of producing electronic music. He had imagined the sounds before he was able to produce them. The liberation that this proved to be for Varèse's creative faculties, and the renewed productivity of his last years could easily trap us into viewing everything that went before as a preparation for his electronic works. But to listen with such hindsight would be to falsify so richly inventive and self-sufficient a score as *Arcana*.

Varèse began *Arcana* in 1925, the year when he bought the house on Sullivan Street in New York City which was his home for the rest of his life. The title, *Arcana*, or its original French form, *Arcanes*, was an afterthought. It came to him while composing, when his wife showed him a copy of Paracelsus' *The Hermetic Philosophy*. This suggested the title for the work that was taking shape. In addition he prefaced the score with the following quotation from Paracelsus: "One star exists higher than all the rest. This is the apocalyptic star. The second star is that of the ascendant. The third is that of the elements—of these there are four, so that six stars are established. Besides there is still another star, imagination, which begets a new star and a new heaven."

In order to avoid misunderstanding, Varèse later said of the above quotation: "This extract is equivalent to a dedication; it makes of my symphonic poem a kind of tribute to the author of those words; but they did not inspire it, and the work is not a commentary upon them."

Much of Varèse's work on *Arcana* was done during the summer and fall of 1925 in Paris. Since Mrs. Varèse had shouldered the responsibility for remodeling and furnishing their Sullivan Street house, she could not accompany him. So Varèse's numerous letters kept her posted on the progress of *Arcana*. One of the most interesting, dated Friday, October 9 [1935] enclosed several bars of fanfares, with the description of a dream in which he heard them. On the reverse of the scrap of music paper with the fanfares he wrote:

> *The two Fanfares I dreamed—I was on a boat that was turning around and around–in the middle of the ocean—spinning around in great circles. In the distance I could see a light house, very high—and on the top an angel—and the angel was you—a trumpet in each hand. Alternating projectors of different colors: red, green, yellow, blue—and you were playing Fanfare no. 1, trumpet in right hand. Then suddenly the sky became incandescent—blinding—you raised your left hand to your mouth and the Fanfare 2 blared. And the boat kept turning and spinning—and the alternation of projectors and incandescence became more frequent—intensified—and the fanfares more nervous—impatient . . . and then—merde—I woke up. But anyway they will be in Arcanes.**

On a subsequent postcard he jotted: "*Arcanes*—Never have I written music as solid, as joyous—as full of force, of life, of sun. *Arcanes* is developing in a new phase—"

Then, on October 29, Varèse wrote that he had destroyed everything he had written and was beginning all over again. But the dream-fanfares persisted intact. The curious listener can hear fanfare number 1 at the very beginning (measures three and four of the printed score) precisely as recorded from Varèse's dream, while the second bursts from the brass and woodwind in measures nineteen through twenty-two; literally a dream come true!

The very foundation of the work is a single idea, which Varèse called an *idée fixe* (a term he borrowed from Berlioz), rather than a conventionally symphonic theme. This "obsessive idea" consists of three notes: an ascending minor third repeated in a syncopated rhythm. It is given out at once in the first measure, almost like a motto, by the dark combination of Heckelphone, bassoons, tuba, cellos, and kettledrums.

The structure of the score has been compared with the repetitive pattern of the Baroque passacaglia. The *idée fixe* returns in a hundred guises, from jazzy syncopations to jaunty Gallic marching tunes, to moments when, as Stravinsky himself observed, "perhaps some of *me*

---

* Translation by Louise Varèse, from her *Varèse, a Looking-Glass Diary*, Vol. I: 1883–1928 (New York: W. W. Norton and Co.) p. 238.

peeks through . . . too. . . ." Many listeners would agree with Stravinsky that there are fleeting echoes of his *Rite of Spring, Petrushka*, and *The Firebird*. But the totality of *Arcana* does not sound derivative. Varèse's originality, especially his imagination in the new world of sonority he created, dominates from start to finish.

The first performance of Arcana was presented at the Philadelphia Academy of Music on April 8, 1927, by the Philadelphia Orchestra, under the direction of Leopold Stokowski. The New York premiere followed four days later. Berlin and Paris both waited five years before they heard the revolutionary score of Varèse, who already loomed as a major figure on the international scene. Varèse revised his score in 1930 and again in 1960, deleting certain bits which he may have felt referred too obviously to American jazz idiom, and altering a conclusion of the score, which may have seemed too obvious in another sense.

The orchestra required for *Arcana* is enormous: some 120 instruments with especial emphasis on percussion, which almost balances the strings and winds in importance. Specifically the score calls for 3 piccolos, 2 flutes, 3 oboes, English horn, Heckelphone, 2 high clarinets in E flat, 2 B-flat clarinets, contrabass clarinet, 3 bassoons, 2 contrabassoons, 8 horns, 5 trumpets, 2 tenor trombones, 1 baritone trombone, 1 bass trombone, tuba, contrabass tuba, 6 kettledrums, 2 bass drums, side drum, snare drum, string drum, 3 tambourines, medium gong, high tam-tam, low tam-tam, 2 pairs of cymbals, suspended cymbal (with drumsticks), Chinese cymbal, 4 triangles, slapstick, 3 Chinese blocks (both high and low, with drumsticks and metal sticks), 2 coconuts, 2 guiros, rattle, xylophone, glockenspiel, bells, 16 first violins, 16 second violins, 14 violas, 12 cellos, and 10 basses tuned to low C.

7: Leonard Stein

Growing up in Los Angeles had a big effect on my musical experiences and career choice. I started playing the piano at the age of five and a half, and I always imagined that if I had lived someplace else I might have become a performer. But it's terribly difficult to succeed as a music maker in L.A.; somehow, the cultural climate's not right. I have thought a lot about why. We can and do generate tremendous talent out here; conditions are very good for that, especially in areas like Beverly Hills among the children of doctors, lawyers, and other professionals. Fine private instruction is available. But after studying here for a few years, an aspiring musician must be sent on his way to Juilliard, to the eastern establishment. Few who live in this part of the country have full-time musical careers unless they do commercial work or teach.

As it turned out, I became primarily a teacher, probably because I worked closely with Arnold Schönberg during the thirties and forties, assisting him when he taught at the University of Southern California and helping him write books and articles. I guess I'm known as something of a Schönberg authority. Over the years I've done much more teaching than anything else; I've also written, composed, and organized concerts—this last because of my interest in the performance of recent music. In fact, all of my activities relate directly to twentieth-century music.

When I was young, it wasn't easy to hear new music in Los Angeles. Fortunately, I had a very fine and enlightened piano teacher, Richard Buhlig, who studied with the great Theodor Leschetizky around the same time Artur Schnabel did. Buhlig was among the first to play for Schönberg in Berlin. He came to L.A. from Chicago, bringing contemporary pieces in his fingers. At his recitals he played pieces by such composers as Schönberg and Ruth Crawford Seeger. I became increasingly interested in the avant-garde under the influence of Buhlig and Roy Harris, the composer, who was one of Schönberg's first pupils in L.A.

The concert scene had other gaps besides recent music. Oddly enough, I don't think I heard my first live Beethoven string quartet until I was sixteen. There were some chamber concerts in Pasadena—the other end of town; going to them was a big event. I

Leonard Stein, who teaches composition at the California Institute of the Arts, and is the Director of the Arnold Schoenberg Institute at UCLA, was interviewed at his home in Los Angeles in April 1975.

remember taking the "red car," the train over there. I was taking piano lessons all along, and by the age of ten, I was participating in glee clubs and accompanying singers. That's how I became a good sight reader.

I first met Schönberg in 1935 at USC. I was 19 years old. He'd just arrived in the U.S. It astounded me that none of the people in his class—and most were teachers—actually knew much about the rudiments of music. I was the only one who could sightread a Beethoven sonata! I always felt close to the kind of disciplined teaching method that was more European than American. So I hit it off with Schönberg right away, since he saw I had the kind of background he expected. But remember, he was fresh from the Akademie der Künste in Berlin, a professional school and fine conservatory, where his students were accomplished young musicians like Schnabel, and other master pupils provided by the musical academy. Suddenly in America he had to start many more students from scratch.

Schönberg was such a marvelous man and so passionate a teacher that he immediately readjusted and wrote appropriate exercises for those trained in this country. He soon decided to write textbooks on harmony, counterpoint, and composition. We worked on several together. I inherited some of the drafts after his death, with his express wish that I should finish them. There is a tremendous lot of material. I've always regretted that he didn't get much beyond elementary studies. To this day, if I'm asked to give students advice on counterpoint books, I recommend Schönberg's *Preliminary Exercises in Counterpoint*, the only text I know that treats the subject at levels beginners can grasp. Strange, isn't it, that the great master of complex music contrived a successful way to start from the beginning. Others would throw novices straight into Bach, into intricacies they couldn't begin to comprehend without a basic vocabulary. Schönberg hit home in teaching the fundamental principles of musical logic. I recognize his stamp on almost anybody who came under his influence or who studied with one of his students. When I compare notes with someone like the composer Leon Kirchner of Harvard, I can tell immediately that he belongs in Schönberg's circle of ideas. Not too many people stressed the basics as Schönberg did—and this emphasis shows in all who came in contact with him.

Teaching helped Schönberg as well as his pupils. Many new ideas occurred to him in the classroom. Unfortunately, he was sort of isolated in America. A strong nationalism dominated music in this country during the late thirties and forties, which probably faded with the wave of emigrants during and after World War II. I'm thinking particularly of the "national group," as I call it, around Serge Koussevitzky, Aaron Copland, and others on the East Coast. They were young and rather opposed to anything from central Europe. They seemed to project their dislike for Wagner onto the present day. They preferred France; they were all taught by Nadia Boulanger to have French esthetic viewpoints. They had their own fish to fry.

So although his compositions and theoretical writings didn't materialize entirely in a vacuum, Schönberg simply wasn't in close contact with important American musical developments—he was artistically cut off from the mainstream. Then, language was a problem for him; his ideas were difficult to write about even in German. And when he *did* put down his thoughts in English, there were not many intellectual organs which published such things. Above all, Schönberg's music wasn't popular. Not many people played it. Of all the great composers of this century, I think he's been the most neglected. For a great deal of his life, he never heard many of his works performed, which I'm sure was a shock to him. He always downgraded or soft-pedalled his theoretical contribution—yet many people talk of Schönberg more as a theorist than as a composer. This began to grate on him toward the end of his life; just after the war, Europeans discovered Schönberg's prize student, Anton Webern, and passed over poor Schönberg, even though he was still active and Webern died in 1945. Then, those who had positions of importance in musical life, like Leonard Bernstein, did very little for Schönberg. His contacts with some older conductors weren't bad; Frederick Stock, the conductor of the Chicago Symphony, was a man he admired. He intensely disliked Koussevitzky and Bruno Walter, who he felt were real reactionaries.

Why all the resistance to Schönberg's music? It's hard to say. In his article called "Self-Analysis" he ascribes it to the complexity rather than the dissonance of his music. Pieces like his first string quartet must have been quite a puzzle in their time. There is a great quantity of ideas, and the ways Schönberg works them out are complex, which makes his explanation plausible enough.

At any rate, his life in America was an uphill struggle. Many of his colleagues at USC didn't appreciate him, and when UCLA made him a substantial offer he went there. I think Schönberg would have felt much better in a city with a more receptive and open musical environment. Would he have fared better in New York? It's a question I have discussed with many people, including members of Arthur Weisberg's Contemporary Chamber Ensemble. The name of Stefan Wolpe came up—he had his own circle—and several of us agreed that he was a kind of surrogate for Schönberg. Had Schönberg been in New York, he might have been the central figure in new music. True, Béla Bartók lived there, but he was a very private person—so people have told me. He didn't enjoy teaching composition. Schönberg, on the other hand, was gregarious—he liked to surround himself with pupils and thinkers. He might have flourished in New York—except for the weather. Sunshine brought him to L.A. He expected to supplement his income by teaching studio musicians. He did teach some of them the first year or so, people like Dave Ryan and Oscar Levant. George Gershwin was a good friend of his; they played tennis together.

Schönberg knew many people in show business. Performers like the Marx Brothers and Fanny Brice were his friends and would take him around. What a strange bunch. These people were all temporary transplants from different places; they came and went rather frequently. I remember when Schönberg wanted to raise money for scholarships at UCLA, he asked his show biz friends for help and they all pleaded poverty; they said they had gambled their money away. Quite a sign of the times!

At that time, UCLA didn't even give a degree in music. I had to get my BA in history. I was among the first candidates for the MA in music, which I received after writing a thesis on one of my compositions. As an undergraduate, I studied enough history to get through the requirements, but mostly I took music. Schönberg taught many more courses than any professor would nowadays, mostly undergraduate classes in counterpoint, harmony, beginning composition, and analysis. As his assistant, I corrected his students' papers and put together composition exercises.

After I left school, I would see Schönberg several times a week. A peak experience for me was watching him conduct the L.A. Philharmonic in a concert of his own music.

Around this time, I was organizing and participating in many concerts. Along with Peter Yates and others, I helped to found the

"Evenings on the Roof," an unprecedented effort to present chamber music of all centuries. Remarkably, the series is still going, under a new name—"Monday Evening Concerts." One of our earliest concerts was an all-Schönberg evening, and I remember that Schönberg came and was very gracious. He was always very kind to anyone who played his music. I believe he didn't expect much. When I played his music for him, he would pay me a compliment, then add a big "but" and continue with suggestions for improvement. He went straight to the point. Remember, In Vienna he had the Verein für musikalische Privataufführungen with private concerts where many musicians were trained to play new music. And Schönberg always had the last word. Although not essentially a performing musician, he was full of practical advice for the performer. In his sketches and manuscripts he's very careful to write explicit dynamics. Schönberg realized that he had to make his music as understandable as possible.

On the other hand, he saw no reason to teach his twelve-tone system. He believed he could take students only so far—give them the fundamentals and put them on their own. I still believe in training people in the classics first, to give them some kind of vocabulary, a language to work with. And it is important to study harmony and counterpoint, along with other musical disciplines, maybe from a variety of viewpoints. Later one has time to learn a system *per se*, such as twelve-tone or what have you.

I have found that Schönberg's approach to counterpoint isn't as old fashioned as it might seem on the surface. Instead of reconstructing the polyphonic style of Palestrina or Bach, his counterpoint exercises are designed to create a neutral language which teaches the student to control basic contrapuntal materials. You see, composition students often don't have proper backgrounds. They don't want to get well-acquainted with the musical heritage; they prefer to improvise, make up their own rules as they go along. Theirs is a very limited perspective. Many can't go beyond a certain point because they confuse technique with substance. Others are led into a rigidly systematic approach to music and think that's all there is to it. But they should remember that it is essential to be well-versed in two areas—fundamental theoretical principles, *and* the classic musical literature. Each takes time. In fact, they're harder than learning foreign languages. But everybody is in such a hurry these days.

Schönberg and I didn't agree on everything. We didn't agree on

Stravinsky, for instance, who arrived in L.A. around 1940, a little later than Schönberg did. I met him through a friend who told him I copied music; Stravinsky needed a new edition of *The Rite of Spring*. His personality was not at all like Schönberg's. Perhaps this led people to assume that there was antagonism between them. People would say "Isn't it a shame that these two musical giants live in the same town and don't speak to each other or move in the same circles?" I reflected on this and concluded that genius doesn't like the company of genius unless the two individuals are in different fields. Schönberg had enough to keep him busy in music; the fact that I was interested in other modern composers neither excited him nor bothered him. I knew there was no use discussing Hindemith or Stravinsky with Schönberg. He didn't study their music. He was most knowledgeable about music of past masters. He even said very little about his two outstanding pupils, Berg and Webern. I found some of Webern's scores in Schönberg's library, but he never referred to them. He wasn't trying to hide them; they just weren't his main interest. I was fascinated by them, though; I was among the first in L.A. to present some Webern songs and to play some of Berg's early pieces.

Schönberg thought of his own music as part of an evolutionary process. His teachers, as he writes in the article "My Evolution," were Brahms and Wagner, and this is evident from the early Schönberg songs we have uncovered. You can trace the constructive principles, the handling of polyphony, the interest in development of material. The continuity's there. Schönberg's a Viennese traditionalist. What looks like a great rupture turns out to be part of a process. Hostile criticism of new music was a fact of life in Schönberg's world. Wagner had been a polemical figure and more than anyone helped produce an argumentative atmosphere in Vienna that lingered for years. Almost any new art or music provoked devastating criticism. The music critics were mostly scholars or operetta composers and they were terribly antagonistic to musical developments. Schönberg says in one of his articles, "I was never a revolutionary. The only revolutionary of our day was Richard Strauss." And he may be right.

People too often forget what Schönberg did for all modern composition. Because of him, listeners are not so instantly hostile to new music as they used to be. If anything, it's the opposite. Complex composers like Elliott Carter and Pierre Boulez are just as difficult to understand today as Schönberg was in his time. But because listeners have struggled with Schönberg's pieces, they don't dismiss anything new and unfamiliar out of hand; instead, they say, "We have to wait a while in order to be able to judge this work." Such tolerance is a relatively recent phenomenon.

In fact, sometimes tolerance gets out of hand; when after one hearing of a new piece critics tell us enthusiastically all about it, I suspect they've been deceived by the composer's propaganda, which some take as gospel. I feel like crying out, "Well now, wait a minute. You can't *really* know this piece all that well." Upon first hearing the Bach B minor Mass, I knew that I couldn't digest it all at once. Now it seems that some reviewers are jumping on the bandwagon right away. It's quite the thing to accept a new work instantly, or just as often to reject it as quickly, without listening, examining, and really experiencing it.

I don't downgrade all critics, but they usually don't carry out their function too well. More of them should be like Andrew Porter of the *New Yorker*—know music well and write about it with enthusiasm and grace. Nine out of ten critics I know are either frustrated tenors or were once involved with opera in some other way. You have the sad story of Martin Bernheimer of the L. A. *Times*, who would thrive in a city with an opera house, where he could write about the things he likes instead of having to travel to find them. L.A. isn't the place for him. But *someone* should be investigating what does go well here, such as certain kinds of new music. And someone in L.A. should be criticizing film music. My advice to critics is: Be part of your own community. Our critics tend to be carpetbaggers who have no faith at all in L.A. or what goes on here, for better or for worse. Everything's always more important to them when it comes from somewhere else.

I deeply resent the paucity of different critical opinions in L.A., where there's often only one review per concert, if that. It's not fair. I myself would hate to have to go to all the concerts one critic must attend and then make on-the-spot judgments of all of them. Sometimes by chance you get an intelligent review; often you don't. Either way, that lone review reflects a single critic's prejudices. I wish there were some others around to balance the situation. Out here we lack cultural give-and-take. I always associate culture with literacy. That's why, even if there's no more music played in certain cities, you have a feeling that they are more important places because lots of people talk and write about whatever gets performed. That's probably true of Paris, where there isn't all that much great music performed, of London, a tremendously literate town, and of course, New York.

Yet our musical situation in L.A. is peculiar. In the past some of our finest orchestras belonged to Fox and other studios. Many so-called serious musicians deeply resented the way Hollywood soaked up talent. To a great extent we scorned film music because it seemed to interfere with great music. And yet the same people who played a commercial date one day would the next day be playing in the Roof programs or recording with Bruno Walter. They earned a terrific reputation for versatility. I had students at UCLA who were wonderful jazz players on the side, which is only natural for young Americans. They played every kind of music. It's a strange state of affairs; there is a pool of outstanding individual players, but not many ensembles, like string quartets, wind quintets, and the like. Every major group comes here to visit, but none seems to grow naturally out of the soil. One cannot talk about a Los Angeles style. And I guess the truth is we're a little bit jealous. We envy the well-established groups that are based in the East.

Now we *do* have some excellent schools and quite a few good composers connected with them. These people get their works performed. Often they receive grants. But generally, those who teach would like to drop out occasionally to concentrate on composition or performance. Teaching full time is no particular hardship in my case; I've taught in many different schools and enjoyed most of them. Even so there *are* times when I'd like to be closer to professional playing and not involved just in its preparatory phase. For those who are constantly composing, though, or who want to play more, there are great inducements to be in the East. A school like Eastman gives its performers a lot of time off to perform, and the market down that way is good for first-rate performers.

Another good reason to be East is that recording is not as feasible here; all the big companies are there. And we suffer for it. For instance, a few years ago I uncovered some early Schönberg songs and made a tape of them with Marni Nixon, an exceptionally fine singer. The songs seemed to suit her voice beautifully. We couldn't find any company to market it. Recently she sang the same songs in New York and immediately there was interest in recording them. Now we've been approached by at least two very large companies. You have to be there on the spot. Despite all the great music making in colleges and universities in L.A.—and there's a lot—you are still no one until you're in New York.

But it's not a total wasteland. At the California Institute of the Arts, where I teach, I've been able to invite a number of excellent composer-lecturers who pass through these parts. One of them this year was Krzystof Penderecki who was in town to hear his symphony played by the Philharmonic. His works are often commissioned and performed here. He told me he is astounded, in his travels around the country, at the amount of talent he finds in out-of-the-way places where his music is performed. There are nooks and crannies of activity all over the place that most of us don't know about. Why not? Lack of communication in newspapers, magazines, radio, and television. The media simply don't focus on the multitude of regional developments. Sometimes I know more about European composers than American ones. I've had to tell publishers from abroad like Schott's that they're not reviewing American music very well in their magazine *Melos*, what with only one reviewer in New York who occasionally takes note of L.A. I said, "You're certainly not covering the whole country, which could be broken up into six regions each as large as the largest country in Europe, excluding Russia." They don't seem to realize this. A publication like *Numus West* tries but it cannot get the distribution. *Numus* is Seattle-based. Who's heard of it outside of people in the West? *I'm* not even on their mailing list. There should be more writers like Tom Willis of Chicago, who sometimes move out of their home bases, and go on the road to see what's happening.

We need a closer-knit musical community in which people across the country exchange ideas frequently, in which somebody says something thought-provoking and somebody else responds. It's this kind of interchange that we are entirely lacking in our neck of the woods. And we don't have a national journal that comes out often enough to serve the purpose.

Tuck (Hubert) Howe, our contact in New York on the *Contemporary Newsletter*, put out by NYU, specializes in computer music.

He manages to get around the country quite a bit. Tuck is originally from L.A. and he's on the ISCM [International Society for Contemporary Music] board. Now, that organization hasn't played much of a role in this country but it does have one chapter out here and another in New York. Every year we try to get works performed at the ISCM European festival and never succeed, often because sending people to Europe is just too expensive. In 1976, though, the festival was located in Boston and people like Howe solicited money to bring groups from around the country. The ISCM has three American members—Howe, Gunther Schuller, and Elliott Carter. We're trying to add someone from the West Coast, to further understanding between the two ends of this country. In order to get any of our composers played in the festival we'll have to send a performing group from here. So other Americans may hear our music. But how's the world going to hear it?

Given all the difficulties, it's still not so bad being a composer today, even if you live in L.A. If you're decent you get performed somehow or other. When you're associated with a school—and most composers are these days—you usually have performers right there, on your local territory, which is something like the situation in a European small town. Then, you can probably get your music published. The trouble is, performance and publication don't pay. I have some young students at Cal Arts who are practically ready to publish their music, but they can't make any kind of living. Roger Reynolds, a composer from San Diego, told me last year, "Yes, I got a grant from the NEA, but it was only $4000. I can't afford to take time off from school to work seriously on a composition."

But sometimes there are other sources of funds. After seeing enough scores, going to enough concerts, and listening to enough records I have found that at present, as in all periods, music is being commissioned by groups who want to perform it, like the New York Contemporary Music Ensemble. So many new pieces are tailor-made to fit a certain combination of talents, taking into account their predilections and strengths. In London you might be writing for Peter Maxwell Davies' group, in Germany, for Karl Stockhausen's group. This situation is both good and bad. Music written for a specific ensemble may not be exportable because it is tied to certain surroundings and special conditions. On the other hand, one positive consequence might be a closer tie-in between composers and performing groups, which means that new works will get more than one performance apiece. This could be a major trend of the future.

Do I see any rise in the level of understanding of contemporary music these days? I guess there's more general awareness of what's going on. More publicity and recordings are sure to have an effect. But it's still true that most composers have a hard time reaching a broad public. I'm not referring to contemporary heroes. I'm sure that Elliott Carter or George Crumb will get a large audience wherever they're performed, but others may not be so lucky. The two or three hundred people who hear a new work in New York's Carnegie Recital Hall or Alice Tully Hall resemble the two or three hundred who listen to new music concerts out West.

The whole process will always go this way: Music filters down to a larger audience as people learn that they have choices about what to hear. This is bound to happen more and more.

We made an interesting discovery when "rock culture" descended on us. Before rock, no contemporary music was reaching the masses of youth. Jazz had gotten more rarefied and progressive and less comprehensible. Young people wouldn't have much to do with ballads and love songs that were considered popular at one time; these became associated with a kind of commercialism that repelled them. The majority of young people were not being tapped. I didn't consider it amazing when the Beatles came along and did so well. It seemed so natural—they were filling a tremendous gap. There has to be something for everybody in every field.

But what we still need in music is more recognition of serious composition in the intellectual community. The serious artist or musician always fears, perhaps rightly, that he isn't really connected to such a community. He's not necessarily looking for popular approval—maybe ultimately, but not at first. Rather, he wants the understanding of, for example, scientists and philosophers. It's terribly ironic that when we do get into academia, there's as little communication between artists and intellectuals as outside the academy. Your colleagues don't particularly respond to new music or new ideas in music; they respond to scientific developments. The indifference to composers even extends to many performing musicians, who in turn are not as narrow as people in the other arts. At Cal Arts, where we have several departments, it's the musicians who travel between film, art, and theater and get to know people in each area. The people in other fields tend to be more limited.

The musicians' broadness is rather encouraging, and it's making me begin to believe that in some ways musicians can be and often are the most alert and curious of people. Perhaps it's because they go back and forth between the private and public worlds, in contrast, say, to a painter who might never have contact with people or to an actor who is always on display. I must say, I gain renewed respect for performing musicians when I meet somebody like the pianist Alfred Brendel, not only because he plays Schönberg but because he happens to have a brain. He looks at music as a person who reads outside of music *and* keeps aware of what's going on in the field, even if it has to do with music that's not part of his repertory. Then there's Edward Cone, the philosopher of music at Temple University, and Charles Rosen, the pianist and writer, who sometimes gets irritable because he wants to deal with ideas more than most musicians do.

Such people have broad humanistic viewpoints. I share their predilection and try to instill that spirit in my own students. "You should go beyond music," I tell them. It's a revelation to them when even Wagner or Mahler is presented in a broader cultural context. It's incredible how little they've absorbed of general culture. They might know the notes of Stockhausen's latest piece, but they really can't understand it because they are unable to relate it to the realms of philosophic speculation or scientific investigation. Devoid of the historical sense that's so essential, they also lack a literary and poetic background. Unfortunately these gaps are often reflected in the music they write. Ah, for a community of thinkers and artists!

8: *Carl Schachter*

I always wanted to go into music. As a youngster, I thought of becoming a concert pianist and trained accordingly. I never heard of theory until I was thirteen, and I didn't begin studying it seriously until college. As it turned out, a solid foundation in piano was probably the best possible preparation for becoming a theorist; I believe very strongly that theory and practice in music are closely related and mutually dependent.

I had no such sophisticated thoughts as a kid growing up in Chicago, though I showed a love for music very early. Apparently I sang a lot when I was little. We had a maid who was a graduate of one of the Chicago conservatories and she sang quite a bit in many different languages. So by the time I was two or three I knew about forty songs. That's how I started. Then I played the piano by ear—we didn't have a piano but my grandmother did. I would pick out tunes and play them over and over. So my parents started giving me lessons when I was five.

My father was a great music lover. He used to usher at the Chicago Opera. Sometimes he carried a spear in *Aida*. He studied the violin a little as a boy but never went very far with it. Both my parents encouraged me in my musical interests. My main teacher in Chicago, Sara Levee, was a very fine, serious musician. I learned an enormous amount from her. I worked with her until I was sixteen.

Then, intending to perform, I came to New York. Very briefly I studied with Karl Friedberg, a magnificent pianist and musician. But I went on to study with Isabelle Vengerova; lessons with her took away any thoughts of becoming a pianist.

I'm grateful to her for one thing, anyway: She thought I ought to get a general musical education and since she was on the faculty of the Mannes College of Music (then the Mannes Music School) she suggested I enroll there. That was a fine experience. At that time I was quite interested in conducting; I had started buying orchestral scores when I was thirteen or fourteen. So I became a conducting major at Mannes. I studied with Carl Bamburger, and I had marvelous theory classes with Felix Salzer, a student of the brilliant theorist Heinrich Schenker. It was Salzer who introduced me to the Schenker approach. That opened up so much to me that I began to think of

Carl Schachter, professor of music theory at Queens College and the Mannes College of Music, was interviewed at his home in New York City in October 1977.

doing something in theory. And indeed, as I started teaching, I got more and more interested in it.

I think everyone now agrees that Schenker is the greatest music theorist of the twentieth century. Making use of a lot of earlier traditions, he put music theory on a totally new basis. He not only pointed out single features of a given piece of music and showed how they resembled or contrasted with other features in the same piece or in different pieces, but he also pointed to what made the piece as a whole a unified work. By dealing with the issues a composer raised in a piece and how they were worked out, Schenker could at least begin to deal with whether a piece was great music or not. Greatness is not something one can totally conceptualize but I think one can get closer to understanding it with the Schenker approach than with any other.

Schenker's way of dealing with theory very profoundly influences the way one hears and plays. It's rooted in the idea that the rules of music flow from certain conditions imposed by the nature of the tonal system and, beyond that, reflect what the greatest composers were able to achieve. It's very difficult stuff, and not everybody should make Schenker analysis the prime interest in his life, but some exposure to it is very helpful to any musician. Every one of Schenker's detailed analyses of pieces of music contains a long section on how to perform the piece; he considered that an absolutely integral part of each analysis.

Presumably, many performers would use theoretical insights to deepen their interpretations. But unfortunately, the marked separation of theory, composition, and performance into different disciplines has become a key feature of modern musical life. In contrast to the past, people in different walks of musical life often have very little to do with each other. I find this development rather sad.

Most of the great performers throughout history were also composers. Some, like the violinists Wieniawski and Vieuxtemps, wrote virtuoso concerti for their instruments; others less talented wrote silly little salon pieces. But still they all had the experience of putting notes together into coherent wholes. That gave them a kind of insight into the way music works that they couldn't have gotten just by playing. So there was a close relationship between what was composed and what was performed: there was continuity between what one played, what one listened to, and what one wrote oneself.

Then, traditionally, teaching theory was entrusted to composers. That was so in the past because there was a connection between what the composers were writing and the tonal theory that underlies our greatest music. Since composers were putting theory into practice, they were very often the best people to teach it. This was true even into the twentieth century. In much early-twentieth-century music there are demonstrable links between what happens there and in earlier music; even if the connections are rather vague, the composers themselves were very well trained in the classics and put a high priority on teaching them to their students. As far as I know, for example, Schönberg didn't teach twelve-tone music at all; he was more interested in having his students analyze Mozart quartets and do counterpoint. He had a traditional understanding of what it meant for a composer to teach theory.

Now, what happened in this century was nothing less than a musical revolution. This can't really be described briefly, but it has meant simply a greater discontinuity between recent music and earlier music than at any time in the past. Composers who lived as far apart in time as Bach and Brahms—Bach died in 1750 and Brahms in 1897—different as their music is, wrote in the same basic musical language. But there is no unified basis that I can see for most compositions of the recent past. Certain fundamental things about the way the notes combine with each other and what these combinations mean are quite changed from the past—and vary from piece to piece. John Cage's *Four Minutes and Twenty Eight Seconds of Silence*, for instance, is not built on the same set of assumptions as Milton Babbitt's *Semi-Simple Variations*. Yet somehow these two pieces and countless others, are all regarded as *music*, a term that's become much more broadly defined in this century than ever before.

When I was a kid in the forties, everyone who wrote on new music agreed that the first half of the twentieth century was a period of experimentation and that undoubtedly the second half of the century would be a period of consolidation. Well, that period has not arrived; as a matter of fact, things are much more fragmented now than thirty years ago. This is true of twentieth-century life in many ways; I think the musical trends relate to and reflect general trends. Certainly, not everything that happens in music has social causes—there *is* an internal musical dynamic—but music and society are connected.

In any case, the music being written today is quite divorced from the earlier repertory most performers play. And performing musicians these days don't compose much. Thus they would do well to study some theory, so they'd have some real grasp of how pieces *work*, not only how they sound.

But most performers don't want anything to do with theory. It's very difficult to understand why not, and the reasons probably vary from musician to musician. First of all, performing is a very ego-threatening activity all by itself. So submitting oneself to something like theory, which is very exacting and difficult and somehow not completely necessary, seems to many people like too much to ask; after all, one *can* play the notes and create some effect without really knowing how the piece is put together. Then, it may be that performers see theory as just one more pressure in an already pressured life. Also, the highly competitive nature of modern concert life gets in the way of objective contemplation. Many people are afraid that if they are too conscious of what they're doing, the spontaneity may be lost. That may be partly true, though I think talented musicians can transcend this self-consciousness. The great conductor Wilhelm Furtwängler discussed scores with Schenker over a 20- or 25-year period; he was willing to put himself through that kind of discipline and it showed in his interpretations. But I think very few people nowadays are willing to take the trouble.

On top of all this, there's been a pervasive anti-intellectualism among young people over the last couple decades which seems to be a bit on the wane; these days one doesn't find students interested only in non-intellectual activities; there is more of a sense that, after all, the mind *is* part of the human makeup.

Taking all these issues into account, I think that many modern-day trends in performance make it difficult for musicians to incorporate much significant music theory into their playing. Nowadays performers aim for two ideals—one of them a little old-fashioned, the other more recent. The first is imitating a machine. This is so pervasive because of the mechanization of modern life in general, and because it is possible to achieve a kind of artificial surface perfection on records. When I say imitating a machine, I mean having a mechanical ideal of perfection, and aiming for a certain smoothness and uniformity in your playing. However, I think that seriously incorporating theory into performing requires a non-uniform, sometimes irregular way of playing with quite a lot of rubato and use of different colors and shadings, not just for their own sakes, but for what they show about the composition. Thus theory and current practice are at odds.

The more recent trend is a little harder to spot. The so-called "Romantic Revival" might seem to hold out hope as a counter-balance to the first trend I described; people involved in it personalize their playing, take slow tempi, and change tempi within a piece. Certainly, this is encouraging. But I'm afraid that a lot of this freedom in performance, good as it is, is not as significant as it seems; many people are applying "Romantic" mannerisms indiscriminately, without knowing whether this or that interpretive choice makes sense in the context of the piece as a whole. Thus gesture for its own sake comes to replace gesture as part of an overall interpretation; it implies a kind of mechanical freedom, if you will, rather than the real freedom that comes from knowledge. Again, if you're using this or that mannerism whenever the spirit moves you, you have no need for theory.

Of course, there are always some naive geniuses, who understand so much intuitively that they achieve depth without knowing quite what they're doing. There are never many of those though. And of course there are performers who *do* have a good deal of knowledge about how pieces work; I'm not trying to paint an altogether bleak picture. But the balance certainly does not fall on the side of interpretive depth.

In terms of this whole discussion, the issue of "fidelity to the text" becomes very complicated. I believe strongly in the concept; not only do I believe in playing the *notes* the composer wrote but also in being very conscious of slurs and dynamics and the implications of such things. The fact is that one can still be enormously free while being faithful, because composers have left a tremendous amount to the performer's discretion. One doesn't exclude the other. Look at someone like Artur Schnabel, who was more text-conscious than most and was also in many respects a free performer.

Then, it's well to know something about the aural world in which the composer worked, but trying to re-create it exactly has some dangers too. Compare it with drama—say the performance of a Shakespeare play. Certainly it might be interesting for us to see a young boy playing Juliet or Lady Macbeth, and hear people pronouncing the English language in the Elizabethan way—we know quite a lot about it all. But it would not be a very live performance; the whole tradition that animated male performers in female roles, which is still alive in the Kabuki theater, has gone out of the Western world. There would be something terribly artificial about it. I don't think any boy today could play a Shakespeare heroine in a natural way, nor is anybody learning to speak Elizabethan English going to speak it naturally. Therefore, in a performing art, one has to accept that certain things in the world change, and one can't really reproduce any given performance practice. While it's worthwhile to revive old instruments, old performance techniques, and the like, it's also important to recognize that there are limits to what can be achieved. The very limitations of an old instrument, which the best performers of the day might have tried to overcome, are sometimes the very things that people who try to play with great historical accuracy mistakenly emphasize. I'm sure that gives a totally incorrect picture.

And I think that a talented performer playing, say, a Bach French suite at a concert, knows that this music was written to be enjoyed by the performer and perhaps a few people sitting around listening, and that it was to be played in a room and not a huge hall. If he's any good, he can convey that intimate feeling even in a larger space. I think people can be too literal about these things—they feel that the original conditions must be reproduced exactly or one can't get an accurate impression of the work of art as a work of art. But that's like saying that if you look at a painting at New York's Metropolitan Museum of Art that was intended to be hung in a church, you can't appreciate it. That's wrong; there's something in a great work of art that transcends the specific conditions under which it was created.

Related to the question of fidelity to the score are some very odd oversights on the part of many performers. For example, there is an early version of the C-Major Prelude and Fugue from the second book of the *Well-Tempered Clavier*, for which Bach provided fingerings. These are most interesting; they reveal certain nuances about articulation and phrasing, if one studies them carefully. You can see, for example, that when you go from the dominant to the tonic at a cadence Bach prefers you to keep the bass disconnected. Many performers do this anyway, but it's rather nice to know that Bach's fingering bears this out. There are many other such subtleties, not nearly as obvious as that.

Now, this version is extremely accessible; it's been in pocket format for fifteen years. But how many people who play Bach care about the composer's views of the finer points? Very few. It's rather amazing that a young pianist who would think nothing of spending fifty or sixty dollars for a lesson with Madame Somebody-or-other won't spend one dollar for what would amount to a lesson with Bach. Now, this has nothing to do with theory *per se*; I'm just observing that people don't think about avenues to interpreting music other than listening to other performers, or taking lessons; they don't seem aware that one can find out things, and grow as a musician through closer study of the music itself. This phenomenon relates to the lack of interest in theory. I'm at a loss to explain it. You'd think every piano teacher would encourage such exploration. As it is, even if pianists happen to have the miniature score, they don't bother to look closely at what's in it. Very strange.

Again, I'm afraid this harks back to the fact that people who are involved in different aspects of musical life have less to do with each other than they ever did. Exceptions are composers and those performers who are really interested in contemporary music; these people do occasionally talk to one another. And probably there is some contact among certain Medieval and Renaissance music historians and performers who specialize in early music; they need each other. But with the central tradition, the historians go their own way without any concern for what theory or analysis might have to offer; performers are usually interested in neither. I don't know that this situation is inevitable, though I'm not sure what can be done about it in a large way. I think the kind of community I'd like to see exists to some extent in England; maybe because it's a smaller country, people in music connect with each other more than their counterparts do here.

Overspecialization is a very serious problem. I think it has many causes. Again, it's related to the state of composition nowadays and the fact that most performers are very detached from what most composers write. Then, there is certainly a pervasive tendency for people in academia to intellectualize about everything and to feel that collecting quantities of information and categorizing it is in itself valuable. And of course there's the widespread use of computers, which keeps many people in music far away from real music. One finds many people going into the field of theory who may not have much musical talent—who have bad ears or don't play anything or don't know the literature very well—but who do have the kind of self-discipline and intelligence that enables them to get through graduate courses, write some kind of dissertation, and teach. Specialization is meant for such people because it means they can work with some little corner of music theory and thereby hide their general inabilities. The same thing happens in every field. Of course, music theory deals in abstractions—that's what it is—but the person who's doing the theory ought to know what an abstraction is and what it is being abstracted from. For many of these people, the abstraction is the only concrete aspect of music. I think this is very bad.

Specialization is not the only distressing trend in contemporary musical life. Related to it in some crazy way is a tendency toward too much diversification in university music curricula. Musical education in many places has become extremely broad; it encompasses much more than the study of the history and theory of tonal music, which would take four full years of study all by itself—and then some. Nowadays one has to learn not only about medieval music, and very recent music, but also about all sorts of exotic musics, rock, jazz, and so on. Sometimes one even has to teach people how to take a tape recorder into a public toilet and make music out of it. (I didn't make this up; it took place in a freshman theory class at a very respected university.) We are forced to ask, what does the field of music consist of? What concerns me is that if all these things have to be taught, then students end up knowing next to nothing about anything, and least of all how to deal with what is, after all, the heart of the musical literature, masterpieces of the sixteenth through the nineteenth centuries, which I think most people in their innermost hearts feel constitute the bulk of the greatest music, certainly in the Western tradition, and probably of the whole human race. I feel it is necessary to give students the kind of training that will enable them to deal with this great music. After all, it is still partly a living tradition; I studied with somebody who knew Brahms fairly well and who was able to say, "When Brahms played this piece for me, he pedaled like this." That's just a tiny point, but it's true that there are a lot of people around who still understand this music intuitively and don't have to re-create it completely intellectually. What a tragedy if that tradition were to die out—and it easily can. We can't really sense how sixteenth-century music should be performed. One might have opinions about it, but not much more. It would be horrible for the living link to disappear with somewhat later music.

So, in the most serious music schools and music departments, I would like to see a concentration on the central part of the repertory, at least for undergraduates. Once they have a really good foundation, they can go on to other things.

Maybe then performers would start writing some tonal music on a modest and simple scale, not necessarily with hopes of its being performed, but the way Chinese scholars in the nineteenth and twentieth centuries still practiced ninth-century calligraphy, not for commercial purposes but just because it was beautiful. As I've said, I think if performers could write music this would help their playing. And I see no reason why such pieces could not be performed occasionally, though they probably wouldn't become part of the standard repertory. One can't bring back another era. But one can at least develop for oneself a personal relation to writing music.

Somehow PhD programs in theory and musicology prefer students who are university graduates but not necessarily performing musicians. Unfortunately this is a self-perpetuating phenomenon—a kind of professionalism, academization, or what have you. What a shame this is! It should be a rule that nobody be admitted to a PhD program in music who can't play an instrument or sing, at least well enough to begin to think about interpretive matters. The way you analyze a piece of music is very much connected to the way you play it. If you have no sense of music as a performing art, there's no hope for you as a theorist or even as a musicologist. Also, we should make sure incoming students have at least trainable ears, and know some of the literature.

Amidst all the gloomy trends, a positive one is that there is a great increase in interest in Schenker now; many universities and conservatories are offering courses in Schenker analysis, though a lot of people who teach it abstract it much more than he intended. It's sad that with this increasing interest in Schenker's theory, you have so many people going into music who are musically illiterate. I know of a student who was trying to transfer to Mannes from another well-known conservatory. She wanted to be a theory major. She'd been at her first school for two or three years, had analyzed George Crumb's use of sonority—and she couldn't harmonize a basic chorale melody.

It wasn't completely her fault; she wasn't given the tools. It's very depressing.

Nowadays I'm doing more university than conservatory teaching. I teach at Queens College and [the] Mannes [College of Music], and I also have a few private professional students. I've seen a greater change in the university than in the conservatory student over the last decade or so; I find the students in general more serious and interested now. But I don't think that has anything to do specifically with music or music theory; it's just the way students are now. Next year this might change.

Unfortunately, musical illiteracy among college students seems to be on the increase. I think trends in teaching have a lot to do with this. During the "Academic Revolution" of the sixties, everything taught had to be "relevant"; thus there was no special priority given to plain ordinary great music. Another tendency was to allow students to do whatever they pleased, without requirements. For a number of years, one very well-known and in some ways quite good conservatory hardly required any courses in theory. But you could study Josquin or Wagner—without any tools to enable you to make judgments about them. I find this ridiculous. A seventeen-year-old kid who comes into a music department doesn't know how best to proceed; there's no way he can. And it's an absolute abdication of responsibility on the part of teachers to leave it to him.

How would I do things differently? I would start to fix the situation at younger age levels first. I think it's very important for young musicians in elementary and high schools to have many opportunities to play and to sing. Then, kids who are gifted in instruments other than piano should study some piano—it's incredibly helpful for any musician. An overly intellectualized abstracting regimen should not be undertaken too young for most people. What they need, and what most music education fails to provide, is acquaintance with a lot of literature, and solid training in reading and hearing.

The first thing I would insist upon on the college level is that students be taught how to read and how to hear. These are not so simple. By hearing I mean being able to discriminate pitches accurately; by reading, knowing how to make one's way through an orchestra score. Many musicians can't do either; a lot of literature is closed to them because there's a limit to what they can get out of listening to records.

Then, there has to be a really thorough grounding in tonal counterpoint and harmony, and that's not something you can get in just a semester or two. One has to accept the fact that it takes a couple of years. There are various approaches one might take to theory, but however it's taught, students should come out being able to harmonize a folk tune, or a hymn or chorale, and write some two-, three- and four-voice counterpoint. And I believe very strongly that some kind of work in Schenker should be available to all serious musicians. It doesn't have to be taught everywhere—in fact, there may not be enough people around who can teach it—but every part of the country should have some place that does it well.

In graduate music programs, more harmony and counterpoint writing should be the norm. But for the most part, it's not. There is a fiction that one learns how to write fugues and such as an undergraduate and then one theorizes about theory later. The fact is, many advanced students haven't done enough writing; the ones who have had some should do more. This situation used to be better—when Walter Piston, say, taught graduate courses at Harvard. People got a lot out of his fugue class.

I'm not asking for anything outlandish. I'd just like music students to be able to hear, read, play, and write at least simple examples of music that make sense. In one harmony book, the author says you shouldn't teach tonal compositional techniques any more because they're passé. After all, he continues, if someone acts in a Shakespeare play, he doesn't have to be able to write a play like Shakespeare. Which is true. But you would imagine he could form an English sentence or write a simple letter in a way that someone else could understand, that makes some sense. That's all I'm talking about in music—I'm not asking anyone to write a symphony in the style of Beethoven.

When teaching rudiments, it's good to use as many examples from real music as possible, though sometimes one has to create certain artificially simple situations in order to focus on particular problems. One of the difficulties with the approach developed at Juilliard is that every example comes from a real piece. Sometimes the music is so complicated that if one doesn't simplify things a little, one can't do anything with it that can be built upon. On the other hand, elementary theory is often taught in such a way that it is very much divorced from real music. Both extremes are bad. You can't throw somebody at a Bach chorale and say, "Derive some rule for four-part writing from this," or inversely, "Here's one rule after another and never mind how composers use them." The problem with the French approach, which Nadia Boulanger and others follow, is that it constructs a terribly elaborate artificial language that has some connection with music but which goes much too far along its own path without really connecting with what actually happens in great compositions. It's much better than most other systems; you learn something from it. If you're an intuitive musician and you perform, you can eventually learn to draw your own connections.

But the French system isn't the best because it can make people terribly rule-conscious in a bad way, so that they're afraid to express anything musically and are inclined to feel that any departure from contrived conventions is earthshaking—which it's not necessarily. Very often people with such training look at real music and say, "Why isn't it following the rules?" And because the system is admittedly artificial, there's a tendency to feel that there must be more specialization between theory and practice than really has to be. I think the theory programs at Queens and Mannes are good because they manage to avoid this pitfall; at both schools there's a healthy balance between playing and thinking.

Teaching in such places makes my life very satisfying. It's very pleasant to have some influence over talented people. Music students, whatever problems thay may have, tend to be deeply interested in their subject and very often select it because of some inner compulsion to do so. If one believes, as I do, in the way one is approaching a subject, then giving others a better foundation than they might otherwise have is very gratifying.

Then, think of rich people who spend millions of dollars to own great paintings, so they can live with them and get to know them. Nobody can own a piece of music in that way, but it's possible through study and hard work to get close to some of the greatest works. And people pay *you* to deal with this wonderful body of music. What could be better?

I *love* music of all kinds. I've always played the violin, and still play quartets every week. I go to every concert I can manage. But it was probably my passion for history rather than my fondness for music that made me take so strongly to the harpsichord, an instrument widely used by composers before 1800, and in virtual exile since—until the recent and growing interest in the authentic performance of early music. I see my work as one small aspect of a broader drive in our time to unearth facts and sensations from the past. I derive special pleasure from trying to bring to life the *art* of the past, because the task has esthetic as well as intellectual rewards.

Of course, complete success in my field is unattainable. It's true that good musicians in general are never satisfied; they are constantly seeking an unreachable ideal, a Holy Grail of some kind. But we in old music—medieval, Renaissance, even Baroque—are faced with an additional dimension of unreality: We hope not only to achieve abstract and timeless musical goals, but also to recapture a long-forgotten sound world. We're trying to resuscitate periods of music, styles of performance, and instruments that are dead or are not in the living consciousness of most musicians and audiences. Furthermore, the conditions under which this music was composed and performed no longer exist. Since there is no aristocracy, as distinct from a bourgeoisie, no music is designed specifically for Church or Court: we don't go to court to take part in a Masque and we don't have the leisure to go to church on Sunday for four hours to hear a Bach cantata. We can't possibly perform such music properly, that is, in full conformity with the original conception. So there has to be a larger component of imagination in our music making than in any other. We need all the enormous imagination any musician needs, plus an added fairyland quality—a tantalizing desire to do something that can't be done.

Music doesn't stand alone. It's very hard to revive ancient, medieval, and Renaissance dramatic forms as well. The common problem is tearing "art" out of its cultural context. The semi-religious athletic games of the Greek theater, for instance, were part of a sacred ceremony. Or take a miracle play done on the steps of a cathedral—that is hardly theater in our sense. Entertainment was one element, but the pedagogic and ritual purposes were more important; and neither of these is as meaningful to viewers today.

Frank Hubbard, the harpsichord-maker, lived in Boston, and was interviewed in October 1974. He died in February 1976.

Then again, you may have slightly less trouble putting on a Shakespeare play than performing Elizabethan music, because today people still go to the theater as they did in Shakespeare's time. They still sit down and watch the play. Sure, the audience, the theater, and the stage were different four hundred years ago. But to some extent you can duplicate the experience. Not so with old music. Why, the whole idea of a *concert* is relatively new. Music making in Shakespeare's time involved a group of amateurs in a certain social setting that's long been extinct.

I've always felt an affinity with the past. One of my favorite children's books was a boy's how-to-do-it from my grandfather's generation. I remember it told you how to take butter churns and turn them into paddlewheels for steamers. Of course I couldn't find a butter churn anywhere but I'd still pore over the pages of that volume. I didn't realize at the time that the book combined two strong fascinations of mine—the past and technology.

It took me a while to put my three greatest loves—music, history, and making things—together into a career. In graduate school at Harvard in the 1940s, where my field was English literature, I began to realize that my particular talents were probably factual rather than critical, and that I might make a good historian. I wanted to discover *new* information, not simply interpret known data, and English literature had been pretty thoroughly worked over. There's plenty of interpretation to be done, but one's not likely to find out a great deal more about Chaucer's birth year than we already know. As an amateur violinist, I had read a good bit on the history of violin making; suddenly I found myself reading more and more on the history of musical instruments. I began to feel that this was a field that could be freshly studied. Thank heavens I didn't know then how much work had already been done in the area. I had a friend at Harvard, who shared my enthusiasm, named Bill Dowd. He was very interested in old instruments—especially the harpsichord—and evolved a grand scheme to revive the whole Baroque orchestra. But we never got beyond harpsichords. First we decided we needed some training. Dowd went to study with John Challis, the Detroit harpsichord builder who in turn had studied with Arnold Dolmetsch, the great European pioneer in reviving music of the past. I went off to England to become an apprentice with other successors to Dolmetsch, who had died in 1940. I came back to Boston with the notion of dividing my life between the workbench and the library table. As it worked out, over the years, despite a couple of long stints in the library, there's been much more time spent in the workshop, which I sometimes regret.

But many mechanical matters needed to be dealt with. For some perverse reason, it hadn't occurred to anyone making harpsichords simply to look closely at antique instruments and try to duplicate them. We were the first to do this, starting in 1949. It was just the right moment; both Dowd and I became famous because we were in the right place at the right time. We worked together until 1958, and then went our separate ways.

Now, harpsichord *playing* had been revived some fifty years before we came on the scene, by Dolmetsch, Wanda Landowska, and others, who thought that music written for the harpsichord should not be played on the piano. I suppose these musicians were as keenly aware as Dowd and I that the conditions of modern musical life are very different from those of earlier centuries. It seemed impossible to them to re-create an eighteenth-century performance atmosphere; thus they tried to translate the experience into relevant modern terms, and some of them compromised on the issue of instrument authenticity. Public curiosity was excited by this taste of the musical past, and by the time we came on the scene listeners were eager for an even more genuine representation of the past. Nonetheless, the world owes a lot to Dolmetsch and friends for moving us a giant step closer to literal quotation of history.

Dolmetsch worked mainly in Europe, though he came to America for a few years at the turn of the century and made harpsichords, virginals—the oldest and simplest members of the harpsichord family—and a few viols (early violins and cellos) at the Chickering instrument factory. This got the ball rolling in the making of early instruments in this country. As far as the performance aspect, a group of Landowska's students were very influential here— several in Texas, a few in the Midwest. Then there was a group of musicians in the Boston Symphony who repaired some old instruments from the Casadesus collection at Symphony Hall, used old-style bowing, and so on. So activity in early music in the 1930s and 1940s was scattered around the country. Some of these efforts were rather dubious, but at least they signified real interest in old music.

Probably World War II provided the biggest impetus in this direction. When Hitler came to power, many German musicologists escaped to the U.S.; this exodus led to the beginnings of American musicology as the broad scholarly discipline we know today: our practicing musicologists are the students of the Germans who came just before the war. Fortunately for my interests, many of these scholars were interested in medieval, Renaissance, and Baroque music.

Then, around the same time, the Columbia-Victor record monopoly collapsed, and many small recording companies sprang up; competition developed. But where Columbia and Victor still had enough money to hire Heifetz on violin, or the New York Philharmonic to record orchestral works, the smaller companies had to look for a cheaper repertoire. The obvious cheap repertoire was Baroque music performed by small groups of unknown players; that way, there would be no head-on competition with Columbia and Victor, neither of which recorded much early music. The little outfits began to record early music en masse, and almost every piece recorded required a harpsichord. This gave the instrument an enormous boost.

Other factors have contributed to the rise of the harpsichord as well. One was and is that people often turn toward the past to escape the present, which may be menacing, and the future, which may be terrifying. A strong motive for looking back is that this takes your mind off nuclear weapons, the population explosion, urban decay. I know that's where a lot of my energy comes from. Recently I went to climb Mount Monadnock. It's hard to imagine a mountain being jammed, but this one was, with a parade up and a parade down and people screaming in your ears both ways. It was almost a relief to get back down to the car and onto the highway. After an experience like that, you begin to feel there are no places to hide on this planet now, except in the past. Perhaps for this reason, the harpsichord revival had been germinating in Europe more slowly but over a longer period of time. The American seeds, after all, came from Europe. It's curious to recall that Europeans like Landowska and Dolmetsch got the harpsichord movement going, but that the most recent developments have been American.

Learning how to duplicate old instruments was a relatively

straightforward process. I had studied woodworking and instrument making in England, but knew almost nothing about the history of the harpsichord when I started out. While in London, I searched the British Museum on my own, picking away at whatever I could find of a documentary sort. I happened to run across Donald Boalch, who is the author of a dictionary of harpsichord and clavichord makers and a superb bibliographer. He gave me a lot of leads to sources where harpsichords are mentioned. So, without really realizing it, I was doing research for a book on harpsichord making. I measured every antique instrument I could find and then came back and made some with Dowd. By the late 1950s I felt I wanted to write a book. Since my subject was fresh and unusual at the time, I got a bouquet of fellowships to go back to Europe for two years—a year in Paris and a year in Brussels—and I measured hundreds of instruments. I travelled all over Europe in a VW, went everywhere there was an instrument collection, and worked in the Bibliothèque Nationale in Paris and the Bibliothèque Royale in Brussels. I came back to the States with a rough draft of the book and a lot of documentation on instruments, which influenced both Dowd's and my work and subsequently affected all the people who have worked with us. [The book is *Three Centuries of Harpsichord Making*, Cambridge: Harvard University Press, 1965]

The next information-gathering expedition came about ten years later in 1967, when I was invited to Paris to set up a workshop at the Conservatoire de Musique. They have a fine collection of musical instruments and I was to start a permanent place to restore them. This work at the Conservatoire on old instruments themselves gave me a much more intimate knowledge than I had previously had of some of the finest vintage keyboards. Basically, the work was a matter of examining, measuring, getting all the figures, and then organizing the data, the way any historical research is done.

Deciding which instruments to duplicate requires some thought and experience. My original inclination was to pick harpsichords that were widely used in the mainstream of musical history. After all, if you want to reproduce music by François Couperin, a late-seventeenth- and early-eighteenth-century French composer, you want to find a good sample of a typical harpsichord of this time. After thinking about typicality, you want an instrument that enjoyed a good reputation, and, if this is possible to ascertain, one the composer might have had in mind when he wrote. You have to know which instruments that have survived are freaks. A freak may be interesting but it is not the first thing to copy. Now, though, we're beginning to branch out in my workshop as a matter of course. We've become knowledgeable enough to judge instruments on their own merits. Some by minor makers happen to be better than those by famous names.

With eight people in the shop, we make about two hundred harpsichord kits a year for amateurs to put together, plus twelve or so finished harpsichords. Up to now, half the finished instruments have been bought by individuals and the rest by institutions. But institutions usually mean state universities these days, and I refuse to sell them any more instruments. Life is too short to deal with their business managers. They're too big and we're too little and there's too much hassle. As a result, we now sell only to individuals.

A few years ago I would have said we make close approximations of the originals. After all, our measurements are exact; every detail is identical. But copies of anything from the past can be easily identified as products of the period and place the maker comes from. That's mostly because the elements you choose to copy reflect your own taste and that of your time. I'm sure this is true of my instruments. However, I inform myself as completely as I can; I try to make instruments in which every important part has a parallel on an old model. But sometimes it's difficult to decide what aspects are most significant, and there are so many considerations—the type and age of the wood, the tools, and so on.

Not being a harpsichordist imposes obvious limitations on me, but it also has certain advantages. I have discovered that many harpsichord makers who do play the instrument tend to build harpsichords to their own weaknesses. They make actions that are comfortable for their stiff fingers, whereas I am forced to listen to what professional players say. Whenever one comes through Boston and plays an instrument of mine in concert, I make sure to find out what he really thinks of it.

I never deliberately compromise on instruments in order to meet concert requirements—say, that the sound be audible in a large hall. These instruments were simply not originally designed to be heard over vast spaces. On the other hand, I *do* compromise on mechanical matters to make an instrument work better. I don't change the way the harpsichord sounds or feels, but I do make it easier to adjust and less likely to stick and fail. We have certain environmental factors today which didn't exist in the eighteenth century, like heating.

Restoring ancient instruments and building new ones from scratch are two quite different matters. No matter how careful you are, a copy of an old instrument will never sound quite like a restored original. The new version has a tendency to be purer, more equal, with fewer funny sounding notes or unevennesses. But it lacks a kind of warmth and immediacy that the old instrument has. I suspect that these qualities come with age. Harpsichords become uneven but interesting, rather than plain and boring.

I'm afraid that too many instrumental performers these days have fallen into a rut. Most pianists and violinists play the same literature over and over in roughly the same way. Their students follow suit and it becomes pretty hard to distinguish one from another. But new possibilities have been revealed by performers such as the harpsichordist Gustav Leonhardt, whose "new" attitudes toward rhythm, improvisation, and phrasing actually hark back to original performance practices. You find these same aims in groups like the Concentus Musicus of Vienna. This is very refreshing and will probably influence performers of such later music as the Beethoven quartets to consider old conventions more seriously. My guess is that the next generation of quartet players will not sound quite as modern as the Juilliard Quartet. But in another sphere, it's my impression that today's composers are deserting the human instrumentalist for the synthesizer. So my work and attitude may be a little irrelevant to their efforts.

It's hard to say exactly how many harpsichord makers there are in this country. Wallace Zuckerman, in a book called *Modern Harpsichords*, lists a hundred and fifty or so. But the category fringes off into amateurs. There probably are not more than ten or twelve first-rate builders in the U.S. There's a lot of shoddy work. Also, many people only make a few instruments in a lifetime, while others assemble other people's kits. Then there are harpsichord makers who do not try to duplicate old models as closely as we do. They are descendants of the Pleyels, the famous Parisian piano manufacturers, and make "modern-style" harpsichords. These people do not pretend to be making antique replicas. Of course everything they do is anathema to me. Nevertheless I must admit that what they're doing may be just as rational—or irrational—as what I'm doing. It's a matter of choice and temperament.

As for demand, ours is a nation of over 200 million people. We make about 12 finished harpsichords a year, hardly an adequate sample. But our order list keeps growing. The kits give us some idea of the interest—and last year we doubled our sale of kits. For every kit we sell, there are about 25 inquiries. In other words, there are 25 times 200 or 5000 people who are interested enough to write a letter asking for a brochure, which begins to be a fair number. Magazine ads apparently have an enormous pull. Most mail-order houses wouldn't dream of getting as many responses per reader as we do. We started out advertising in the *Saturday Review* and *The New Republic*. But you can only go so far with that readership. We've now turned to quarter-page display ads in *Scientific American*, the New York *Times* Sunday magazine, and the English magazines *Early Music* and *The Harpsichord*. From one ad last summer in the *Times* we're still getting responses into the fall.

A kit varies in cost according to how finished it is. The range is from $950 to about $2700. The average kit we sell costs somewhere between $1500 and $1700. My feeling is that most of the kits get finished somehow or other. I don't know this for sure, but nobody throws away $1500 lightly. Most of the people who buy kits are amateurs. And a fair number are bought by university music departments and are assembled as a class project or by a piano technician or beginning harpsichord maker. Some of these work out beautifully. The University of Illinois has one and the University of Washington has several. Then there's one in the Royal Festival Hall in London, another in the Conservatoire in Paris, and yet another in the Conservatorium in Amsterdam.

When institutions buy kits I don't always get followup reports. We ask individuals to send us pictures of the finished instruments. The ones who succeed send in photos, but you never hear from those who fail. It would be fun to contact our lists of customers and ask them, "Is your instrument finished? Are you satisfied with it? Has it ever been used in a a public concert?" A questionnaire like that would probably elicit some interesting responses. I might just try it.

We keep learning how to improve both the finished and the unfinished instruments. Our design is always changing. The kit instructions often need rewriting. I've enjoyed refining the kits as an intellectual game. It's fun to get your own thoughts sufficiently collected so you can tell somebody else exactly how to do something. Also, it's challenging to work out methods of crafting the parts so they can be made at a reasonable price. And there's been another spinoff. Since we make nearly all the parts, we've been forced to make better tools. We don't make keyboards; they are made to our specifications in a German keyboard factory. A man from the factory came to our workshop and we gave him a crash course in keyboard making.

In the future I want to make instruments nobody today has tried, such as a seventeenth-century German-style harpsichord. So much music was written for this instrument, but there's nothing genuine to play it on! As a matter of fact, as yet no one has made a good eighteenth-century German-style harpsichord, which is even more of a shame. I'm also becoming very interested in early fortepianos, the direct predecessors of our modern pianos. We've started bringing out kits for a 1784 Stein, an instrument Mozart might have played or heard. We might move on to other fortepianos. The field remains an open and exciting one, and there's a lot left to do!

Part Three: Conductors

10: Eugene Ormandy

Photo by Louis Hood, The Philadelphia Orchestra

I *don't* think the Philadelphia Orchestra or its audience has changed much since I became music director in 1936. Possibly there is a greater demand for contemporary music than was true a generation ago. But the great Classical and Romantic works still fill the house when they are performed.

I did not always plan to be a conductor. I was born in Budapest in 1899. My family was not musical but my father was a music lover and always hoped to have his first son become a great violinist. Hence he named me after Jenö Hubay, the famous Hungarian violinist of the day. I began to study the violin at the age of two with the aim of some day becoming a concert violinist, which I indeed became. I also played the viola and piano. Unfortunately I did not become as great an instrumentalist as my father dreamed of.

As a boy I had many fine teachers, among them Zoltán Kodály in composition and harmony, Leo Weiner in music interpretation, counterpoint, and form, and David Popper for coaching in chamber music. I toured Europe as a violinist and then settled in the U.S.A. Musical life in America was different from Europe in many ways because everything in America was done on a large scale.

I never made a formal decision to become a conductor. My fate was decided for me when I substituted for an indisposed conductor in 1925. In 1931 I became the conductor of the Minneapolis Symphony Orchestra, where I stayed until 1936. Then I came to Philadelphia where I've been ever since.

People sometimes speak of the "Philadelphia Orchestra Sound," but this was and is actually nonexistent. It is up to each conductor to create his own sound by the way he approaches the music. The so-called Philadelphia Sound, I believe, is the result of our orchestra's having had only two principal conductors in sixty-five years—Leopold Stokowski and myself. Naturally, in both cases, the orchestra and the conductor got to know each other well.

Some things remain the same, others change. I agree with the late Gregor Piatigorsky that the pace of musical life has quickened today. I personally have felt that the jet age is harmful to most musicians, especially conductors or soloists who jump on planes right after concerts and have rehearsals the following morning on another

Eugene Ormandy, music director of the Philadelphia Orchestra, was interviewed partly by mail and in Philadelphia in October 1977.

continent; they have no time to adjust to and acquaint themselves properly with all the different orchestras they work with. Because everyone today is in such a hurry, the quality of musical life has changed considerably, and perhaps for the worse.

Other aspects of musical life have become more difficult as well: For instance, the problems young conductors face in trying to get positions are greater than ever. It is difficult for an unknown conductor to get opportunities to perform in public, because managements must keep a sharp eye on box office sales in order for orchestras to survive. On the other hand, it is of course true that not all would-be maestros have that spark of genius which the great conductors of the past have had, and which audiences respond to so strongly.

I would advise beginning conductors to perform as often as they can—after studying all aspects of their art thoroughly. They must understand that the conductor functions on three levels, each dependent on the others. The first two, personal study and rehearsal, culminate in the third, the performance itself.

During his period of study, the conductor prepares himself both technically and artistically. On this level he must be musician, historian, stylist, orchestrator, and listener. He must study the score so that he "hears" it in his mind. As he does this he evaluates the music and begins to balance the many strands of musical line. He must understand the historical context in which a particular work is conceived and bring to bear upon the growing interpretive edifice a thorough knowledge of the stylistic requirements inherent in the work. To study such a masterwork as Beethoven's *Eroica* Symphony without some knowledge of the composer's response to the ideals of the French Revolution and Napoleon's unique political position in 1806 is to study music in a vacuum. Among the elements of stylistic validity are tempi and dynamics. A Mozart allegro differs greatly from a Tchaikovsky allegro. Similarly, a Haydn forte is an entirely different matter from a Wagner forte.

A thorough knowledge of orchestral colors and timbres enables the studying conductor to "hear" the orchestral sound while he studies the score. It is very important that every aspiring conductor play at least one orchestral instrument and have experience playing in various orchestras, thus getting many chances to watch different conductors while they conduct.

When conducting older composers, the conductor must sometimes compensate for the technical inadequacies of the composers' times by delicately rewriting certain passages in terms of today's more complete orchestras and more highly skilled players. Present-day performances of such works as the Fifth Symphony of Beethoven, the "Great" C Major Symphony of Schubert, the symphonies of Schumann, to mention but a few, are rarely given without many instrumental changes. Even so "pure" a conductor as Toscanini did not deny the composer the benefit of today's heightened instrumental resources.

While he studies, the conductor must "listen" objectively to the work as a whole, pacing its progress, spacing its climaxes, deriving a general aural concept of the musical architecture.

In rehearsals, the conductor prepares the orchestra to perform the concept of the work he has developed through close study. On this level, he acts as a guide to the orchestra, building up in the musicians' minds an interpretation of the piece parallel to his own; the eventual public performance requires a group of musicians that play *with* a conductor rather than *under* him.

During the rehearsals, the conductor clarifies all problems of metrics and tempi, elucidating his own pacing of the work. He must temper all original dynamic markings so that the instrumental sound is balanced; the older composers always wrote the same dynamics vertically (for each simultaneous part, straight down the page) in their scores. It was only composer-conductors, like Mahler or Wagner, who realized the pitfalls of dynamics incautiously marked.

As he rehearses, the conductor checks his ideas about the music against the actual physical sound. When the two do not fit, he must alter one or the other. There are some places in certain scores, such as the lengthy oboe solo in Richard Strauss' *Don Juan*, where the prudent conductor who is fortunate enough to possess a highly sensitive oboe player, permits him to "have his head," and acts almost as an accompanist rather than a leader.

It is in performance that the conductor operates upon the highest and most demanding level. Here the work is finished technically; the orchestra is prepared. The conductor, his study and preparation behind him, now immerses himself in the music. It is at this crucial time that the most difficult function of the conductor comes into full play. He must, while identifying with the music, keep a constant watch upon the progress of the work, allowing a portion of his analytical mind to constantly evaluate the sound and pace of the performance. He must be prepared to instantaneously make any adjustments, large or small, that the actual performance requires for the fullest realization of his inner concept. Many factors make this necessary: a different hall, a player's momentary inattention, the effect of several thousand persons upon the acoustics, even the understandable enthusiasm of the moment which might affect the tempo. It is on stage that the conductor meets his greatest challenge, for the progress of the work must not suffer in the slightest; there must be no detectable "hitch." At such moments the experience of a conductor tells, for the young conductor, new to such emergencies, tends to do one thing at a time. Music does not permit this, for it flows in time, and all adjustments must be superimposed upon the uninterrupted continuum.

11: *Margaret Hillis*

I *live* many lives, all of them in music. I direct the Chicago Symphony Chorus, teach at Northwestern University, and conduct the Elgin Symphony Orchestra. Each of these activities enriches the others, and all of them give me great pleasure.

I'm from Kokomo, Indiana. I've known I wanted to conduct ever since I was eight or nine years old. I had music in my blood: Grandmother was a church organist, Grandfather a great music lover. Father was a lawyer, Mother an amateur musician who took me to every kind of concert when I was little. I heard Paderewski and Josef Hofmann—in Kokomo! They came on the old Chautauqua circuit to towns all over the state. If anybody worth hearing came within one hundred miles, Mother bundled me into the car and off we went. Kokomo was a very civilized town, settled by people from Massachusetts who carried the New England spirit and love of culture with them. Poetry and book clubs abounded. From my earliest years Mother took me along to the meetings and I heard books reviewed and poetry read, as well as music performed.

At age five I began piano lessons. Afterward I played several instruments, including the French horn and the string bass. I studied voice a bit, but not much. My background was mainly that of an instrumentalist. My college was Indiana University, which had a fine music department but no classes in conducting. I entered as a piano major, and switched to composition so I could take courses in counterpoint and fugue writing. During the war I dropped out of school for two years to teach flying in the Navy.

I never thought about the absence of women conductors from the professional scene until my senior year in college. My composition teacher wanted me to go to Yale to study with Hindemith. When I told him that I was taking composition only because of my interest in conducting and felt that no conductor was worth his salt unless he knew counterpoint and could write a fugue, my professor was appalled. "But you're a composer," he said. Well I was conducting a little concert soon after, to which he came. When it was over, he said, "You're right, you're a conductor." But there was more: "Don't go into orchestral conducting. Go to Juilliard and study choral conducting with Robert Shaw; maybe that way you can get into the orchestral world through the back door." Now, I had never even sung

Margaret Hillis, Director of the Chicago Symphony Chorus, was interviewed in Chicago in March 1975.

in a chorus, much less worked with one. But I took his advice, the more so when, on graduation day, in 1947, the Dean, himself a very good conductor and composer, approached the table where I sat with my parents and greeted them with this statement: "Your daughter's a talented conductor. Too bad she doesn't wear pants."

That's when I opened my eyes and saw that there really weren't *any* women conductors around. Until recently, I guess, girl children weren't supposed to develop professional skills like their brothers. Just think of the *two* Mozarts for instance. Who knows how talented the little girl was? All the father's time, care, guidance and attention were lavished on his son. The girl was expected to master certain musical social graces, like singing or playing the piano, as if they were sewing and cooking. Dilettantism was encouraged. Professionalism was practically unthinkable for leisured and cultured ladies who could blamelessly dabble—and not much more. After all, we didn't even have women *singers*, in public anyway, until the latter part of the eighteenth century. All the opera roles were sung by castrati. The situation was almost Arabian; women were not allowed to perform outside their homes.

So, at the time, my teacher's advice was probably sound. I'm not sure it would be today. And yet even now the social atmosphere is such that a woman conductor has to be better than her male counterparts to get anywhere. My advice to young women is, study your fool heads off; learn the repertory so thoroughly that you have full command of the material. Authority in the arts *should* be based only on what you know and what you can do. Nonetheless, I would warn them that the path is still treacherous, and that irrational nonartistic factors may be responsible for their success or failure.

In the documentary movie *Antonia*, Antonia Brico, the veteran conductor, remarked that strangely enough, most of the people who stood in her way were women. Generally speaking, it's women who don't want to see another female on the podium. Oh some do and they cheer for her—but many are opposed to it. These are very conservative ladies of the leisure class, who often serve on symphony boards. Somehow, it's improper for a woman to be so active in public. What's acceptable in front of a private chorus becomes unacceptable in front of a real orchestra. I do think, though, that this attitude is dying out and that a big shift is on the way.

However, when I began, choral conducting was a good solution;

what *would* I have done without it? But I hardly knew the choral repertory at all—Bach's B minor Mass, for heaven's sake, or the *St. Matthew Passion*. There was so much to catch up on. I had the orchestral but not the choral masterpieces in my ear. I soon found, to my surprise, that a large chunk of Mozart's total output was vocal. Then, when you take into account operas, masses, choral works, motets, and so on, you find that many other great composers wrote largely or mostly for voices.

It didn't take me long to discover that rehearsal procedures, though not conducting technique, are different in orchestras and choruses. Choristers usually don't have a great backlog of repertory. A symphony player who auditions for a place in the Chicago Symphony knows the orchestral repertory through and through and can play all the important tricky solos from memory. On the other hand, people who come new to the symphony chorus may be able to sight-read like whizzes and sing like crazy, but have a grasp of no more than four or five major choral works. They don't have a hundred-odd pieces at their disposal as instrumentalists do; they don't know all of the big important works. Choruses don't have the same professional tradition that orchestras do. Frequently when choristers sing a work, it's their first exposure to it. A violinist who hasn't played Brahms' Third Symphony shouldn't audition for the CSO. But a gifted singer who hasn't sung the Brahms *Requiem* comes into the chorus regardless. My job is then to fix the *Requiem*—or any other work we're doing—firmly in his ear and his throat. That takes time.

One of the first things I point out to my singers is the close relationship between text and music in vocal works. Take a piece like the *Requiem*. The interplay between the words and the notes is extraordinary. The text may be describing the morning and evening rain—and the music responds most appropriately. I would go so far as to say that the music *reacts* to the text and vice versa; when they are so beautifully wedded you have a great masterpiece.

I learned a great deal about such issues at Juilliard from Robert Shaw, the great choral conductor, who has the most incredible rehearsal technique I've ever seen. He didn't give lectures; I learned by sitting in at rehearsals and analyzing everything he did with a chorus and then trying it out myself.

After Juilliard, I had many jobs in New York. I founded a professional chorus of my own which soon had a concert series at Town

Hall; did a lot of preparation work for the Little Orchestra Society and the American Opera Society; helped get choral groups ready for recording sessions. I also prepared choruses for Stravinsky and many others, and toured with a small professional group, taking my chamber choir several different years to perform at the Library of Congress. It was darn hard work to learn so much music so fast. I conducted my first big piece, my first Bach B minor Mass, in 1955.

When I started out, I was in the same position as most conductors, male and female, who have to support themselves—pretty broke. My family had some money and they helped me out. I couldn't have managed without them. For an American musician, especially a conductor, to get off the ground, "angels" are essential. When it comes to opportunities for young talent, our biggest problem in this country is that we don't have many opera houses running fifty-two weeks a year. Even the Met is cutting back. Germany, on the other hand, has sixty-odd houses going year 'round.

A young German conductor usually begins as a rehearsal pianist. Then he becomes an assistant conductor—he does some coaching and is probably responsible for the chorus. He spends a lot of time crawling around backstage, giving cues to this one, that one, the other one. Dirty work. But soon he becomes a real assistant to the principal conductor, maybe conducting one opera in its tenth performance that year—by then nothing's likely to go wrong. If he succeeds at that, the following year two or three operas may come his way earlier in the season, when it's necessary to have a responsible conductor. Finally, in the fourth or fifth year, he gets his own opera to work on from the ground up. By then he's gone through a true apprenticeship program. In those very early years, he learned how things work, and by the time he gets his own operas into shape, he has matured as a conductor. Then his career starts to take off. Many great conductors worked their way up; Bruno Walter, for example, was first a choral director in an opera house. Unfortunately, in the U.S. today, we don't have anything like that kind of rigorous training.

Anyway, my family sustained me until the late fifties, when my pride got in the way. I figured I should be on my own. I was teaching at Union Theological Seminary and doing choral preparation for various groups, but when Fritz Reiner invited me to build the Chicago Symphony Chorus I decided to do that too. Now, it's unusual for an orchestra to have a permanent chorus attached to it, but

Reiner decided he wanted one; he'd heard me conduct in New York and he insisted I organize and conduct his new group of singers. Thinking it over, I realized that I could board a plane on Sunday night for Chicago, do the Monday night rehearsal and catch a midnight flight back and be able to teach at the Seminary on Tuesday. I did that for five years. Then I settled permanently in Chicago.

Reiner was very impatient with mediocrity, but no one was kinder and more encouraging if you did your job well. Often after a performance he'd call me backstage. I'd wonder if he were dissatisfied. "Dr. Reiner, you wanted to see me?"

"I wanted to thank you."

If members of the orchestra weren't up to snuff, he was merciless; if they were good, he was highly appreciative. In a way, Reiner transformed the Chicago Symphony, which had been fundamentally excellent but leaderless. Morale was very low after Frederick Stock's death in 1942 and the musicians felt like the servants who sat below the salt, as it were. Bluebloods on the board acted like nobles. And when I arrived the musicians' salary was around $6000 a year, which didn't help morale at all. Many objectionable things had taken place and some carried over even into Reiner's time. Eventually, all that led to great upheaval and some basic change.

There I was, having to build a chorus as good as the Chicago Symphony. There were problems. The singers had no real sense of professionalism. That was a lesson I had to teach. When I first took on the job, a few people from Chicago cautioned me, "You'll never find anybody with a good voice." Others said, "If you find a good voice, the person won't be able to sightread." What about the rare bird with a good voice who *can* sightread? "He'll never come to rehearsals." To guard against this, I carefully set up auditions designed to engender immediate respect for the chorus. Everything was precise and everyone was punctual. I had to teach rehearsal procedures from scratch. I expect a small professional choir to do its own vocalizing or warming up. But it's different with a large group. Just to get the voices going, we start in unison with several different vowels and, as everybody begins to match, I move them on to some triads, just to get a little bit of agility going. Then, once it's hooked in, I don't use more than two or three notes to finish warming up. When the bass and the alto voices no longer sound "huffy," I begin the rehearsal.

At first singers in Chicago didn't want to join the Chorus be-

cause they still suffered from that awful Second City syndrome: anything originating in Chicago has to fail. But by the end of the first
year we succeeded very well and the caliber of those who auditioned
went up. Then, for a while, the symphony board protested against
paying for a permanent chorus. Each year for four years I was uncertain about whether the chorus would last for another season.

You see, Chicago had never really had a great chorus; it was
primarily an instrumental town. Choral groups weren't taken as
seriously as orchestras. I understood the feeling very well because,
before I went into choral work I shared it. Most of the choristers I
had heard would have been better off knitting at home. They were
ineffective, lazy, out of tune, never phrased and lacked strength, piz-
zaz, or real musical courage. With this image in mind, for the better
part of fiteen years some symphony subscribers refused to come when
the Chorus was singing. Six years ago, Carlo Maria Giulini conducted the Mozart *Requiem,* and for once these particular subscribers didn't turn in their tickets. They listened—and they were
flabbergasted. Since then they're a regular part of the audience.

This past fall I had 165 new auditionees and room for fifteen.
Eighteen of them were put on a waiting list. Some people come into
the chorus and find that our schedule is too heavy for them and they
either go on leave or resign. Many re-audition a year later. In the fall
we lose about five percent and fill up the gap with people from our
waiting list. About half the chorus is paid; the rest are volunteers. I'd
love to take in more singers—some have auditioned three or four
times—but we just don't have room for all of them on stage! I hope
I've built the chorus well. The test will come if and when I leave. If
the group holds together, then I'll know.

I'm quite proud of how well the chorus has handled some very
difficult music in recent years. When we did Schönberg's *Moses and
Aaron* several years ago, I first sent out a packet of materials to the
chorus members—a copy of the tone row Schönberg uses in the
opera, in its original order, backward, and upside down, plus program notes so they'd know the history of the piece. I asked them to
read the libretto carefully, and for God's sake, to come to the first rehearsal having thought about the text and with the row memorized in
all its versions. Somehow they learned the piece in six weeks. I'm
sure that's a world record that won't easily be broken!

There's a kind of family feeling among the chorus members and a real sense of commitment. Otherwise they'd never turn themselves inside out for the group as they do. When we were rehearsing the Mozart C minor Mass recently, I noticed them leaving rehearsal with their faces just breathing smiles. Its not unusual for them to tell me, "We came in tired and we leave exhilarated."

I have noticed the same spirit in my Elgin Symphony Orchestra, which is sponsored by the Elgin Community College with some help from the State Arts Council. It's a volunteer operation except for the principal strings, who are paid. My concertmistress is an excellent violinist.

With my encouragement, some of the Elgin kids are now playing in the Civic Orchestra, a training ensemble sponsored by the Chicago Symphony. I'm one of its staff conductors; Gordon Peters runs the operation. We each conduct one concert a year and bring in guest conductors for two or three more. I guest-conducted the Minneapolis Orchestra this past December and found four ex-members of the Civic Orchestra there. It's not generally a direct feeder for the CSO, though the assistant first flute, Louise Dixon, came directly into the Symphony from the Civic. She's exceptional. Young people from the Civic usually go to Denver, Winnipeg, or another one of the less demanding orchestras for maybe three or four years of experience, acquire repertory, then audition, and often make the CSO.

As I watch people come and go from these different ensembles, I perceive slow but pronounced social and ethnic shifts in the musical world. We're in the ashes right now and haven't yet seen quite where the phoenix will rise again. In general I'm pessimistic intellectually but optimistic emotionally. We're in great difficulty when it comes to string players because the fine old Russian Jewish tradition is dying out in this country. In music, as in everything else, the Russian Jews are becoming assimilated, which is fortunate in some ways but unfortunate in that some great values are being lost.

Since music is something you eat, sleep, and drink, many professional women I know often have very great problems. I'm aware of some female singers and a few instrumentalists who are married with children and manage to do right by both their families and their careers. It depends entirely on what kinds of marriages they make. Betty Lambert, a violinist in the CSO, has an exceptional relationship with her husband. They have two children, both grown now. She didn't come into the Symphony until her younger child was fifteen or sixteen and could pretty well take care of herself; she had kept up her playing all that time. During rehearsal Betty will sometimes think, "Oh Lord, I've got to scrub the kitchen floor today." Then she'll get home and lo! the floor is clean. Her husband scrubbed it. He does many things around the house to help her out. As men take on more and more household chores, women in music, as in other fields, will be freer to pursue careers.

As for blacks, I would say that black singers, more than black instrumentalists, have "arrived." One reason for the discrepancy may be that singers can start training a little later. If you start playing the violin much after the age of eight, you've had it as far as a career is concerned; the same is true of the piano. And most black families can't afford, or have not in the past been able to afford, early instruction for their children. It seems that the Japanese are coming up in the musical world, largely on account of the Suzuki method, a technique that starts children on instruments at a very young age, getting them really involved in music at age two or three. It's fantastic!

Teaching has always interested me. Besides my conducting posts I'm a professor of conducting and head of the choral department at Northwestern. From that position I can help the most gifted youngsters bridge the gap from amateur to professional life, a transition that's mighty scary, as I know from personal experience. Our best singers at school go into the Symphony chorus; one was a soloist in the Mozart C minor Mass just last February. Then, Stanislaw Skrowaczewski who conducts the Minnesota Orchestra asked me to recommend someone to sing Stravinsky's *Les Noces* and I sent him one of my students; she was a great success. Things like that come up all the time; I'm glad to be able to help the most talented gain some experience in the professional world. In the classroom, there's a certain discipline I try to bring to the kids' musical awareness, a knowledge of basics like instrument transpositions, score reading, and analysis that every musician needs.

I can usually tell young musicians with a spark from those who should be doing something else. One way to differentiate is to see whether they make music perfunctorily or with passion. Sometimes young people ask me whether they ought to go into music and I tell them, "If you have to ask, the answer is no." Fortunately I come across many who are driven, who couldn't do anything else but play or sing. It's a great pleasure to help them on their way.

12: Neville Marriner

Photo by Clive Barda

I started the Academy of St. Martin-in-the-Fields Chamber Orchestra with some colleagues in 1959. It seemed to us that in England, particularly, we were lacking a small orchestra of the eighteenth-century type. I was a violinist in those days, and as concertmaster of St. Martin's, I directed in the conventional eighteenth-century way—from my front seat.

I think that our enthusiasm stemmed mainly from our shared need for more personal responsibility in music making. As one member of a symphony orchestra, you are useful, but not especially responsible. Even the principals have a relatively small amount of influence on any one performance. If you are ambitious, or you are a normal extrovert musician, you want to affect a performance. And the smaller the group, the more individually responsible you become. St. Martin's started out with about fifteen players, and one continuo instrument.

Actually, in founding St. Martin's, we were part of a movement that had started a bit earlier. The revival of interest in chamber orchestras probably began in the late 1930s and early 1940s in Europe, when a few people turned their attention to the performance practices of the seventeenth and eighteenth centuries. In England, in the 1930s, a man by the name of Anthony Bernard started the London Chamber Orchestra. Strangely enough, his group was in demand for private social functions rather than public concerts. People would hold musical weekends and employ this ensemble. It was very chic to have your own chamber orchestra—a bit like having your own house band.

Another fellow, Boyd Neel, put his chamber orchestra in the concert hall. His concerts were enormously successful. Overnight, he became a key figure in the chamber orchestral world of England. Then there were the Europeans—the Stuttgart Chamber Orchestra, the Virtuosi di Roma, which became I Musici, the Zagreb Chamber Players, the Jacques Pailliard Orchestra in Paris.

In some sense, all this activity was a replay of history. Princes, archdukes, and bishops used to have house bands. The Margrave of Brandenburg had his own orchestra, and so forth. As private pa-

Neville Marriner, Founder and Director of the Academy of St. Martin-in-the-Fields Orchestra, and founder of the Los Angeles Chamber Orchestra, which he no longer directs, was interviewed in Los Angeles in April 1975. He has been appointed Music Director of the Minnesota Symphony, effective September 1979.

tronage fizzled out, music went public. As soon as it moved out of the house and into the concert hall, the orchestra got bigger. Mozart and Beethoven came toward the beginning of the transition. Mozart still conceived his symphonies in terms of six or eight first violins. In a letter to his publishers, Beethoven wrote, "Please, for the premiere performance of my Sixth Symphony, may I have more than six first violins?" This gives you some idea of what the size of the orchestra used to be. Beethoven might indeed have liked more instruments, but the repertoire through the turn of the nineteenth century was written for a small orchestra.

As the nineteenth century progressed, everyone wanted as many instruments and as big a sound as possible. All the sections of the orchestra grew. I can't think of a composer who didn't take advantage of the larger ensemble. So, very little music for chamber orchestra was written during the nineteenth century. Also, in that period, earlier music, written for a smaller group of instruments, was played with the expanded orchestra. And when you use sixteen or eighteen first violins where six or eight were intended, you lose a certain athleticism. Though the larger group has a much greater power of sostenuto, all the tempi have to be slightly slower. A performance becomes, shall we say, portly in feeling, even cumbersome. Most of Bach's choral works suffered greatly at the hands of nineteenth- and even twentieth-century choral traditions. You know, those vast choruses of 200–300 people.

In our own day, the chamber orchestra is coming into its own again, for two main reasons. First is the desire for authenticity in the playing of older works. Second, since the 1950s, the economy has compelled many composers to think twice before writing symphonic works. Those in charge of large orchestras usually feel they can scarcely afford to program, much less adequately rehearse, many new pieces. Scheduling a contemporary piece is likely to half-empty a hall. Add to this a couple extra rehearsals specifically for the unfamiliar work, and you are really into pocket.

But with chamber orchestras, which often perform in the same halls as bigger groups, all things are possible. Composers are gradually realizing that the smaller ensembles, which operate on much lower budgets, can afford to promote new pieces and rehearse them more satisfactorily. I imagine this is much more rewarding for composers. In fact, I just discussed this issue with John Cage. He said that he now makes a habit of withdrawing his music from programs if rehearsals have been insufficient. He doesn't care how angry people get with him: if a conductor leaves a ten-minute piece for the last fifteen minutes of rehearsal, Cage isn't interested.

Now, if you add the rapidly increasing twentieth-century repertoire, the little nineteenth-century material there is, and the vast quantity of seventeenth and eighteenth-century works available to us, you end up with a large and varied assortment of pieces to choose from. In fact, I would say that of all orchestral and chamber music bodies, a group like St. Martin's is perhaps the most colorful and flexible. However, purely in terms of decibels, some audiences find our sound difficult to accept, compared to that of a bigger orchestra. Rock musicians have got exactly the right idea: Emotionally speaking, decibels count. Our size group can't build the blazing climaxes that are possible with symphony orchestras. You can't quite tear people out of their seats with the purely physical noise that you make. Therefore, dynamically, we must have the most polished pianissimos possible; these should be of extraordinary quality, so that they are exciting in themselves. Then, whatever forte or fortissimo you can produce is effective. You can create the same passion that you experience, for instance, in water colors as opposed to oils.

As a young professional musician, I gravitated toward small groups. But one cannot always pick one's spot in the musical world; jobs are often hard to come by. Not that I'm very strong on security, necessarily. I'm not even sure that security and being a musician are compatible. There is a sort of restlessness, a perpetual dissatisfaction, to contend with. You've always got to look for something, even if it's only a better standard of performance. Security seems to have a flattening effect on personality and lifestyle. If you're the sort of person who demands security, you shouldn't have become a musician in the first place.

I myself never thought of becoming anything else. I started playing the violin at six. Music has been my life since then. Both of my parents were amateur musicians. They encouraged me. The only way to get children to do anything—the only way they ever learn—is for the family to take part in their activity. Mine did with me. They didn't stick me in front of a television set and say "Get on with it." They liked the idea of my becoming a musician—thought it was great. They gave at least an hour or two a day of their lives supervising my practice or playing along with me. Nothing gave my father more pleasure. He was a builder in the cathedral city of Lincoln, where I spent my early years. He played violin and piano. As soon as my father came home, he strode into the music room and we played.

When I left Lincoln, I studied at the Royal College of Music in London. After the war, I went to Paris. Upon returning to England, I taught at Eton College, which, I can assure you, is no cradle for young musicians. But it was a job. I needed the money. I was in a string quartet, and nobody's ever going to make his fortune that way. I stayed with the quartet for seven years. During that time I also played with the Boyd Neel orchestra, and with various small groups.

By this time I had met Thurston Dart, who probably has had more influence, musicologically, than anyone else in England. Dart was not only an extremely perceptive musicologist; he was also a professional *performing* musician. He played the harpsichord. He and I had a group, called the Jacobean Ensemble; we made our first records together. We were a duo, on harpsichord and violin.

Ours was an excellent working relationship. Dart had great knowledge, so his performance practice ideas always made a strong impression on me. But at the same time, he was quite open to suggestions and other views.

Our collaboration tapered off a bit when I joined the London Symphony Orchestra in 1956. I stayed with them for quite a while. After I formed the Academy of St. Martin's with some other London Symphony members, I invited Bob, as we called him, to work with us. (His first name was Robert.) We did many projects together, such as Handel's Opus 3 and Opus 6, and the Bach suites. He died while we were recording the Bach Brandenburg concertos. Stylistically, he made an enormous impact not only on me, but on all who attempted to play authentically.

St. Martin's income derives mainly from the record industry. Through the wide distribution of our gramophone records, we have become well known. The orchestra is invited to give concerts in many countries every year. This is fortunate indeed, since studios get sterile after a while. Musicians need a public. Making immaculate records is never quite as rewarding as giving outstanding live performances. And the public needs concerts. I suppose it is the wide availability of gramophone records that makes listening to them less exciting. Going to a concert is a special event, but you know exactly what a record is going to be like after you play it once. There's no question mark hanging over the experience, none of the marvelous excitement of *not* knowing exactly how the music is going to sound. And people's ears can be easily hardened. If you get to know a Brahms symphony as conducted by Toscanini, on a record, and listen to it over and over, and then you hear someone else perform the piece in concert, you may be so conditioned that you think there's something wrong with the live performance.

But records can have positive consequences.

People who wanted to start a chamber orchestra in Los Angeles several years ago had heard many discs of the Academy. They consulted those who knew about chamber orchestras, and soloists with whom I had worked, like Isaac Stern. Eventually, I received a letter asking whether I would be interested in becoming artistic director of a new orchestra in L.A. I said, "Of course, in principle I am," though I hadn't the foggiest idea what musical life on the West Coast of America was about. When an Englishman thinks of the western part of North America, he pictures Vancouver or Seattle, towns on the edge of the continent, beyond which it's impossible to venture. Going there is a one-way journey; it's not a through route to some other spot. Therefore, you suppose that things probably stultify a little through lack of traffic. When I arrived in L.A. in 1969, I was presented with a mixed orchestra of about 35. That number has remained fairly constant. The orchestra was originally made up of people from the universities and the studios, all professionals. The first thing that struck me was that although instrumentally they set very high standards, stylistically they were rather a mixed bag. Now, with a chamber orchestra, you play a lot of music which dates back a couple hundred years before symphony orchestras existed. You have to put yourself into an earlier aural frame of reference. The pre-symphonic style of playing didn't come naturally to American musicians.

Why? Well, I think that the environment has a great deal to do with it. This awful pollution of the air affects the sound. Humor aside, musical currency has been downgraded by the endless stream of sound that's in every elevator you enter in the States, in every store, every hotel. Anywhere you go you find a slightly soupy sentimental noise, which I suppose is soothing in some ways. But it does color one's natural aural perception; everything one then plays is just a little too sweet, a little too smooth. When you consider the style we're aiming for, the currently accepted "conventional" eighteenth-century sound, the articulation has to be immaculate. You might say it all has to be slightly more aristocratic. There lay the first battle—to refine the players' style. Some were too deeply entrenched in Hollywood sounds; however fine they may have been as instrumentalists, one would have had to change their whole attitude toward music in order to "reclaim" them for early works. About 49 percent of the orchestra today are survivors from the early days. The average age of the orchestra members has gotten steadily lower. Now there are many more young players. Obviously, it's better to get them before they're hopelessly engrained.

After you work with players a short while you can tell many things about them—what their general possibilities are; how flexible they are. You notice that some may be instrumentally less brilliant than others, but are more perceptive or responsible in ensemble circumstances. Having all virtuosos does not always result in a great orchestra. You need people who are sensitive to what's going on around them, as I think all the Los Angeles Chamber Orchestra people are by now.

The L.A. group compares favorably with its European counterparts, and it has special qualities of its own. The players in L.A. have more bravura. In Europe they often achieve a cooler atmosphere, which particularly suits much of the Italian music of the seventeenth and eighteenth centuries. Both the St. Martin's and L.A. orchestras play Haydn, Mozart, and twentieth-century works well. This is their common bond. The Americans seem to be able to play nineteenth-century music far more imaginatively, possibly because it's the repertoire with which they're most familiar. On the other hand, English musicians seem to assimilate difficult scores more quickly.

The English reach a certain level of achievement rapidly, and stay there. The L.A. orchestra members are a little slow off the mark; the players have to take their material home and do a little woodshedding. But then they improve, sometimes strikingly. Every time they perform a piece it can sound better. Their technical virtuosity pays off.

One big difference between England and America is the quality of music criticism. Much more than in England, American critics work for the newspapers—for the journalism profession—rather than

for the music profession. The critics in England tend to be more involved in musical life, and some get too much involved with the
musicians on a personal level, so it becomes difficult to be objective.

Perhaps I find some American critics a little harder to accept because the quality of their writing, their journalese, is something that
offends me. I'm sure this is rather prudish or bigoted on my part. But
I would like to see beautifully written notices, and well-turned phrases, as well as opinions that I can accept. Also, I wish more critics
would keep concert reviews matters of opinion. Why can't they simply say that *they* didn't like a particular performance, rather than stating categorically, "It *was* a bad performance." As if that kind of dec-
laration were a judgment! No one can be so exact. There are too
many extraneous factors that might affect them—their metabolism
might have been high or low that day.

Then, I think it's a pity when critics are "brutally frank" in cases
where their word may influence the careers of young people. Critics
can be very destructive. At the same time, they can be sycophantic
about musicians who have achieved great success. Very rarely do
they give an objective view of performances by really successful people. But critics are human just like the rest of us. And if every
musician were honest, he'd admit he pays attention to them. It's intriguing to read what other people have to say about you, whoever
and whatever you are.

I wish more critics would come to rehearsals. Then they'd know
exactly what sort of problems we face, and how we attempt to solve
them. They would see how we try to achieve the tone quality of the
period in which a piece was written, whether it be the seventeenth
century or our own.

As far as twentieth-century music goes, we have a policy in L.A.
of commissioning at least one composer a year to write something
specifically for us. For example, Paul Chihara of L.A. has done one
piece for us, and will do another. We rehearse a new work
thoroughly, and give it first and second performances. The second is
the important one: if a piece is only heard once it disappears into
oblivion. We can give a new piece as many as half a dozen performances, which gets it off the ground immediately as a performing
work. We then know more or less accurately whether it's successful
enough to go into the permanent repertoire. I think you have to give

the composer the benefit of half a dozen performances to discover if his piece is satisfactory.

There was a time during our early recording days in England when we dug up as many unknown older composers as we could, purely because record companies were interested in having names in their catalogues. But you discover that if music has gone unperformed for many years, there are usually very good reasons why. And after all, we have been playing for six years in L.A., and we still haven't bitten very deeply into the standard repertoire.

I must say that in terms of audiences, there is a lot to be thankful for in L.A. The city is in many ways uniquely European. There is a large Jewish community, which has brought Europe to the States with it. I should think that next to New York probably L.A. has the highest concentration of European Jews in America. And their tastes have come with them. The result is a discriminating audience who have probably heard music at home all their lives. The tradition of listening to and making music stays in families. The chamber music sound is no novelty to them. They've been exposed to it, certainly in the European parts of their lives. So life in Los Angeles has been fairly easy.

The ensemble travels a bit, especially to different campuses. Young people are very much open to the sort of music a chamber orchestra plays, and the style in which we perform. It is usually middle-aged, middle-class people whose tastes are restricted to the larger symphonic sound.

I have started to do more symphony orchestra conducting myself, though not for one moment do I intend to neglect the chamber orchestras. St. Martin's takes about five months of the year, L.A. three; [in 1975]; that leaves a third of my year available for symphonies. It makes sense from an artistic point of view not to keep a chamber orchestra in session for an entire year. In St. Martin's we've always maintained that to retain any freshness in our kind of organization, you must perform for a short period, then break up for a short period. In between you do other things. Our repertoire in St. Martin's has expanded since our early days; we've added more musicians. In order to give individual members a certain amount of freedom to move about, we have a pool of 20 violin players, of whom we rarely use more than 14 at any one time. The other six are free to fulfill perhaps more prestigious, if less remunerative, engagements. I think all musicians like to be able to go off and play concertos occasionally, rather than always doing ensemble work. Sometimes concertos are artistically less important, but they're still rewarding for the individual, more of a challenge, I suppose.

I now conduct with a baton, standing on a podium, as normal conductors do. But of course that means I tend not to conduct much. A small number of players only need someone to hold them together physically, geographically.

The group grows and shrinks, depending on what we are playing. I went with the Academy to Germany, where I conducted four performances of the Bach B minor Mass, in Berlin, Hanover, Hamburg and Düsseldorf. Then I came back to London to conduct the London Symphony, leaving a smaller part of the orchestra in Germany to do a tour in the way we used to, with the concertmaster directing. This has been acceptable to them only since I've become rather busy conducting other people's symphony orchestras. Last year I stopped being involved in everything St. Martin's does. But it works out fine.

They were away for the rest of January, while I remained with the London Symphony. I then went to Italy to work with the Soloisti Veneti, a similar group, and then to Portugal to work with a largish chamber orchestra in Lisbon. After that, I came back again to England, just as they came back from Germany, and we made a couple of records in London. Then we went on to Paris together for some concerts there. I conducted one of them, and I actually played the violin for one of them, at the Théâtre de Champs Elysees. I'm rather embarrassed by the state of my violin playing; I have played rather infrequently over the past six or seven years. If I were to choose members for my orchestra, I probably wouldn't choose me. I only take out my violin on occasions that I think can stand it, musically you know. Finally, after Paris, we came home and gave a concert at Royal Festival Hall. Following that, I went off to conduct the Bonn State Orchestra, and from Bonn I went to Kansas City to conduct the orchestra there. Now I'm in Los Angeles to start the season with the L.A. Chamber Orchestra.

There are significant differences between rehearsing and conducting small and large orchestras. Obviously, with a chamber orchestra it's a much more intimate affair. As I indicated before, each musician has to deliver almost on a personal basis, as a paid-up member, you might say. You can ask for specific things from specific players on a personal basis. On the other hand, in a symphony orchestra, you still have to work in blocks, really. Your first violins are a large unit. You can't individualize them. In fact, if there are any personalities that stick out, you're rather sharp about quieting them, because you want a homogeneous sound. You simply have to think in bigger musical terms. To rehearse a symphony orchestra with the detail at your disposal when you rehearse a chamber orchestra would be very arduous indeed. Just geograpically, you can't get as fine detail across to so many people. You make broader gestures. You accept more imperfections. Of course, the sound level is so great that many of these never reach the audience. You clarify as much as you can with a symphony. Still, when rehearsing, you must always stop short of taking the enthusiasm out of the musician's part in his performance.

I think that the conductor's job on the podium at a concert is simply to remind the players of what's been rehearsed, and to stimulate them into producing at their optimum capacity. It's *not* his job to act out the music for the sake of the players or the audience. And I think the conductor has a certain duty not to get too involved in the emotional part of the music. Otherwise he becomes less than effective. If you get carried away with your own charisma on the podium, you tend to fall down on the job.

I think the role of the conductor now is quite interesting. There was a time, maybe in the 1930s, when you actually taught orchestras the notes of a piece. Nowadays, musicians are so sophisticated, they're so extraordinarily professional themselves, that you no longer do that. No one bullies an orchestra any more. Those days are gone. The most you can hope for is the cooperation of your musicians. A conductor must count himself very lucky to be in a position from which he virtually exploits a lot of very talented people.

I am always careful, when I conduct a large ensemble, to reduce the orchestra if we play earlier music, say, a Mozart symphony. Otherwise, I don't think I can give it a fair presentation, certainly not one that passes a plausible Mozart style on to an audience. I want to be fairly true to the composer. And I can't produce the Mozart sound I am committed to with vast numbers. It would be something else than Mozart—a different animal altogether.

Americans have perfected the symphony orchestra. They have prettied it up far more than we have in England. Your big glossy orchestras—*the* big five, really—Boston, Philadelphia, Cleveland, Chicago, and New York—are trendsetters. Boston was the first major American orchestra I conducted. I believe that in Europe, the Berlin Philharmonic is the only ensemble that has attained comparable perfection. Both of them are a little more brutal than English orchestras in the way they are administered. Hiring and firing are rather more ruthless. If you want to have good products, perhaps that's how it has to be.

There are differences in the way big orchestras sound in Europe and America. The tone quality of the wind sections is not the same; for example, in the U.S. the oboe players cut their reeds much thicker, and get a much soupier sound. The result is marvelous. I love it. But the dynamic extremes are missing. You can't really play pianissimo with an American oboe reed. In England, where reeds are cut much thinner, oboists get a much thinner sound, but they are capable of the most incredible pianissimos. Each reed is good for a different kind of music, I guess.

It's interesting to compare American orchestras to one another. There are varied traditions. The Boston Orchestra has much more of a French tradition—or at least that's how it sounds to us. It's because of the conductors they had. The Chicago Symphony is more Germanic. Overall, the Cleveland Orchestra under Szell was the most remarkable and precise instrument.

No English orchestra is quite like that. The London Symphony Orchestra has a spirited presentation; the London Philharmonic has a traditional sound which is quite good. The BBC Orchestra is, for me, a little civil servant orchestra, you know. It's a bit too bureaucratic—and it suffers from playing too often in the studios, to no audience. Nevertheless, and all in all, I'm afraid government support is needed to keep orchestras going, on both sides of the Atlantic. Thus far, the L.A. Chamber Orchestra has survived with private patronage, which is truly noteworthy. Now, when music is economically one of the last items you would expect to be considered, some people clearly care about it—and about the actual quality of life. They are prepared to invest in an organization like this which, however minimally, does something to improve the quality of life.

As to the quality of my own life, I think that by moving on into different spheres of musical activity, I am continually growing as a musician. When I virtually gave up the violin to take up conducting, it was a landmark of sorts, in my life, anyway. I spent the first 20 years of my life learning to play an instrument. The next 10 years or so I spent playing orchestral and chamber music, and teaching. Next I conducted chamber orchestras, and gradually worked back to a large orchestra, this time on the other side of the fence, as conductor, not instrumentalist. I hope soon to be ready to become the musical director of a symphony orchestra [in 1975]. This brings the discussion back to where we started, with the desire among musicians for more responsibility in a performance. When you conduct, if the musicians are responsive, you are largely responsible for the overall performance.

I'm convinced that it's good for a conductor to be involved in a variety of experiences—else he becomes too constricted, too limited. If you live in your own little backyard, you can deal with problems rather easily and quickly. Having no new challenges tends to turn you into rather a dull musician. You need to be in situations where you're permanently on trial. Even if you fail, I think it's most important to go on trying. It produces the kind of growth I admire.

13: Michael Tilson Thomas

Photo by Arnold Newman

This is my story. First I am a human being alive in the late twentieth century. Next I am a musician. Then someplace under all that I am a symphony conductor, a pianist, a composer, who does this or that kind of music. I am interested in figuring out how I can use music to express and to testify to the feelings, the realities, the problems, the states of being that I go through or discover as a human being of this time.

In my early life I fluctuated between science and music. As a kid, I was interested in geology, mineralogy, chemistry, and crystallography. I started out fascinated by rocks and got involved in serious aspects of the subject, taking classes in the mineralogical laboratories of the Los Angeles County Museum School. They were at the university level. This took place during the Sputnik terror—"Oh my gosh, you have to have science courses now!"

At the same time I did a lot with music, playing the piano a great deal, but using the oboe as my around town instrument. I joined the musicians' union when I was 16 or 17 and began playing in community and semiprofessional orchestras. We even had some recording dates. I was a teen-age free-lance in L.A.

So I was torn between alternate visions, pulled in two directions. While respecting each, I chose art—specifically music—over science. My parents had encouraged me to be a scientist precisely because they were theater people who knew how difficult and uncertain the artist's life could be. They knew that society is not really open to the serious artist. It makes certain token gestures toward him, but does not appreciate that to a great degree its soul rests with artists, as it does with philosophers and religionists—people whose concerns intersect with those of artists. My parents' view was practical. They could not have foreseen that if I were a scientist I'd be out of work right now; ironically, I am employed because I became a musician instead. But they used to tell me, "Become a scientist and you can still love and play music. You will suffer no economic insecurity, and all will be well." After all, they continued—and I agree—science *is* the major force of this century; science as a whole has raised the most important questions.

Yet meanwhile I was getting powerful genetic messages in the

Michael Tilson Thomas, music director of the Buffalo Philharmonic, was interviewed in New York City in August 1976.

opposite direction. I knew my grandmother very well. She was just as famous on the Yiddish stage as my grandfather, Boris Thomashevsky. In fact, I was surrounded by Russian actors as well as Viennese psychiatrists. (Believe me the psychiatrists were just as eccentric as the actors.) These were friends of my parents and grandparents. The atmosphere was theatrical—with an overlay of psychology and much talk of conscious versus unconscious motivation. Against that backdrop, in our house there was a constant, if unspoken, question. It was the ontological question: "What is real?" Or: "What do you want to be real?" Decide that first and then make it real. This was conveyed to me in little ways during my childhood. For instance, I was addressed by constantly changing names that included every version of Michael: Misha, Mishinka, Mitch, Mickey; but also I was called Jingo, Jehosafat, Agamemnon and Alcibiades. After a while certain moods and personalities came to be associated with each of these names.

Then there were the Russian-Jewish actors. One minute they'd address me in their own persons—and the next they would be the Inspector General and Ivan the Terrible. From a very early age I was able to assume whatever dialect and manner of presentation they simulated. I'd dish it right back at them. It was an environment where either by direct action or by discussion and description a lot of fundamental questions were raised about the nature of reality. I saw some people proceeding analytically, others spontaneously.

But I decided to become a musician finally for two reasons—or two *groups* of reasons, like A and B groupings in a romantic sonata. For one, there was the enormous joy I experienced through music, a sense of exultation unavailable to me in science. I said to myself what a wise friend of my father's had said to me: "You should not go into music unless it is a compulsion. In the end all you really have as a center is the music itself. Make sure that you really love music, that you have to be with it every day. If that's true then you should become a musician."

And it was true. I made my career decision unconcerned with whether it meant being a musician in a university or a small town or in a big city. If I could work on music, be involved and live a life with those notes, then I'd be happy. I wasn't motivated by a dream of a specific professional success, something I knew might or might not happen.

Secondly, I had a feeling that our world, because of its obsession with numbers, was quantifying itself out of existence. I thought about the value of *custodianship,* that some people needed to guard what has been passed down to us in our best humanist tradition. For me, the great pieces of music are statements of witness of a particular condition of soul. Somebody has to be there to watch over these things and make them new again for successive generations, to perpetuate and *re-create.*

Still, my dilemmas were not easily resolved. As a teenager, I was most confused, going through the unhappiest period of my life in public school, particularly junior high and high school. Having little in common with most of my classmates and unresponsive to all but a few of my teachers I spent my time reading Dostoyevsky and Marx and Brecht and Euripides, Flaubert, and Jung, practicing the piano, playing the oboe, and writing music. I felt isolated but I had started feeling that way in fourth grade, so I was used to it. From the beginning I mostly associated with adults. My friends tended to be thirty or forty years older than I.

While still in the tenth grade I was accepted at a few universities on the basis of my playing. But my parents rightly wanted me to finish high school. We compromised. I went to the high school for four periods and spent the rest of the day at various state colleges. I graduated from high school in 1962. Strange when you think about it. There I was good enough to study at university level, and yet within the high school context, I was such a mess! I didn't fit in at all.

Fortunately, I had my music. From the age of ten I had spectacularly good piano teachers. They did not force me into being a prodigy; I did not have to learn a million little pieces; they simply taught me to play the instrument, which meant that I could play a bunch of written pieces, but at the same time, since I've always been good at improvisation, I could spend time at the piano playing anything I wanted by ear. Maybe something completely made up, as if to say in music, "This is how I feel now."

I heard much more music on records than at concerts. All kinds of music. I heard some cantorial music, especially on an old Jan Peerce record. I liked those melodies. And my grandmother sang a lot of the Yiddish repertory. My home, although it was intensely Yiddish, had no connection with a temple at all. However, Bible stories, and tales of the old days and the old ways in the old country, re-sounded through the house. Playing Russian card games with my grandmother was part of it; if you lost you had to climb under the table, stand on one foot and crow like a rooster. That kind of thing was a separate education all by itself.

My tastes were certainly always eclectic. From the very beginning I not only liked ancient musical works but also the most dissonant complex modern pieces as well. My musical and gastronomical tastes were interestingly of a kind. I liked dissonant, complicated recent music and I liked sour or bitter or spicy food—but never sweet food or music. And I was a very mystical child off in a special little world with Aristotle or Dostoyevsky or Debussy or Varèse or Stravinsky. I was always out *there* somewhere. In general I was much more interested in listening to Varèse or Schönberg than I was in listening to Beethoven.

Besides the Yiddish music and the new music I had another love—theater music. At home a strong theater or show music influence was at work on me. My parents were very much into that scene. Many of their friends had been on the Broadway stage during the 1920s and 1930s. So there was frequent playing at home of Rodgers and Hart, Gershwin, Kern, Berlin. I know all that music very well, and not too many people my age do. Six or seven years ago, the Mamas and the Papas did a remake of "Glad to be Unhappy" and people were saying, "My gosh, who wrote that song?" Well, it was Rodgers and Hart. There were a million more where that came from. It represented the zenith of American songwriting. Between Gershwin and Rodgers and Hart, I think they were really it.

Given the wide variety of influences on me, plus my endless curiosity, I became a Heisenbergian creature. I am an electron cloud and every part of me floats in all of it.

Well, I wound up at USC where I'd been going anyhow because my teacher, Ingolf Dahl, was there. I had him and other fine teachers who accepted me like a member of their families. There was endless work interspersed with conversation covering every conceivable artistic and intellectual area. And a very interesting circle of people around the university was connected with the Monday Evening Concerts in Los Angeles, where Igor Stravinsky, Aldous Huxley, and the manager, a man named Lawrence Morton, were the prime movers. As a result of contact with that group, I was exposed to and learned to play much more contemporary music than I would have on the East Coast. But not only contemporary music—also Monteverdi, Schütz, and other very early composers. I was really gaining a sense of Western music as a totality and learning that ours was a musical civilization composed of more than Mozart string quartets and other endlessly played pieces.

I was also always greatly attracted to Asian studies. A strong religious and philosophical quest is still going on in me. I don't know exactly how to describe it. When I was growing up I was mostly exposed to analytical empiricists, atheist and agnostic intellectuals. Their views were very fashionable at the time. In addition, my family's circle was very much committed to the socialist cause in some way or another. All this had a marked effect on shaping my world view.

While in college I became an established Los Angeles musician. John Crown, my piano teacher, was supposed to play a piece at a Monday Evening Concert; he did not have time to learn it. In my usual shy, retiring manner I said, "Oh, I love that piece; I have plenty of time to practice, and I'd be happy to learn it." The piece, for piano and ensemble, was *Over the Pavements* by Charles Ives. Crown was relieved, "Well fine, okay." He called Lawrence Morton: "I have a student who will do a fine job. There's no time for me to get it together." Ingolf Dahl conducted. I played the piece very well—or well enough for Morton to ask me to play a piano concert soon after, at the Spring Festival. After that experience, one opportunity to play followed another.

I started conducting in junior high school. The music teacher was sick one day and they sent a phys. ed. teacher to substitute; he didn't know what the hell to do. So somehow or other I ended up conducting. I was *chutzpahdik*, throwing myself in wherever I could. I officially began to study conducting in college—that plus music history, performance practice, and analysis. Dahl was an inspiring teacher; over and above the subject matter, he showed his students about the practical application of humanism, that is, how to let humanistic concerns infuse your daily existence.

I really didn't plan it, but all of a sudden I became a big-league conductor. It was a crazy dream, full of happenstance, a condition with which I was already quite familiar. I had resolved to work at music until I was 20 and if nothing definitive happened by then I'd go into science. And what happened? Exactly on my 20th birthday, Gregor Piatigorsky called to tell me that I'd been selected as conductor of the Young Musicians Foundation in L.A. So I felt, when this clicks and that clicks, I am being *led* somewhere. If so, I might as well go along with it and see where it takes me.

So I won a prize, got some attention, blah blah blah. Then there was a series of weird little coincidences, strange meetings. Okay. Then suddenly there I was, 23 years old, on the East Coast as assistant conductor of the Boston Symphony. Seemingly overnight I started conducting big-name orchestras all over the place, desperately trying to get together enough repertory, suddenly having to do 40, 50, or 60 concerts. I didn't know all that many pieces. I had to study scores night and day. I had to learn more and more all the time. Sometimes I'd be so depressed and scared I couldn't eat. One day I was high, the next low. I alternated between elation and despair.

Boston disappointed me in some respects. For one, I did not meet musicians who knew or cared about all the music of Western civilization. They were focused just on Mozart, Beethoven, Brahms, and Liszt; what is more, they had a certain limited way of viewing and playing even that music, namely, the "traditional" way that Koussevitzky or whoever had taught them. That was my first direct encounter with tra-di-tion: "This is *the* tradition, this is *the* way. You are a kid. So get with it and learn the tradition." If only they had said, "This is one way." There was very little room for individual interpretation, or for the view that maybe there is more than one "correct" way to play a piece. The truth was, the BSO had become very conservative during the Charles Munch and Erich Leinsdorf eras. Besides disagreeing with the conservatism on aesthetic grounds, it was in my nature to resist rigidity. If somebody insists, "You *must* do this, you *must* do that," even if it's something I like, my reaction is to bang the table, stamp my foot and say, "No, I don't want to. There are other ways to explore."

Hence, although I loved the orchestra and could sometimes do wonderful things with those fine instrumentalists, I was also interested in discovering other, less rigid aspects of music and life. Members of the orchestra reacted negatively to this inclination of mine. They were not happy, for instance, when I went on the road with James Brown, a black soul singer. I'd always enormously admired that man, and learned so much from being with him even a few days. It wasn't only how he worked and the kind of music he made and what his shows were like, but also the wonder of being on tour with an intense black soul figure and his entourage. In all-black theaters in downtown Washington, and all over, this milieu was a revelation—who was with him, whom he saw, the audiences, what it was like to do three shows a day, a whole sense of self-actualization on stage. I came back from that trip with James Brown awed at what I had seen. The spectacle of musicians on stage in a state of ecstasy governed by one idea: Put it out, get it across the footlights, say it, do it, all that was extraordinary. I remember trying to explain some of this to a member of the BSO who reacted as follows: "I never heard anything so disgusting. You are a symphonic conductor, you have a serious responsibility, you should be at home listening to Toscanini and Fürtwangler records, studying your scores. You shouldn't be out on such nonsense." What moralistic, judgemental wrath!

I was at variance with so many people simply out of my interest in many things, not only black music, but gamelan music and folk music as well. And all the time I went on exploring within the western repertory and *outside* of it too, searching for an answer to the question: What actually is music? What has our species done with sounds in different cultures? What is the *whole* literature like? And in all that I used to meet resistance, not from everyone but from a certain element on both sides of the footlights. Some were very enthusiastic too. But I began to perceive very much that the situation of big musical organizations, and a large part of their audiences, spelled a proprietary interest. They were more concerned with the orchestra as an institution, or in a concert as a kind of ceremony, than they were in the art, the message, what the music was saying. A lot of people were coming to concerts as a way of distracting themselves from their own insecurities about stocks and bonds or whether the servants would stay in line, or whatever troubled them. Their problems were swept away by coming to the Symphony, sitting in the same seats every time to hear the same pieces played in the same noble, everything-will-be-beautiful-and-nothing-will-be-disturbing way. There they could feel that all was right with the world, but only as long as those pieces were played that way, with their everlasting melodies and eternal sentiments.

Now and then you could change the repertory to shake them

up. Or once I had a concert series in which we wore T shirts, no ties or formal clothing at all. I got an indignant letter from someone who was "never so insulted in her life" as when she saw the orchestra without coats and ties. "It's shocking. How could you do this to me? I've supported the orchestra all these years," and so on. A real *shanda* (scandal).

What is this all about? We have wonderful institutions, but they are living in never-never land, deliberately reclusive and insular, with an overall attitude borrowed from another century. We are locked into an obsolete musical and social tradition. This is no particular reflection on Boston. It's essentially what the big classical music scene's all about.

I wasn't sure how to proceed with my life, what my role should be. Trying for perspective, I looked at it this way: A magical thing has happened to me. Normally I wouldn't have had the opportunity to do this until I was 40 or 50, and by then I'd have been ground down to being a perfect product of the system. But here I am still in possession of many of my crazy ideas, concepts distilled from an untraditional upbringing. In spite of everything I have recognition. It must mean I'm here to change things that are getting to be more and more a caricature of themselves. To do something about them: that's my job. Well, there were disappointments, but I went some distance toward expanding the repertory and doing things with concerts that had never been done in Boston before. Whenever I got in trouble during my Boston years it was because I tried to do too much too fast. I was encouraged to do a lot, and I wanted to do everything. Sometimes it got excessive, the more so since I was also occasionally living my own life, or trying to, all the while struggling with a million unanswered questions.

During this period, my two most important teachers died. This left me feeling temporarily but utterly at sea. Here I was, a young touring artist, with my foundations suddenly gone. The people I most trusted on musical matters were no longer around. That was scary; it made the whole context of my professional life a little shaky. For a while I could hardly see anything but the bad side, especially being overworked. After all the big ups and downs I went through, it became apparent to me that the conducting profession by itself was not totally fulfilling. To be sure, at first I'd been ecstatic, and then it all began to turn around. I told myself: "This is your work, your craft—

but your spiritual development and enlightenment rest with what's happening to you *as a person* in relation to others."

Surely so much time invested so intensely in work and practice would shrink the soul of a man who still had a lot of progress to make.

Then I went from assistant conductor in Boston to conductor in Buffalo. It's the most wonderful thing that has so far happened to me. I actually started to run an orchestra myself, and learned by running it and through other people, by working and rehearsing with them. The Buffalo Philharmonic has been the joy of my life. We have grown together, playing, touring, recording.

And Buffalo's no wilderness. Morty Feldman, a brilliant composer and a sensitive man, very important in esthetics, lives there. There's Harold Cohen, dean of architecture at the University of Buffalo who's also excellent. All along I've been passionately in love with the visual arts, and the Albright-Knox Gallery is in Buffalo. I spend long hours in that gallery, and in getting acquainted with Buffalo arts people too. I also had more time for New York City. I began to discover my real circle—people in music, in theater, in the media, in design and fashion, even in carpentry, who were as curious and restless as I was. I could get across to them—we communicated.

At a certain point, not so much when I started out as a conductor but sort of midway along, Leonard Bernstein and Pierre Boulez exerted a real influence on me. Although I've been compared to both men at various times, I more and more realize how unlike them I am. But they're people I can talk to. With Lenny I have great talks because of course he's well-read, a musician involved with ideas. We can talk about music in its relationship to what else is going on in society. It's a great pleasure because there aren't so many people around like that. Alexis Weissenberg the pianist is another who's more than very well read. He knows what life is in all its complexity—what the street is, what the library is, and how all the component parts make up a whole.

Rather than learning from other conductors, I have learned most about the art of conducting from the pieces of music I conduct, from the pages of the score. I have a system for learning a piece, a kind of broad analysis, that came to me partially on my own and also from my teachers at USC. I am refining it all the time. I am much more interested in the spirit of the composer than in whether a

$30,000 viola section sounds gorgeous every instant. I am very will-
ing to sacrifice "beauty" to idea, to communication, to articulation.
Of course if you work with great instrumentalists they do play beautifully, but at the same time you must let the text and its essence
have the upper hand. Too many concerts feel to me like hearing a
singer with the world's most beautiful voice whose tongue has been
cut out. There is absolutely no bite, no sense of steady motion to a
cadence threading its way through a piece. What's very important to
me is the thought, the idea behind or within a piece, and how the
composer works it out.

Even though technology helps us so much by transmitting information efficiently, it's done some really awful things. For instance:
"Tell me Mrs. Jones, do you know the Beethoven symphonies?"
"Oh, of course I know them. I *own* them, I have them all at home,
right on my shelf."

"Oh you *own* them, eh? Isn't that interesting. You *own* all the
Beethoven symphonies."

Imagine such a distorted perspective! A Beethoven symphony,
with its universal message, is a calculus interrelationship of ideas set
forth in tones which can be expressed in many different ways. But
what happens? Why do people think they own the Beethoven symphonies, when in fact they own one recording of one interpretation
of these great works? Well, there is a record of a particular performance. It is a possessible object. Once a person possesses it the dis-
putes start: "My object is better than your object. My performance is
the performance. Such-and-such is the ultimate performance." What
nonsense!

This condition is related to the fact that musically we are now in
a state of tremendous uncertainty. How we reached this point is not
such a mystery if we look at the situation historically. The primary
interest of music is getting a composer's musical ideas across. Its
subtlest version can be heard when one person plays a solo piece and
every little nuance, every little shift, every little control, is brought
close up to us. It's a direct individual projection of the soul.
Chamber music can also be quite subtle, because each musician involved has his own very specific musical task to fulfill. Even in pieces
for somewhat larger groups, subtlety need not be sacrificed. When
Haydn, under Count Esterhazy's patronage, composed for an orchestra, he had in mind one, or maybe two or three, musicians on a part.

When the bourgeoisie developed and got actively into music, they brought it to the fast-growing towns, saying, "We are going to create a concert life more in tune with economic developments. We'll show those aristocrats how to provide music for more people— at a profit, no less." Pretty soon you have concerts for 600 listeners instead of six or twelve. You start selling tickets. The composer is forced to conclude, "It's nice to put one musician on a part, but in a big room people in the back will be too far away to hear. If we have eight guys playing in unison, we lose an awful lot of subtle phrasing, but everyone will be able to hear." Progress marches on, with halls for a thousand people, and ten guys on a part instead of eight. Big spaces beget big orchestras.

Now, what happens to repertory? By the end of the eighteenth century, when Mozart wrote, the middle class was just beginning to feel its oats. It dawned on them that they had new power in many fields, including music. So they began commissioning piece after piece, first by Haydn, Mozart, and Beethoven, and then by Liszt, Schumann, and Brahms. Thus these composers were constantly writing new pieces, and 90 percent of the music played was contemporary. But as the middle class became stronger and stronger economically, it was on its way to becoming the new proprietary class. They were most impressed with the conditions they were creating, and the music they were commissioning. The interest in more and more new music couldn't last.

Farther along in the nineteenth century, most remnants of feudalism collapsed entirely. The *haute bourgeoisie* enjoyed an unchallenged triumph—and composers' output for the most part got smaller and smaller, partly because the new ruling class, like all classes in power, was more interested in preserving the past than in fostering change. So we behold a musical society memorializing itself. By the end of the nineteenth century, Mozart, Beethoven, Mendelssohn and their contemporaries predominated on the concert scene. Sure, new music continued to be written. But there was also terrific resistance—both to newness, and to the fact that the musical language was becoming increasingly complex.

And then what happened? At the beginning of the twentieth century there were great musical breakthroughs—but not in the symphonic literature, which had become fairly standardized and was no longer a feasible form for experimentation. Most of the innovations come in ballet and theater music—these are the arenas where Stravinsky and Schönberg and Bartók did their major work. They moved into a sphere that wasn't completely stultified, that hadn't been made into a memorial to certain home virtues. And then when the theater stagnated music was written for little chamber groups, and in later years, in the 1950s, many composers were attracted to the electronic studio, where they work alone. So in some convoluted sense we've come full circle.

If you look at the aesthetics of music and ask, what is music written for—what is it trying to express? you'd have to admit that the really great days of music-for-other-than-commercial-purposes ended with Johann Sebastian Bach. Before Bach, most music was written either for the Church or for an enlightened nobility. Its purpose was to express certain ideas and testify to certain truths; there was no question of tickets. The minute musical performance became a public event, a subscribable event where people were making money, we had a revolution on our hands. It was manifest first perhaps in the Italian opera houses. Entrepreneurs made money by investing in the Venice Opera House. With new pieces to hear, audiences were storming the opera houses. It was a business opportunity, like investing in a Broadway musical today. The inward spiritual force of Western music declined. Music tilted toward entertainment, as the visual arts did toward interior decoration. It's true that some of the greatest music was written during more recent periods. But by whom? For the most part by people who had had disastrous experiences which blocked their entry into the most lucrative and financially rewarding spheres of musical culture.

Mozart was a superior genius and as a kid he wrote marvelous pieces, but the decline of his career threw him into contemplation of other questions, other languages—which led to his most mature work. Beethoven, when he began to go deaf could no longer appear as a touring virtuoso for the entertainment of rich people in drawing rooms; he could not even appear as a soloist with the orchestra any more—which turned him around. His art changed—it became much more abstract, much more a matter of, "I am writing for the ages, not for Mademoiselle Schnasky's living room and the party the day after tomorrow. Never mind external titillation; everything you need is in the music itself." Beethoven was among the first to be conscious of this distinction. Or take Schumann. He hurt his hands and couldn't be a virtuoso pianist any more.

So many have some version of the same story. Or else it's like the case of Bach, who remained an obscure struggling musician his entire life—employed, but certainly not revered. But my, the earlier giants were prolific! Nowadays there are very few composers who in their entire careers have composed anywhere near as much as let's say Mozart or Haydn or Bach. This again relates to specificity and complexity. As the musical language became more complex, creating music required more and more decisions all the time. Before the twentieth century, if you decided to write a piece in G major, a lot of your choices were made before you started because of the G major scale structure and what it allows. These days you can write a piece in any number of different serial systems—either pre-existent or newly devised—or in free dissonant counterpoint. The range of choices is so enormous that you begin to find composers who write basically one extended piece over their lifetimes. Through a series of pieces they try to arrive finally at *the* piece which is *the* definition of what they believe. Edgard Varèse is a classic example. Carl Ruggles is another. And Charles Ives. After many pieces that explore the same theme again and again, he got to one which says it all. The pieces that came after that are like further footnotes or an additional commentary on the same text.

For music of this century, direct contact with the composer is certainly of great help to the conductor. For example, every time I do a piece by Luciano Berio, I first go over it in detail with him. He even sits there at rehearsals with the score and sings and explains what he wants, telling us which sections to watch out for and why. Besides going bar by bar through a score, Berio analyzes the total work for us. You have to understand a piece as more than simply individual notes on a page—you have to realize what's important in the work as a whole.

With the standard repertory we are heir to traditions which are often absolutely inapplicable in light of current musicological research and esthetic values. Mozart is usually played in a tradition that developed somewhere around 1900. It has nothing to do with Mozart's performances in, say, Prague in 1790. Somehow a later version has come to be considered *the* tradition, the way Mozart should be played now. I don't do much Mozart or Bach any more—except when I'm prepared to spend considerable time on a piece. It takes a while to develop an interpretation that incorporates the composer's expectations and your own understanding of the piece. If someone says to me, "Would you like to do the Bach *Mass in B Minor* next season?" I say, "Oh, I'd love to, but I can't right now because it would take a year of solid work, of studying and editing and making endless decisions about rhythmic mutations, ornamentation, instruments, the character of the instrumental playing among the musicians who carry the bass line, and so on and on." Without all that you can't begin to grasp what Bach's stylistic language is all about. Then, how ironic it is to see that the famous Maestro X, Y, or Z is putting on the Mass with a chorus of 200—a much bigger ensemble than Bach had in mind. Isn't it really amazing that in this day and age, knowing what we know about performance practice and esthetics, that such a thing can still go on and that it can still be taken seriously? I'm not saying that you must return to exactly the same number of players and the old instruments, but you do have to develop an understanding of the original style and how to project it through whatever instruments are at your disposal.

People always ask me—"but what about your own interpretation?" Interpretation is a polite word for distortion. You take something universal and look at it as a person of your own time. Or rather, you first look at what it was originally, and then you look again from where you stand now. You need stylistic fidelity to the composer's era, but at the same time, one idea within a piece can be emphasized over another—and that's my job. An exciting interpreter obviously is somebody who emphasizes those ideas which communicate most directly to the audience of his own period. That's why there is no such thing as *the* ultimate performance. The primary interests in another fifty years might be different from today's; then the revelatory performance will show you other aspects of the work, different approaches and directions.

Unfortunately, none of these issues dominates the commercial world of music. Currently, the paramount question is, "Will it sell?" That's what the record business and the concert business are all about. At first, during my "jet set" years, I was very much caught up in all that. I discovered that they can put you in London today, in Paris tomorrow, in Berlin three days later, and in New York three days after that. You can go on doing it forever. You have a repertory of pieces that you know well, you can rehearse, and interpret so that multitudes will respond. You can go all over the world doing those pieces. They sell you here and there and everywhere. I did it for a few years and stopped dead with the realization that it meant nothing. This frantic activity does not contribute to music or even to the places where you make music; it does not allow you to develop any real relationships with other musicians; it leads nowhere very important.

As for recording, that too is dominated by commercial concerns. Whatever repertory you record is almost always a tradeoff. There are certain works that you very much want to record. So you push for those. And usually there are some works that the company wants you to record. So you make a deal: "Okay, if you want me to do this, fine, I'll do it for you, and you do me a favor by letting me record something a little less well known." It feels good to bring out records that nobody else would do, and by that I mean repertory which will be heard on records for the first time. Like what? Well, like the complete works of Ruggles, or Beethoven's late choral music. I'm most interested in bringing new music into the world, whether it's old but unknown music or music that's just been composed.

I haven't had much time to compose up to now, but I plan to do more. In these next years I want people to know me more through the music that I write. Through this they will gain a greater understanding of what I believe, though already many people have caught on to the fact that I have a certain off-the-wall perspective with regard to how pieces of music are put together, how they work, and what they mean.

I try to write a kind of music which is shaped by all the music I love, by classical music, by contemporary experimental music, by folk music and traditional blues and jazz, and also by Asian music. I submerge myself in such music and delight in it. When I go home I listen to African tribal music, Bulgarian folk music, Javanese gamelan and gagakoo, blues and rock, whatever. I want to be able to say through my work, "Listen everybody, these other peoples you think are so strange, their ideas that you think are so alien, come on, they are *you*; the longings, the yearnings, the quests are yours as much as theirs. Only the expression, the approach, maybe the priorities are different. But the essence is not."

I went to a synagogue in Jerusalem, and the first thing I had them do after Friday night services was to sing a bunch of Catholic pilgrims' hymns from fourteenth-century Spain. That caused some consternation. I said, "We know all about the politics and the persecution. No one is forgetting. But that's a whole other story. Meanwhile listen to the notes, to the cadences, to the vows, to the commitment, to the joy and sob *in this music*. Are you going to tell me that all this comes from some other kind of people?" In Israel two of the most favored composers are Tchaikovsky and Chopin, both of whom were quite anti-Semitic. And the Israelis won't play Wagner, though he was possibly less anti-Semitic than the other two. I tell people, "When it comes to the music itself, such things don't matter; forget them. You've got to have enough compassion to say, 'This person is ignorant in a social sense, his politics can't be ours, he was a repugnant type, whatever; the point is, his *music* embodied really important emotions that we all feel.' "

The trouble is that music, like science, can be merchandised not only for commercial, but also for political and social purposes. Nazi Germany represents what happens to a society when it attempts to deny the nonrational. There was Germany, a tremendously literate, highly rationalist, completely controlled nation. Everything was fine, and then overnight the economy collapsed. Because the German people had never squarely faced any issues bearing on what they believed, on their central values, on what measure of faith and of reason to embrace, they were wide open to manipulation by any little myth-maker, who could put the arts at his service without a murmur from most of the populace. What happened with Hitler is a danger to any society that gives no consideration to its spiritual values, that drifts, directionless, unanchored, panting for a phony savior.

To counteract this, education is essential, but education has a very low priority in our country. The teacher's position is laughable; the curricula are abominations. At some point it will have to be said that we are committing cultural suicide. Young people have a right to something better. We've got to spend the money, pay attention, wake up, not just in the arts, in everything.

My general advice to the aspiring young is: love music, and use it to speak of those bigger truths that you are experiencing in your own life, so that after a performance, even in some small way, the hearts of those who've listened will have been opened a little bit.

After all, most people are not lucky enough to be living a life of contemplation and growth, grappling with the greatest thoughts that man has ever had. They push papers from one side of a desk to the other, or have to do more strenuous but equally mindless work.

I am socially conscious enough, thanks to the politics of my family, to add, "Look, I am living in this society, and I am supported by it in a most extraordinary position. I do have a great life." As much as I may complain about it, groaning over too few rehearsals and crammed schedules, my life *is* spent with great thoughts and visions and revelations. Now, if this society supports me in leading that kind of life, I have a responsibility to give whatever I absorb back to it. The responsibility could be most easily discharged by doing some kind of bread-and-circus events that have always been done— playing the same familiar pieces in the same familiar way, and playing a pops concert every now and then. That would make everybody happy. But we have to keep social pressures from stifling our souls. My job is *not* to make everybody happy. My job is to open people up and move them upward, to nurture some of their sensitivity. I know it's there in all of us.

Part Four: Performers

14: Gregor Piatigorsky

I *must* say I have had an extremely hard life, hard but fascinating. As a little boy in Russia, I heard music at home all the time. My parents played, without really being musicians. They didn't especially encourage or discourage me to become a musician—I was absolutely determined about that myself at an early age.

Before starting the cello, I played a little piano and violin. The cello was too big for me at first. But it was soon my favorite string instrument. I found it the richest of the strings, with the biggest range and the most extraordinary possibilities.

I started to earn money for the family before I was eight years old. As a youngster I had all kinds of jobs. I even wrote music for the silent movies, in Russia, when I was nine or ten years old, and later in Paris. Before I knew much about love and kisses, I had to put music together so people would respond romantically. Oh, I have done many things.

My formal education approaches zero. How could I coordinate school with work in night clubs and other such places? I was forced into a kind of self-education. I sought the company of people from whom I could learn something. I was ashamed of my ignorance, of not even knowing elementary geography. I must have been quite a bore to some very nice people. I would come to them with strange questions: What is life? What is love? What is hate? Fortunately, a few wonderful people were not put off by my questions. I was interested in so many things, and I never had time for them all.

I learned from nearly everyone I met. Musicians taught me formally and informally. First, at the Moscow Conservatory, a beautiful man, Professor [Alfred] Von Glehn, deeply influenced me. He had been a student of the great cellist Davidov. Davidov was a close friend of Tchaikovsky's. Even *I* am not old enough to have heard him. When Davidov was director of the conservatory in St. Petersburg, he engaged Tchaikovsky as a composition teacher. In my class there was a big photo of Davidov.

I prefer the Davidov school of cello playing, because he was such an extraordinary master of the instrument. His playing was not based on theories. It didn't derive from what people refer to as "technique." He had no "method." Or you might say that his "method" was simply to make music and that, for his time, such an idea was

Gregor Piatigorsky, the cellist, was interviewed at his home in Los Angeles in April 1975. He died in August 1976.

most advanced. Although he didn't have many outstanding students, one of the best of them, Professor [Julius] Klengel in Leipzig, later became my teacher. One Davidov pupil taught me in Moscow, and then another in Leipzig.

I ran away from Russia, to Germany, before my twelfth birthday. The revolution sped me on my way. At that time, I had no sense of geography, of where I was going. I only knew that I had left Russia.

No matter what part of the world you inhabit, if you are a musician, you *live* in music. But I was never totally one-sided, and in Germany one needed to learn a lot. First there was the language, the literature—Goethe and so many other great writers.

I took a course in philosophy at the University of Leipzig. My choice was rather unfortunate—you know, trying to absorb all that heavy metaphysical German philosophy. I spent much of my time with strange philosophers, like Max Stiller and Otto Weininger, the woman-hater, who killed himself when he was in his early 20s.

Imagine: There I was in the midst of the rich Weimar culture of the 1920s, with a chance to pursue many other interests besides music—literature, politics, oceanography, and so on. I must say, my favorite sport was to sit and to think, or alternatively to walk and to think.

While still very young, I became the first cellist of the Berlin Philharmonic, where I remained for several years. It was difficult to concertize as a soloist and at the same time to play in an orchestra. But those in charge of the Philharmonic were marvelous about my doing both; I had full freedom. It was fine. I ate. I worked. I'll soon be 72 and I still don't know the meaning of the word vacation. I just can't understand it.

My son is a biologist for the National Institute of Health. He has always been a tremendous worker. Yet I used to be astonished at how many holidays he and other children had—national and religious holidays, and then the worst—summer vacations of three months! That's still the case. Why? Have they worked so hard? Kids should have a few days free, but whole months? What for?

I don't think we've learned how to bring up children. It's very difficult to be a parent, and it's very difficult to be a child, always to be told, "Don't, Don't, Don't." Resentments are bound to develop. I have found, however, that my children, though they are not musicians, have always known quite a bit more than I do in certain areas. For instance, my daughter would tell me that my English was not very good. I said, "Well, that's true, my accent and all that." She said, "I can teach you." She would come home from school and say, "Father, time for a lesson." My son has also taught me countless things, for example, about sports. I learned a lot from my children and it gave them satisfaction to be "father's professor."

They grew up right here, in California. My daughter was born in Paris, my son in New York State. I first came to the United States on a concert tour in 1929. Later, when I got married, I became a citizen, I think in 1940 or something like that. Well, I'm very bad at dates. For a while, I was even vague about my birthday. I didn't know the exact date I was born, only that it was sometime in April of 1903. I kept it a nice round date, April 20, until I discovered that was Hitler's birthday, when I changed it to the 17th, which turned out to be the correct date!

Life in Germany—for any musician, let alone a Jewish musician—became impossible under Hitler. One couldn't stay there. It was barbaric. Artists were stifled. You know, music, art—these are not just little decorations to make life prettier. They're very deep necessities, which people cannot live without. And every musician, every artist, has a heavy responsibility.

Though not all of them realize this, to be true to art they must really forget themselves and devote their lives to something larger in which they believe. Just look who stands out in the history of humanity. It's hard to discover who was the richest man in the Middle Ages, and you cannot easily remember the names of all the kings and princes of the Renaissance; there were quite a number of them, but now they hardly matter. But who will ever forget Michelangelo, and later, Mozart or Beethoven? We can judge the whole history of mankind by such great people. We see that art is what matters. It may not look that way at the moment; people are much more ashamed to *feel* anything now than they were in the past. Children must be rough and tough. If they talk about flowers, they're considered sissies, and poets are called softies. We should remind ourselves that their greatest strength may lie precisely in so-called softness.

Frustration for a musician begins, continues, and ends in the fact that somebody is selling him. The commercialism is most disturbing. So, what's the alternative? Well, we artists must try to forget about drawing large audiences that make a large profit, and concentrate on giving wonderful performances. Attractions and sensations are not our business. About all this, I would have little advice for musicians, only for those who organize music—the managers, the critics, the women's clubs. I'm afraid I would want to advise those who are usually deaf. They only look for glamor.

Many fine artists whose names are not well known get few engagements. Many of my students are superbly equipped. Some can play anything that has ever been written, and do it magnificently. They could give fine concerts anywhere in the world. But who gives them the opportunity to perform? They're lost to the world. These people ought not to have such a hard time. Their only obligation should be to art, and if they are good everybody should listen to them.

Luckily, I have always had plenty of work. Whether I enjoyed it depended on what I played, with whom I played, and how I played. If my playing wasn't satisfactory, how could I enjoy it? Recently, I have very much liked playing with younger musicians. Of course, my playing has changed over the years. One's personality keeps developing; I'm certainly not as messy a musician as I once was. I'm different and better. I continue to improve. As time goes on, one obviously has more knowledge, more experience—one has had more time to think.

A performer must be a man of many loves. With a composer, the less he is influenced by others, the better. But a performer has to understand a large number of composers.

Interpretation is very creative. The interpreter doesn't lose his personality to the composer. Sure, he plays what's written. But what *is* written? Very little, actually. The few indications—tempo, dynamics, whatever—what are they? Take "piano"—it means soft, but *how* soft? That already is a question. Now let's say there's a hold, a fermata. How long a fermata? It doesn't say. Maybe there's time for you to have lunch, and then to continue. How long the fermata? How short the fermata? *You* decide, and when you do, it is absolutely impossible to hide your personality. What an absurdity to say, "Here is a performer who *excludes* himself," or to insist, "A performer plays Beethoven well only if he himself disappears." If he disappears, he is a corpse. No one disappears. The performer is a human being. His judgments might be right or wrong, but through them he is always there.

It is too late to think about all this during a performance. You must think about it all your life. You must live with pieces, and try, with all your sincerity, depth, and knowledge to understand what composers really meant, and what their pieces say to you. That's quite a responsibility. How gratifying it is, though, when you reach people, when they respond strongly.

But remember, public or general taste is a complicated matter. I have played for audiences the world over, and have found few differences between one group of listeners and another. I often find the public's intuition remarkably sound. I think the public feels something. It differentiates.

But on the other hand, the public likes sensationalism. And pride enters into their judgments. You will find people who like something and are ashamed to admit it, others who hate something and are ashamed to say so. But very few people are truly knowledgeable. I'm afraid that applies even to musicians.

You have probably heard this story, but it's worth repeating. Once I played several Beethoven sonatas with Furtwängler in Paris. Ravel was there. He said, "You play so beautifully, but why do you play such rotten music?" I said, "Wait a minute, this is Beethoven." He said, "Yes, that's what I meant." Well, if Ravel could not understand or appreciate Beethoven, what can you expect of amateurs? This goes on and on and on. It's very difficult to say who *knows* and who does not *know*. I would put more trust in intuition.

Ignorance is not the only problem. Unfortunately, musicians are arranged in ranks. It's worse than the military—there's a general, a lieutenant general, a brigadier general—and at the bottom there's a private first class, who plays in the orchestra. For me, this is illusory. I have met so many wonderful musicians who played in orchestras. Look, even Dvorak played viola in the Prague Symphony. Also, many very admirable people do not choose instruments with large solo repertoires. They may prefer the clarinet, the oboe, or the horn. They become soloists *in* the orchestra. No one seems very anxious to know their names or to celebrate them very much. But they have all my admiration.

Ours, however, is a world of champions. Music gets to be like tennis or football. You have to be the best, the biggest, the greatest, the most. In art, that's a catastrophe. Thank goodness I never needed to play in competitions. I have never won an official prize. I am not a boxer. You know, in a fight, one man is laid out half dead on the side, with a broken nose—he's the loser. And the other dances around him—he is the winner. That's prize-fighting, a bloody, competitive, hit and knock area. Why should it interest an artist? Art is not competitive, but, alas, artists are. They're made to be. My students go all over the world in order to *compete*. In that way, they hope to gain some recognition. What a misfortune.

I refuse to do it any more, but in the past I often served as a juror in competitions. Now, it is very embarrassing to have to judge who is the best, the second best, the fifth best. Though they may play the same instrument, even the same piece, each musician is unique. As soon as people reach a certain level, it's preposterous to make comparisons. I am seldom able, myself, to compare one artist unfavorably with another. The only thing I can say is, "There's a wonderful artist," not, "this fine artist is better than that fine artist." Differences are good. They're interesting. It would kill me to try and say who's "the best." I can say X is good at Beethoven, Y is good at Mozart. But how does anyone number them one, two, three? It's not possible in music or any other art. You can't say, so and so's *the* greatest poet or writer or painter. Look at the paintings on my wall. That one is Toulouse Lautrec, this one Roualt, this is Fragonard, there's Modigliani. Would you ask me, who is the *best* of these? Wouldn't you say to be excellent is enough?

Of course, I feel closer to some painters and composers than to others. Most of the time, I know which of them I can play best at a given moment. Actually, for me, the greatest music is whatever I have just played.

I was not always comfortable with music I didn't understand, with new music that I didn't grow up with. Lots of recent pieces are full of gadgets—electronics and all that. Too many people are annotating music, just making noise. But I have always been very interested in contemporary work. We must remember, Mozart and Beethoven didn't hear all of the sounds we hear. They never heard the sound of a car motor starting, running, grinding, stopping. They never heard a telephone ring, or an airplane roar. It's like painters who didn't see what our astronauts have seen. In every period, there are thousands of new sounds, thousands of new vistas. So how can one be super-conservative and say, "I'm just used to some music that I call classical, and it's the only good music."

In point of fact, I have played new music all my life, although people sometimes laughed, especially once in Berlin, let's see, in 1926, I think. I was always curious, and some works fascinated me: Schönberg's *Pierrot Lunaire*, for instance. I remember the first performance in Berlin, with Artur Schnabel at the piano, Fritz Stiedry conducting, in 1923. We got a big standing ovation because it was a home product. Nowadays, *Pierrot* is almost classical, as are many other pieces from earlier in this century. Also, I find quite a bit of uninteresting music by the greatest composers. I know some pretty dull pieces by Haydn, Mozart, Bach. They count more as creators, because really, they were not quite human. They were gods. But let's be reasonable. Their output was not all of equal quality.

Schnabel and I played a lot together. We had a regular trio: Schnabel, piano; Prof. Carl Flesch, violin; and me, cello. We travelled a great deal all over Europe. The group itself didn't have a name; each of us had his own name—we were just known as Schnabel, Flesch, and Piatigorsky. Schnabel and Flesch were much older than I, and we never played as a trio in America. But later, Vladimir Horowitz, Nathan Milstein, and I, pretty much the same age, played together, here and in Europe. Rubinstein and Heifetz were my partners in my last regular trio; we played together only in America. Nowadays, I play with various friends; it depends on who's in town. Heifetz and I play quite often together. We do "chamber music," whatever that is. I have never cared for the way people label the activities of a musician; when you think about it, what *is* chamber music? The opposite of military music or street music? Is it every kind of music played in chambers? No, no. Remember that a big orchestra can play very intimately; it's able to produce a "chamber music" effect.

Worse than the term "chamber music" is "virtuoso." To me, that's a dirty word, used much too loosely. "Virtuoso" should be applied to *any* person who has mastered his instrument, not just to flashy soloists.

From the beginning, I have only wished to be a good servant of music, a good servant in any capacity. I don't know how to pinpoint exactly what I am. You know, I think I'm simply a musician—not a "chamber musician," not a "soloist." "Musician" is a real category; I am not so sure about the others. My goodness, I'm full of titles. I don't know how many doctorates I have—but thank God nobody calls me "doctor." Ah those titles. So superficial, so meaningless.

Of all the titles applied to me I like "teacher" best of all. Though I believe one remains a student of music as long as one lives, I like to teach very much. I like young people; I like to share my experiences and, if possible, to help them. I was one of the few concert artists in this country to do a lot of teaching as well. First I taught at the Curtis Institute in Philadelphia for about ten years, when Zimbalist taught violin and there were many great piano teachers. Currently, and for the past ten years or so, I have been at the University of Southern California. Many of my friends, men like Rachmaninoff and Kreisler, never gave a lesson to anybody. Such people were astonished at my teaching, and they asked me, "How can you do it?" To many of them, teaching is somehow a lesser activity—only concerts matter. Certainly the world looks at it in that light. Therefore, an artist gets thousands of dollars for one concert, and only a few dollars for one lesson. Furthermore, being a teacher seems to reduce his rank. Now, I find that deplorable. Money, large audiences, standing ovations—they're all false and ridiculous criteria to a true servant of music.

I have been teaching for a very long time. I started when I was sixteen or so; there's been no respite since. One thing I would never do anywhere was to take money for giving private lessons. Not even in Russia. Because, look, nobody made me pay for lessons when I was a kid. I teach for pay at a conservatory or university.

On the whole, teaching has been a positive experience, but unfortunately I never had beginning students. I'd like to have them one day. I want to start someone, to make it good from the beginning. Most of the time when students come to me they have already played many concerts, studied with many people, and developed many bad habits. It takes a long time just to help them get rid of those habits, which sometimes are purely physical. A student holds the bow in a peculiar way, or places fingers in the wrong way, by which I mean in a way that's not natural. There are many things in life that people do naturally: walking, gesturing, holding a fork. Actually, many people do everything well that they have not studied. Well, the moment they learn something about string instruments they encounter *methods,* according to which you must use a certain finger here, you must stretch there, you *must* do this or that. All that is unnecessary and should be unlearned if possible. The point is to be natural. Technique is nothing more than the capacity to express whatever you want to express.

But some teachers are still dictators. So are some conductors and some critics. It's so difficult to find quality in any of these areas of music. Also, the individuals involved so rarely coordinate their activities. Whether they know it or not, artists and critics have a common purpose, and that is to spread the love of music. They should help each other, understand each other, make other people understand. But they don't work together very much. In all my life, all these years, I may not have spent five days with critics; I have hardly ever met one. Now, that's not natural.

On the other hand, I have known many composers. I was very close to Stravinsky, to Ravel, to Prokofiev. There were many, and I knew them everywhere—Milhaud in Paris, Richard Strauss in Vienna. I played with Strauss when he conducted, and with Hindemith; he was a fine musician. At Curtis, I liked Menotti very much, and Barber was often there. It was a stimulating group of people.

I left Philadelphia for California, first, because I liked it. I knew it from playing concerts here. Also, my son had an ear inflammation in Philadelphia—terrible climate there. Besides, I was packing all the time—packing, going and coming, packing again. I decided life would be nicer in a place where at least you didn't have to pack to go away for the summers. Here, even if you want to ski in July or August, you can find a spot. As for the children, in California there ears didn't hurt. All in all, I'm very happy with the choice.

When impresarios were sending me 'round and 'round, I did, oh, 100, 120 concerts a year. Before starting at USC, I still travelled most of the time. Years ago, I used to have a manager; now I don't want one. I'd rather not travel like a madman, as I used to do.

Sometimes I didn't know where I was. Once I played in London, I think on Monday, and on Tuesday I had a rehearsal in Missouri with the St. Louis Symphony. Imagine the time difference, jet lag, and all that. For me, it's, shall we say, less than ideal to live this way. I realize, though, that some people love it. They are mostly the young but already famous musicians. Some, for instance Barenboim, can tell you exact schedules for concerts around the world, months, years in advance. It's fantastic how the youngsters come and go. I played some concerts in Israel—"chamber music," as it's called—with Barenboim and Pinky Zuckerman. Think of this: There I am. I look out the window 30 minutes before the concert, and there's Pinky playing tennis—but he comes to the concert on time, and everything's fine. This is so different from older musicians, who generally have to think and compose themselves. They sit around for hours before a concert. It's as if they face a tremendous ordeal every time. But also, they like to sit and talk. All they want is more time. Oh, there's a lot to discuss.

I never liked running around so much, doing many activities in a given day. I like sports, but I never mixed my professional activities with sports or extraneous pleasures of any kind. I did everything, but each at its own time. Now, if I decided to climb a mountain, I couldn't attempt to do that just before concert time. Sometimes I envy the young who make nothing of it. But I prefer a little more time.

Today, everyone's in such a hurry. Last October, I went to Washington to play with the Israel Philharmonic under Mehta. So I arrived there the day of the concert, not knowing when the rehearsal was, where the concert was, and what time it was to take place. At 5 o'clock I started to put on my white tie; then it was 6:30. I found out the rehearsal was at 7:30, the concert at 8. As it turned out, I just had time to arrive and say a quick "hello, how are you, everything is fine with me," to my friends. Then we tuned our instruments, rehearsed, and played the concert. This isn't so bad if you're playing with friends, with good musicians—an orchestra of people who know what you want in a performance. But it's so fast! In my youth there was time. We didn't produce instant concerts. There were no airplanes. You arrived a few days before the concert. You went to look at the hall. You made new acquaintances, spoke to interesting people; you walked around. You saw how people lived. You got more out of life. As the speed and communication increased it became airport, hotel, concert hall, and that's that. Instead of being able to describe a town,

I can only describe its airport: "Well, that airport was very bad. You have to walk for 40 minutes, and then drive to town, which takes an hour and a half." What a big change!

But still, there's nothing better than life, no matter what life. One shouldn't complain. Life is absolutely fascinating. And altogether, I wonder if I would have preferred to live in another age. It was never perfect. I wouldn't mind living a long while yet, to see what is going to happen.

To me, my work is life-giving, but you cannot live only for yourself. In the end, everything you see and hear is for people—not only the table, the ashtray, and so on, but art and music as well. Music makes life better. People who have no contact with music are to be pitied. Music is a necessity. It is rich. It is imaginative. It is magnificent. And it is for everyone.

can't remember the time when I didn't play the piano. It's always been the center of my existence. No matter where in the world I am—and I've travelled all over—when I sit down at the keyboard I feel at home.

I was born in Chile, in the small town of Chillan, in 1903. I started my career as a child prodigy at the age of five, with a recital in Santiago. I hadn't had any lessons at all; I taught myself how to read music. The urge to play the piano was very strong. When people asked me what else, if not a pianist, I would have wanted to become, I couldn't say, because I have never doubted for a second that I was born to play the piano.

After performing in Buenos Aires at the age of seven, I went on to Berlin to study, with a ten year scholarship from the Chilean government. So I owe my early musical training to an early form of socialism. After that money ran out, I had help from wonderful wealthy patrons in Europe, who saw that I was still too young to earn a real living.

My mother, sister, and brother came with me to Berlin. Mother was an excellent pianist; while she never performed in public, hers was the first classical piano playing I heard. My sister could have become a very good pianist, but she was a little older than I and when she saw I was getting on faster she felt disappointed in herself. In any case, my family was wonderfully supportive of me in my musical career.

Nothing shaped my intellectual and cultural outlook as much as Berlin. At first I went to a gymnasium, but left after six months; it was impossible to improve my piano playing unless I stayed at home most of the day to practice and work with tutors on my general education. Nonetheless, I managed to imbibe a great deal of the spirit and the substance of the city.

Berlin of the twenties was unique. Many factors made it that way. Above all, the cultural atmosphere was incredibly intense and manysided. We had four fine opera houses going at the same time, plus a marvelous orchestra, and an incredible number of creative interpreters—William Furtwängler, Bruno Walter, Erich Kleiber, Leo Blech, Otto Klemperer. Also there were extraordinary people in the theater—Max Reinhardt, Erwin Piscator, Kurt Weill, as well as won-

Claudio Arrau, the pianist, lives in Douglaston, New York, and was interviewed at his home in August 1977.

derful museums. Weill was my composition teacher for a while and we were good friends. He had a brilliant mind, was an unusually pleasant person, and a great teacher. Unfortunately, I never saw much of Weill in the United States.

Such a setting will not easily be duplicated. Unhappily this ambiance only lasted for about fifteen years. Then came the horrible man who destroyed everything. In three months Berlin went from a leading cultural center to a provincial backwater, due to the lack of culture and the general stupidity, not to speak of the brutality, of the Nazi leaders. The many marvelously talented Jews had to leave— Weill, Reinhardt, Piscator and so many more. They all made new lives here, but somehow the richness of the Berlin experience could never be recaptured. Piscator lived in my house here in Douglaston, N.Y., before we bought it. He was a remarkable person; in Berlin, he was known for his outstanding stagings, though in the U.S. he mainly taught.

As for my becoming a concert pianist—I first went through a very successful European prodigy career, making my formal Berlin debut at the age of eleven. I had a brilliant teacher, Martin Krause, who died when I was fifteen. I adored him and would go to no one else for lessons. It seemed to me that everything he had told me was so right that any other teacher would spoil it. After Krause died, I again became an autodidact.

I remember Krause's teaching very vividly. He didn't concentrate only on music; he tried to develop my total personality, integrating music with a cultural life that included considerable knowledge of other arts. He didn't want his students to be specialists on one instrument and know nothing else. He thought that the wider a young musician's cultural base, the greater he would be in his own field. That's the essential point and what made him different from most other teachers.

It is not enough for an interpreter to know a score. He must know as much as he possibly can about the spiritual and intellectual atmosphere of that moment in which the composition was created, not least the possible influence of literature and other arts. All this surrounding content gives us deep insight. It's important to know what a composer said and thought and wrote at the time when he was developing a particular piece. Take a well-known example. They

asked Beethoven what the titles on his *Tempest* and *Appassionata* sonatas meant. These names seemed crazy at the time. So he said,
"Read Shakespeare's *The Tempest*." It's important to see what Beethoven said about his music to Czerny [who was a pupil of his] and
others. Letters are invaluable. One should really be acquainted with
every major composer's complete correspondence.

Krause was a pupil of Liszt. As a youngster, I was made very
conscious of learning in the Liszt tradition; I knew I was being encouraged to perpetuate a specific legacy. But my teacher didn't believe in imposing dogmas on youth. Rather, he allowed the pianist's
talent to develop naturally, leaving a lot of room for one's own initia-
tive. In musical matters he was a spiritual guide. Then again, in
technical matters he was a very strict disciplinarian. He pushed the
young student, not excessively, just enough.

My gift for rapidly learning a lot of repertory showed up very
early and my teacher urged me to develop this capacity. By the age of
fourteen I already knew the 48 preludes and fugues from Bach's *Well-
Tempered Clavier* by heart and I could play them in any key. If you
said, "Play the E Flat major fugue in D Flat or D," I did it—a very
helpful exercise, both for remembering music *and* mastering technique, since when you transpose, you put your hands in different
positions. Every day I tried to memorize something new. Such discipline developed the memory, and helped me to pile up repertory. It
was never my nature to be lazy, nor could I have been under my
teacher's influence. He believed—and now I also do—that to understand a composer's musical language you have to know most of his
output. If you come upon enigmas in a certain piece, they may be
unraveled by analogy to a composer's other works. Even if you compare piano sonatas to string quartets or symphonies, you can understand and dispel many puzzles.

It became my aim to be at home with a wide range of pieces by
each of the great composers. I never performed one work by a composer over and over and over again. It's wonderful to have so many
works at my fingertips. They enrich each other. Sometimes I feel a
little stale in relation to a certain work, so I lay it aside for a while
and take it up again later. Playing the entire *oeuvre* for piano of many
composers helps you develop a sort of creative capacity for true musical understanding. And I can get most pieces back into my fingers

very fast, even if I haven't played them in a while. This too is a question of discipline, and it's a very useful skill.

Krause inspired in me an enormous admiration for great teaching. I myself have had pupils ever since I was a young man in Berlin. I guess you could say I belong in a line of succession from one great master to another—Beethoven, Czerny, Liszt, Krause; I hope this tradition will be kept alive not only through my own playing but through that of my students. I have always enjoyed teaching; I think of it as a very creative activity. I love to awaken young talents to their own possibilities. I agree with Krause that it's not the teacher's function to impose opinions on a student. Rather I try to make students aware of technical and musical issues and let them solve their interpretive problems however they choose.

One of the first things I try to show young pianists is that one actually has four musical memories—visual, muscular (touch), aural (sound), and analytical. The last of these eclipses all the others. If you've got that you know exactly how one phrase follows another and contributes to the piece as a whole. However, this memory comes last. First comes sound, second muscular, third visual—and yet these three develop more or less at the same time. Finally comes the analytical—looking at the form, the ups and downs, the development from one key to another, the climaxes. It means understanding how the piece is put together, ultimately providing a more complete perspective. Acquiring these memories is not easy—but then, it's not easy to be a good performer. In fact, it may be a miracle.

In one's early years, I tell my students, one learns so much from great and experienced artists. The most exhilarating experiences of my life may have been performances with great conductors like Wilhelm Furtwängler and Bruno Walter. In Berlin I worked with so many fine musicians—Arthur Nikisch, Charles Münch, Felix Weingartner, Willem Mengelberg, all the fabulous maestros of that day. My favorite was Furtwängler. Besides everything else, he was an extraordinary accompanist, who listened carefully to the soloist and matched his interpretations. I don't agree with the people who say there were many greats in the past, but the age of the great conductors has passed. There are plenty around, like Carlo Maria Giulini and George Solti. And they are not alone.

I am also encouraged about young pianists these days. Ours is a time of tremendous talent—perhaps more than ever before. I don't know why it should be so, but the number of gifted young pianists is appreciably greater now than when I started out. And many of them seem to feel at home with the great pianistic traditions of the past. I have quite a number of first-rate students in different parts of the world. In Europe, several young pianists actually travel with me when I tour. I would like to think that my relationship to my pupils is something like what my teacher's was with me.

Unfortunately, while there's more talent there's less opportunity. Fewer individuals today will step forward to help a young artist. A certain amount of money is essential for young people to organize concerts of their own before management has taken them on; in the past, many more rich benefactors were willing to give novices sums of money. Such people helped me enormously. This kind of personal assistance has largely disappeared, and has been replaced by institutional support; and the institutions just can't keep up with the number of young performers. Thus, there simply aren't enough chances for young people to play in public. Prize winners are an exception, but I'm sorry that our system has had to get so competitive. I accept it, even though contests develop an unhealthy and selfish spirit that shouldn't exist in any artistic activity. That mentality is more suitable for sports, where one runner gets a medal because he can run faster than another. Realizing all this, I still accept the system as it is because winning prizes is one of the few ways for young artists to start careers.

And I myself won prizes when I was young. I was awarded the Liszt Prize twice in a row, when I was sixteen and seventeen, and my adult career was launched. I was then able to earn a living as a pianist, chiefly in Germany, but also in Scandinavia, Eastern Europe, and Great Britain.

I left Germany for good in 1939. After a Latin American tour my wife and I went back to Germany for our little girl, who had been left with her grandparents (my wife is originally German), and then went straight to Chile. We stayed there for several months before moving to the United States, which is still our home base. During the forties I was mostly in the U.S. or traveling elsewhere in this hemisphere, with many trips to Canada, Mexico, and South America. I am still a Chilean citizen, though I am not in agreement with the present regime.

Doing so much moving about, I have been in a good position to compare audiences. I used to find that listeners were different in various parts of the world. As you moved from country to country, the public more readily accepted or angrily rejected certain composers. This is changing now, because the music world has become increasingly international in its tastes. Until recently they couldn't stand Brahms or Bruckner or Mahler in Paris; now they're crazy about all three. In Germany they didn't like Sibelius; in England they never cared for Debussy. In general one could say that Latin American audiences were more spontaneous, more emotional; but even that differed from country to country. Today such national differences are less and less noticeable.

I find young audiences very sophisticated these days. They have strong preferences, definite likes and dislikes. For them music isn't simply entertainment or just a way of acquiring "culture." For some young people music is gradually replacing religion—the musical experience means that much to them. I see this everywhere, and it's very encouraging.

I think audience sophistication in general has increased over the period of my career. Thirty years ago you wouldn't have played a whole Schubert recital, say, because people would have disliked it. They wanted variety. When Artur Schnabel played a complete Schubert cycle, it was the first time such a thing had happened in New York. But even the great Schnabel had to play this cycle in Town Hall; he wouldn't have attempted to fill Carnegie Hall. Today the idea is far from outlandish; program selection has become much subtler and more refined. I like very much to do programs of works by one or two composers; I like to show different aspects of a composer's genius in one concert.

Most listeners *do* have one blind spot—contemporary music. People have such trouble with recent works because they don't provide what they've come to expect from music. This is roughly formulated, but I'm afraid that what they expect is to be put into a certain mood—one of daydreaming, of pure lofty and romantic feelings unavailable in mundane everyday life. People should realize that emotion in contemporary music means something else entirely. New pieces are like music from other planets, that is, vastly different from earlier music. Modern music asks for a lot of effort from the listener, to open up, listen again and again until the meaning of the music becomes clearer. Twentieth-century compositions are simply not what commercial audiences have been trained to enjoy.

I believe in including a small amount of avant-garde music on concerts of mainly traditional music—but this should be done cautiously, so as not to frighten people away. Some efforts have been made to give people a lot of new work all at once. This won't work. It has to be done carefully and slowly, so that gradually such music comes to be part of their consciousness and they don't reject it so completely.

I myself was not shocked by Schönberg and Stravinsky when I first heard their music in the twenties. I generally love their music; it's quite exciting. I was present at the premiere of *Pierrot Lunaire;* we literally had a riot in Berlin. People booed, they fought, they came to blows. I enjoyed the piece—and the disagreement. The audience was *alive,* full of pros and cons.

I don't learn as much contemporary music as I'd like to. There's not enough time. Memorizing avant-garde music is exceedingly slow and difficult. Then, audiences don't expect Claudio Arrau to play that kind of music. I don't like the stereotype they have of me at all. An interpreter should be able to understand and perform absolutely any kind of music he chooses. I would very much like to perform Elliott Carter's piano concerto, which I greatly admire, some works by Stockhausen, and Boulez's piano sonata. And much more. I am 100 percent for modern music and open to new developments. Why don't people expect new music at my concerts? They like to put a stamp on an artist: "I go to hear him play Beethoven or Brahms or Schumann" or whatever.

Perhaps I've been typed so strongly because I've done a tremendous amount of recording of the classics. Making records is not like playing for an audience. Certain things one does in public performance may sound exaggerated on records. Even tempi that are right in concert sometimes have to be changed a little for recording. In a concert hall there's an element of improvisation, of spontaneity, of creativity of the moment. Every performance should be, and is, slightly different. But a recording becomes a kind of document—it stays the same. It's a different medium and requires a different thought process. And listeners should remember that since a record is a document, it's valid as the expression of one particular moment in an interpreter's life. It's instructive to listen to records from different stages of your career, to hear how you've developed and changed. As it turns out, I seldom listen to my own albums, but those of other performers from various points in their careers interest me.

How have I matured as a pianist? The only answer I have is that my approach to interpretation has gotten more and more pure; I do things more for the sake of the music alone, and not for the sake of success, for glamor. As you age, personal vanity should mean less and less. If in your youth you wooed an audience and sought to please it, with years, that tendency should be overcome. I think I am pretty free of it now. As a young man I was very unhappy if critics didn't like my playing. Once in a while they were unkind. Even then I didn't let myself be influenced by what a critic said. I did have friends and advisors to ask about a performance—highly cultivated people whose judgment I trusted. But it's very difficult to talk to others about your playing. I was cautious; I only took the comments I thought I needed. After all, you are your own best critic.

Through the years, I've thought a lot about the musician's end-less quest for balance between fidelity to the score and personal in-terpretation. My own conviction is that the basis of any interpretation must be absolute faithfulness to the text and to the composer's inten-tions as far as we know them. On top of that, one can build one's own creative superimposition—but *only* on top of that. For instance, I always say, "Never play a measure *fortissimo* when the composer writes *piannissimo,* **never play** *staccato* when the composer writes *legato.*" Such freedom of choice is a distortion, a real departure from the original conception. But of course there is the opposite school of thought that says, "Play the music exactly as it is written and add nothing else." Also wrong. An automaton could do that. Why have human interpreters? First I accept loyalty to the notes, and then the flight of one's own imagination.

With this reasoning in mind, I decided to do a new edition of the Beethoven sonatas. Peters is putting it out. I thought it was time for yet another one. There had been so much new research since the last edition—many facsimiles of the manuscripts were published and many things came to light that we didn't know before. Only recently, a new copy of opus 109 was found. It contained a very important change in one of the variations. Then, there was the London edition of the *Hammerklavier* Sonata, Opus 106, in which the order of the movements is different: After the first movement, the London edition had the third movement, then the second and the fourth.

My version is different from the Henley; I think I'm even more faithful to the original. Now, not all the original manuscripts are available, but I looked at as many as I could. I also studied all the previous editions. Schnabel's for instance is marvelous, but it doesn't have the benefit of newer findings. The system of the Peters edition is that all of my additional comments will be printed in a special booklet with no notes alongside the music. I make a lot of suggestions about the meanings of different passages. I indicate my own metronome markings and also those of Czerny. And so on.

I have very much enjoyed putting together my edition. I did most of the work at our summer place in Vermont, where I spend as much time as possible when I'm not touring. Though my house is only forty miles from the Marlboro, Vermont, festival I met its director, Rudolf Serkin, for the first time only six months ago. He was very nice—cordial, warm, a marvelous person. Wherever I've lived or visited, I've seen musicians less than other people. I like to meet and get to know novelists, poets, and psychologists—all kinds of people.

My main advice to young pianists is to be well-rounded human beings. First, I tell them to look after their emotional well-being. Too many artists are arrested in their development by psychological blocks. I have had pupils come to me with what seemed like very small talents, and suddenly, under the influence of many factors, they started to unfold and become worthwhile young musicians. Artistic progress has a lot to do with one's psychological state.

Then, further, I would tell young people to develop all facets of their personalities—to spend time in the theater, at museums, to read a lot. I read three hours a day and I would feel very bad if I didn't. I've been reading Goethe all my life. I love Herman Hesse and Heinrich Böll. I read and speak five languages—which is a tremendous help. Not only can I read literature in the original, but I can speak to people in their native language when I visit their countries.

It still gives me pleasure to travel. I enjoy seeing different places. I have been almost everywhere in the world except China, where I hope to play some day. Although there certainly isn't enough time in any one place, even a short stay is nice. In today's world everything is faster than ever before. The jet has made a big difference; now you can get anywhere very quickly. There used to be more time to spend in every old memory-laden place where so much had happened to you. Now there's less time—but by moving such a lot one learns to perceive more speedily what's going on and what changes have taken place. I'm writing an autobiography about it all, but this too will take time.

I've had a rich life, with many satisfactions. As for frustrations, in any large sense they're hard to think of. I've liked my life just the way it was. Putting it negatively, I'm an uprooted man, but in positive terms, I'm a citizen of the world. This is the way I always wanted it. I hate nationalism; I just abhor it. I think the world is too small for such things. We should all aim to be citizens of the world, sharing a planetary culture.

16: *Lydia Artymiw*

In some ways, I feel I grew up too fast. There was just never enough time to be a child. I'm grateful that things have worked out so well and that I'm happy now.

I was born in Philadelphia in September 1954. My parents are from the Ukraine and emigrated to the U.S. in 1952, as displaced persons. Ukranian was my first language.

My father studied violin but was injured during World War II and could not pursue a musical career. He became a pharmacist, but he never lost his love for music. My mother studied guitar, mandolin, and a little piano—in a popular way, just for fun. I have a younger brother, Orest, who is a gifted violinist.

I started ballet lessons at three and responded so strongly to the music that my parents bought me a little piano, and I began piano lessons at the Ukranian Music Institute the following year. My father came to each lesson, and practiced with me every day until I was thirteen. He would notice my errors, make suggestions, and remind me of what my teacher had said. From my experience and that of many musician friends, it seems essential that at least one parent devote him- or herself to helping a child in music—even a very gifted child can't gain the self-discipline required alone.

As a child, my life consisted of school and music. Once, I remember I wanted very much to go to a friend's birthday party, but my father insisted I stay home and practice, and go to bed early, since my piano lesson was the next morning. I was so upset! On the other hand, my father made clear from the start that unless I loved the piano, there was no reason to keep playing. And I did love it! I knew I could never give it up.

At the age of eight I began to study with Freida Pastor Berkowitz of the Curtis Institute of Music in Philadelphia. That year I played the recently discovered Haydn C major Piano Concerto with the Philadelphia Orchestra, after winning their children's auditions. Though I had played in public before, this was my first big concert.

I didn't have many friends as I grew up. Most of my schoolmates had little respect for piano playing. This was especially true from seventh to eleventh grades, when I was awarded a scholarship to the Stevens School, an elite and demanding private school. I got straight

Lydia Artymiw, the pianist, lives in Boston and was interviewed in New York City in November 1973 and November 1977.

A's and a very solid academic background, but socially life was difficult. Sports like hockey and ice skating were the big things, but I couldn't participate because I had to leave school early to go home and practice. Also, until recently, we had no TV at home, which shocked the other girls. "My God," they would say, "How can you live without a TV?" When I said, "Well, I have to practice the piano," they responded, "What? How boring! How awful! We feel so sorry for you." Our interests were so different that we didn't get along well.

Let me tell you about one special diversion from schoolwork and practicing. My father worked nights in a big pharmacy across from the Academy of Music. Musicians came in and out, and occasionally he went backstage to hear part of a concert. On Friday or Saturday nights I would sneak into the hall with an usher, who usually found me a seat. So I heard lots of concerts, and went backstage afterwards, autograph book in hand, to meet and speak with the artists. Those were my uninhibited days. These meetings really inspired me. I met many Philadelphia Orchestra members and some famous soloists, like Artur Rubinstein, a great musician and a wonderful man. He left a profound and lasting impression on me. I loved his playing—and he took the time to speak with me and signed my book. I've come to feel that communication backstage is as important as onstage.

My first encounter with Gary Graffman, my teacher since 1967, was backstage after he had played. By the time I was thirteen, it was time to change teachers. Mr. Graffman taught at the Philadelphia Musical Academy (now the Philadelphia College of the Performing Arts) and he accepted me as a student through this school while I still continued at Stevens. He came to Philadelphia once every two weeks or so from New York—what a change from one-hour weekly lessons to more infrequent two-hour sessions. I worked on longer pieces; my concentration span had to increase. And I realized that my father could no longer help me as much as before. Since he's a violinist, he couldn't really relate to everything that went on in advanced piano music, especially from a technical standpoint. Nonetheless, I still like him to be one of the first to hear me play a new piece. He is very sensitive and critical and can tell me whether or not I'm musically convincing.

Mr. Graffman is a very thorough teacher. For example, he's always insisted that each hand be able to function on its own. He would often ask me to play just the left hand, by itself. Independence of the hands is essential.

Mr. Graffman also believes very strongly—as do I—in orchestrating at the piano—that is, making the piano sound like different orchestral instruments, bringing out each line distinctly and coloring it in a special way.

Another Graffman rule-of-thumb is something that Artur Schnabel also stressed: Before you can execute a sound, you must have it firmly fixed in your mind. Then you must work at reproducing this sound at will.

Mr. Graffman always encouraged me to develop my own ideas. What is most important is that they be musically convincing. I believe very strongly in maintaining individuality in my playing. Although I no longer have regular lessons, I still play for Mr. Graffman occasionally.

When starting a new piece, learning the notes is only the first step. One should also investigate as much musical and historical background as possible in order to gain a deeper understanding of the work. I have spent much time comparing various editions and studying whatever facsimiles of the original manuscripts are available. Sometimes it's also important to examine the literary influences on a composer. For example, I read E. T. A. Hoffmann's novel *Kater Murr,* an acknowledged influence on Schumann's *Kreisleriana,* while working on the piece. The dramatic and romantic implications of this story provided me with vivid images which have a direct impact on my interpretation.

Since I was ten, I had been learning other aspects of music besides piano—ear-training, counterpoint, harmony. One needs more than just piano lessons—an understanding of form and harmony is necessary in order to formulate a total interpretation. So, when I entered the Philadelphia College of Performing Arts (PCPA) at the age of fifteen, I passed out of most of the theory requirements. Juilliard had accepted me, but living arrangements in New York City were a problem; going to PCPA, I lived at home, had my own piano, and could still continue to study with Mr. Graffman. As with high school, I graduated in three years.

Besides music, I took related art courses at the Philadelphia College of Art, across the street from PCPA. The Romantic period in the arts, the nineteenth century, intrigues me most. Romantic music

is very much a part of me. This includes anything from late Beethoven through Schubert, Schumann, Brahms, Chopin, plus Russian and Slavic composers like Dvorak, Tchaikovsky, and Rachmaninoff.

Schumann, by the way, is a perfect example of the completely
rounded artist, the kind I aspire to be. He was a pianist, a great composer, and author of many excellent essays. I myself enjoy writing. At
one period, it was poetry; then I kept a journal. As I get older, I
frequently find that there are things I must express in writing—not
only emotions, but musical ideas as well.

As for new music, PCPA is very strong in this. I took a twentieth-century music course which ended with the contemporary
scene. We discussed the multiplicity of areas composers are probing.
People like John Cage are experimenting with chance elements—
getting away from form altogether, or creating forms as they
happen—by playing around with pure sound colors. Then there is
electronic music and tapes, and layers of sound, and attempts to see
what kinds of sounds aside from the usual ones an instrument can
produce. If I have time, I am always ready to perform works by young
composers, to give them a chance.

Two teachers at PCPA, good friends of mine, are composers.
Theodore Antoniou, writes very intriguing music. I have played
some of his compositions. Then, in 1975, as part of the Bicentennial, I had the opportunity to commission a piece from my other
teacher-friend, Andrew Rudin, who studied with George Rochberg.
This work, *Museum Pieces*, is a set of short movements which are very
pianistic and were enthusiastically received when I played them at the
Kennedy Center.

Certainly, new music with strong ideas should be taken
seriously. It is tragic that it always takes years for new things to be accepted and understood. When you read the reviews Beethoven received for his late piano sonatas and string quartets, you realize he
was way ahead of his time. Though it seems ironic, often the composers who are accepted immediately and are popular during their
lifetimes fade out after half a century.

Until I was seventeen, I concentrated on solo pieces. The Marlboro Music Festival opened up a new world of repertory—chamber
music. I knew some Marlboro recordings; to me it was sort of a
dream place—a chamber music paradise with such greats as Pablo

Casals and Rudolf Serkin. I spent three summers there, the first in 1972. It was quite an experience. I learned many beautiful pieces. Playing chamber music is terribly important—it teaches you how to listen, and how to balance the sound of your instrument against others. A couple of summers ago, for example, I worked on Dvorak's *Dumky* Trio, a very difficult piece to perform because it's so sectional. It's based on Slavic folk tunes and dances. In the middle of this great trio, after tremendously rich writing for all three instruments, the piano has a simple melody that can be played with one finger; it's supposed to sound like a shepherd's flute. How do you project this simplicity? One of the main problems with the piano is achieving a singing tone, and getting one note to lead right into the next. When you play a note, and it begins to die, how do you continue the sound? Mr. Serkin has the gift of willing one note into the next—making a crescendo on a note with his body, so you *feel* that one note really connects with the next.

Playing together with older, more experienced musicians who had only been names before, I realized what wonderful dedicated human beings they are, with many ideas, but ready to listen to yours—to share and communicate. If you work with people you admire, they naturally leave their mark on the musical character traits developing inside you. Pablo Casals was an overwhelming influence. His presence and his whole being communicated warmth and love of music.

The Marlboro community is like a large family. I formed many close friendships there and had wonderful long talks with other musicians about music and personal life, about the problems of growing up, and about how to reconcile your career with the rest of your life.

I am indebted to Marlboro for more than musical reasons. It was there that I met David Grayson, one of the recording engineers, who later became my husband. David is a graduate student in musicology at Harvard and he has been a tremendous influence in my personal life as well as in my musical development. A relationship with someone and your musical career are both serious commitments, and I have learned how to balance them. It hasn't always been easy.

Marriage can interfere with a woman's career; that's why male performers predominate, I think. Then, if you're a woman muscian, people attach more importance to your appearance than if you're a man. People think it's cute and charming when a little blonde girl walks out on stage and plays; they've always made a big fuss over this, and I've grown to resent it. I should be evaluated by how I play and by what I have to say as a musician, not by my physical appearance.

Frequently, even reviewers, who are supposed to be impartial, get back at you if you're female. They assume for example that you don't have enough power to play difficult so-called "heavy" pieces. Once a critic wrote, "Ms. Artymiw is a wisp of a girl who *nevertheless* has great power." He would never have said such a thing about a man.

As for the question of masculine and feminine styles of playing—there are so many factors by which to judge a pianist's playing that I think these categories are meaningless. Some women are very percussive pianists, and have enormous strength in their fingers. And some men play lyrically and sensitively. Gender has nothing to do with it.

My age used to be another problem. People would say, "You're still so young." It was nice to be young, but at the same time I was not always taken as seriously as I should have been. I'm glad this is no longer a problem!

Getting concerts has not been difficult so far. I am now under management in both the U.S. and in Germany, have played recitals in major cities throughout the U.S., and will be playing with several important orchestras, including the Boston Symphony and the Cleveland Orchestra. I'm very pleased with how my career is progressing.

Sure I've had periods of great crisis. I imagine everyone does. I've wondered, "Why am I spending all my time playing the piano? Shouldn't I be doing something more constructive—something to help other people?" But I overcame this doubt when I realized that I was reaching others through my playing.

Nice things have happened to confirm this. In 1973, I was on a Music from Marlboro tour. I love traveling and meeting new people. When we played in Williamsburg, a group of students heard me rehearsing and encouraged a group of friends to come to the concert. I spoke to them afterward. They were very inspired by our concert and full of enthusiasm and questions. They wanted to know more about my musical activities and where to apply to study music. I really felt as if I'd gotten through to them. Too often, there is an artificial barrier between listeners and performers. We could overcome this by having performers get together with students at universities and schools, meeting after concerts, holding special sessions to share ideas.

Now I feel content with what I'm doing—personally fulfilled and socially useful. To put it abstractly—as the ancient Greeks realized—man strives for a certain measure of immortality. He wants to be remembered throughout time, to go beyond time's limitations. And art lasts. Music, great music, has been passed down through the years, grows even greater, and is always a new challenge—as are all great works of art. They give us a special, spiritual kind of satisfaction.

There are times when I think music is everything—when a certain phrase is so incredibly beautiful that, at that moment, it must be the most important thing in the world.

17: Doriot Anthony Dwyer

Before becoming first flutist of the Boston Symphony in 1952, I lived in many different places and had a wealth of musical experiences. I come from the Midwest, I've spent time on the West Coast, and I'm now on the East Coast. You might say I've been well positioned for comparisons.

I was born in Streator, Illinois, one hundred miles outside Chicago. As far as culture went, Chicago was everything. In the thirties, we would rattle off the hundred miles in an hour and a half, door-to-door, city traffic and all, going pretty fast over flat country. My family thought nothing of making the trip to Chicago for a concert—and coming home the same night. In my little town there was no music except the high school band and a city band in the park. Midwesterners are very band-oriented.

There were four children. We all played different instruments, and I remember that as youngsters we played at church all the time. Mother was a wonderful flutist. She was a tremendous example to me. Her flute playing had a unique singing quality which even now I try to emulate. She was almost completely self-taught, so she saw to it that I had the finest teachers around.

I didn't get deeply interested in the flute until I was eight or ten years old. As a small child, I had been forced to sit by the radio and listen to all the opera and symphony broadcasts, and all the children's concerts. I listened and listened every weekend for two whole days, and nothing seemed to jell. I was a hopeless case until the World's Fair came to Chicago. There were two symphony orchestras at the Fair—the Chicago and the Detroit. Mother was just dying for more live music and was entranced with having two orchestras around at one time. It was heaven for her to run up to Chicago for two concerts a day. That meant double concentration for me, and somehow with all that exposure something clicked. I remember it was the *William Tell Overture* that overwhelmed me. From then on, I was highly motivated to play, and to play well. I had one lesson during the summer of the Fair with the first flutist of the Detroit Symphony, but for the winter, mother sent me to Chicago to study with the first flutist of the Chicago Symphony.

I had a wonderful teacher in Mr. Liegl. He gave me thorough training in the interpretation of music, and I learned a lot of reper-

Doriot Dwyer, principal flutist of the Boston Symphony, was interviewed at Tanglewood in August 1975.

tory. He had me play certain works by Liszt that I have never yet played with an orchestra. He took me through the Beethoven symphonies. And all the time he told my father, "It's ridiculous for this girl to expect to have a career, because women just don't go very far in music—they can't." But he never compromised his standards, and he gave me everything I could take.

And I *did* plan for a career. I really prepared myself in a practical way. My exaggerated idea of the difficulties stood me in good stead. I *over*-prepared, practicing very hard. But without more performing experience, it was hard to make any headway. So I went to the Eastman School of Music in Rochester, New York, and during the summers, I went out to some of the smaller orchestras in the West, including the Oklahoma City Symphony Orchestra, where I symphony-apprenticed.

It was in Rochester that I first heard people like Gregor Piatigorsky. I never dreamed a cello could sound like that. I just couldn't move while he played; it was hard for me to breathe after I heard him. And Rachmaninoff used to play on the same concert series. I remember hearing so many great singers and instrumentalists. I was starved for concerts, never having lived in a center where all the big artists came. When I went to school at Eastman, I bought tickets for all three series and went to a concert every night. I heard everybody.

There were many women at Eastman who wanted to be professionals. There are always a lot of women in music schools. Most of them don't get anywhere, but then neither do many men. The vast majority of musicians of both sexes have to become teachers. But it was and to a large extent still is exceptionally difficult for women. It's not so bad for flutists and it's getting better for string players, because there is a big shortage of them. But it's very difficult for women brass players, who must confront a real male stronghold. Nevertheless, two of the early first-chair women were brass players. The first woman to hold a principal position in the U.S. played first horn in the Chicago Symphony during the second world war. She was there for about three years. In addition, there was Dorothy Ziegler, a first trombonist in the St. Louis Symphony for many years, who used to be my classmate. And there was a woman first flutist as well as first oboist in the Indianapolis Symphony. But of the major orchestras, it was the Chicago Symphony that pioneered.

My father supported me while I was in school. It was no hardship for him. Even though he didn't understand music too well, father encouraged me to move in a stable direction. He'd see that I had certain recordings, talk to my teacher and other musicians about the music world, and caution me about the hazards that lay ahead.

But heaven help me if I'd been a boy. In my youth, American businessmen, of whom my father was one, considered male performing musicians as effeminate men inappropriately pursuing the arts. That's changed in our time. More businessmen understand the need for art; they or their corporations support us a great deal more than before. But father supported me in my pursuit of a musical career because I was a daughter. My brothers were equally musical. One was a very good cellist—father really worried that he would become a musician.

Coincidentally, I am related to Susan B. Anthony. My maiden name was Anthony. I am something like a great-great-grand niece: her father and my great-grandfather were brothers. It was a big joke in our family that we were related to the person who got the vote for women. To the men she was some sort of freak. Mother, on the other hand, was very proud of this lineage and kept telling me, "Never mind what they say. She was a great woman." Then came the New Deal, and father was very hostile to Roosevelt. But FDR got out a postage stamp in honor of Susan B. Anthony, and my father was a great stamp collector, so what could he do? He bought the stamp and became proud of her.

When I finished at Eastman, I went to Washington D.C. to play second flute in the National Symphony. The war was on. There were a lot of women around and I remember going out to lunch regularly with six or eight male colleagues and getting terrible stares from envious women. Many of them were lonely. But those of us in the National were not. They took many women and kids straight out of school because at that time it was a training orchestra, not nearly as good as it is now. During this period in Washington, the Navy Band Orchestra had some of the finest young musicians in the country; they were there to be saved from being cannon fodder. To be in a Washington marching band was then a great honor and a great niche. We played on Thursday nights and so did the Navy Band Orchestra. They had wonderful soloists. After our respective concerts, we'd get together and talk over our conductors and our music. It was very stimulating and lots of fun. I remember an Italian restaurant owner who was an aged but fearless French horn player. He and his daughter did their own versions of operas for the guests far into the night. He'd play the tenor or baritone parts on his French horn. Sometimes we'd stay there till three in the morning.

In the National I played under big name conductors, like Antal Dorati, for the first time.

When I started out, many conductors were wild. Some were real brutes. They were brought up in the Toscanini tradition, but like so many disciples of brilliant masters, they didn't live up to their mentors' genius. Musicians could stand Toscanini's quirks because they really respected him as a musician, but quite a few conductors were both cruel and incompetent. So for musicians who had to play under them, there was little reward and life was hard. Some of the arbitrariness bordered on sadism. The New York Philharmonic had a new conductor back then who fired half the orchestra, more or less at whim, it seemed. That was routine. Management couldn't get away with that today. The union is too strong and the musicians are much more highly educated than they used to be. Nowadays conductors behave themselves.

We all thought the big thing was to play in New York. In order to do that you had to reside there for six months. At one point our first flutist in the National wanted his union card in New York and went there to live for half a year. While he was gone, I played first flute—a very good experience. During this time, the orchestra played for a while at Watergate. To me, the name means something rather different from what it connotes to most Americans. We gave concerts on a barge exactly where the Watergate Inn is now. The musicians sat on the barge, and listeners would sit on the sidewalk or in stadium seats on the land. Our audience grew when boats draw up around the barge. It was lovely!

But when the regular first flutist came back, I decided to go to New York. Since I had to wait half a year before I could look for steady work, I went to Columbia and had a fine old time. I was dating a doctor and thought, "I know nothing about science. I'd better learn some." I took botany and zoology, enjoyed them and got good grades. I didn't have much to do directly with the music department at Columbia, but I heard a lot about it from friends. Many composers I knew from Eastman ended up at Columbia when I did.

Wherever I go, I know composers; they always seem to be the wittiest, liveliest and most creative people around.

What excited them—and me—about the Columbia department was its interest in opera. Now, the U.S. is terribly backward as far as opera goes. We have marvelous singers who usually must go to Europe to get experience and that's awfully sad. L.A. was another haven of operatic activity; when I was there they had a first-class workshop to train singers, which was unheard of elsewhere. It was run by Carl Ebert, the well-known opera director. I remember someone asking Ebert if it was important to do opera in English and he said, "I don't think it's important—it's essential." Yes the music sounds better in the native language, but it's so important for the public to know what's going on. More people will take to opera in a meaningful way. And we need a more musically sophisticated public, people who don't attend operas primarily as social events.

Anyway, at Columbia they were presenting American opera— Virgil Thomson's *The Mother of Us All,* an opera by Douglas Moore, and lots of others. They had many premieres. Out of that department emerged a composer who specializes in opera, which is rare these days—Jack Beeson. Jack was my classmate at Eastman. Today Indiana University and several other universities have opera concentrations. Yale has finally started a vocal department; Phyllis Curtin, a fine singer, is involved there. It's all rather encouraging. I haven't played a great deal in opera orchestras, but I've played some and loved it. I vastly prefer the symphony orchestra as a full-time occupation but opera is exciting too and the pit is a very good training ground for young musicians.

The first musical job I had in New York, which the union got me, was the typical gig they gave women musicians—marching in a Chinese New Year's Day parade, alongside a most distinguished female flutist who was also having trouble getting jobs. We went all the way up Fifth Avenue to 72nd Street. That was my only job in the city until I got my residency. Then I worked at CBS, playing on a radio show, which caused a big scandal. Many people were up in arms that CBS had hired a woman musician. Somehow a CBS stockholder managed to get me an audition with the contractor, who had to admit I could play. So I got some short-term employment on a lovely show—all serious music. We had a small orchestra with about six players; they amplified the strings to sound like a whole orchestra, and there was one flute. I went regularly to listen to the CBS Symphony rehearsals and concerts. My friend Julius Baker, who is now first flutist of the New York Philharmonic, was a member of the CBS Symphony.

After living in New York for a while, I got sick of the city and not being able to find any serious, steady work. Then somebody called and asked if I'd like to go on tour with a fine ballet company, run by the legendary Leonide Massine, one of those people from the golden age of ballet. Well, I am a balletomane and I thought, "What an opportunity to see this man in action." Besides, I was very happy to tour all over the country. This was right after the war, before the big dance companies reassembled. We had eight dancers, four male four female, and a little orchestra. The whole company hardly filled one railroad car. There was no scenery and only a few costumes. The show was called "Ballet Russe Highlights." It was a series of great solo dances from the classical ballet repertory. This lovely little operation went bankrupt after two months because most of the country was then indifferent to ballet. Today such a program would be mobbed. But at the time it was too concentrated for the American public, who wanted circuses and acrobats and plenty of scenery.

There we were, stranded in Texas. I got money for a railroad ticket and went to California. Friends and relatives in Los Angeles had urged me for years and years to come on out. They said there was a big killing to make there and that was true. But the film studios didn't interest me very much—movie music was really only watered down classical. I *was* interested in the Philharmonic, though, and in Los Angeles itself. I had wanted to go West all my life. I got a steady job immediately, which was most unusual, but it was connected with the University of Southern California which did not come under union jurisdiction; I was paid by the school. I didn't know many musicians at USC but I later learned that they were all clustered around Schönberg. I hadn't yet gotten into modern music except in school where I learned a few sonatas, like the one by Hindemith. At the time, Hindemith was almost a dirty word. He was one of those horrible sounding "modern" composers, I was told. But when I learned the Hindemith Sonata I felt that there was indeed something to be said for contemporary music.

The University job was a very funny one. It could only have existed in Southern California. A 73-year-old oil millionaire had almost completely endowed the USC school of music. He even had part of his home taken and planted in the university as a sort of museum to himself. In return, the administration allowed him to use the school auditorium every morning, Monday through Friday, for his chamber music sessions. For these he hired twenty young women to surround him and play. It was like having an old-fashioned patron, in the sense that he paid us very well. This man, our "sponsor," started to learn the cello at age 70; he was miserable at it. His idea of playing a solo was holding one note while we did runs and trills around him. He "played" the Saint-Saens cello concerto by starting the first note and letting the violins play on from there. Sometimes he wouldn't quite hit a low note, but one of our bass players, would supply the right pitch. After doing one piece this way, he'd take a bow, and wouldn't appear for the rest of the program, when we'd play arrangements of symphonies. The ensemble director was the captain of our patron's yacht and was quite musical considering his nautical background. We rehearsed every morning and gave one concert a week in a public school or some other institution. It was a depressing job with comic aspects.

In due time I became soloist and first flutist at the Carmel Bach festival. That meant great music and lots to do. Afterward I just couldn't go back to USC. The same summer there was a vacancy for second flute in the Los Angeles Philharmonic. I tried out and got the position! Alfred Wallenstein was the conductor. He wasn't really too tyrannical, but he did use terrible language. I have rarely heard a conductor swear so much. He would continuously shout, "For Christ's sake, do this or that." One time we played so well he couldn't get mad and all that came out was, "Well, let's do it again, just for *security*'s sake." Somebody turned around and remarked, "He's become an atheist!"

Wallenstein wasn't as mean as Arthur Rodzinski—who was also a good conductor, as I discovered when I played at the Hollywood Bowl. The Bowl concerts were the first big summer musical festival in this country where international musicians came and played. For some complicated reason, the Bowl Association didn't hire the Philharmonic as such, but employed Philharmonic players on a freelance basis. One summer there was an opening for first flute; I auditioned for Bruno Walter and got the job.

Now I played with wonderful conductors—besides Rodzinski—

Eugene Ormandy, William Steinberg, Erich Leinsdorf. I played in the Bowl for many summers; it was great fun. Also I got an exciting radio job on the Standard Oil Symphony Hour, where again, a lot of people from the Philharmonic were hired. I was first flute for several years and loved it; Bruno Walter also conducted that orchestra. After joining the Philharmonic, everything opened up. The situation for women in that orchestra was never too bad; there were always three or four others. Perhaps that's because it wasn't considered a major orchestra. I got a lot of good experience, anyway.

And the musical situation in L.A. fascinated me. On the one hand, L.A. had the first big summer music festival, which had been going for 25 or 30 years before I got there. And there were a lot of good musicians around. But not only did the taxi drivers not know about the L.A. Philharmonic, but musicians in the film studios looked down on orchestra players because we earned so little and they made big money. It was always money. And yet, when they had something really difficult to play in the studios, like the *Nutcracker Suite* (don't laugh—it's not so easy), they'd hire Philharmonic people. For that reason I did quite a bit in the studios, which was lucrative.

Then, we had a wonderful chamber music series in L.A., "Evenings on the Roof," now called "Monday Evenings." The roof concerts were started by an industrial architect who was putting an addition onto his house. After he finished the first floor, the roof looked so pretty that he never finished the second floor. He decided instead that the roof would be a nice place to have concerts. He loved music and his wife was a pianist who wanted a chance to perform contemporary music. So they started the "Evenings on the Roof" literally on their roof.

It was a musician's paradise, a place where music was made by musicians for musicians: musicians made up a large part of the audience; our purpose was to play for each other. The series got so popular that we had to hire a hall and secure a little financial support. The musicians were paid all of $10 a concert. That's been raised to maybe $25 or $30 now, but it's still a pittance. One does this sort of thing *con amore*. And the spiritual rewards were well worth it; the evenings were like my second college. I met composers as well as performers and encountered many new ideas. Also I gave several concerts that I put together myself, which included some Mozart quartets

which were a delight to play. The programs usually consisted of unusual or little heard music, mostly new, but also older music. It's interesting about the relationship between very old and very new music;
to this day I find that most avant-garde composers are extremely well-
versed in old music and their own music and have a marked disdain
for Romantic music.

The Evenings introduced a lot of important twentieth-century
music. When I arrived on the scene, they had already finished a
major Schönberg festival, when hardly anybody in Boston had even
begun to perform Schönberg. When I came to Massachusetts in
1952, the Evenings were celebrating the 25th anniversary of their first
performance of a work by Schönberg; they were doing repeat performances of *Pierrot Lunaire* in L.A. and it had still not been played in
Boston. When Leinsdorf did the piece seven years later at Tanglewood, it created quite a stir. L.A. certainly is a strange city, full of
contradictions and surprises. Even though the East Coast is the home
of music in the U.S., I always remember L.A., crazy as it is, as a
place where a lot of new and innovative things go on.

In the summer of 1952 I heard that the first flute position in the
Boston Symphony had opened up. There wasn't much else doing
that summer. So I trained hard for that audition, practicing well into
the night every night. Orchestras have what they call standard repertory—all the Beethoven symphonies; all the best known Mozart and
Haydn; some music by French, Russian, and Italian composers;
some Bach. You have to master them all. Back then the conductor
usually knew in advance which performer he wanted for a given position. He might go through two or three auditions, but not the thirty
or sixty they're now required to do by the union.

Charles Münch, who was then conductor of the BSO, did
something very unusual for his day. He insisted that he would not
hire anybody on reputation alone. As a rule conductors inquired of
their managers or contractors, "Who's the best musician you can
get?" Then the order was, "Go get him." For example, I don't believe there was any auditioning for the NBC Symphony. But Mr.
Münch would have none of that. When the first flute position came
up, everybody had to audition on an equal basis. Consequently some
very famous flutists stayed away. Their reasoning was, "If we're not
selected it won't do us any good." And they felt it was beneath their
dignity to try out. Take those people who had played on radio for

twenty years in the New York Philharmonic or one of the radio orchestras—why should they audition for the Boston Symphony? Why go to Boston anyway? That attitude eliminated a number of competitors.

My audition in July for Mr. Münch was very difficult, but I was really ready for it. Münch had guest conducted for the L.A. Philharmonic and I had liked him very much. I thought to myself, "It's going to be all right. I know what he's like." But I didn't think I'd actually get the job. I just knew that if I was ready the audition would be a pleasure. And I was prepared. Mr. Münch had a Ladies Day for women flutists. It was a whim of his because so many women had applied for the job. This usually didn't matter; most orchestras wouldn't even answer women's letters. Many of mine went unanswered. I had thought that maybe I'd just stop playing in orchestras after the Boston audition. Why? Because I'm a *first* flutist; I have the soul of a first flutist. I wasn't going to play second flute all my life. Yet I had no high expectations of successfully storming a male stronghold like the BSO. They had thought of every excuse in the world to exclude women—excuses I never dreamed existed.

But I was thrilled with the opportunity to try. My audition was very long, maybe an hour. I realize that sounds unbelievable. Most auditions last fifteen minutes or, at most, half an hour. When mine was over, I was asked if I could come back next week to play again. I refused, saying, "You've heard me play and I can't just take off and leave my own orchestra again. What would you think of me if I kept taking time off from your orchestra to play at the other end of the country?" They offered to pay my fare, but I wouldn't yield. I felt they had heard enough of me. Evidently they had; the decision took two months, but I got the job!

In L.A., they were most surprised that a *second* flute would become a first flute any place. In musical circles that produced a big scandal. There is or was a caste system such that second players never become firsts. I broke that barrier and I enjoyed it very much.

Münch honored me by hiring me and treated me well when I got to Boston, but he also was very hard on me. He made me work hard. I don't resent that; I think I learned a lot by it. Fellow musicians in Boston were no great problem. Not that they particularly wanted women in the orchestra, but when it was an accomplished fact, they behaved wonderfully well. The board welcomed me with open arms. The local critics, however, didn't see how a woman could handle the job. That didn't surprise me. I too had my doubts since my predecessor, Georges Laurent, was a great flutist. Laurent himself came to my audition and encouraged me. I had the utmost respect for his playing and didn't expect to fill his shoes, but I had something to say and I stood on that.

Since then, it's been pretty smooth sailing. But there are things that never got solved for me. After a year in Boston, I got married. My husband was a doctor. We were divorced nine years later. I have one daughter. It's extremely difficult to be a family person and a professional musician. I am very happy to have a child, though, and I consider her the biggest miracle of my life, an even greater miracle than being a member of the Boston Symphony. She's a terrific kid who's naturally not too interested in music. A lot of musicians' children are that way. They see all the practicing that goes on. She really is musical, has many artistic instincts, and is also very good in science and math and sports—an all-around type. I'm sure she'll do very well at whatever she goes into.

I suppose I paved the way for other women players, but change was in the offing anyway. It is probably easier for women to get into the BSO since I got there. Starting next fall, we'll have ten. Originally, as far as the wide world was concerned, the shock was to have a woman in such a responsible position. The *inside* shock, as I said, was that a second flutist, regardless of sex, had gone on to first flute. To get into a major symphony is difficult in and of itself, and I know how many *males* not to speak of females, haven't made it—so I have a broad range of sympathy for anyone trying to get in. But of course I'm glad that my success has helped other women. L.A. has a woman flutist, Montreal has one. Lois Schaffer who is in the BSO now was in New York as first flutist at the New York City Opera after having been in the Chicago Symphony. In the New York Philharmonic their second flute player and assistant first is a woman, Renée Siebert. The situation is also better for string players. It's possible that male homosexuals in music helped each other and made it harder for women. But this is a problem in every art, not just music.

All along I have taught, at Pomona College in L.A., at the New England Conservatory, at the Berkshire Music Center in Tanglewood and now at Boston University. I love to teach. And, from my exposure to students, I feel pretty good about the coming generation of musicians, and music lovers. Are audiences getting any more sophisticated? Well, they are certainly getting larger, and when that happens, there gets to be more of a sophisticated nucleus. There are many more symphony orchestras around the country than there used to be. In some ways, the music business is prospering. Even though very little new music is played by big institutions like orchestras and opera companies, you hear 100 percent more now than before. For various anniversaries the Boston Symphony has commissioned new works. And of course at the Berkshire Music Center at Tanglewood we have a contemporary music festival every summer. I always find new music a challenge.

It's been a busy life. When I first got to Boston, I must have played a recital a month somewhere or other, besides my orchestra commitments. Last year I had a series of three recitals in New York at Carnegie Recital Hall, and I'm doing the series again this year with different programs. It amuses me that people say, "Oh yes, we heard you play at your contemporary music concerts." Well, I played other music too, but the new pieces apparently stuck out. I love to play solos with orchestras and I do quite a few with the Boston Symphony. Walter Piston wrote a concerto for me, and I have the Walter Piston chair in the orchestra. That means somebody contributed a certain sum of money to the symphony which enabled it to name a chair for one player. Such a chair is often named in memory of some relative. But this contributor told the management, "We want a chair for the first flutist and you pick a name for it." They knew I admired Walter Piston, and that I was great friends with him. So why not call it the Piston chair? He's written copious flute music, all of which I love and have played at one time or another. He wrote two versions of his flute concerto for me, and I've played them both.

I'm doing fine, and I think women performers are doing better than ever. Will women ever flourish as conductors and composers? I hope so, but it's very difficult for them. Much of the problem lies with the women themselves. Granted exceptions, there probably has to be another generation of liberated women before the true female creators come forward. I have a friend who teaches performers. When I told him how talented some of them sounded, his rejoinder was, "I don't use that word anymore because, with the right tools and the right attitude, almost everybody is talented." If women are brought up with more respect from their parents it will show. Now, to my father, I was always a woman, something different; any time I had a good idea, he'd say, "You know, she really thinks!"—as if that were so remarkable. When great groups of women are treated as whole people, eventually they will become "talented," so to speak, or their talents will become manifest, their creative ideas will have a place. Let's say you're a writer with an article to write and you just can't think about it because you're so busy moving from place to place. What you have to do from moment to moment absolutely interferes with the creative process. Then, when you are all settled and your house is in order, you get a free flow of ideas. Well, I think that's what will happen with the next generation of women. As soon as their houses are in order.

Of course, there are many women composers right now, many more than before. Then again, there were some in the past too. For instance Felix Mendelssohn's sister Fanny wrote beautiful songs. She wasn't as prolific as Felix and maybe not as good, but she did compose. I'm sure archivists will find more and more women like her. As for conductors, the problem is perfectly obvious. All the fine orchestras in this country are essentially male orchestras. To have a woman cracking the whip over them is not yet accepted. Some day it will be. I have great hopes for women!

18: Kurt Loebel

Photo by Robert Newman

*L*et me start by saying I may at times sound cynical and disillu-sioned with my professional experiences. Perhaps my current attitude is a reaction to the over-idealistic views of my youth. Of course, I will always continue to fight the negative tendencies common to all professions. With maturity one comes to accept the fact that social change is slow but inevitable.

I guess you could say I'm a union man. For several years I was chairman of the Orchestra Committee of the Cleveland Orchestra. I joined the American Federation of Musicians in the early 1940s, soon after arriving in New York from Vienna. Without joining the union, I soon discovered, it would have been impossible for me to work as a musician in the United States. I have been active in orchestra affairs ever since I joined the Cleveland Orchestra in 1947–48.

There was no musicians union when I was a youngster in Vienna. My real problem in that environment was being Jewish; even before Hitler, the idea of ever landing a steady job in music was more or less unthinkable. That specific problem of the Jewish musician in Vienna has always existed and probably *still* exists. Those few Jews who did succeed, with some exceptions, converted to Catholicism. Gustav Mahler and Bruno Walter are famous examples. There was no way a Jew could join the Vienna Philharmonic, let's say, which was and still is a state-supported organization.

I started to study the violin as a child because I loved music and decided early on to become a professional musician. When I was about 14, both my family and friends said, "You're very unrealistic; as a Jew, you're not going to get into a good orchestra. Unless you become a virtuoso soloist like Fritz Kreisler or a first-class chamber music player, how are you going to make a living? Do something else!"

I said, "But I love music and that's what I want to go into." So I went to music school. I was 16 when the Nazis marched into Austria, and my studies were interrupted, of course. Like so many others I had to flee to save my life.

I came to New York alone and penniless. I brought my parents over six months later. I had many odd jobs to scrape together a living—peddling ties, washing dishes in a drugstore, working for

Kurt Loebel, a first violinist in the Cleveland Orchestra, was interviewed in New York City in February 1976.

Western Union. At first it was a matter of sheer survival. Eventually I spent two years in Bridgeport, Connecticut working in a factory. After I was on my feet a bit, I saw that it was necessary to continue my studies in order to be able to work as a musician. Music was the only thing I had studied intensively and I knew I wanted to pursue it as a career. But I had not completed my schooling in Vienna and was not really equipped to be a professional when I got here. With the encouragement and support of American friends I auditioned and was accepted as a scholarship student at the Juilliard School of Music in New York.

While still a student, I joined the musicians union. I remember going up to the Union hall in 1942 or 43. I had led a sheltered life in Europe. Here I found a dog-eat-dog, commerical, non-artistic, rough atmosphere. It was noticeable right away, even when I simply went up to pay my dues. It was clear that in order to find a job, you had to know somebody, to be aquainted with guys who could pull the right strings. Knowing a good contractor meant you'd get some kind of work playing somewhere, even if not in a symphony. I was familiar with this situation; personal connections counted just as much in Europe as in America. Maybe more. But I was better off here, where conditions were essentially free and at least the Jewish question was irrelevant.

I wasn't in school long before I was drafted. Since I spoke German I was placed in the U.S. Army Intelligence Service, serving in Europe as interrogator of German prisoners. After my discharge from the Army, I had a couple of lucky breaks. First I got a job playing in the Dallas Symphony, which at that time had a 22-week season. After two seasons, when I was 26, I auditioned for George Szell and got a job playing first violin in the Cleveland Orchestra. Szell had just taken over in Cleveland and as a result there was quite a turnover of musicians.

I soon found out that the symphony musician is part of a small minority within a union. In most American cities a large percentage of the membership consists of part-time musicians, who play occasional jobs but make their living primarily in another profession. This distribution of membership has a profound effect on union policies, locally as well as nationally. Thus any effort to make significant changes in the union structure on behalf of those few in the symphonic field is difficult. Our ranks are too small. How can such a small proportion of the total membership do anything in its interest, without support from other members? In Cleveland, two members of the Symphony have run for election to the union executive board, hoping to represent the problems of the symphony musician. Both were defeated.

Until approximately 10 years ago, the symphony contract was negotiated between the orchestra management and the union leadership, without serious participation by the orchestra members. When discussions on working conditions, salary, the conductor's rights, and the duties of the musician, were completed, the orchestra members were informed by a notice on the bulletin board to sign their contracts by a certain date. Aside from personal negotiations about conditions not stated in the master agreement between union and management, there was no way for the orchestra members to be involved in negotiations. When I joined the orchestra we had no ratification of contract, no strike vote or other alternative. The contract was settled and we could take it or leave it. This was standard procedure all around the country and still exists in a few cities.

When it occured to musicians that milkmen and others ratify their contracts, they became more militant. This took place on a local level as well as nationally through the formation of the International Conference of Symphony and Opera Musicians (ICSOM), who organized themselves as a separate organization, because they felt that the American Federation of Musicians did not fully understand and represent their unique problems. In recent years ICSOM has become a conference within the Union working with the Union leadership for common goals. In the 1950s our aim was contract ratification. With the enactment of the Landrum-Griffin Act [in 1959, which regulated internal union affairs] we hired a lawyer and started a lawsuit to give us the right to ratify. Not only did the court rule that the Landrum-Griffin act did not spell out such a right, but I was one of 10 musicians who served on orchestra committees to be taken up by the union on disloyalty charges. Eventually the lawsuits were settled out of court. Although we in Cleveland pioneered in this matter, we were among the last to win the battle of contract ratification and also gain recognition of the orchestra committee as participants at the negotiating table. Within the last 10 years it has become standard procedure to hire a labor lawyer to assist the orchestra members and the union in negotiations. Philip Sipser, legal counsel for

ICSOM, has been involved in negotiations for most major orchestras as well as opera companies. We now share all the labor problems common to other professions. Historically speaking, these are new to the musical profession.

I think that some of the resistance to gains for symphony members is easily understood when we consider that we who can earn some kind of living in classical music are a minority. The generation gap rears its ugly head when some old timer says: "You guys are unreasonable! You make wild demands. You want it in your contract that if you travel so many miles it must be by plane! You want it stipulated that there must be no more than so many miles of travelling a day prior to a concert!" The musician who made his living 50 years ago might say: "You guys have rocks in your heads. We used to sit in drafty trains, without sleepers, and ride 12 hours straight!" which, incidentally, even the Cleveland Orchestra still did in the 1950s. There were times when we sat up all night, got off the train and then played two concerts. Even today, some orchestras might travel from 9 A.M. to 6 P.M. on account of bad weather conditions, and play a Carnegie Hall concert that night. Some orchestra contracts prevent this from happening, some do not. The audience is unaware of such problems, and will surely make no allowances for them, nor will the critics be merciful.

When, 10 years ago, people would ask us what we wanted, our answer was basically that we wanted to make a living wage ($10,000–$15,000 a year at that time) and get vacations, Blue Cross insurance, protection and redress in case of dismissal, severance pay, and a pension. Only recently have these gains been made to varying degrees—sometimes against opposition from within the orchestras. When I first joined the Cleveland Orchestra in 1948, the only orchestra in the country providing a semblance of full-time work was the Boston Symphony—and perhaps the Philadelphia Orchestra and the New York Philharmonic. At that time we were paid less for our work in the summer than in the winter. Management contended: "You don't play under George Szell then; you have less pressure; you give pop concerts; therefore you should earn less." Our weekly pay might have been $140 in the winter and only $115 in the summer. Our answer was: "We have to eat in the summer just as we do in the winter. We pay the same rent and use the same utilities." It took us years to get that concept across.

My first impression of James Petrillo, the powerful head of the AFM for many years, was positive. I felt "Here is a man trying to help musicians!" Over the years, as I learned more about the profession, I saw some of his limitations. He was more concerned with bread-and-butter issues than quality-of-life issues. Nonetheless, I do think Petrillo helped musicians a lot. He was certainly aggressive, and was a spearhead of progress on many fronts. There's no doubt about that. It was under Petrillo that for the first time some royalties from recordings went to musical organizations and eventually to the players as well. He fought hard for the musician, but by the mid-1950s his type of fight was becoming outmoded. By then we had much greater expectations of what place musicians should have in society.

The Union has sometimes been blamed for the disappearance of live music from the radio, but I don't know whether any Union leader could have prevented it. I would put equal responsibility on management. Take the discontinuance of the NBC Symphony, which was created specifically for Toscanini. When the great maestro died, NBC let the orchestra fall apart. Even before that there were big battles with radio stations over how much live music should be broadcast. The NBC Orchestra was followed by the Symphony of the Air. When it died after a short existence, so did live quality music on American radio. The union could have done little to prevent it.

Nowadays, when I hear the phrase "NBC Orchestra" on the Johnny Carson show ("Here's Johnny and the NBC Orchestra") I still see Toscanini at Studio 8H in New York. I am sure the Union opposed the death of the NBC Symphony Orchestra. Management probably considered union demands excessive and thought it better (or at any rate cheaper) to have no live musicians. But how could one believe that argument, when they spent millions on all kinds of inferior programs?

In any case, the result was a net reduction in the number of opportunities for musicians. A great many worked in radio stations and I believe by the time World War II ended, so did part of their livelihoods. Lately live bands have enjoyed something of a resurgence. They were also killed off in part by the recording business. It used to be that if people wanted to hear music they had to attend live performances. Now, with records, tapes, and a host of electronic devices, you can listen to music without leaving your home. For dances or parties, people use records instead of live bands. To what degree can we call this "progress"? There can be no doubt that music now reaches many more people, especially in isolated parts of the world, and that electronic means are often used for good ends. One might argue that recently concert attendance has been up and thus records have helped the performing artist. But we also feel a backlash from the record-buying concertgoer, because the gimmickry and splicing of tapes make for a sound quality and perfection impossible to achieve in live performances. Furthermore the communication between artist and audience cannot be re-created on recordings. One hopes that the positive aspects of the Electronic Age will outweigh the disadvantages.

Many things have changed since I entered the profession. One of the most striking is that the conductor's dictatorial powers, in some cases involving abuses and temperamental outbursts bordering on cruelty, have been steadily reduced; by now there are few Szell-Toscanini-Reiner-Stokowski types on the podium. I have been told that in the 1930s a man might show up for rehearsal one morning and find his chair missing. He would ask: "Where is my chair?" his colleagues would reply, "Mr. Stokowski has removed it." I have witnessed similar flareups by certain conductors; however, such arbitrariness is no longer customary. Nowadays there are steps that can be taken against unwarranted behavior on the part of the conductor as well as the musicians. Both are union members and can be brought up on charges. There are clauses in the contract dealing with the use of abusive language. Tyrannical behavior is out of fashion. This is not so much the result of organized efforts for change, but a reflection of our time and our psychological orientation against extreme authority. Toscanini would scream and break batons, Krips would throw the score onto the stage, and some conductors would walk out, threatening to cancel the concert. Permissiveness as a reaction to autocracy has taken over—in some cases too much perhaps, and is on occasion counterproductive. But the situation today is definitely more humane and the absence of tyranny need not be an artistic detriment. There were always conductors who succeeded in getting good results without resorting to extreme tactics. Dmitri Mitropolous and Ernest Ansermet seemed gentle human beings who didn't order people around at whim, and they got pretty good results. There may not be as many superstar conductors as there used to be—but I think this

is largely due to the loss of almost a generation of potential con-
ductor-giants during World War II.

A man like Szell insisted on absolute power on and off the podium. At first we couldn't budge him, but eventually he became
more flexible and willing to listen to certain requests. In some areas
he was the musicians' friend. He saw that increasing salaries and
fringe benefits and lengthening the season were artistically beneficial
steps, and in his interest as well as ours. Thus many of the orchestra
committee's activities had his blessing. You see, the better the conditions, the better one's choice of good and well-educated players.

Over the past half century or so, the profile of an orchestra
musician has changed enormously. In the old days musicians were
not necessarily college-trained, often coming out of conservatories
where there was little emphasis on academic subjects. Today the
younger people in our orchestras are college graduates. In most instances they are the products of a university or a top conservatory,
where substantial academic courses are required. It is perfectly true
that some superior instrumentalists may have chosen to neglect academics somewhat in order to concentrate on their playing, but that is
the exception rather than the rule. I would like to think that a musician combines intellect and emotion and that therefore the education
is necessary. Fritz Kreisler, who was a mathematician and a Greek
scholar, is more typical than a few great artists of the past, who let
themselves be guided exclusively by instinct and native talent.

While some things on the musical scene have changed during
my lifetime, others have remained almost the same. Some of our best
conductors still tend to be European-born or trained, mainly because
opportunities for conducting in the U.S. are comparatively restricted.
Germany, for instance, has an opera house, possibly two symphony
orchestras, and a radio orchestra even in medium-sized cities, thus
providing several conductors with work. A city of comparable size in
the U.S. is unlikely to have an opera house, and may not have a
symphony, let alone a conservatory.

Musicians, on the other hand, tend to be native Americans.
When many great musicians were forced to leave Europe in the
1930s, this country experienced a tremendous influx of outstanding
talent, and as a result American students no longer needed to go to
Europe to be trained.

Women and blacks have made minor gains in the serious music

field in my time. For many years the Cleveland Orchestra had only one principal woman player—our harpist. That was then standard procedure all over the country. The Boston Symphony's acceptance of Doriot Anthony Dwyer as first flutist caused a mini-revolution. Perhaps it started a trend. If Boston had a woman first flutist, there was no reason not to have women in the Cleveland Orchestra. Szell was at first reluctant to hire women, but he was intelligent enough to realize if qualified women were catching on in the United States, he should go along with the times. In 1977 there were 12 women in the Cleveland orchestra. New York has [at least] 4, Chicago 9, Philadelphia 8, and Boston 10.

The picture is not as bright for black musicians. When Szell hired a black cellist many years ago, he took a poll of the musicians' reactions. The players overwhelmingly approved; however, to this day we have only that one black player. In the past there have been legal battles over racial problems in the New York Philharmonic and San Francisco symphonies. In the fall of 1977 the only black member of the New York Philharmonic resigned, stating that he had been in the orchestra for 15 years and was "tired of being a symbol." He also stated that the problem was not a local one, "but part of a national social problem." I believe prejudice is still at work, because there *are* qualified black musicians around.

On the economic side, the lot of symphony musicians has been improving in the major cities, but it is still meager in many smaller although no less important communities. Of course our persistent feeling is that we are underpaid in relation to the plumber, the lawyer, the doctor, and to certain other professionals whose training period might be shorter. The battles involve the cry for more money. Today's salaries in major orchestras are adequate for subsistence; however, that was not the case until a short time ago. In the early 1960s one of our outstanding players sold Fuller brushes during the summer to support his family, while others drove taxis and buses, worked in department stores, sold insurance, and so on. Then as now we fill out our incomes by teaching.

In a society where material values are so important, they can't help but penetrate even a non-profit organization like the symphony orchestra. Depending on the player, the conductor, and the orchestra, a first-chair soloist might earn twice as much as a section string player, who usually gets union scale. Sometimes there are premiums on certain chairs. Along with the increased monetary income come psychic rewards, like attention in the press. Now, added responsibilities and exposed positions fully justify the salary differentials. But the built-in economic and sometimes social distinctions create a conflict situation which can never be entirely overcome, even when everyone's good will is at hand. Of course all orchestra members realize they have much in common—working schedule, travel conditions, and so on. But you cannot always expect a saintly attitude toward group solidarity on the part of the principals, because they have to consider their own self-interest, prestige, and survival in a competitive soloists' market. Naturally, this has some unfortunate results. And when a large segment of the orchestra is somewhat anonymous, a certain military atmosphere comes into play; for most of us individuality must be sacrificed for the sake of the musical product. As you can see, a sensitive and complex interplay is at work between conductor and orchestra and among the players themselves; the danger of dehumanization is ever-present.

Then, orchestra members still have little say in artistic decisions. In the last few years artistic advisory committees have been formed throughout the country to voice players' opinions to the conductor, management, and trustees. One important function of such committees has been participation in selection of conductors, but there are many situations over which we have no control. Suppose we have to perform a work with insufficient rehearsals, because the budget does not allow for overtime. If the performance turns out well, the additional personal effort on the part of the players and the conductor is neither recognized nor rewarded. If the performance turns out badly, the performers are blamed and feel imposed upon and frustrated, since they have no opportunity to explain the situation to the public or the press. It is maddening to have no control over such matters—especially for those players, often strings, who did not originally plan to play in an orchestra, but spent many years on solo and chamber music repertory hoping to make their livings outside an orchestra. Wind and brass players usually plan on an orchestra job, knowing that a solo career probably can't support a family. Anyway, there are fewer winds and brasses in an orchestra, so each one stands out more than an individual string player.

Perhaps the greatest frustration for all of us is that we have no voice and no choice: We are told what to play, when to play, how to play, under which conductor, and under what conditions. In American orchestras, the musical director has the power, as opposed to some European symphonies which are self-governing. Which system is preferable? Each has inherent advantages and disadvantages. The best we can hope for here is a reasonable balance.

If musicians had more of a say over repertory, would they play more new music? The age-old dispute over recent music rages on among musicians, audiences, and critics alike. George Szell, who felt most at home with the Classics and Romantics, would jokingly refer to contemporary works as "temporary" music; his appraisal would certainly cause violent protest by Pierre Boulez. Now, to fill the halls we must perform the masterworks which appeal to a wide public. Failure at the box office endangers the orchestra's existence. But from an artistic viewpoint programming must be innovative and experimental as well. As far as inflexible concertgoers of either persuasion are concerned, you are damned if you do and damned if you don't. The musicians themselves are divided between those who are interested and challenged by new music and bored with doing the so-called warhorses time and again, and others who resist experimentation, which admittedly involves trying some inferior new works. This disagreement is less a matter of the generation gap and more of temperament and outlook. Be that as it may, input from the orchestra might result in a more open attitude toward expanding the repertory.

And orchestra members would welcome the chance to air their views. Unfortunately, too often players are not given credit even when their suggestions *are* adopted. This makes them bitter. A little more recognition would go a long way!

19: *Julius Levine*

Musically, I was born at my first Pablo Casals festival in Prades, France, in 1951. Biologically it happened in the Bronx in 1921. I was brought up there and in Brooklyn, part of a nice Jewish family. My father, who was first a cabinet maker, then an architect and contractor, with his ups and downs, had also been something of a cantor. He loved music and had a natural voice. The story they tell is that he got a fiddle at a pawnshop and tried to teach himself to play, but the sounds were awful. My mother said that one day she heard him cry, "Sophie, Sophie, come quick, take it away from me." He had smashed the fiddle in a rage and sat there crying like a baby. That was his musical education. But for the children it would be different. They were to acquire skill in music on their way to becoming doctors or lawyers.

So I had piano lessons from some cockamamie violin teacher of my older brother's. The piano was not my instrument. I can't explain why, but it may have to do with vertical reading. I don't know if his makes any sense, but did you ever look in a stereoscope? You look with both eyes at two pictures and you see one. Well I don't see one I see two, each of them separately. Anyhow, for me vertical reading was always slower than horizontal. But I struggled on with the piano until I got to high school.

While in my teens, I planned to go to the mountains with a band, a group of friends, and since two of us played the piano, it was agreed that I should take up the trumpet at school. We already had a good trumpet player in the group so I would play second trumpet. I went to my first trumpet class and right away the teacher said, "Levine, blow a D major scale." When the teacher tells you to do something, you don't argue. So, though I knew nothing about the instrument, I put the trumpet in my mouth and out came Splat Splat. He asked me, "Didn't you learn anything last term?" And it turned out that they had registered me for the advanced class by mistake. Well, that wouldn't do and the beginning class was filled. What was left? The bass. They desperately needed someone to play the bass in the orchestra. I wanted to know, can you play the bass in the mountains in a band? The answer was yes, and I said, "I'll take it." The music chairman asked to see my hands which I opened as wide as I

Julius Levine, the free-lance bass player, was interviewed at his home in New York City in October, 1974.

could to make them look big. He said O.K., and they gave me a bass and a book.

So I came to the bass very much by accident. Luckily I am suited to it; possibly I would be more suited to the cello, which plays essentially the same bass line part of the literature at most times, but offers a richer chamber music repertory. Many cellists don't want or understand how to play their proper role in an ensemble situation; they tend to compete with the violin, because the cello in the upper register in the hands of a master can sound like a violin, and they want to stand out. I've heard very fine cellists criticize a piece they're playing because they don't have more than a continuo part. That's rather an egocentric attitude, and doesn't do much for the music. I've always been a group musician—it's an art to be able to blend your instrument with others to achieve a musical whole.

Even before high school I felt vaguely committed to music. My parents were very ambivalent about this. The first crisis occurred when I took a bass out of school for the summer. My father had to sign it out. He and my mother were very reluctant to do that; they felt it meant getting too serious about music. But they went along with me. The second crisis occurred when I wanted to *buy* a bass and my father told my mother, as she reported, "Papa said, if you're going to be a musician you might as well quit college and go to work with him. Why should you waste your time getting an education?" But my older sister came forward and lent me the money to buy the instrument.

I repaid the loan on the bass quickly. But my parents were shocked when I had a summer job with a dance band playing on the boardwalk at Coney Island and then elsewhere in Brooklyn. My mother was sure I was being unrealistic, heading for a tragic future, because my aunt Sylvia knew a performer who claimed that even if a musician is a genius, he still starves. Sure, you *can* starve very easily as a musician. But I didn't accept this as necessarily so. Early in the game, when I got that first bass, I had the feeling that *this* was my instrument, and I wanted to spend my life making music.

I went from New Utrecht High School to Brooklyn College to the Army. The year before I was drafted, a friend of mine who played the violin pointed out that you couldn't get into an Army band playing a string instrument. So we both took tuba lessons. I couldn't play the tuba then, in between, or later, but when I played the bass for them, they took me in the band as a tuba player. I blew well enough to play the formations. I played in the dance band and did some arranging.

Eventually I went to India in the Army as a musician, stationed at an air transport command base. Musically the experience was worse than a total loss. When I came home on furlough, I'd go to a concert every night. Back on the army base, if I was in the service squad and somebody put even a semi-classical record on, I'd get such a horrible feeling, I'd rush out immediately. I couldn't be in the vicinity of real music or anything close to real music while I was serving my time in the Army.

When I came out, I lacked direction, but I was glad to go to Juilliard for a year on the G.I. Bill. There for the first time I came in contact with what I would call a real bass teacher in the person of Fred Zimmerman, who was also in the New York Philharmonic. He was probably *the* leading bass teacher at that time. What I learned from him was an organized approach to the instrument—too organized, too worked out for me. When I was picked to be the first bass player of the Juilliard orchestra in mid-semester, he congratulated me, but I got the sense from his favorite pupil that his other students were shocked and surprised. They wondered how I ever came to be picked, since I was not exactly the type of student he turned out. I was a little too much of a dreamer.

Meanwhile, I was working in New York as a freelance musician, making a modest income, picking up work wherever I could. Some jobs were semi-regular, others less than that. I never had more than a couple thousand dollars in the bank as summer began and I never had more than a few hundred by the end of the summer. I was never ahead. If I ever got sick for a month, I had to borrow money; and there was my mother, who was getting old. Was my situation typical for musicians? It certainly wasn't atypical.

Then again, it depends on the individual. Some musicians are businessmen from the day they learn to play their instruments. They know how to make contacts in the recording and television worlds. They wouldn't dream of doing a concert—it might interfere with a recording date. I hate to do commercials, but, see, if someone called me to do a commercial tomorrow and I was free, I'd probably accept because of the pay. This wouldn't bother some people but it worries me. I have to watch my bank account—but I also have to look after my soul.

Many people think of musicians as living in ivory towers and having endless time to concentrate on their art. That's ridiculous. I have a life's work to write, what with my peculiar education and the way I got to music and then to Casals—and I have no time to do it. All I've got so far is a bunch of notes. I can't get a block of time to sit down and make sense out of them. That's a musician's life.

Let me give you a concrete example of how bad it can be. In 1950 or so I started working at CBS. What was that all about? Well, you sit in a studio and you wonder why. They're busy coordinating you with a camera in another room and somebody in headphones is trying to figure out what they're doing—and you wait. It's an awful waste of your time—you don't play much. But you're being paid much more for that than if you were rehearsing for a concert—though less than if you were recording. A little half hour show might be rehearsed in two and a half to four hours. An hour show would take longer. Sometimes they spread it over several days, three hours one day, three hours the next; or maybe you come in at ten and the show is at eight that night. It goes on like that, day after day. You make a living—but oh what a spiritual price you pay!

Against my nature, I was starting to do more of that when a window was opened for me which let the breeze in. Pablo Casals was that breeze. I went to my first Casals festival (it was Casals' second) in 1951 in Prades in the south of France, a few months after I started psychotherapy. I saw a very unusual, humane, and gifted man who, in a few months, had opened a window in me. I went off to Casals and what poured in during those six weeks was a once-in-a-lifetime revelation that I don't think anybody can explain.

The single most shattering musical experience I ever had was my first rehearsal with Casals. The Festival orchestra I played in had been with Casals for one festival the summer before. This group was not like the one in Puerto Rico later on, which was hand-picked. The Prades orchestra included professionals, amateurs, and less than amateurs. All they had in common, generally, was the love of music and the appreciation of Casals as a musician.

Until that summer music was a rather vague thing for me. It was a collection of notes that I didn't know why I played relatively well. I

knew what music meant in terms of harmony, of certain formal organizations. But beyond that I didn't know what it really meant, on a
deeper level. Like why do we have this formal organization, what's its
purpose in life? How did it come to be—what's it all about? I remember in a high school math class, another student once made a
derogatory remark about a question I asked, saying "He's always asking questions which go so far back that they have nothing to do with
what you're talking about." And the teacher said, "You're dead
wrong. He asks the questions that mathematicians ask." But I was not
really mathematical. It's just that my mind tends to work in equa-
tions.

In any case, at the first rehearsal, we did Mozart's *Eine Kleine
Nacht Musik*, one of the warhorses of chamber music that has been
played so badly so many times. The orchestra read through the first
movement, and there was Casals, with the magic that his wordless
communication inevitably produced. And there I was participating in
this. It made me very happy. I thought, "This is great. Now I understand why people come from everywhere to be with Casals." He
would sing the first phrase, echoing the orchestra, without any derision. Only as Casals got older did he start to be a little negative and
mimic what you were doing to show how bad it was. When I say
older I mean up in his nineties. At this time he was merely 76 or so.
Anyway Casals gave you a representation of what you had done, and
then he sang the music again in his own way, opened it up, slowed
the beats, so that you could *see* the undulation between notes. You
could perceive in slow motion what guided him, how he got to a particular feeling, what made sense for him. Then he went on to the
next little section and repeated the process. It might be a bar or half a
bar or two bars. In this way he sang through the whole movement.
That's when a fairy godmother touched me and turned me from a
pumpkin into a coach. Only I didn't have to come back at midnight.
It was mine forever!

Casals tore the world I had apart and showed me another one. It
was shattering in a positive way, but still shattering. I'd always put a
little layer between myself and spontaneity, but after experiencing
Casals, I didn't do this in music any more. While at the festival I suspended all preconceptions. I was a willing prisoner of the situation.
When it was over, and I toured Europe over the next few months, I
found musical thoughts just started coming to me. I sensed some

deep meaning, though for many years these thoughts were very disorganized, mere intimations. Upon my return, I said to my therapist, "One thing I have learned is that music is not sharp. Music is round." I still believe that, though today my philosophy of music is better formulated and I can say more precisely what the Casals "breeze" did for me. When I met him, music was a total abstraction to me and when I left him, it was as concrete as this chair. Casals' basic message had to do with energy. When he talked about making a diminuendo "so that the note lives its natural life," he was discussing sound, but what he was really saying was that when you express energy in an artistic way, there comes a moment of resistance or tension followed by a sense of release. That process was his diminuendo. People to whom he didn't personally transmit this idea of energy often don't get it. They don't know how to shape sound in terms of a life process. They just get softer—a much less compelling musical solution. I must say, Casals really turned my life around. I finally felt confident and started fulfilling my potential.

As I went through festival after festival, I began to think of Casals as the parent—you might say my mother. The violinist Alexander Schneider was the midwife. I met him at my first Casals festival and we've been close ever since. He has in common with Casals the belief that music is a completely uninhibited expression of life's energy. Over the years I've played many concerts with Schneider; I owe him much of the recognition I've gotten.

I didn't see Casals again until 1953, two summers later, at another festival. Then again perhaps in 1956, when he inaugurated his Puerto Rico festivals. In 1960 I spent a week at the Marlboro Music Festival where Casals was in residence, coaching chamber music, giving master classes, conducting. I remember doing a Mozart piano concerto under his baton.

In 1961 I started coming to Marlboro for the whole summer; I'm still doing so. There I met my wife-to-be, Caroline, a fine violist. In 1962 we got married, in 1964 we had our first child, Dena, and in 1968 Amy was born. There are professional advantages and disadvantages to having a spouse who's also a free-lance musician. I guess the main disadvantage is that when things go badly in the music world, you starve. You don't have somebody who works in banking to keep you going. There might be other disadvantages for some people. I know I'd be miserable with someone who didn't understand music.

My wife's the same way. Some married musicians are competitive. We wouldn't feel that way about each other no matter what fields we were in.

Making our living as free lances complicates family life. A nine to five worker can at least apportion time with the children; his home and his office are two distinct areas. But my home *is* my office. When I play a concert or rehearsal I'm simply out on a case. I come back home to practice, to teach, in other words to work.

A free lance, when you come down to it, is someone who wants no master and finds out that he has many. Of course, there is the relief of knowing that if you can't stand the idiot you're facing on the podium today, tomorrow you'll be facing a different idiot—for whatever that's worth. It's true that I chose this course. I had to give up financial security because with it I would have been smothered. That would have ended musical independence for me. I gave up the one thing that I couldn't imagine any son of my mother giving up—stability. I have two brothers and a sister, and all three of them are in civil service, two retired, the third not yet.

What other options did I have besides becoming a free lance? One was a job in a symphony orchestra. Too confining. Another, which I didn't really take seriously until recently, was teaching. I'm doing more and more of it and enjoying it enormously. Early on I never wanted to teach. I was afraid to; my ideas about music were not clearly enough worked out. So I got into it very slowly. At first I was dragged into it when somebody asked me as a special favor to teach his doctor's son. So I took him, and in due time I took another student. I found that teaching does not mean knowing everything and passing it on. Teaching is being curious enough to learn yourself, being able to get down in the mud and scuffle with someone else until you help him find something neither of you realized was there—and possibly what's wrong with it. After that, *you* know more than you knew before. It's having the equipment to go looking rather than having all the knowledge to convey.

It's gotten to the point where I feel I have some very important things to teach besides the bass. I give bass lessons at home as well as at various schools, like the Mannes College of Music and Queens College. But it's the making of music that deeply interests me right now, more than the technical aspects of this or that instrument. Casals affected me very profoundly on that score, investing every note he played or conducted with a special expressive energy. The beautiful way he directed his vitality to produce such striking results became a major preoccupation of mine. Somehow or other, as somebody who was distorted musically until I met Casals, I felt that I understood him in certain ways better than people who were much more sophisticated when they first met him. What I learned from him was so meaningful that I feel I want to pass it on to others, whether through teaching my instrument, coaching chamber music, writing the book I hope to get to someday, or teaching the course in musical expressivity I'd like to teach.

This is what I hope to get across: In order to make music on the most meaningful level, you must know how to invest the sound with expressive energy. The sound is nothing but acoustics until a life energy makes it say something. The engine between the emotions which are invisible and the sound which is nothing but acoustics is the human body, in which breathing and pulsation are the important and inseparable reflexes as far as music goes. Emotionally, and I suspect physically as well, we have a cardio-respiratory system. You cannot breathe a stiff one-cell breath. It's invested with pulsation. And you cannot have a sense of pulsation without breathing. It's one process. Now, once you understand that the two function together, you stop breathing as if your body is a tube that goes up and down, at least when you're making music. Rather, there's a sense of pause; your breath creates an atmosphere which surrounds you, encompasses you and your instrument. It's not easy to put into words. Casals communicated it without words; I try to do the same.

I divide musicians into those who play on their instruments and those who *include* their instruments when they play. This is not to disparage the first group—they just don't say much to me. Of course, some cross over. I can think of one very great pianist who goes back and forth, depending on his mood.

Now, for me, chamber music is the epitome, the essence of all music. I would modify that remark only to include solo compositions played by people who have the musical understanding of a chamber musician and then only if they have that something extra which a soloist needs. I can't stand the cult of personality that surrounds somebody who may have plenty of charisma but is basically a musical idiot.

A chamber music performer is generally thought to be one who understands the discipline of playing with others, who needs no conductor, who knows when and where to listen and follow and lead. I have a somewhat different conception. To me, the chamber musician is someone who understands how to *breathe* with everyone else. It's not enough just to listen and play your part. You might say that chamber music is an ideal form. It's a group concert. Now, you hear people claim that no great masterpiece was ever created by committee. But with chamber music you have to recognize that you're not a committee of creation, you're a committee of reproduction and interpretation. You must know before you think, sense when and what the others will do, where you can incorporate the others' idea within your own, so that you give a little and they give a little and all reach for something similar.

There have been some very great quartets, like the Budapest String Quartet, in which the personnel were really quite individualistic musicians. I think what brought them together was a chemistry of three rather than a chemistry of four. Joseph Roisman, the first violinist, was extraordinary. There was something patrician about his playing, something very elegant that gave a special quality to the first violin part. He was not an aggressive leader, but the way the other three followed him as a team made it clear that they understood Roisman's talents.

As my reputation around New York was growing, I was called to the Library of Congress to play with the Budapest. In chamber music, that was like having your name in lights on Broadway. By now I've played with every major quartet, but playing with the Budapest was the stamp of approval. I had arrived.

That concert was a peak experience for me. I was thrilled at being received into the world of chamber music. It always had a special aura for me; I'm tuned into that atmosphere. Getting involved in that world has made it possible for me to avoid some of the great frustrations of a free lance's life, such as being a "telephone artist;" you pick up the phone and maybe someone you never heard before starts to talk dates, places to go, and amounts of money. You look in a book and if the spaces are open and the conditions are satisfactory, that's your commitment for the moment. Taking such jobs can have unpleasant consequences. You might find yourself in one of those less-than-amateur amateur orchestras where nobody plays in tune. I'm not one of those people who stands there like a Rock of Gibraltar and plays in tune when everyone else around me is not. For days after, sometimes, I'm not able to find the notes on my instrument. What a nightmare! I'm a very good chamber music player, but in bad company I play poorly.

Something I still find frustrating is that there isn't more chamber music with bass parts. I wouldn't be so unhappy if the limited repertory I have were done more. I enjoy looking deeper and deeper and deeper into a single piece. I was playing Schubert's *Trout* Quintet, one of the greatest pieces with a bass part, last spring at the Library of Congress with the Juilliard Quartet. Speaking to the first violinist, Bobby Mann, afterward, I said, "I must have played the *Trout* two thousand times in my life and every time I see something I never saw before. Maybe that proves I'm slow and stupid." But I really feel that I'd rather play the *Trout* for the two thousandth time than play something that's not much good even once. I *will* do it once; I want to find out if there's anything there, and when I'm not sure, I'll do it twice, but if there's obviously nothing there, I'd prefer to do a work I love once again. It's like going out with a girl who's terrible company only because you've never been out with her before, instead of seeing somebody you enjoy. What for?

Now, contemporary music is harder for most of us than the standard repertory, so it's necessary to give new pieces time before you render a judgement. Some recent music is great, but not all of it is even music. Not all music in any period was music. We need time to cull out the good from the bad. Meanwhile, I feel it's a bit presumptuous of people to say that you're unfair if you don't give new music a proper hearing, and give yourself time to understand it. By that they often mean you have to take something you realize is garbage and play it again and again, since each time that you don't like it, it just means you haven't understood it yet. This is a circular trap. Some things are just plain bad; some composers really have very little to say.

I've played a fair amount of twentieth-century music. During my year at Juilliard I became associated with a group much like today's Speculum Musicae, a bunch of first-class players very dedicated to contemporary music who usually play music worth playing. Stravinsky indirectly sponsored my group even though he was on the West Coast. Robert Craft, who organized us, was at that time a sort of East Coast secretary for Stravinsky, whose constant companion he later became. It was good experience, and I recognize value in many contemporary compositions, but I was and remain more fulfilled in the older literature.

You see, I have more of a gut-level feeling for older esthetic questions and aims. Put too simply, the creative minds of 200 and even 100 years ago were most interested in exploring *life*. Philosophers asked, "What is alive?"—and artists answered the question in various ways in their works. Of course, creators necessarily deal with timely questions. In today's society, the machine—a lifeless amalgam of nuts and bolts—predominates. Artists are forced to ask, "Where will machines take us?" Sadly, this inquiry results in a lot of cerebral—and to my mind not very musical—music.

This trend toward the mechanization of music is really most distressing. It has ramifications in other areas besides composition. What has happened to music departments at many universities is that the historians, the theorists, and the musicologists are like an army behind a fortress, their guns trained on people who know how to make music. They'll shoot them dead before they'll let them in. The performer is a threat. The academics talk on and on; if they really have nothing to say, they make it sound important with fancy words. Then along comes somebody who actually knows how to play a phrase, who knows how to make music come to life. What a threat!

Musicology and performance departments should exist side by side in the same schools. Musicians should learn more history and theory and scholars should learn how to listen and play. I wish universities without performers would find themselves abandoned by people seriously interested in studying music; it's really a scandal that "musical" academia often has no musicians as part of the community.

Even in schools with both concentrations, the two worlds often remain far apart. I remember being asked to visit the University of Hartford to determine whether I wanted to come up there one day a week to teach bass. I was introduced to the members of the music department. I recall one fellow who wore his hair like a mad professor. When he heard that I played with Casals he said, "Casals? Oh yes. Casals." He vaguely remembered hearing Casals play something many years before in a European city. On that occasion, Casals did this or that in a certain piece, and this professor remembered that some remote musicological stricture had been violated. When he heard Casals go "bloop" instead of "bleep" he was delighted at catching the Master in a mistake. I thought, "My God, what a phony. He probably builds a course on meaningless statements like that and the pupils think they're hearing about music." I don't know how many like him there are.

I have one categorical remark to make about all this: Overspecialization is dangerous. That's why I want to teach about the craft of musical expression in a university. I want to show people that notes on a printed page should be read not as abstractions, but as musical expressions that come straight from the composer's viscera. Historians and theorists today hardly ever listen; even those who do don't always realize what they're hearing. Our ears are just a channel right down to the gut. They may tell you something superficial, like "how interesting it sounded," or "how beautifully he played." But there's more to the musical experience, and most people are missing too much. In my own way I'd like to help them find something deeper.

Kermit Moore

My life in music has been a very satisfying one. I grew up in a musical home, studied with fine teachers in the U.S. and abroad, know many wonderful performers, play a lot, and conduct and compose as much as I can. Though modern society is in many ways quite troubling, ever since I was small I've felt lucky to be alive and have so much beautiful music at my fingertips.

I was born in northern Ohio. My father came there from Jamaica to study at the University of Akron. I was the third child. Though father was in business, he had a marvelous baritone voice. Mother taught all of us piano when we were five or six. Since she also conducted choirs, I began to sing at an early age, as a boy soprano in the Episcopal Church. Both parents encouraged me in music; they took me to the Cleveland Orchestra children's concerts where I was fascinated by the cello. I decided to study it when I was about eight; they made me wait two years until I grew a bit.

My first teacher was a student of Charles McBride, a cellist in the Cleveland orchestra, who soon after became my second teacher. Mr. McBride didn't baby me. Even though I seemed to be catching on very fast, he was extremely strict, spare with praise, always stressing discipline. While in high school, I continued to study with Mr. McBride at the Cleveland Institute of Music. Then I went to New York, to Juilliard, to study with Felix Salmond. He was remarkable—energetic, emotional, thorough and sometimes unreasonable, a quality that forced you to defend yourself with greater skill. For a long time he taught many fine cellists at Juilliard and at Curtis.

I knew very early that I also wanted to be a conductor. When I was ten or eleven, my father made a record player with huge speakers. I'd put on a record and conduct to it! I studied conducting rather obliquely in New York. I was attending NYU and Juilliard at the same time; however, there was a conducting class at Columbia taught by Rudolf Tomas and he needed musicians to play for the class. A number of now-well-known musicians played for him. We made very little money, but got conducting lessons thrown in free. And Dr. Tomas was an excellent teacher. While playing in his class, almost thirty years ago now, I picked up all that he said about conducting, and sometimes I was allowed to conduct for him. What a treat!

Kermit Moore, the free-lance cellist, was interviewed at his home in New York City in October 1977.

At sixteen, I had begun to play concerts. Because I came to New York by way of Tanglewood, I got a manager who was fairly successful in getting me concerts—not big prestigious ones, but concerts to grow by—in colleges, in the sticks. My parents still supported me, but I had enough engagements to be able to earn a little something.

I soon learned that a career wasn't so easy. Practicing alone or playing for friends was one thing; sitting on stage after a trip when you were tired was something else—it meant you had to grow up in a hurry. You had to meet a schedule, play well, go somewhere else, and play well again.

I was unusually lucky to get as many concerts as I did. You can't rely on concerts at an early age unless you win a big contest. You might get a lot of publicity, or notoriety, from public performances, but they don't pay the rent. And while trying to make ends meet and finish school I was also figuring out how I could play, compose, conduct, and earn a living all at the same time. I had a lot on my mind.

Fortunately, at 21 I got a job teaching at the University of Hartford. By that time I had been concertizing for a number of years. In Connecticut we had a string quartet in residence and I played in the Hartford Symphony, which I didn't enjoy because it wasn't too good an orchestra. You could hear and feel that some of the players were not as developed as others.

I stayed in Hartford for three years before moving on to Europe. In a sense, that's when I began to live. I had felt something was wrong before. There were elements in American musical life that weren't what they seemed. For one thing, the music establishment was hard to penetrate. I suppose it's hard making it to the top in any business—but in music I had hoped people would be wiser, more sensitive and humane. But I found, like any other business, it was a little crass. Unfortunately, that's truer than ever.

Now I didn't find Utopia abroad; there are a lot of problems in Europe too. But my focus was different. I went to a conservatory and studied cello with Paul Bazelaire and Form and Analysis and Composition with Nadia Boulanger. That study in composition and fugue writing was probably the best educational experience I've ever had. And Paris was in many ways an eye-opener for me. Musically it was very lively. Even before my Paris debut, I played in the recording business—which sounds crass but it wasn't. This is how it came about, a Schönberg devotee, René Leibowitz, became a good friend.

I was a "grand-student" of Schönberg's because I had studied with Marcel Dick in Cleveland. So meeting Leibowitz was for me a bit like meeting Schönberg himself. Leibowitz was recording the *Gurre-lieder* and asked me to play in the orchestra. Delightful! But I didn't have a work permit. So he worked that out. We had a fine musical relationship. Just meeting him and playing chamber music at his house was a splendid experience, because the level of musicianship was so high.

What people always say about Nadia Boulanger is true—she has a genius for bringing out her students' unique gifts. She helped me tremendously with composition, and found work for me in Paris. I was a guest in her home about every two weeks for teas and dinners. I like her very much as a person. I think she is probably lonely. She once told me she had no living relative; her sister Lili had died in 1924, and they were the only two children of parents who were only children. So her students were her children. The housekeeper had several children Miss Boulanger treated like her grandchildren. It was very touching. Some people think she's hard, but they just don't know her. She is actually warm and sensitive. And so knowledgeable it's overwhelming. Under her tutelage, I got out of the Schönberg bind. You must get out of any bind in order to be yourself. You cannot become a miniature Schönberg, or a miniature Brahms. I had been writing twelve-tone music and though I continued to admire it and would not have written any other way at that time, she could lure me out of a rigid mold. Not by damning serial music, but just by making me myself. I still write twelve-tone music, but now I have the freedom to do it if I want to and not if I don't.

I lived in Europe for seven years, three of them in Paris. Besides Bazelaire and Boulanger, I played for Casals during his last summer at Prades in 1954. Better than anyone else, Casals made you feel a link with the whole history of cello playing. It's hard to verbalize what he communicated—I'm not sure he ever did. Casals was always conscious of style, the *kind* of sound you were making, and what your musical intentions were. You never just played the instrument; you had to play the music, and it had to be delineated properly. He conveyed his attitude by the way he stopped you and asked you why you did something—and then showed you another way to do it. He was very thoughtful and kind—and very critical.

Another wonderful experience was meeting Georges Enesco.

Nadia Boulanger had him to dinner one night; I was there and we spoke. He said, "I'd like to hear you play." So I ended up, over a period of several months, playing my entire repertory for him. That was probably as deep a musical experience as one could ask for. He invariably told you what the composer himself said about a certain piece. Enesco seemed to have known Monteverdi. He knew what Brahms or Mendelssohn or Tchaikovsky had to say. He actually did know many composers. So I had the pleasure of playing works for him that he'd played or discussed with their composers. At Tanglewood I had studied with the first cellist of the Boston Symphony, who had played the Fauré Elegy for Fauré, and the Saint-Saens Concerto with Saint-Saens. These living links with the past are crucial for maintaining musical continuity from generation to generation. Exposure to a living musical heritage gives you some basis for the way you play, and makes you feel part of a tradition.

The link that must be there is lacking in a lot of performances where you'd expect it. I go to certain concerts and wonder what the players are doing. They sound as if they're building a house of sand. The performances are shallow; there's no connective tissue; the phrases don't mean anything. There's a whole element of musicians who want to show you how brilliant and flashy they are. It's sad. They don't make music for the right reasons. Music is really the architecture of sound. You have to build a structure—but there's nothing that connects what they do. It so easily crumbles. If you're building a structure of sound it must have a basis—a plot or a plan. The composer had that in mind. Why shouldn't the player?

After Paris, I moved to Brussels and radiated from Belgium to the other countries. I went all over Europe, then Africa and the Far East. I gave solo recitals, travelling about a great deal. Finally, I came back to the States to play some concerts in 1961, and suddenly decided not to leave for a while. I never quite knew why I stayed. I just decided to see what was going on here. And I had begun to dislike all that travelling. There got to be too many hotel rooms, too many trips to the airport, too much of the same. I know there are people who've done it for forty years, but I want to do things on my own terms. When you move around so much you don't have time to penetrate the music. You start looking for easy ways out. Now I like to travel periodically—for the right purpose, at the right time.

Soon after returning to New York, I got into the American

recording industry. My musical life here was fairly well established in about two years. I wrote to colleges where I'd played in the past, and got some responses. I played commercials. And I began to earn a living. Word got around that I was in New York and people started calling me.

I never minded playing commercials. Some of the finest musicians around do it, and it's a pleasure to be with them. We enjoy each other. Sometimes you are given music that's technically difficult—and you have to record it within three hours. That's challenging. There's also an army of well-trained composers who write commercials. They've made their choices. I'm not saying that work is ideal, or that I'd like to do it all the time, but it is sometimes fascinating to see how the musicians involved solve certain problems. And as a free lance you can choose exactly what you want to do. You're master of your own fate.

It's hard for newcomers to penetrate the commercial world, though. It's a tight little family. I've tried to bring pupils in—some make it but most don't. A few of them get into orchestras. But there are many marvelous instrumentalists these days who have to do other things to earn a living—sometimes in another field. There should be an additional symphony or two in New York. Look how many there are in London, Paris, and Tokyo. I conducted in Tokyo and they had something like five different symphony concerts that week—all Tokyo orchestras. I don't understand why the NBC Symphony couldn't still exist, or why they did away with live musicians at CBS. It's a sad reflection on our culture. I think the level of taste is lower than ever. Television has probably done it. People want to be entertained. Classical musicians on TV have to be clowns—they're made to stand with violins and play fast pieces very badly. And I don't like the idea of opera singers going on the Johnny Carson show. They don't come off well in that setting. They have to tell jokes, try to show they're ordinary guys, and vulgarize themselves a little bit. If they simply came out and sang an aria and said thank you very much and left, that would be all right. But by acting like everyday Joes, they diminish themselves without attracting any more people to the opera. I hope that literature and writers don't go down the same drain; so far they've managed to avoid it.

Of course, I'm fighting the trend, trying to get people to see the danger. But the truth is, if more people could get work in the arts, we'd have a higher standard of culture. There should be two symphonies in each of the big cities, and more opera companies, as there are in Europe. Not enough jobs in music, plus the fact that everything costs so much money to attend, are destroying us.

Some musicians blame our union for all our woes. I think they're mistaken. I joined when I was eighteen. It's a must. We would never be able to negotiate as effectively for pay and working conditions, royalties, and so on, as our officers do. With all their faults, they have to more or less represent us or they're not reelected. But the real fight is not between musicians and their union, or the union and orchestras or opera companies. They should all be fighting in Washington for more government subsidy. We're battling in the wrong arena.

Every other civilized country has more government subsidy of the arts than we do. Here there's a lot of ignorance about art and how much we need it. Everyone should be able to go to the opera without having to pay $25 for a ticket. Our leaders ought to be more concerned with art. I think it would be better for the community, and make for less tension, if people could attend more art events.

This is the spirit that Dorothy Maynor is trying to foster with the Harlem School of the Arts. My wife Dorothy Rudd Moore and I were among her first teachers. I put in the cello department for her; my wife, who is a composer, taught piano and theory. We enjoyed it very much. That school is working as well as anything I've ever seen in the music world. It's because Dorothy Maynor is unbelievable. She really knows what she's doing, as a singer and as a teacher. How sad that she couldn't sing at the Met.

The situation for blacks at the Met has improved, though it certainly could be better. There *is* discrimination, not only against blacks but against Americans in general. The Met should go out and get native singers. If they don't come in for auditions, they should be asked to come and sing. The Met has alienated many good American singers and even some great Europeans. The best Americans may not even have auditions—they probably don't want to. That's why they should be sought out. Rudolf Bing ran the Met very cleverly; he breathed new life into it. But Bing should have made American singers feel more welcome.

There is not much I can do directly to improve the situation in opera. But in an attempt to increase opportunities for instrumentalists, twelve of us founded the Symphony of the New World in 1964. The goal was to open doors for deserving musicians who couldn't get into symphonies. There were—and are—very few women in orchestras, very few Latins, blacks, and Asians. We thought, well, if they're talented, they can play in our Symphony. And they did. There was some emphasis on black musicians because they've been hit hardest by discrimination. And the situation's not really getting any better. Black players may be feeling it less, probably because they can find other things to do—they can get into colleges and teach, they can play jazz, they can get an MA or a PhD and do fairly well.

Why is the orchestra such a conservative bastion? On that question I have many thoughts and they're not all polite. I believe that those who control the symphony societies are too much alike. And they've coddled the wrong musicians, those who have already proved themselves to be indoctrinated with questionable values. The powers-that-be are discriminatory not so much because they exclude minorities as because they favor musicians with shallow musical personalities.

Then of course auditioning practices are unfair. Musicians are supposed to be auditioned for orchestras anonymously, behind a screen, but there are signals to indicate who's back there. It's totally dishonest. Auditions are held for positions that are already filled, because the authorities must go on record as having held them. How can they get the best by selecting friends and cronies? Pettiness is rampant.

Symphony board chairmen and managers are too business-minded and clique-oriented. I would feel better about it all if there were more cultural organizations around, to allow for more diversity at the top. At the moment there is no allowance made for the maverick or the person from Podunk who may be inspired to do something creative in the arts. Everyone favors the status quo. It's a bit like politicians who want to make sure they get reelected by stroking the right people.

Black musicians often say that in order to win an audition they have to play forty times as well as whites. But even when they do, they don't get jobs. I know this to be true in case after case. I've never taken an audition that I didn't get—but I never auditioned for a major symphony because I haven't wanted to play in one. I know many people who *have* tried to make it; when they know that they played better than anyone at the audition and don't get called back they're very disillusioned and depressed.

My response is to tell them "Look, just make a living. Don't be discouraged. Some limited and petty person has kept you out. That shouldn't bother you too much." I think that if Leopold Stokowski had auditioned a black who was much better than anyone else he would have hired him. Stokowski had integrity. He didn't bend under social pressure.

I suppose those in charge of musical institutions feel that if they start loosening up, things will get out of their control. The nature of their own operation would change and they'd lose power. And I'm afraid that black people pounding on doors and complaining might have stepped on some people's toes and made them even more hostile. When they went to the Human Rights Commission a few years ago, I was subpoenaed because one of the people who had auditioned used me as a witness to his ability. So I went down and testified to his ability. But I imagine he stepped on hundreds of toes. It's a vicious circle.

The Symphony of the New World helped for a while. If it had continued according to the original conception, we would have made a much bigger splash on the musical scene. At the moment it's a bit directionless. The orchestra has provided work for those who can't get jobs elsewhere, but there are financial problems now. It's not a job if you play without pay, and that's been going on of late. It's no one's fault—but unpaid musicians get very disillusioned.

Conducting is a very tight door to open—it's hermetically sealed. You really have to struggle to get conducting assignments. That's probably the hardest area to penetrate because it's the biggest plum. And there too you'll find discrimination, as in every area, not only by color or sex but by personality, by habits. I've known conductors who have nearly lost their minds trying to get jobs. Fortunately, conducting is not the only thing I do. So I can wait, or I can do whatever conducting comes along. I'd like to do more, but I don't have to to survive.

There are more well-trained black and women musicians today than ever before. I think we're on the threshold of a breakthrough. College staffs are changing their colors. We'll probably get better integration of orchestras outside New York first—in Cleveland, perhaps

Boston. But some damage is done. An orchestra job lasts a long time—and there's been reluctance to give blacks a permanent job. I can't imagine being in a symphony for good because then everything else I do would have to stop. It would be stifling. I couldn't compose or conduct. But I encourage my students to audition for symphonies. As far as our field is concerned, it's a good job. It has dignity, you meet good musicians, you're involved in the real core of the musical literature. I tell people to persevere, and try to help as much as I can; if I know a symphony conductor I put in a good word. Atlanta has more black players than the New York Philharmonic; so does Richmond—their first flutist is black. What's wrong with New York? I repeat—it's that little clique of people with similar vision, or lack of it, similar culture, or lack of it—narrowness, conservatism, call it what you will.

I don't advocate court cases. The Symphony of the New World *could* have proved to the world, "We don't need you," so to speak. I prefer that kind of gesture. I don't believe in begging. You shouldn't have to beg for your rights. If somebody moved me out of my house, I'd go to court, but I would first try to find other ways of defending myself. And musicians should be as independent as possible. They should have pride in their work, preserve their integrity, and make sure that every time they play a note, it's worthy of them. Let them work their way in to places where managers are not so narrow and petty. Make a living first; don't try anything out of desperation. That is not an artistic approach; it only leads to bitterness. You don't have to stoop to the level of your oppressors. There's enough bitterness as it is.

As for programs of all-black music—why not? No one shies away from an all-Beethoven concert, or one of music limited to German or French composers. A concert is a concert. If the program consists only of works by women or blacks, it's still a concert of pieces by people dedicated to what they're doing. If there's no other way certain works can get aired, that's unfortunate, but such a format can obviously do more good than harm because at least the works get a hearing. People have the right to use whatever organizing principle they want. I have put on concerts of music by black composers, three with the New World Symphony in 1974. It's a means to an end—it cannot be an end. We must not try to be giant killers with music. I say, "Play the concert, whatever the program. Its beauty is what counts."

You can get extreme though. At Donnell Library [in New York City] once I played my wife's piece *Dirge and Deliverance*. My accompanist was Patrick Mullins. We went backstage and a woman pianist said to us, "I thought this was an all-woman concert." I said, "We're not composers, we're players." She resented us anyway. She had expected the concert to be all-women through and through. Her attitude was a little too militaristic and dictatorial for me.

But I can be philosophical about it all. I'm not bitter. I love what I do. I recognize our cultural enemies, and I absolutely refuse to tolerate some things; but I won't waste my time hating them.

The contemporary composer has also been an object of discrimination. People are afraid of new music. They've been burned by bad new works and thrown by their failure to understand good new works. Ignorance is always the problem. Audiences are afraid of what they don't know. They're comfortable with Elgar and Tchaikovsky. Boulez took some positive steps toward acquainting audiences with new music. He tried to bring the public along by the hand—but maybe he went a little too fast.

I believe you have to play new music on recitals as much as you can. Instrumentalists and singers alike should do more new music. We're people of the present and it's our responsibility to do music of our own times. Some will like it, some won't—but some don't like anything after Beethoven anyway. Sometimes you're asked by concert managers to play no contemporary music. That's bothersome; by complying you feel as if you've sold your soul. The Fromm Foundation Concerts are a great antidote. And I think commissions by orchestras are an excellent approach to getting new music heard by the widest and so-called most knowledgeable audience. It's the only way to get new works systematically integrated into the repertory. So if a composer can somehow get a commission from a symphony, or possibly from a major chamber group or soloist, he's probably done the best thing possible for contemporary music—always provided he delivers a good work.

I don't get much income from my compositions—just a few royalties here and there. Most of my income comes from performance and private teaching. I have kept up with my composing, although not as much as I might like. I played my cello piece in Alice Tully Hall [in New York] last year. Then there's my timpani concerto which I like very much. I'm going to conduct it next year. My music is a little far out.

I have founded an orchestra of people, drawn mainly from the recording industry, to play my concerto and other pieces. I call it the Riverside Orchestra. Many performers in the commercial world are among the finest players in existence; they usually play only in recording studios. But just ask them, and they'll jump at the opportunity to play in a chamber group or in your home or any place. These people never say no, and they're the best you can find. Getting all these musicians into a permanent orchestra would be a multi-million-dollar operation. They're too busy—they're making a fine living and don't want to change their way of life. If you have an orchestra concert to give, though, they're available. In fact, I just conducted a concert at the Cathedral of St. John the Divine and had many of them sitting in my orchestra. I conducted a concert at the UN last year and again the orchestra comprised some of the finest players. Ask them to play and you don't even have to finish the sentence or offer triple scale. They're hungry for such things.

My main frustration in life is that there's not enough time to do everything I like to do. Also, I guess I'm disappointed in people. Even though, not being a teenager, I know what to expect from human nature, I am still surprised when someone isn't what he seems to be. I can still be fooled. I think I'm blasé and totally existentialist—and then someone I'd put some hope in does something wrong. We have to look for ways of improving mankind; going to the moon isn't enough.

Since I'm primarily a performer, I derive the greatest satisfaction from performing well and getting my message across. This happens on occasion. Sometimes getting a student to understand something about the left hand is very satisfying. Gratification is cumulative. If you feel you're thoroughly living your art, that's great satisfaction.

I come from a showbiz background. My father was a vaudevillian who did the Eastern circuit from Maine down to Florida. After he married my mother, the two of them had an act together, and they remained in vaudeville for many years. I was brought up in that environment.

One way or another, I heard and made music all my life. Mother was an organist in a Catholic church in Norwich, Connecticut. I sang in her choir. Both my parents were singers too—Mother was a coloratura and Father a high baritone. They put on many musical plays for the church, and every year Mother did a musical for the Hadassah Society. So you see, at an early age I'd been exposed to all kinds of music. I heard arias, religious music, an awful lot of show tunes, some good music, some bad. With all that listening, music came to me naturally. I'm the youngest of three and the only one who became a singer—though it had never entered my mind as a youngster to become one.

Mother was my first music teacher. She taught me voice and piano. After high school, the natural next step was to come to New York to study. I had no intention of staying; I'd never been away from home and the idea seemed ridiculous. However, Mother thought I had some talent and she wanted me to further it. So I moved to the big city in 1939.

I started taking private lessons right away. And I needed a job. In those days, everybody auditioned for radio; I tried out for a job with the CBS Chorus and got it. I started working for CBS in 1940; by 1941 I had my own show, a half hour a week. I'd usually do an aria, a couple of art songs in German or French and a song in English. I loved it. Every broadcast was marvelous. With the advent of TV in 1947, live radio was phased out, but by then my name had gotten around, so I wasn't hard to sell.

Singing over the air was great—but very fatiguing. Remember, at that time if you did a commercial show in New York you repeated it three hours later for the West Coast. I did those repeat performances all year for seven years. And in the summer I did the Prudential Family Hour once and then once again. I did many other national shows twice-over. It snowballed. Of course, that left no time for the concert hall. At the very least, I had to learn a program a

Eileen Farrell, the singer, lives in Bloomington, Indiana and was interviewed in New York City in May, 1976.

week and that's a lot. But when TV came in I started concertizing and singing opera.

What a difference! For seven years my audience had been an imaginary one. All that while the microphone was the only thing in front of me and now here I was before live people. It was wonderful, but I don't think it altered my performance very much. I'd always been taught that if you sang the words with conviction you'd get your message over, whether through a microphone or before an audience.

Adequate preparation for an operatic role is much more time-consuming than preparing for a radio show, though. Say I'm learning an opera. If somebody asked me to be ready in four months, I would say that's preposterous. Give me a year and I'm willing to go ahead. It takes time for an opera to become part of you. On radio, in contrast, I always had the music in front of me. I didn't need to memorize anything. Nothing I sang was very long. Broadcasts and opera performances are different kettles of fish.

The way I learn a role in an opera is to *speak* it as a play, with somebody feeding me my lines, before I even touch the music. When the time comes to sing I know every word. My father was an actor and taught dramatics, so a feeling for drama rubbed off on me. I'm glad, because poor acting is a common deficiency among opera singers. It's important that we be able to act and dance as well as sing. I took dancing lessons for years, starting when I was five. Dancing is wonderful for your body. You become more graceful on stage when you have some idea of how to move and can be more supple. You really must be an all-around performer to do opera properly.

Unfortunately, many opera conductors seem to emphasize music over drama. Not all conductors are singers' conductors; they conduct opera scores as if they contain only music and no words. Others, though, are a pleasure to work with. I'm not sure I have a favorite, but I loved Dimitri Mitropoulos, whom I sang with a great deal. He was a very sympathetic person and marvelous with singers. Sure, I was afraid of some of the conductorial tyrants, but they never turned their wrath on me. Maybe this was because I was trained not to do anything unless I was very well prepared; I always told myself, if you know what you're doing, not much can go wrong. And not much does.

I sang at the Met for five years, but since I declined to sign a contract I wasn't at Rudolf Bing's beck and call. I could make five times as much money singing a recital as singing at the Met, and I couldn't imagine just being an opera singer. My God, to sing only opera would be so dull! I mean, after awhile, what roles are left to do?

I didn't have a hard time with Bing. We talked very seldom. The problem was simply that he seemed to dislike American singers and unfortunately I happened to be an American. I think Bing did American artists a particularly great disservice. The Metropolitan is our opera house and should be primarily for American singers, who I think are the greatest. He needn't have brought so many foreign artists over. During my last years at the Met, Mr. Bing told me that if I wanted to do an additional opera, he would ask one of the foreign artists to relinquish a role. I told him not to bother.

Almost the only really modern opera I've done is Alban Berg's *Wozzeck*, with Mitropoulos. We also did some Janáček, which is pretty far out. On the whole I don't care for twentieth-century operas. Give me Verdi, good old grand opera—cornball opera—that's for me.

Though I love the stuff, I must admit that those nineteenth-century opera composers wrote about an awful lot of dumb broads. They really did, you know. Their characters amount to nothing, really nothing. It's hard to know what you can do with them to make them more substantial. For instance, in *La Gioconda*, the heroine loses her mother; in every act she's finding her mother; by the fourth act when everybody's gone home, she's still on stage with, "Good God, where's my mother?" For me, one of the most interesting operas is *Maria Stuarda*. I enjoyed gathering material about Queen Elizabeth I and her era; she was quite a gal. I have also enjoyed doing Cherubini's *Medea*. I did it in concert form many times, and with the San Francisco opera on stage. It's quite a tour de force, a magnificent opera with Medea coming across as a tremendous woman. As for most of the other heroines, they just sing and die. You can make them more believable by stressing certain lines and not others—but it's hard.

Maria Stuarda was the last thing I recorded and I'm not eager to record any more. The whole process is terribly difficult. Every time you sing, it's a performance, and you might have to do five, six, seven takes for one aria. It's most exhausting. Suppose something sounds great to you but the conductor says, "That note's not right." You've got to do it all over again. Or you'll be recording a song and it's going along fine—when all of a sudden a guy in the orchestra hits something very flat. Once more you've got to do it all over again. Or you're singing with somebody else and you may feel, "Gee, this is OK," but your partner disagrees: "I don't like this—we gotta do it again."

I'm pretty dubious about records anyway, and whether they convey a singer's true sound. Last year Luciano Pavarotti came to Indiana University, where I teach, as part of a big concert series. The kids were telling me about him for weeks. "Had I heard his records?" they demanded.

"No and I'm not about to either," I retorted. Records are not the way to judge anybody's voice; sometimes the sound is all electronically contrived. But the students insisted that Pavarotti had the biggest, most gorgeous voice. Pavarotti, Pavarotti. OK already. I went to the recital. This big man came out on stage and began to sing. He had a charming lyric tenor voice, by no means a big voice, lovely but not likely to give you goose pimples. Here my kids had built this whole thing up, this is the greatest tenor alive and all. I thought, "Well, I mean, he's not bad, he has a nice voice, but to me this isn't a great voice." You've got to hear a singer in person to know for sure.

And you have to make up your own mind. There was a time years and years ago when I paid attention to critics, but I don't any more. I don't care what they say about me or anyone else. Nobody should decide anything on the basis of one man's opinion. The public, people like you and me, are at fault whenever we ask about a performance, "What kind of review did it get?" You may discover someone's great even if a critic pans him. The reviewer may have had a fight with his wife or might have indigestion and wish he was the hell out of the concert hall. Readers have no way of knowing. And too many critics are frustrated musicians—not all, but a lot. Virgil Thomson was good. And there's Alfred Frankenstein in San Francisco who is very good, a great opera lover. Then of course there was the famous gal in Chicago, Claudia Cassidy. Oh my, she could be awful to people, but she always said something nice about me.

Whose opinion does matter to me? Originally, my teacher's did. She was very honest, and I could never stand flatterers who invariably say you sound great. Well, you don't sound great all the time—that's impossible. For the past twenty-odd years, Edgar Vincent, the man who does my publicity, has been someone I could rely on implicitly.

He's always correct. I have good reason to trust his reactions—they've always been honest and accurate. I really think, though, that you yourself know whether you've done a good job or not. You don't need someone else to tell you.

I know that I've always tried my best—and I've done many things. One thing I never did was a musical comedy—never got around to it. But I once did a soundtrack for a movie, *Interrupted Melody*, a film biography of Marjorie Lawrence. That was easy. All I did was sing in a studio with an orchestra. We recorded a great deal, much of which wasn't used. Then Eleanor Parker, who did the acting, had to watch me, listen, mouth the words and so on. I didn't get on the list of credits. I got paid. What did I need with credit? But everybody wondered, "whose voice is that?" Eventually it came to light.

I sang popular songs as well as opera excerpts for that movie. Popular music comes naturally to me, since I have show business in my blood. And I've been exposed to a great deal of jazz. Don't forget, I lived in New York from 1939 on, and the 1940s were a great period for jazz. There was the Blue Angel and many other marvelous places where people performed and sang jazz. And the first score I ever bought was *Porgy and Bess*. I've seen it at least five times. Most of the records I play at home are jazz, instrumental as well as vocal. I hear Ella Fitzgerald and melt all over the floor. She's fantastic. What technique! Ella's never had a voice lesson in her life and she can tear you to pieces. Because of Ella and many many others like her, I've come to think that popular and jazz singing can't be taught. It's a flair. Either you have it or you don't. But a teacher can certainly help with other kinds of singing.

I've been teaching with great pleasure at Indiana University for the past five years or so. A dean had been after me for several years to come out and teach. I had never thought of doing so before. However, as I got older I got more critical of singers in general. I'd say to myself, "Now, if they would only do *this*, *that* would happen." I started analyzing different voices and I thought, "well maybe I *do* have something to offer budding singers. You never know." So I agreed to try.

Indiana has perhaps the largest music school in the world. And the faculty reads like Who's Who in the Music Business. Furthermore, they have a lot of performing teachers, on the assumption that we're very good for students. I think that's right.

I hope I've grown since I've been there. At first I had to figure out exactly what it is that I do when I sing, which wasn't so simple. I know intuitively, but for the first time I had to explain it to other people. And I think I can. But I never sing for my students. They will never learn by hearing me, but only by applying themselves.

One of my teachers used to sing a scale and then tell me to sing it and I would. I hadn't the slightest idea what I was doing beyond imitating a sound. She would say, "That's fine," and I was supposed to have learned something. But my most important teacher, whom I studied with for years and years, didn't work that way. She explained to me that I had to apply myself, my mind as well as my vocal cords, not imitate. That's when I really learned how to sing. You see, singing requires complete concentration and tremendous discipline. That's hard for kids. Some start out with no concentration span at all. The first thing I teach them is to discipline themselves not to be distracted, to concentrate entirely on singing. They soon discover how exhausting it can be!

Many of them don't realize that you can't just get up and sing. Musical talent helps but you also need brains and some depth of character. One of my students who graduated this month had everything. The day she walked into my studio I knew there was something special about her—I just knew it. And in four years her voice has developed beautifully. She has all those qualities we sum up as, "that certain something."

Indiana's really a special place. When voice students apply, they have to pass an entrance exam and sing for the whole faculty. There are seventeen of us in voice alone. We might admit them to the music school but they also have to be scholastically acceptable, which is a separate business. Those we take are of very high caliber. Then we have a brand new $12 million opera house right on campus. We do five operas a season, four performances of each opera, with two separate casts. It's utterly fantastic. Here we are in a little town, Bloomington, Indiana, out in the middle of nowhere, with this big opera house and people coming from all over the region. Prices help draw audiences I guess—no ticket's over $5. We have two dress rehearsals, one for each cast and anybody who's attached to the university can listen to them from the balcony for free—which is great! I wish opera around the country were as accessible.

I'm glad to have a job that keeps me settled in one place much of the year. I've certainly travelled in my time. Have I ever! Yet I never left home for months and months at a time. My son was born in 1947 and I didn't want to stay away from the family too long from then on, so I would only leave for maybe two weeks at a time. My career was important but my family was more important. My children appreciate music, though they're not musicians. One's in medical school and the other's in law school—she'll keep me healthy and he'll keep me out of jail. They *were* exposed to a lot of music as kids, and I know that will stay with them.

Juggling home and professional life hasn't been easy. However I have a very good, patient husband. We just celebrated our thirtieth wedding anniversary. Let me tell you, I gave him a medal for his patience. I *did* have live-in help to stay with my children because my husband worked too—as a New York City policeman.

Even so, at the beginning we always had money problems. When I started, managers took a heck of a big cut. It takes at least fifteen years before you can begin to save anything at all. And singers do need managers, especially those like me. I'm not the type of person who can go out and sell herself. Now finally, after 35 years, my manager doesn't have to sell me either. He answers the phone when it rings and then calls me to ask whether I want to do such and such a date. He never accepts unless I say yes and I only say yes to symphony dates these days.

From now on I want to focus on teaching, but it isn't so easy to extricate myself from the concert world. I've already done four performances this month, two *Tristans* and two orchestral dates; last month I did six. That's a pretty full schedule. And for some engagements I'm booked a couple of years in advance. I'm generally busiest at the beginning or end of the season, in other words, opening or closing a series. Tomorrow night I fly to Miami, then I go to Daytona Beach, then back to Maine; next month I give a week-long master class at school and go on to St. Louis and Ames, Iowa—and then finally back to the country—Maine—until school opens again.

It's a hectic life. Always has been. But I've had fun. I've done radio, concerts, opera, television, recordings, teaching. I've done it all. I just love variety.

Photo by Daniel Rosenberg

I took up the harmonica as a lark. I grew up in Baltimore, and when I was fourteen the Baltimore *Evening Star* ran a harmonica contest as a promotion stunt. I bought a mouth organ and found it was easy to play. Then I learned a light classical piece, which won me the prize because all the other kids played jazz and popular numbers and the judge was a classical musician. I wasn't the best player, but I won the contest. About three months later, I just left home without telling my parents. I had money because I sold *Liberty* magazines. My "fortune"—twenty-five or thirty dollars—was enough to buy me a ticket to New York and then some.

Now, I had met a New York musician passing through Baltimore named Nat Brusiloff, who had said to me casually, "If you ever come to the Big City, kid, look me up." That's all the invitation I needed. The minute I got to New York I looked him up and he was astounded and rather horrified to find this fourteen-year-old kid on his doorstep. But he was a nice, kindly man, so he took me around. He was a violinist with the NBC Orchestra and had a lot of contacts. He took me to meet Borrah Minevitch who had a harmonica band. Borrah auditioned me (I remember all the boys in his band standing outside the dressing room listening). I played *Poet and Peasant*. When I finished Minevitch said, "Kid, you stink."

I walked dejectedly out of the dressing room and the boys just sort of patted me on the back, trying to be sympathetic, but what could they do? I started for Penn Station, to take the train back to Baltimore, because if Minevitch rejected me, what hope was there? But on the way I passed the Paramount Theater and saw Rudy Vallee's name in lights and something—I don't know what—made me decide to play for Rudy Vallee. I checked my bag at the Astor Hotel, sneaked in at the stage door of the Paramount, past the doorman, found Rudy, and started playing the mouth organ at him, just like that. All he could say was, "What the hell are you doing?"

And I told him my story. He said, "I can't do anything for you." I said, "I've heard you on the radio—you are always presenting new talents." He thought a minute and said, "Well look, I tell you what, come back tonight. I'll take you down to the club where I'm working and put you on there." And he did—but I flopped. Nobody listened

Larry Adler, the harmonica player, lives in London, and was interviewed there in April 1973 and in New York City in May 1976.

to me. But Rudy Vallee had taken some notice of me. That gave me the encouragement I needed to stay.

I still had about eighteen dollars left. Nat Brusiloff let me live in his house rent-free. Within a few days he got me a job synchronizing music for an animated cartoon called "Pony Boy." And soon after that I was signed up for a travelling road show. There I was, fourteen years old, with a contract for forty weeks at a hundred dollars a week! So I was in show business. I played two songs—"Button Up Your Overcoat" and "I Want To Be Loved By You." During those forty weeks I learned what I needed to know about handling myself on stage, and became quite a pro.

At one point we were playing in Chicago at the Oriental Theater, and were invited after the show to a party at the Croydon Hotel. The host, whose name I didn't know, started talking to me: "You're Jewish, ain't you?"

"Yes."

He said, "I'm Catholic," and I said, "That's nice."

Next: "You go to shul?" [temple]

"I do five, six or seven shows a day and I can't go to shul."

He was outraged and made me promise that the following Saturday, no matter how many shows I had, I would get up early and go to shul. He also wanted to know if my mother and father were living? They were. "You write to them every day, huh?" No, I wrote once every two weeks, maybe. Which also displeased him. "I don't like that. Look, get your coat, go on home. I'd rather not see a kid like you here. At home, you're gonna sit down and write your parents a nice letter. You promise?" I promised. So I went over to the comedian Harry Ross (who's still alive, by the way) and I asked, "Who's that busybody?"

"Come on, Larry, you've got to be kidding."

"No, no—what's his name?"

The name was Al Capone. I went to shul and wrote to my folks.

While growing up rather fast, I was also developing as a musician. I was deeply influenced by people like Duke Ellington and Louis Armstrong. Later on, when I played "Ain't Misbehavin'," I'd imitate Armstrong. And Ellington—I would listen every night for his broadcast from the Cotton Club. To me "Mood Indigo" was like a Schubert melody. I thought it was wonderful. It was quite a thrill, some years later, when Ellington and I went to the Grand Terrace in

Chicago together. He played the piano and I played the harmonica and we did "Sophisticated Lady." I'll never forget that night.

Now, I didn't play any classical pieces at the beginning of my career, but after a while I got tired of playing popular songs—and remember, in those days popular songs were written by people like Gershwin, Kern, and Porter—but even so, I yearned for the kinds of things I heard Rachmaninoff play, for example. He was a great idol of mine. As a kid, I studied the piano for a couple of years, but I was a poor student. I never practiced. Unfortunately, no one ever made clear to me the value of a really good musical foundation; I am still a bad sightreader. By ear I can play almost anything. But to read notes is still a painful process for me.

The first classical piece I played professionally was Ravel's *Bolero*. Then I learned things like Kreisler's *Caprice Viennoise*, de Falla's *Fire Dance*—nothing too profound. I wasn't anywhere near ready to play Bach. My passion for Bach started when a girlfriend of mine gave me a record of the Double Violin Concerto, played by Menuhin and Enesco, for my 21st birthday. It didn't get through to me right away, but because she had given it to me I played it a few times and one day I found I was singing it without the record. I realized that the concerto meant something to me, and I got more and more into it until I really started to appreciate Bach. Now I'd rather play Bach than almost anyone else. In the early days I preferred showier pieces, novelties. Depth comes with maturity.

In 1937, when I was in my early twenties, I gave my first solo classical recital, with piano accompaniment, at a place called Grotian Hall in London. It no longer exists; it was bombed out. Cyril Scott, a composer who is still alive, wrote a piece for me for that recital. I don't know what happened to the piece—disappeared I guess. The critics took no notice of the concert. They thought it was a stunt. Even so, I was now bitten by the idea of getting more into the classical field. My accompanist, Arthur Young, taught me many things, including the Vivaldi Violin Concerto in A minor. He played it on the piano and I learned it by ear. The next year I was in Sydney for a benefit concert with the Sydney Symphony Orchestra. They had asked me to be soloist. I chose to play the Vivaldi. They were amazed. They expected me to pick something like "Smoke Gets in Your Eyes." The concert went over very well.

When I came back to the States in 1939, I met my old friend Paul Draper, the dancer. I suggested to him that we try doing a joint recital, which we did at the Lobero Theater in Santa Barbara, California. I remember my agent coming up to hear it and saying, forget it. Nobody is going to pay good money to listen to a tap dancer and a harmonica player doing classical music. And it looked as if he was right. Because, although we got good notices and a pretty good house, and then did another concert in Chicago, everyone still thought it was a stunt. When we tried to hit a serious concert manager—we approached Columbia Concerts—they thought we were two night club performers who really wanted to use the concert platform for publicity.

Finally they were persuaded to take us on—that is, to lend us their name and nothing more—and they booked us about six or seven halls that we had to pay for. We didn't get any fee, but we came out of the six concerts with a profit of about $75, which amazed Columbia because they thought we would be heavily in debt. They then started to book us at fees and within three years, Paul Draper and Larry Adler were the hottest concert attraction in America. We were getting fees like $3500, $5000 a concert and in some places, like Los Angeles or the San Francisco Opera House, we wouldn't take a fee—we just took over the house and did beautifully. At the City Center in New York we played for a week between Christmas and New Year's in 1948 and we took in $52,000, which was the biggest gross on Broadway that week.

Then I proceeded to ruin the whole thing when I got into political trouble. First, I supported Henry Wallace in his third party candidacy for President; anyone who did so was considered ipso facto to be a Communist. Then the Hearst papers waged a campaign to drive Draper and Adler out of show business. We were a *cause célèbre*, front page news and all. But as far as performing was concerned, we were through. We couldn't work. You couldn't have booked me for free benefits. It was so ironic; just a few years before, The Chicago *Tribune*, on its radio station WGN, had the Chamber of Commerce nominate me as an outstanding young American, worthy of having his life story dramatized over WGN. Later on, I should have threatened to expose them: "Oh, what I could tell McCarthy about you."

Anyway, with all that notorious publicity, my only recourse,

and Draper's also, was to go to England where I was known and welcome. I had been in England for a few years in the thirties, and
found no difficulty getting back into the swing of things.

In 1952 I came back to America briefly and decided to put on a
recital to see what the reaction would be. So I hired Town Hall and
was told the next day they were cancelling my reservation—one
member of the Board had decided I was a Red and that they mustn't
let me play there. Though I had never met him, I called Norman
Thomas about this, because he was also on the Town Hall board. He
was very indignant and got me Town Hall back. I gave the recital and
the press went absolutely mad—in fact, the notices I got were far in
excess of the program I played. I wasn't that good. I did a good recital, but honestly, you'd have thought it was the greatest musical event
since Heifetz's debut. They were just glad to see me back. But Sol
Hurok couldn't book me further, even with such good notices. I
thought it was the end for me in America.

But in 1959 I was invited back and played the Village Gate and
a few other places. Very recently things have been picking up in the
States again. I played a long engagement at the Rainbow Room in
New York a couple summers ago, and just finished some concerts
with George Solti and the Chicago Symphony.

This time around, as in the past, critics have generally been very
good to me—so good that I actually remember the bad notices,
they're so rare. A critic on Montreal's *La Presse* thinks I've got
nothing—no talent, no musical ability, and also that I play a lousy
instrument. "Eh." That's his opinion. I really think he could head-
line his reviews with an "eh."

The critical reception in the U.S. has been excellent for the
most part, but not entirely. For instance, when Draper and I were a
team and did our second concert together in Chicago, a long time
ago, Cecil Smith, a critic for the Chicago *Tribune*, wrote in effect that
I don't seem to be a musician because what I play is not an instrument; Draper doesn't seem to be a dancer because what he does it
not, strictly speaking, dancing. Also, he remarked that we were "two
people who do whatever they do like a house of cards that will very
shortly collapse." Claudia Cassidy of the *Tribune* always gave me
good reviews though, as did the Chicago *Daily News* critic. Likewise
the New York press.

But I had problems from another quarter. For a long time the

Musicians Union didn't recognize the mouth organ either. Then in 1943 or so, the union went on strike against the recording and broadcasting companies, and for a while, if you wanted to make a record, you could *only* make it with a mouth organ. So suddenly the union decided it *was* an instrument after all.

A little earlier, when Margaret Case Harriman did a profile of me in *The New Yorker*, I told her that the mouth organ wasn't recognized by the union. She called them and they confirmed it. To them the mouth organ was a toy. That provoked her. "What do you mean, a toy?"

"Well, there is no music written for it."

"I beg your pardon, there *is* music written for it. Larry Adler has had a work written for him by Darius Milhaud and he plays it with symphony orchestras."

"Oh Larry Adler, that's different. He's a freak."

When the union decided that the harmonica was legit, they insisted that mouth organ players join up. I was the first one accepted as a member, and Jimmy Petrillo touched little fingers with me. Petrillo wouldn't shake hands because he was afraid of germs but apparently the little finger doesn't carry germs, so that was O.K. The night I was "admitted" he took me with him to a banquet. As guest of honor, he talked about orphan children and started to cry. Real tears rolled down his face. He was like Louis B. Mayer. It was synthetic emotion. He could really turn it on. He'd use up five handkerchiefs in one speech to the membership.

For all his foibles, though, Petrillo sure changed things in the music business. When I started out, musicians worked a seven-day week in cinemas, playing four, five, six shows a day for $18. Petrillo surely did a lot for them.

But it wasn't the union that helped get me back to these shores. It was one of those personal quirks of fate—being in the right place at the right time and all that. A few summers ago I met Fran Cole, a harpsichordist from America, when she was visiting England. Upon her return to New York, she heard a record of mine (she hadn't even known I played the harmonica). Fran figured, "Jesus Christ, the guy's got talent." She wrote me a letter inviting me to come to New York and play in her harpsichord festival. I was glad to. Since I was going to New York for a concert at Carnegie Hall, it seemed like a good idea to get Paul Draper as well. I suggested it, and she got

Paul. He and I did our "act" at Carnegie. It was a very emotional evening. Both of us got standing ovations on our separate entrances. And a Rainbow Grill engagement came out of that. I was to have been there three weeks, but they extended it to five. Those were the first local performances in many years.

Sometime soon I'd like to do a tour of my one-man show in universities. I think it would go over well. It's a two-hour presentation, and in a third of it I use taped accompaniments, with people like Django Rheinhardt on guitar and Herb Alpert on trumpet. It's more or less an autobiographical study. I do the *Rhapsody in Blue* and talk about knowing Gershwin; I do some Bach, usually the unaccompanied violin sonatas, or some of the vocal pieces like the *Sicilienne* or the *Vocalise*. Even if it's extracted from a piano sonata, almost any Bach fits the mouth organ fantastically. He wrote a melody like *Bist du bie Mire*, the sadness of which tears your heart out. It's beautiful. So is *Jesu, Joy of Man's Desire*. How can people say that Bach didn't write melodies? The middle movement of the Double Violin Concerto is one of the most beautiful melodies in the world.

I even play Bach in jails. I'm active in an organization called Radical Alternatives to Prison, which tries to improve things for prisoners. I play the prisons every year.

Despite my long political involvement, I don't think of music and politics as necessarily intertwined. There used to be a famous expression: "If you have a message, send for Western Union." I don't think any creative artist should *insist* on having a political reason for his creation. You may have a good reason for putting politics into your work, as Hans Eisler did, or Pablo Casals, who made one of the greatest political gestures, I think, in refusing to play in Spain so long as there was a Fascist government there, even though he himself was a loyal and devoted Spaniard. Or look at Picasso and the Guernica mural. These were very inspired acts, and one can only admire, applaud, and even envy them; but I think it's wrong to say that you *must* have a political reason before you can create. If I am composing and a melody comes to me, I don't say, "Hey, that's a left-wing melody." I may be able to turn it to a left-wing purpose, but I don't think it was a left-wing idea that put it into my head.

Now, the way politics and art get mixed up can sometimes get rather sticky. I remember being asked to picket Carnegie Hall when the pianist Walter Gieseking was going to play, soon after the war; he had lived in Germany through the Nazis and not opened his mouth. And I said, "I don't like Gieseking's opinions, but my protest is best made, I think, by staying away from his concerts, not by keeping him from performing." He was one of the great pianists and, anyway, I don't think one artist should try to keep another artist out of work because he doesn't like his politics. So I wouldn't picket. But if Gieseking had asked me to do a joint recital with him, let's say, I don't think I would have. Or if I were asked to be soloist with Herbert von Karajan, who I think is a great conductor, I don't think I could do it. Not that he has asked me to. But I couldn't actually work with a man I felt to be a Nazi.

I remember how I used to feel about Richard Strauss. I was in Garmisch-Parten-Kirchen in 1945, about three weeks after the end of the War, doing shows for the troops, and an American colonel there said to me, "You know, Richard Strauss lives about two miles from here. Would you like to meet him?"

I replied vehemently, "I don't want to meet that Nazi." I regret to this day that I said that. I would have loved to have met Strauss. I would have said to him, "I play the mouth organ. I'd like you to hear me. Would you consider writing a piece for me?" Well, I lost that opportunity.

Many composers *have* written for me, though. Ralph Vaughan Williams, Arthur Benjamin, Gordon Jacob, Malcolm Arnold, Alexander Tcherepnin, and Darius Milhaud. When composers compose for me, I give them a diagram, showing what the mouth organ can and can't do. It is no use, for example, for a composer to write an interval of C and F because you exhale for C and inhale for F. Unless you've got some special kind of lungs, you can't play these two notes together.

My harmonica has three octaves, starting at middle C. There's a larger one with a four-octave range, but it's correspondingly bulky, and I can't handle it easily. I prefer to sacrifice range for greater mobility and ease of movement.

There are very few chords on the harmonica, but composers tend to be fascinated with what there are. The second movement of the Milhaud is almost all in chords; most of the Vaughan Williams is too. When you combine the limited chords of the mouth organ with the right kind of orchestral background, it sounds quite fascinating.

Most of the composers who have written for me didn't realize beforehand how versatile the harmonica is. When Stewart Wilson, the former director of Covent Garden, and a great friend of Vaughan Williams and mine, introduced us for the first time, the composer and I had the following exchange.

Williams: As I understand the mouth organ, you play one note by exhaling and the next note by inhaling.

Adler: That's right.

Williams: Then it's impossible to get a smooth legato; when you change breaths, surely you break the line.

Adler: Well logically, yes, but I'll play you a piece by Bach. (And I did.) Could you tell where I altered the line?

Williams: No. That's amazing.

The first piece of mine the BBC Orchestra played was the Vaughan Williams. After that Arthur Benjamin told me that if the BBC would commission him, he'd write a concerto for me. It was partly at Vaughan Williams' urging: "Arthur," he said, "Now it's your turn. You must write something for Larry." Next day I called the BBC and they gave Benjamin the nod.

It was not hard to get the composers to see what the mouth organ could do. Usually conductors are also quite responsive. I felt the tongue lash of a conductor only once. It was Eugene Ormandy, around 1944, when he was doing the Ford Symphony Hour. I heard later that he didn't like the idea of conducting for a mouth organist. It was beneath him. When I got to the rehearsal, not knowing this, he rehearsed the orchestra and kept me waiting. A conductor usually tells his soloist exactly what time to be there, and when he comes, stops everything to rehearse the soloist. Ormandy stayed with the orchestra until only about fifteen minutes of rehearsal time were left, all the time ignoring me. I finally came out on stage, seething. I knew he had done it deliberately. Then I gave the violinist my A, and Ormandy asked, "What's going on?"

I said, "The orchestra has to take my A because I can't tune to them."

He replied, "That's ridiculous."

I told him, "Mr. Ormandy, I've done this work before with *this* orchestra. If conducting me in any way disturbs you, I think we can do it without you." Never in my life, before or since, have I been rude to a conductor. Anyway, he tapped his stand, went on with the work, and never spoke to me again.

I'm doing a good bit of composing myself now. I made a very lucky start in composition some years ago, when I wrote the music for a film called *Genevieve,* which has since become a classic. Since then I have done about twelve films. I've also done the music for a play that was recently in London's West End called *Say Goodnight to Grandma.* About three years ago I did the songs for a play at the Mermaid called *Enter Solly Gold.* That was about a crook-rabbi. It was very funny. Last year I did the music for a BBC-TV play called *The Mad Trapper* and the year before I did the score for another BBC production called *Soda Water Fountain.* I just did the music for a BBC documentary about the East End of London.

The only classical piece I ever wrote is a "theme and variations." I've thought about making a potpourri of my film music for harmonica and symphony orchestra. And André Kostelanetz keeps telling me that I should write the definitive harmonica concerto, but I've not yet been able to do it.

Besides music, I write a lot of articles these days. I review books regularly for the Sunday *Times* of London, the *Spectator,* and *New Society,* with occasional pieces for *The New Statesman.* I've started an autobiography, which was commissioned by Doubleday many years ago, but which I've never managed to finish. I still owe it to them. In the interim, I did a book of jokes Doubleday published in 1962. I write political articles as well. I've written about the Vietnam War. In England the political causes I've been most involved with are the anti-Apartheid movement and the Alternatives to Prison group.

My writing's very important to me. I've always been a thwarted writer, perhaps because I played the mouth organ and felt that I wasn't in the legitimate channels of music; I felt like a musical poor relation. There was a time when I wanted to write to show that a mouth organ player could actually think. I don't feel inferior any more—not since the composers started writing for me. I recorded the Milhaud, Arnold, Benjamin, and Vaughan Williams pieces with Morton Gould and the Royal Philharmonic Orchestra, on RCA, in 1969.

I love playing with symphony orchestras, just for the sheer majesty of the sound. I've played with several in Great Britain and Canada, and in the United States, with the Pittsburgh Symphony, the New York Philharmonic, the Philadelphia Orchestra, the Cincinnati

Symphony, the Chicago Symphony and the Los Angeles Philharmonic. The Baltimore Symphony has asked me to solo. You can't know what that means to me! As a child, I used to go hear the Baltimore Symphony; those were gods up there on stage; the conductor, Gustave Struby, was the man who judged me harmonica champion at the contest that launched my youthful career. Playing with the Baltimore Symphony is almost more of an achievement for me than playing with the New York Philharmonic.

I hope to do more concerts like the one I did in the summer of 1973 with the pianist John Ogdon. We did a Gershwin-Ravel evening and enjoyed it enormously. We played a work Ira Gershwin gave me as a present—an unpublished string quartet George Gershwin wrote around 1919 called *Lullabye*. We made a transcription for harmonica and piano. I had already recorded it—Morton Gould scored it for mouth organ and orchestra.

I met George Gershwin in 1929, backstage at the Roxy Theater. Later he authorized Robert Russell Bennett to reorchestrate the *Rhapsody in Blue* for me, which I recorded. Once, when Gershwin heard me play the *Rhapsody*, he said, "Larry, you make it sound as if I wrote it for the harmonica." Then, in 1944, I moved to Beverly Hills, mainly to be psychoanalyzed. There was a man there who worked with a lot of show business people. It didn't take long before I was in with people like Ira Gershwin, Frank Loesser, Harry Kurnitz (a very funny screenwriter), David Selznick, Willie Wyler, Henry Koster. I found myself in the midst of a very nice, creative group of people. I also met Charles Chaplin—I used to play tennis with him quite a lot. He was in his sixties then but my God he was fast on the court. Also, a few blocks from where I lived, were Stravinsky, Thomas Mann, Hindemith, Schönberg.

While in L.A., I once did a concert with Marian Anderson and Artur Rubinstein at the Hollywood Bowl and later on, with Albert Spalding and Marian Anderson at the Salvation Army. Rubinstein was jealous of me for a very odd reason: people kept saying that I told better stories than he did. Rubinstein has always prided himself on being a good raconteur. As such he has his faults; he doesn't edit, he doesn't get to the point, he loves to wander. But so what? Artur Rubinstein is one of the very greatest pianists.

I never played professionally with Jascha Heifetz, who also lives in L.A. However, in London, Lady Ravensdale used to give parties which Jascha and I attended, and there he would play the accordion while I played the mouth organ.

I met Stravinsky at Chaplin's house, but I never got to know him well, which is a pity because I wanted him to write something for me. I never quite had the nerve to suggest it to him. It was the same with Rachmaninoff. I would have given anything if Rachmaninoff had written for me, but the two times I met him, I couldn't even say "how do you do." That man overawed me, just froze me up. He had a face that looked like the Siberian wasteland. When I was five years old my uncle took me to hear Rachmaninoff play. I remember that concert very clearly. It made a tremendous impression on me. I wanted to do what he did, to be a concert pianist. But I didn't have the discipline to practice by the hour. So, by the time I met the man, he had become such a legend to me that it was nearly like facing the sun full on. I couldn't be natural with him.

Rachmaninoff had fantastic dignity, but he was very forbidding, very off-putting. And yet, I'm told that people who knew him well found him warm and lovable. He showed none of this to strangers.

Getting back to Stravinsky, the only piece I play of his is called *Chanson Russe*, a beautiful little thing. I heard Nathan Milstein play it once on the violin and decided I'd like to try it. Transcribing pieces for the harmonica isn't always easy. It depends. *Afternoon of a Faun* by Debussy was terribly difficult to transcribe. But *Chanson Russe* was not because it was already in violin-piano form.

I'm always looking for new pieces that will work on the harmonica. My practicing is done mainly when I'm studying something new. That is one of my great weaknesses as a musician—I don't practice. I have no steady routine. Every musician should, I know, but I don't. Since I never had a teacher, I learned bad habits.

Nonetheless I teach, but it's only been eight or nine years since I've taken private pupils. Before that I was afraid to; I hadn't had a conventional beginning myself, so I didn't know how to start people. If you knew how to play, I could criticize what you did, sharpen it up, and do a lot for you. But I found—and still find—it very difficult to start from the basic groundwork. I can do it, but it's damned hard.

Also, at one point I had the feeling that no one should be allowed to play the harmonica except me. I was used to being an oddball. But I've since become a more magnanimous fellow.

I have some very good students. Three of my English pupils are already getting professional engagements. I also have students in distant parts, like Japan and Israel. They take lessons from me by sending me letters and maybe tapes of their work. I listen and then write back with suggestions. The last two summers I taught a class in harmonica at the Summer School of Music in Barry, Glamorganshire, Wales. I had about fourteen pupils there. When I played at the Rainbow Grill in 1975, we put an ad in the paper saying that I would teach a master class. I expected about a dozen people to show up. Around 450 came! They were all mouth organ players and I had to listen to every bloody one of them. I listened and criticized, listened and criticized. Three of them wanted to come to England to study with me. One was about fifteen, but the others were grown men.

Despite all this, I still find many people are incredulous about the mouth organ as a serious instrument. For example, I have never done a serious concert in Germany. I have done TV shows there, but they won't invite me to do a recital. The same is true in Russia. Once I met the composer Aram Khatchaturian and played for him. He said to me, "I will have to take your records back with me; otherwise no one will believe me when I tell them about you. No one plays real music on the harmonica."

Mostly, though, people are wonderfully nice. Once in Chicago, for example, I got the most beautiful compliment: Duke Ellington introduced me to Billie Holliday and she said, "Man, you don't play that thing, you sing it!"

Part Five: Music in the Inner City

23: Dorothy Maynor

*I*was born in Norfolk, Virginia, a seaport town surrounded by tidewater. I fell in love with the way one river led to another. Ever since I have been fascinated by water. I know that Norfolk reminds many people of warships, but we did have beautiful sailboats too. To reach most trains you had to catch a boat that went up the coast to New York, to the Eastern Shore, or to Pennsylvania. And going inland you took a ferry. So we were water people who felt very much in touch with the whole world, partly because sailors from everywhere were all around us.

I chose my mother and father very wisely. My father was a businessman and a Methodist minister. He did much to revive old congregations and refurbish neglected old churches in little hamlets. We all used to help him. My sister played the organ. I played the piano for Sunday School (I had started taking piano lessons at the age of six) and my brother was a chauffeur for the elderly. Music was very much a part of our lives. We would gather together with friends and neighbors on Sunday afternoons; our porch and the yard ran over with people who came to sing. It was a great joy to my father and mother to have people come together at the house to make music.

Radio meant a lot to us too. I remember hearing the Damrosch broadcasts with the New York Philharmonic every week. There was a children's listening hour, a great event in my house; everybody had to be quiet and sit and listen to the symphonies.

Then again, in eighth grade, I made another happy choice—this time a school, the academy at Hampton Institute, just across the Bay. There I met two remarkable musicians. One was Ernest Hayes, the organist, whom my mother engaged to continue my piano studies; the other was R. Nathaniel Dett, the composer and conductor. Dr. Dett had a chorus which I joined. The following year, I sang my first solo in Carnegie Hall. I was twelve! Dr. Dett had made a perfectly beautiful arrangement of Thomas Campion's As By the Streams of Babylon; I sang a line and the chorus repeated it. Later on the choir traveled, first in this country and then in Europe for four months.

Hampton was really a special place. Dr. Dett brought to the school many important performing visual artists, to make sure we got a well-rounded cultural education. I remember seeing great ballet— Ruth St. Denis and Ted Shawn both came, each with an entire com-

Dorothy Maynor, the singer, is the founder and Director of the Harlem School of the Arts, New York City, and was interviewed at the school in April 1976.

pany. Where did the funds for all this come from? Dr. Dett thought that if a school could charge students five dollars a year for athletic fees, it could charge them five dollars a year for music and art fees. So he got that ruling through the board. Students paid their five dollars, workers and teachers paid ten apiece. So with 1000 students paying five dollars and 500 adults paying ten dollars, that covered the budget. Once John Philip Sousa's band came to Hampton—which was wonderful for the boys in *our* band. Dr. Dett did wonders for the school. His philosophy of arts education had a profound effect on me.

At Hampton I trained to be a public school music teacher, but I got enormously interested in conducting and went to the Westminster Choir College in Princeton to study choral conducting; I got a scholarship to study there under John Finley Williamson. I then planned to accept a college job in Greensboro, North Carolina, thinking I would very much enjoy handling young voices and helping them grow. Meanwhile I had enough money to spend three months in New York.

This was the summer of 1937; I was in my twenties. I came to the big city and worked with Wilfrid Klomroth, who was well-known as a singing teacher. At the end of the summer, Mr. Klomroth wouldn't hear of my going away to teach—he insisted that I stay and study with him. Even so, I continued to work on teaching techniques. I sang because I enjoyed singing, but I hadn't yet thought of doing it professionally.

After working with Mr. Klomroth for two years, I said to myself, "Oh come on now, it's time to find out whether I should be singing instead of teaching, which is my first love." Generous friends had helped support me in New York but Father had died in the meantime and I had to look after Mother. I needed some kind of steady work. At this time, a friend from Boston, who had been the dean of women at Hampton Institute, invited me to visit, asking whether I'd like Serge Koussevitzky's opinion on my singing. Would I! It was 1939, and I hadn't had a vacation in twelve years. I decided to go to the music festival and try to get an audition. On my second day there his secretary called and said he'd be very glad to hear me.

Just then Koussevitzky was in the midst of auditioning bass players for the first desk; the bass was his instrument and he was quite engrossed in the tryouts. But he stopped everything, and I sang. Apparently, he was very pleased, and asked if I would sing for the whole orchestra the next day at the picnic in the shed. So I got on the telephone and called my accompanist in New York and said, "You'd better come along right away, because I want this to be right." I sang "Oh Sleep Why Dost Thou Leave Me?" from Handel's *Semele*, something from Charpentier's *Louise* and some Mozart concert arias. The press was there, my impromptu "recital" hit the papers, and that was the end of my vacation. I never got another. After those two days in Tanglewood, I had to come back to New York—to prepare for my debut that November.

For my debut at Town Hall I did a lieder recital. It was announced in all the papers. People had great expectations and the place was sold out. So I was under pressure, but I had lots of friends there, which helped, and I remember an English friend came backstage afterward and said, "If you think you are the only person who sang that concert tonight you are mistaken." Everybody was pulling for me. I really felt I was among friends, among fellow music lovers. Often I meet people who tell me they were at that first concert.

That concert went very well. But remember, I'd already had quite a bit of experience on stage. I used to sing in the summers to raise money for Hampton Institute and, before that, in my father's churches. I toured with a quartet. Sometimes I even accompanied myself on the piano. Oh, I loved to sing. I was a bird. And I didn't care if I was singing alone or in an ensemble.

In those days, long tours didn't faze me too much. I was very healthy and had a lot of strength. When I was very young, my group gave seven concerts in nine days. Then we had four concerts one week, three the next. It never let up. Once my solo career was launched, I sang all over North and South America, in Hawaii, Europe, and Australia. I remember going on a South American tour, coming back to New York for three days and then taking off for Europe. What a schedule!

The concerts in South America were really quite different from all the rest. First of all, they do little advance publicity. You come to a city and it's announced that you're singing on such and such a date. Period. You might have very few people at your first concert. But you stay in that city and give anywhere from eight to twelve performances, two a week. If you get good reviews, more and more people come. You can't repeat any repertory, so you go prepared for a dozen different programs. Even *after* your first recital, you have to prove yourself again and again. But once you've built up an audience in Buenos Aires or Rio or Caracas, you never lose it. The South Americans are most demonstrative. They don't clap their hands as much as use their feet to applaud. It's like a stampede, with the dust of the old theaters billowing up at you. At first I didn't know whether to run or stay put.

In this country, there were race problems but I seldom had to deal with them face to face. I had buffers who protected me. But I could not sing at the Metropolitan or any other opera house. At that time Negroes couldn't do opera in the U.S. I studied 27 operas and never could sing one. That was pure racism. Then there were annoying non-artistic things, such as exclusion from hotels. For a long while Negroes couldn't stay in New York hotels and for even longer we were barred in the hinterlands. Many places made exceptions for me, but some didn't. Then perhaps I'd be invited to stay at the home of the chairman of the board. Only it's much better to stay in a hotel room where you have your own privacy, which is important if you've got to work or study and set your own pace.

My managers must have handled a lot of problems I never even knew about. They shielded me from them. I felt bad about the operas. Only once did I perform in opera, in concert form, under Thomas Sherman. No one else ever gave me a chance. At the end of Marian Anderson's career she did what they called a guest performance at the Metropolitan. That broke the color barrier. Negroes were accepted after that, but she was the first; and I think they gave her that honor because she really should have been there years and years before. Finally I think that, at least for singers, prejudice is really breaking down.

Nothing else really stood in my way. Critics were kind to me, I'm told, though I never read them. I felt I knew my own inadequacies better than anyone else. My husband always told me when I got a good review, but to this day I refuse to read them.

I can't think of any one "peak" performance, but I do recall being thrilled on several occasions when I arrived at new insights about a given composition, maybe an aria from Weber's *Der Freischütz*, or something by Handel or Mozart. I love working out new phrasings, new approaches. The search for underlying meaning is constant. I remember my old friend Ernest Hayes telling me, "Remember now, the hit you make today will not win tomorrow's ballgame." Each time you work on a piece it's a brand new experience.

If I went to the piano now and took down a score, any score, the excitement of going through it would just give me goose pimples. I'd think to myself, "Here is one theme, and here's another; now it's up to you to find the key to it all." That's the excitement of music. All musicians should feel it. Too often today orchestras are filled with men who just sit there looking bored, unless they have a Klemperer or Rodzinski to animate them. I can't understand this. Where is the joy? I like to hear orchestras with lots of young people, who bring a kind of abandonment and spontaneity to their playing. They may not play flawlessly, but the spirit's there. Those who take music as a routine activity miss the whole charm of it. That's a big problem in live music—and a bigger one in recorded music.

I recorded a great deal, with the Boston Symphony, the Philadelphia Orchestra and others. It's a process that's not improved much over my life. Oh, there are technical innovations, but they aggravate the problem. The amount of distortion on records simply astonishes me. Record producers mix takes according to their own wishes and conceptions rather than to what you have created and shaped. With a recording of a group I conducted, I insisted on several reprints because I felt the technicians had completely missed my interpretation. They made drastic changes—turned *piano* passages into *forte* ones. It was a disgrace. You would think that with electronics it would be so easy to attain a greater degree of refinement. If only they would let the music alone. Records are hodgepodges of different performances; they are no longer one great, unrepeatable performance. The minute you take the best portions of different tapes and splice them together, you take away from the unique interpretive reading, and the result becomes artificial. Maybe the engineers feel that they are doing a service to the listener, but I'm convinced that interpretation has to be left to the performer. Start mixing elements from here and there— and probably you'll mismatch them.

I remember how Toscanini wouldn't allow anyone besides himself to touch the controls of the recording equipment. Some people thought this was typical of his tyrannical nature. I'm afraid that, in a way, conductors had to be tyrants and still do. Their job was and is to see that magnificent sounds are transmitted by the orchestra, and they can abide no distractions. In order for men like Toscanini and Pierre Monteux to get what they were after, they had to be strict. There's no time for foolishness.

Great conductors are under tremendous strain. They have a pure musical conception in mind that's very difficult to attain, especially when they're trying to achieve it with 110 people in front of them. In that situation you can't expect everything to be sweet apple pie. The creative act never is. If someone speaks scathingly of the conductor tyrants, I just look at him a little strangely thinking, "You don't know what it takes to achieve something worthwhile."

I've heard a lot about the cruelties of some of our great maestros, but I never experienced unpleasantness at their hands; they were always very kind to me. One time, following a rehearsal with Bruno Walter, he and I went backstage, found a piano, and stayed there for several hours playing through some wonderful music. That's the kind of pleasant recollection I have. I feel very strongly that when a conductor demands something of you, he isn't being mean. Such a man is demanding creative fulfillment. You should be glad to comply, and for many years I was.

After a while I yearned to go back to my first love—teaching. So, after being on the stage for 25 years—a brief interruption—I came back to my chosen vocation and founded the Harlem School of the Arts in 1964. My husband, Dr. Shelby Rooks, was pastor of the St. James Presbyterian Church in Harlem and he wanted a program in the community that had more substance than recreational athletics. I came up with the Harlem School of the Arts, since arts education interested me most and the public schools were (and still are) weak in it. The school began right here in the church in 1964. We had to proceed very slowly, since we had next to no money. The first year there were twenty children and I was the only teacher. Then, through the church, my husband gave me funds for a ballet teacher and an art teacher. It was a beginning.

That year we opened for registration on Saturday morning at nine and at eleven we had to close the door. The church looked like a supermarket. We couldn't take more than 80 children; now we have well over 900. They come from all over New York and New Jersey. Clearly we're serving an unmet need, providing what the school systems don't want or can't afford. Some day I'd somehow like to tie our operation more directly to the public schools. There are still too many children whose creative spirits are undernourished.

Now, all the years I'd been performing, I thought a lot about educational matters. A great many young singers sang for me in my travels; for most of them their great tragedy was that they started too late. Unless you have a good solid musical foundation, with subsequent esthetic and intellectual growth, you're lost. Music isn't just playing notes. It's insight combined with the excitement of trying to reproduce while you enhance what the composer intended. Of course, to sing you must have a voice, but that is only a small part of it. The greatest singers did not always have the greatest voices. What they had was interpretive depth and solid technique. None of it came overnight. Good music making takes a long time. I made up my mind when I got back to teaching that I would start with children at the very earliest stage in their musical development—and present them with a variety of artistic stimuli. As a youngster I was simultaneously exposed to all the arts. I didn't just take piano lessons; I had dance lessons, lessons in the visual arts, in drama, and a great deal of singing. I grew up with the philosophy that you are exposed to a lot of things and that you decide only after dealing with them all which give you the best chance for self-expression.

Now, if you take a close look at the children in our school, you'll notice that some of them taking violin lessons are also wearing ballet shoes, or have their drawing equipment nearby. This versatility gives me the greatest joy—our fundamental purpose is adding dimensions to people's lives, not so that all of them will be artists, but so they may be fulfilled in many ways. It's the kind of education most of America has not yet awakened to. I believe very strongly that the arts aren't frills. We can't do without them; they're essential for our wellbeing. Let's say you study dance and then go to a ballet and really enjoy it. You may not necessarily become a good dancer, but you can learn enough to appreciate the perfection of another person's effort, the more so because you have tried it yourself.

We won't teach children dancing until they are five because before that age their bone structure is such that it isn't safe; we don't want to ruin a child with soft bones. In pre-instrumental or piano work we start kids at four. For drama I always felt it was time to start when they could read. But recently we began experimenting with three- and four-year-olds, children in their most formative years. We are getting good results. During the summer we set up a class for those little tots. It met in a very hot room. I went up to observe that class. Guess what they were doing?—imagining a snowstorm. They were actually shivering. Everyone was so serious about it. And I said, "Here we are just sweltering, and they don't know that it's hot out!" So you see, we have found many avenues of approach to the arts, to exercising the imagination, tapping needs, developing potentials.

Now, when you go to the average music school for piano lessons, the first question you're asked is, "Do you have a piano? No? Sorry, we can't take you." But we say, "No piano? Oh goody! That's perfect. You can come use ours every day." In our school kids get supervised practice. If there's an instrument at home, the child might not practice it. But in school he'll practice all right. And the child whose family can't afford to buy an instrument has no sense of inferiority because he plays regularly right here.

We pioneered the Suzuki method in this country for teaching instruments to small children. When I heard that Mr. Suzuki himself was coming to visit the University of Indiana, I went out to meet him. That was ten years ago or more. After that conference I decided that I wanted to try his method with our children. A young fiddler, Dorothy Rothman, a graduate of Juilliard, got interested and she started teaching the Suzuki method for us.

If they had their way, Suzuki teachers would start their pupils prenatally! We do start very early, giving mothers records so that children in their cribs get accustomed to violin sounds. We have enrolled children at birth, although they don't come to school until three years later. The mothers study along with the children. At first we had 25 Suzuki children; now we have over 60. In our new building, which is almost finished, there is a little area just for them. The youngsters involved first learn fingering by rote, but as soon as they're big enough, we teach them to read notes in big sizes. When they're a little older, they proceed to more conventional methods; at that point they've learned how to practice and can go ahead on their own, without their mothers' constant participation.

We've had marvelous results. I'm especially delighted that the Suzuki method provides a natural way for the whole family to be involved in the child's musical life. I believe very strongly that music lessons have to be part of family life, as was true when I was growing up. The family that practices together goes to concerts together and then talks over what it hears, discussing musical issues and getting to the heart of it all.

I take such pleasure in our pint-size violinists, watching them learn how to bow, seeing them hold their violins under their chins without dropping them. Just holding the instrument is such a source of pride. Some of them won't trust their parents with the care of their violin cases. They're taught to respect instruments at our school— and all of them do. As I left the building one day I saw a mother and a child. Little Elizabeth was like a sleepwalker; she held the violin way in front of her in order not to bump it. Her mother expostulated, "Elizabeth, don't you think you'd better let me take it?"

"Nope. You might bump it."

It's amazing what these children do.

In the Harlem School of the Arts students pay what they can. But every child is expected to pay something. I don't approve of free anything. A mother can pay five cents a lesson—I want that nickel and I'll bill her for five cents as readily as for a dollar. I want her child to see the mother go into our office and come out with a receipt; how much is on it doesn't matter. That child knows his parent has invested in him. It's important.

We don't make much money from tuition. We get funds from the National Endowment for the Arts, the New York State Council on the Arts, and other foundations. We've expanded enormously since we started. We needed more room. Also, since my husband was reaching retirement age, he thought the school should have its own home outside the church, because the next minister might want an entirely different program. So the board of directors bought adjacent property and raised most of the funds to complete the building. They're still working on it.

The emphasis in the school is on children, but I also do a master class for older singers. I try to impress on voice students that they're never going to develop as singers without facility in language and diction. And one language isn't enough. They must have several if they're going to do concerts of varied repertory.

So, when they ask to join my class, I audition them, and if the voice and the intelligence are there I say, "All right, we will be delighted to have you. But you must give me every night of the week but one." You ought to see their faces when I say that. And then I add: "You mustn't come with the idea that it's drudgery. You must find it really so exciting that you want to be at it every night; if that will not be your attitude, you've made a mistake and don't belong here." Some protest, "But I just want to take your class." And I reply, "That means commitment to hard work and study, if you want to learn to sing beautifully." So they go to French, German, and Italian classes for diction, and take solfège twice a week. After a while they hate it when we close for Christmas and Easter vacations. They are unhappy when everything stops even for just those few days.

Nothing pleases me more than to introduce my master class to contemporary music. I had the pleasure of presenting the music of a young man from Canada whose work no one had ever heard of until I presented its world premiere. His name is Oscar Morowitz. He writes beautifully. His background is Czech but he has made his home in Western Canada.

I find it challenging to do Berg and Schönberg and their successors. But I also understand audience resistance to twentieth-century music. It's like the children who refuse to taste certain foods they're not accustomed to. You have no idea how harsh Stravinsky's music sounded to the average ear when it was first heard in this country. It took me a long while to get accustomed to him. Anything new is like that. You have to be prepared to enter another world with an open ear, listen repeatedly, work at it—and eventually you'll understand.

We have just done a new opera by Willard Roosevelt at Alice Tully Hall. I threw my students into it for pedagogical as well as musical purposes. They had to confront a strange and difficult score; I put them through the mill. The piece did a lot for them; they all improved as musicians because they had to work so hard. It had hard melodic lines, full of intervals they had never tried to sing before, and the time signature changed every other measure. After mastering the work, they felt wonderful. After hearing it over and over, they became accustomed to it, and it didn't seem so far-out. That's how it is with a lot of contemporary avant-garde music which in ten years will seem quite ordinary. At first new sounds put you on edge and then you get used to them. The same principle applies to painting. For most of us of my generation, anything beyond Matisse was difficult to accept. But it did come after a while.

And the sooner that kids have exposure to the arts of their time, the better. Youngsters are entitled to richer cultural experiences than most of them get. It's time we realized that children are our biggest asset, and that they should be given a high priority in this society. Young people are the real Gross National Product. We invest in the future by investing in them.

24:   Henry Mazer

iano was my first instrument. I joined the Pittsburgh Symphony as a pianist before World War II; after my time in the Army, I went back as first apprentice conductor under Fritz Reiner, as well as personnel manager of the orchestra. I learned a lot from Reiner and from Pierre Monteux, with whom I studied for a summer. After spending about ten years as conductor of the Wheeling, West Virginia, Orchestra, and several more years with the Florida Symphony in Orlando, I came back to Pittsburgh for four years as associate conductor to William Steinberg. Now here I am in Chicago as associate under George Solti.

Every year I lead the Chicago Symphony in a few subscription and numerous popular concerts. In addition, I have what may be a more important job—working with inner-city youngsters as part of the orchestra's youth program. Now, orchestras need young people's concerts in order to raise money, aside from whatever intrinsic worth they may have. But when I came to Chicago in 1970, the program was in such terrible shape that no one seemed to know what to do about it. The situation was so bad that I thought of going back to Pittsburgh, which has one of the few good youth series in the country. Solti himself evidently went on record in opposition to the old concerts. He was right. You can't just take kids off the streets, put them in a hall and expect them to know how to react. The whole concept of taking unmotivated youngsters on "field trips to the symphony" is ridiculous unless you prepare them for the experience. Theoretically the school systems should take charge of this, but they haven't.

So I'm doing it myself. I don't make any extra money going out into the schools as I do; I was never officially told to do so. But John Edwards, the orchestra manager, agreed with me that we had to do something to involve children in these concerts in a more meaningful way or drop the whole program. Unfortunately, I'm more or less on my own in this venture and I've been unable to get enough help; therefore what I do is limited in scope. But it's certainly better than nothing at all.

When I came, in 1970, it seemed almost hopeless. During my first season, while I was conducting a youth concert, one kid went through a plate glass window and two bathrooms were totally de-

Henry Mazer, assistant conductor of the Chicago Symphony and director of its youth concerts, was interviewed in Chicago in March 1975.

stroyed. It was impossible to play the program through without stopping time and again. Debris cluttered the stage; I remember one of the players got a big paper clip stuck in his violin. I'm glad to say that we've made great progress since then; the audiences have gotten better and better.

In conjunction with the Urban Gateways program, I pick 20 schools to work in each year. As it's now devised, I work with 50 or 60 fourth, fifth, and sixth graders. There are several youth concerts at Orchestra Hall each year; I visit the school before and after the first concert, once in mid-season, and a final time after all the concerts are over. I usually bring a musician along. At the beginning I wanted to have college students who played instruments come with me. Forty showed up at my first organizational meeting, four at the second; the number then dwindled to two—and they weren't very good musicians. All this is understandable; people were frightened. When I started out, there was still deep racial tension. I think by today the atmosphere has improved somewhat. I still would not do a regular program in the high schools—I'm no hero. I did try a couple of sessions with the upper grades, and I must say it was rather a scary experience. Besides, kids in high school are too old to start learning about the orchestra from scratch. I do work at one all-black high school, Harlan High, but it's different from others in Chicago because instead of being highly organized in athletics, it has a highly developed music program. But going to regular high schools is a waste of time.

You see, poor children grow up very fast. They mature so quickly because they have to fend for themselves very early. It's pretty hard to introduce Mozart to teenagers who have more pressing concerns on their minds. So my idea is to improve music education in the earlier grades. If I'm able to develop our program with nine, ten, and eleven year olds so it encompasses fifty schools, then maybe after a while we can have the same youngsters continue with music when they're twelve and thirteen.

When you go to as many schools as I do, you get a real sense of what ghetto life is like; you see a lot of lost children, children with no family identity. It's very sad—which makes the struggle to bring something worthwhile into their lives even more rewarding.

The hardest part is getting a reaction out of these youngsters, any reaction at all. From the first day, you have to fight the impassive blank stares. I'll write on the board, "The conductor performed a concerto written by a composer and included a cadenza." There we have four important musical words—conductor, composer, concerto, and cadenza. I make an offer: "I'll give a record to anyone who can tell me what these four words mean." No one ever knows. *No one.* They don't even try to guess. Then you spend thirty minutes kibbitzing around, showing them how the conductor doesn't decide what instruments to use, but the composer does; maybe you play them some Berlioz and indicate how it starts with the drums: "And when you come to the concert, you'll see the timpani. But I didn't decide to use drums; the composer did. I am the conductor and I follow a score." I tell them that when they come to Orchestra Hall they'll hear a concerto and not to applaud too soon because, "In the middle the orchestra's going to stop playing and you'll hear a cadenza."

When I finish speaking I feel sure that the kids have gotten what I've been saying and I ask, "Now, what is a composer?" If it's my first visit they still say nothing. They have been taught that the best way to stay out of trouble is to keep their mouths shut. It's been a way of life for them *not* to learn, not to respond. So, when some kids suddenly start to laugh a little on my second or third visit and say, "Now I know the answer. . . . Hey Mr. Mazer!" I know I'm making big progress. Nowadays, when I come back to schools I've visited before, the kids often have their best clothes on; the boys wear ties, and they all stand when I enter the classroom. I know that's just a beginning, a grain of sand on a big beach, but it's beautiful to feel that something good is happening. Once when I announced that we would play the Haydn *Toy* Symphony at our next concert, one kid went out and bought himself a good-looking tailored red coat just for the occasion. Fortunately someone tipped me off in advance. So I said, "I really like that coat you got for the concert." He was delighted.

I never use big assembly halls for teaching—I like to be in the classrooms with the kids and get to know them a bit. I play as much music as I can on the piano, especially melodies or passages they've heard or will soon hear. I encourage their teachers to play cassettes and tapes that I prepare. And I teach them to respect instruments and the orchestra. If the piano's dirty I'll take them to task: "The least you can do is keep the piano clean, so it will sound as good as it can." I tell them to ask everything they want to know while I'm there at the school: "When you come to the concert, I can't talk with you. I'll come out on stage, say a few words about each piece and then lead the orchestra. I'm there to conduct and you're there to listen."

Sometimes they have tough questions for me. A few months ago a kid asked me, "How much you make on that job, man?" I said, "A lot, man, but I'm good and I deserve it." Then came the hard one: "Why are there no blacks in that orchestra?" What could I say? More and more blacks *are* in major orchestras now, because at last they're getting the kind of training to qualify. I think it would be a great thing if the Chicago Symphony would bend a little and put more blacks in right now—but I'm not in charge. A black bass player made the audition finals last time, but didn't get hired. When I left Pittsburgh there were three or four blacks in the symphony and the radio orchestra had a black woman playing timpani. In most cases these days, except maybe in the Deep South, color is not relevant, especially in the case of good string players, who are very hard to come by.

I'm often asked how I put together youth concert programs. Picking pieces for children is a thousand times harder than doing it for adults. I don't believe there's such a thing as "youth concert music"—there's only good music and bad music. But remember, these are fourth, fifth and sixth graders whose limited attention spans must be taken into account. The time factor is my only restriction. I very seldom take a chance on anything longer than eight minutes. The kids never seem to mind modern music. Sometimes I have them write "reviews" after the concert, and they're generally positive about music of this century. They have more trouble with soft things. Pieces that don't have drums demand more concentrated listening. Still, if you check youth programs around the country, you'll find that ours are probably the most sophisticated.

Last time I did an American program, including Samuel Barber's *Overture to School for Scandal*, a Menotti violin piece, a very new work, and the Ives-Schuman *Variations on America*, which we had done last year, and which I tossed in because so many asked to hear it again. Not long ago, I used the Chicago Children's Choir in a program that included works by Bartók, Berlioz, Hovhaness and Menotti; all good music, short but good.

Every spring we hold auditions to choose young artists who will play solos at youth concerts, with awards of $500, $300, and $200.

The first-place winner, who played Menotti at the last concert, was a marvelous young woman—really a top-notch fiddle player. The young people in the audience enjoy seeing someone their own age on stage; it was a pleasure to see how attentive they were.

In some cities, the orchestra members fool around at youth concerts as much as the kids. When I was in Pittsburgh, I would have meetings with teachers who would say, "How can you expect us to tell our students to behave when the horn players are fooling around on stage?" But the Chicago Symphony doesn't know how to fool around; they only know how to play well. They play well under any circumstances. So they get upset when the audience isn't attentive. You have to get this across to the kids. I tell them, "You know, this orchestra is playing specially for you; it's a real honor for you to be here." At first the kids had to be sort of brainwashed into feeling honored, but now for the most part they behave like seasoned concert-goers.

And some of them get inspired to play music themselves. I give a kid piano lessons, and I got a friend of mine to give another boy flute lessons. I've come to feel very personally involved with these children. Our program is in great need of expansion, but we're reaching more kids all the time. That's very gratifying.

25: Natalie Limonick

I never planned to specialize in opera. I just sort of fell into it, several years after graduating from college. I'm glad opera came my way—I love it. But I had plenty of interesting musical experiences even before I knew a single aria.

I arrived at UCLA from New York in 1944, the semester Arnold Schönberg was retiring, just in time for one stupendous class with him. I felt cheated when he was forcibly retired at age 65. A few years later the thought hit me: shouldn't a bunch of us ask him to conduct a private seminar? Many students loved the idea of continuing to work with him. So we sat on the sofa in my house and composed a letter to Schönberg. I mailed it and two days later we got his response: Yes, he would be delighted. Soon we began a seminar which was supposed to last ten weeks, each class on a Sunday morning for two hours at his home. The subject was musical form and analysis. We all liked it so well that another one seemed in order. The class kept going that way; as soon as one seminar was completed, we'd start another.

There were maybe ten or fifteen of us. It was remarkably exciting to learn from him in his own environment where he didn't have the horror of those awful students at the university who didn't understand him. These were *interested* people. His purpose was to unfold a total theoretical background. He tried out his well-known counterpoint text and others he was working on, on us. When Schönberg died in 1951, Leonard Stein got his notes in order. Those seminars left a permanent impression on me; it was a real privilege and pleasure to study the fundamentals of music with one of the great composers of our time. Schönberg really took his educational responsibilities very seriously; like many great composers of the past, he felt it was his duty to pass on the basics of the musical language to the next generation.

Having the opportunity to study with Schönberg was one of the reasons I never regretted leaving New York. I fell in love with California as soon as I got here. I had been studying piano at Juilliard when my teacher, Ignace Hilsberg, whom I had studied with for two years, visited California and wrote East that he was staying. My teacher not coming back to New York! Tears. Bitter sorrow and all that. I wanted to follow him immediately. He very wisely advised me

Natalie Limonick, general director of the University of Southern California Opera, was interviewed at her home in Los Angeles in April 1975.

to get my diploma first. So I got the piece of paper, went West for the summer—and stayed. With the brashness of youth, I wrote to my mother—my father died when I was eight—that if she wanted to see me, she should come on out to California. And the next year she did; and here we are.

Musically, L.A. was a very exciting place in the forties and fortunately, my teacher knew many of the wonderful musicians around—not only Schönberg and Stravinsky, but many others. I had a grand time.

My interest in opera came relatively late. It was only after the Schönberg classes that I went back to UCLA to do graduate work (I was married by then, and had a seven-year-old child). By some stroke of luck, I took an opera history class with a spectacular professor, Dr. Jan Popper. I had been to one opera in my whole life before that, back at the Met—it was *Hansel and Gretel*. At Juilliard I never had any contact with opera at all.

The next semester, as a complete novice, I took a Wagner class, and then a Verdi class. Two years later I enrolled as a student accompanist in what was becoming a well-known opera workshop at UCLA. I was hooked.

Jan Popper started the opera workshop in 1949, after ten years at Stanford, where he also started a workshop. I entered the program in 1953, but on a minor basis. At the time, the music department shared an old building with home economics and art. We were on the third floor, with maybe three classrooms and no practice rooms. Opera was performed in a big lecture hall. If we wanted lighting, we brought in lighting trees. It was terribly primitive, but great because of that. The audience would always somehow participate by helping out in one way or another. Gradually, the Workshop grew and grew, until it became a major training ground for young singers.

L.A. has a history of good opera workshops. Hugo Strelitzer ran the first one at City Junior College. He came here as a refugee (as did Popper) in 1939 and started the workshop as an evening extension affair, for people from the outlying community. In even more primitive conditions than those at UCLA, he built a workshop of major proportions. George London and many others got their starts there. A whole list of his Los Angeles graduates went to Europe and are singing all over the world now. Then Popper started his workshop at UCLA, and shortly thereafter Carl Ebert, the dean of European opera directors, was involved in a similar endeavor at USC. Everyone knows about the famous emigrant composers who came to L.A., but not many realize that Europeans were responsible for many other facets of our musical life.

Hugo dropped in on his 79th birthday. We were reminiscing, and wondering about the young people who used to come to the workshops as compared to those we have now. For me, the trends are very depressing. And I tried to figure out what had happened. When Hugo's was the only game in town, any interested person headed there. It really became a central force, spiritually as well as technically. Singers worked hard. With his high standards of singing and performing, students knew they couldn't just jump into the professional world after a couple of years of training and expect to make it. Take the case of Ella Lee, a great soprano who started as a chorus member with Hugo at City College. She was there for eight semesters. Each semester she would go one little notch higher, first with a walk-on role, then a little bit part, and after a while, after she'd had lots of experience, a starring role. Everybody in L.A. came to know her. What a marvelous singer! Then one year, Richard Wagner's granddaughter came to L.A. to audition young people for the master classes at Bayreuth. We held the auditions at UCLA; I played piano for them. She immediately offered Ella a scholarship, and as it turned out, a number of us got scholarships to Bayreuth in the summer of 1960. Ella was heard in Bayreuth by Walter von Felsenstein, the great director of the Komische Oper in East Berlin, who signed her for a two-year contract. Kurt Adler of the San Francisco opera, another great director, also happened to be in Europe looking for singers. *He* heard Ella and gave her a contract for his company. Isn't it ironic—as a performer in L.A., 450 miles from San Francisco, she had never had a chance to sing there. Ella went to San Francisco via Bayreuth and East Berlin. That's still the case today, though there are more opera companies around the country than ever before. But most young singers have to get their first professional experience in Europe.

Anyway, the point of the Ella Lee story is that there was a time not so long ago when young singers didn't mind a long apprenticeship; in fact, they relished all that time to learn their craft thoroughly. Today young people move rapidly in and out of workshops and conservatories. They're in a big hurry. They want to take the Met auditions, the San Francisco auditions, these auditions, those auditions. Egotistical teachers push their students into competing, and if the kids win then the teachers bask in their glory. Some years ago I worked with a singer who won the Met auditions. He studied five arias with me, and really learned them well. He could act them as well as sing them. He was brilliant on stage; he had personality like crazy and a voice to boot—and he won. Of course he won. But who knows where he is today? I haven't heard in awhile. All too likely, he's one of those unfortunate cases who burned himself out before he was ready. So many of the powers-that-be push kids before they're ready.

There are other depressing trends these days. Fritz Zweig was a brilliant conductor, head of the Prague Opera House at one time, and also the Deutsche Oper in Berlin. He's now in his eighties and has gone into teaching. Zweig is the soul of musical integrity. He's been training people for the opera for years. I asked him what he thought about the future. He said, "I'm very skeptical." Zweig feels that no contemporary opera of merit and lasting value has been created in the last fifty years. Partly, I agree. Of course, some good operas have been written in this century. But when you think back to a Verdi period or a Puccini period, when the populace at large was born into an opera environment, there's no comparison. Where is the public that would await with eagerness a new Puccini work or a new Verdi work or a new Strauss work? Once produced, such an opera became part of the repertory. In America these days, nobody awaits a new opera with eagerness, and when one comes it never becomes part of the repertory. Not Gunther Schuller's *The Visitation*, which was a big hit when it came out. Or Benjamin Britten's *Death in Venice*, which will never be popular, even if the musical elite likes it.

Is that because the work itself lacks merit or because the public isn't ready, or because these days no new opera is "an event"? Probably they're all part of the picture.

I don't believe that the situation for opera in America, and especially in L.A., has improved much in the last twenty years or so. Nationally, that's related to the overall economy, soaring costs, lack of adequate support; music is just not considered a priority. Locally, there's our notorious emphasis on sports, perhaps because of the beautiful weather. And yet we do have an audience for opera. The

Dorothy Chandler Pavilion tends to be filled when the New York City Opera visits. And when the San Francisco opera used to come down here, the Shriner Auditorium was usually filled. For every abortive attempt to build an opera company in L.A., there's been a solid group of people supporting the effort. I'm sure that all this interest has a great deal to do with the workshops I've mentioned and Dr. Popper's opera history classes, which were very well-attended. But L.A. is peculiar. We can train people well—but we don't provide many outlets for them to use this training.

So I've been working like crazy and getting even grayer hair trying to build a permanent and ever-widening support base for opera—starting with young children. Did you ever hear opera in school? All right, forget about opera. What about any serious music? In L.A., with our beautiful Reagan administration (until the arrival of Mr. Brown) we had budget cutbacks so frightful that music in the public schools was entirely eliminated. But entirely. So now, over a period of years, musically illiterate kids have been arriving at universities totally unprepared for the education they should have received in childhood. If school kids don't know anything and grow into young adults who continue to know nothing, what kind of audience will we have in the future? They've got to be reached, or it'll be really hopeless.

Consequently, we try and try again. Before our big inner-city crisis—symbolized by Watts—when Dr. Popper left for a year, I was in charge of the opera activities. We scheduled a performance of *Amahl and the Night Visitors*, and were backed by "Junior Programs" which has a subscription series of cultural events for children—one month an opera, one month a ballet or a play. We were engaged to tour the production in different parts of L.A. "Junior Programs" was at that time trying to make inroads into an area in the south-central district of L.A. But they were meeting a solid wall of opposition. Blacks, very simply, didn't want whites descending on their neighborhoods to give them "culture."

Well, I had an idea. Since *Ahmal*'s chorus is simple, perhaps some music teachers in schools of that area which had glee clubs could teach it to the kids. I would select youngsters from each group to work with and incorporate those children into our production. When children are in our college production, their parents always come to see them. Thus we would wear down the neighborhood resistance.

It worked like a charm. We were working with kids from two different junior highs. I suggested that both groups of children come up and perform with us in our campus presentation. But there wasn't enough room on stage for all of them, so we had two shows that evening. For the first one, half of them were on stage and the other half sang in the pit. For the second show they reversed positions. We had a party for them in the green room afterward. And the parents came in all gussied up. It was a joy! One of the principals had a story to tell me about a little boy named Leslie: "Mrs. Limonick, you should know that in school he's incorrigible. I have him in my office every hour on the hour for one infraction or another. One day I asked Leslie 'How come you misbehave so in school, and during the whole Amahl project, Mrs. Limonick hasn't had to say "Boo" to you?' And his answer was, 'We've *never* done anything so important at school.'"

Now comes the beautiful sequel to the story. Three or four years later, after the riot in Watts, when it was *the* thing to be on the bandwagon, to provide artistic enrichment in the schools, we were touring an opera. Frequently children were our backstage crew. When we got to one high school, a grinning black boy looked up at me and thank God something clicked. I said, "Leslie, how nice to see you," and he turned to his friend and gave him a nudge, saying proudly, "See, I told you she'd know me. I told you I sang with her." Leslie has gone into drama as a result of that experience.

Somewhat earlier Dr. Popper had left UCLA to take his chances at the new Santa Cruz campus. When he said good-bye I shed bitter tears again. I couldn't imagine working in the workshop or on other activities without him. At the time we were just starting our inner-city school program. Very soon, this had expanded enormously, but nobody in the music department knew it; we who were involved did it on our own time without extra pay, and gained quite a following—outside academia. One year USC, the *other* school, did a production of Alban Berg's Wozzeck—big, big excitement in L.A. musical circles. The chairman of my department, a musicologist at UCLA, who didn't really favor performance much anyway, and certainly didn't favor women, called me into his office. He wanted to know, how come, ever since Dr. Popper (implying, a *man*) left campus, UCLA hadn't done anything important, while here was USC, our rival, doing a great prestigious production? I told him we'd been doing fairly important work—in the schools. What schools, he demanded. I named them. "Nobody knows about them. There's no prestige in it." I said, "But it's community-liaison work. Don't you think that's frightfully important?" No, to him it was kids' stuff. And so I left his office, very depressed. But we carried on nonetheless.

Then came the urban crisis and my chairman sent me a memo: "Do you have any material on your work in the schools, any brochures or whatever? The Chancellor is very interested to know about any faculty doing community-liaison work." And I had a good time retorting, "No I don't have any press releases. We're too busy doing the work to sit down and write about it." At that point it dawned on administrators that in order to gain foundation grants, "the school business" was a good bet. So now everyone's into the schools—but often minus the heart, I'm afraid. Nevertheless, I'm glad for any support we can get.

In a more positive vein, we have several Junior League women, a really sharp bunch who've started an interesting three-year pilot project. They're taking control-group schools in a certain area of the San Fernando Valley and pounding them with cultural events. First they had to find schools which would request such programs, which means they had to find principals who loved opera or drama or art of some sort. But they did it. A long list of performing organizations of merit come into those schools—to be sure, not very often. And only certain schools are involved. But at least it's a start in the right direction. As part of this program, I had a group do short opera excerpts, which I explained as a sort of narrator. We did this in the fall, in the spring another opera group arrived with a full production. There are two performances of opera, two of ballet and two of mime. That's quite a lot of activity in about twenty schools. It's great for them, but sad for the schools that are excluded.

I'm sure, though, that these efforts will have positive effects. We'll see what the statisticians come up with about it all—if anything. I feel that to develop a broad cultural base among children you need at least a twenty-year plan. If that base can be created, it will generate demand and then everything else will fall into place.

The organization sponsoring the three-year pilot program is

called the Performing Tree. They will take care of programming events for this period, and then turn the responsibility over to the schools: "Now it's your baby. We've shown you what's available, and how to get it. Now *you* proceed." Let's hope they do, for the sake of our children and a flourishing cultural life.

Part Six: Managers, Patrons, Impresarios

26: *Harry Zelzer*

I guess I am nearly the last of the impresarios. The term impresario, strictly speaking, refers to one who presents musical attractions with his own money. Maybe there are a few younger guys still trying. But we're a dying breed.

Going into the music business was the smartest thing I ever did. I got myself so involved I work practically every day of the year. I never take a vacation. I am never even away from the telephone.

I've lived within two miles of my office, here in the Opera House building on Wacker Drive, for about half a century. If I had my way, and an apartment could be installed in the office, I'd live in it.

In October 1975, I celebrated 45 years in this office. The carpets are 40 years old. There's nothing fancy here. This is a workplace.

As a boy, I lived in New York. My parents brought me from Poland when I was very young. There's some musical history in my background. My father's great-grandfather, who couldn't read music, played the flute for Napoleon. On my office wall is a picture, which is at least 100 years old, of his grandson, my grandfather Zelzer, from Lublin. He was a fiddler of sorts, but his brother, my great-uncle, was the real musician. He was a friend of Meyerbeer and Halevy, studied violin with Wieniawski, composed music to biblical Hebrew texts, and was musical director of the Polish theatre in Lublin. Unfortunately, I never knew him; he died in 1897, the year I was born.

My father was a merchant. He played a little violin, but out of tune. He used to tell us about a popular Polish slogan, "Everybody to himself," which meant, "Stay away from the Jews." The open anti-Semitism prompted my father to leave. So he came to America and made good. He had been a hat manufacturer in Poland. In New York he opened a shop on East Broadway.

Coming to America meant the end of anti-Semitism for my family, but I remember years later I met Rachel Kaminska, the actress Ida's aunt, in the U.S., with a Polish company. She was posing as a Christian Pole. I asked her, "Aren't you Jewish?" and she said, "Let's not talk about it. They know I'm Jewish, but they let me come along anyway, and they don't want me to talk about the Jewish question."

I went to many concerts when I was a kid in In New York, often

Harry Zelzer, the Chicago impresario, was interviewed in Chicago in March 1975.

at the Jewish National Alliance, which held cultural events subsidized by German Jews. Besides concerts, I heard a lot of good
speakers, in the East, and later here. My friends and I liked to listen
to people who were looked up to—Louis Untermeyer, William Jen-
nings Bryan. The subjects didn't always interest me, but someone
said Bryan was a great orator, so I went to hear him, at 63rd and
Halsted in Chicago, in 1919.

I went to high school and about a year of night college in New
York. I lived with my brother-in-law, who gave me a job while I was
in school. Then, in 1919, I was hired as a bank clerk in Chicago, at
the old City State Bank. I was a teller for nine months, then spent
two and a half years in the trust department. The work was too monotonous. So in 1923, at age 26, I asked for a chance in the bond
department. They made me assistant manager, and in 1925 I became
full manager.

I actually got into music through the bank. One day in 1923
Mr. Paulsen, a man of Danish descent, came in and told the head
cashier, "I want to borrow $600. I come recommended by Mr. Han-
sen, a lawyer. I'm willing to put up my Guarnarius." The cashier
replied, "We'd like to help you, but we can't make loans on fiddles.
We don't know how much they're worth. Talk to Mr. Zelzer in the
bond department. He is greatly interested in music." So I invited Mr.
Paulsen in. We started talking, and by the time he left he had the
$600; he signed a note and I guaranteed it. I knew the value of that
collateral, and I was making good money anyway, since I was build-
ing up the bond department. His situation interested me. Mr.
Paulsen subsidized his own orchestra, the People's Symphony, but he
was having trouble raising money to meet the payroll. He remarked,
"I use fifty musicians, and every Sunday we play in the Eighth Street
Theatre. Would you like to come hear us?" I went. It was right after
Labor Day. I remember hearing Liszt's *Les Préludes* and Beethoven's
Fifth.

I recognized that Paulsen was a dedicated and talented man. He
considered himself a good conductor; he was a great arranger. Also,
he won first prize in a contest for the best symphonic composition,
sponsored by Balaban and Katz, the people who opened movie
houses. In fact, Balaban and Katz's Chicago Theatre was the most
famous and beautiful movie house in the world. It seated 4000 people. Every Sunday morning, 100 musicians played a concert of light

music, before the movies, as an introduction, to get people downtown. Balaban and Katz took the cost out of their profits, and only charged about $1 a ticket.

I was eager to get more involved with music. I had been going regularly to the Chicago Symphony since 1920, and to the opera house since 1919. After the People's Symphony concert, I called the woman who managed the orchestra's affairs into the bank, and said to her: "I understand you are in full charge of the People's Symphony. What do you do for it?"

"I put an ad in the paper every week, and I send out a release."

"What are you paid?"

"$100."

"Consider yourself relieved." And that was that. I put one of my secretaries in charge of the music operation; we used an office in the bank building. I did not know what the hell I was doing, but I did it.

I raised money from my acquaintances to make up the orchestra's deficit. First I called a meeting of bank officers, and got each one to give $10. In those days it took a while to get $10 or $20 from people who were only making between $5000 and $7500 a year. Then I tapped some of the people with whom I did business syndicating bonds. One person gave me $500, which seemed like a lot of money. Somehow I made ends meet. It was a hobby. Instead of playing golf on Sundays, I went to rehearsals, I secured a room in the bank building on North Wells St., and we rehearsed there free. The Eighth Street Theatre charged $85 per session.

Some things could still be done reasonably. The musicians got only $15 a concert—$25 at most for the first-chair players. The conductor worked without fee. Chicago Symphony members were the mainstay of the group. The rest were good freelancers. Students were given free tickets. Local talent got a chance to appear as soloists at the Sunday afternoon concerts. I had a hand in the programs, and we played what the public wanted—the standard works, nothing avant-garde. I became well acquainted with classical symphonic literature.

I also secured radio time for broadcasting the concerts. At this time I met James Petrillo, the big wheel in the musician's union. In the early 1920s he was head of the Chicago local. This is what happened: I sold a broadcast of a performance to radio station WIND for $250. Right in the middle of the broadcast a call came from the union: "Say Zeltz, you'd better appear before the union board tomorrow." I went to Petrillo and explained, "I'm taking charge of the People's Symphony. They have no money, the musicians need rehearsals, and I can't pay for them. Will you permit them to rehearse without pay if they do so voluntarily?" Petrillo said, "Sure." With all due respect, he deserves a vote of thanks for letting us rehearse. He did get tougher and tougher. He was hard on Balaban and Katz, insisting on conditions that forced their orchestra out of work. But Petrillo always gave me a hearing; he sympathized with people who tried to keep musicians working.

Well, I managed the Symphony and worked at the bank until the crash of October 1929. Soon after, our bank, like so many others, got hit as if an earthquake had struck. We closed on Saturday, November 2, 1929, at noon. I thought, "America is America; it'll bounce right back." That was a slight mistake. Fortunately, I myself didn't go broke overnight. With first and second mortgage bonds, and some stock, I was able to subsidize myself for four years or so, until 1934. Soon after the bank closed, I moved into this office, and presented by first Chicago concert in 1930. I simply turned my avocation into a business.

My first artist was Benjamin Gigli, the great tenor, who sang in Chicago on October 15, 1930. The concert went over big, but I had a loss of $1200. Gigli was the greatest tenor after Caruso.

The first performer who put me in the black was a famous Spanish dancer named Argentina. I paid her $3000. By 1934, I had exhausted my private resources, but by then the "Zelzer Concert Management Bureau" carried itself.

I brought many of the big names of the day. Performers like Lily Pons, Jeanette Macdonald and Gladys Swarthout, who played to packed houses. Many artists came under my management in Chicago when my competitor went bankrupt in 1930.

Oh, I knew many greats. I was very fond of Kreisler. With 80 to 150 concerts a year, he probably played for more people than any violinist ever. Even when he was an old man playing out of tune, people came in droves to hear him. I don't think there ever was a violinist more beloved than Kreisler. People adored him not only for his musicianship, but also because he had a certain aura—out on stage, he looked like a saint. In Chicago, Kreisler and I would always meet at the Auditorium Hotel, where he stayed.

Elman was another of the favorites. That man made music

while he was tuning the fiddle. He also played for countless audiences. He was a legend. He never played out of tune. Neither did Heifetz. He elected to retire at an early age, and everybody has missed him. Some people think that he was the greatest violinist, and I am inclined to go along with them.

Critics often don't like an artist the public adores, and vice versa. The best story in the history book about this concerns Paderewski when he first came to America. History says he played in Germany and they didn't like him. He never went back. Then he came here under the auspices of Steinway Piano. He gave a concert in Carnegie Hall. There were few people, and he got a bad write-up. This didn't scare him, because he had had worse notices in Germany, and he had resolved to make good in America, as he had in England. Paderewski persuaded the Steinways to let him give another concert. At this one, 400 people instead of 200 showed up. Eventually he was playing to sold-out houses, even though he started with very bad press. The critics finally had to join the public and admit that he was great. As for myself, I am never influenced by critics—I call them the wrecking crew. I make my own decisions and take my own chances.

No one had a name like Paderewski, except maybe Caruso. He was here in 1921, performing at, of all places, Medina Temple, which is now considered obsolete. It's for circuses. His manager booked him there because the Temple was so big. There were stage seats galore. Perhaps Caruso was more fabulous than Paderewski in that people went to hear him who knew nothing about music. They just loved his voice. No one ever evoked in me the feeling Caruso did.

I like opera as well as concerts—but most of all symphonies and chamber music. I presented grand opera at Soldier Field in 1938, in collaboration with a man named Fortunato Gallo. Also, for many years I brought the Metropolitan and New York City Opera Companies, and the Boston Opera Company to Chicago.

I am interested in cantorial music, but in the same way I like boiled beef. I think it's an inherited taste. I never understood what cantors were singing, but I knew if their voices were good or bad. One day I walked into a Chicago temple when Richard Tucker was singing. I went "backstage" afterward and asked him if he had a Chicago manager. He didn't. So I engaged him.

But I did not engage only big names. Take my piano series—which consists of well known *and* little known artists. For over twenty years the young winner of the Chicago Society of American Musicians' contest has played on the piano series. Year after year, rain or shine, there is a steady, fairly large audience for pianists. Around 1500 out of a 2500 capacity always come. Now with someone like Rudolf Serkin, the place sells out.

The backbone of my operation is the subscription series. Besides the piano series I have a guitar series, a music series, a dance series, and a folk series. If I tried to present lesser known artists off the series, no one would come, but if the performers are on a series, we get an audience. People like ticket packages because they're good buys.

I never took on go-go-attractions, the earlier version of rock 'n' roll. I didn't have to do things just for the dollar.

My one competitor, who called his operation "Allied Arts," went bankrupt, and sold me his "business" if that's what it was, in the 1940s. Until then we had divided the Chicago business half and half; from then on, I was *the* Chicago impresario. I incorporated and became the Allied Arts Corporation. My wife, who was once a piano teacher, and I, own all the stock. She is my vice president and office manager.

I did well from the beginning. But Sol Hurok was always ahead of me. I started in 1930; he started around 1911 in Brooklyn. He had Efrem Zimbalist in 1911 or 1912, and by 1913 he was in the Hippodrome.

I met Hurok formally in 1930. When I gave that first concert he was in Chicago—he wanted to see what the hell I looked like. I had seen him in the bank in 1926. He came in to cash a check. He asked the cashier that day if he'd like to go to the Russian opera, The cashier said, "Zelzer here likes opera." So I went.

Hurok and I became good friends. It was a most amicable relationship. Though we had our differences, we were always honest with each other.

I presented about 99 percent of Hurok's artists in Chicago. The last time he was here, in November (1974) he spent two night next door to us at the Ambassador East Hotel, and we reminisced until all hours of the night.

He was then 85. He died a few months later. I used to call him every Sunday—that goes back thirty years—and if I missed a Sunday, he'd call me Monday with, "Aren't you talking to poor people any more?" He had his own, quite good, sense of humor. He's the one who said, "If they don't want to come, you can't stop 'em." He was smart, for a man with no education, and he had a certain sense of value. He came here at the age of 18. He always kept in touch with Russia. He was Chaliapin's first manager. I was the last one to present Chaliapin, in Chicago in 1934.

All the press came to talk to me when Hurok died. They knew we were close. His death got as much publicity as King Faisal's. Do you realize how much he was responsible for the cultural life in this country? He loved ballet and knew it well. Hurok was just like a German shepherd dog: He could sniff out what people would want to hear. Hurok was a man who guessed 95 percent right. The other 5 percent? Well, he was like any other gambler who, if he does 95 percent right, is OK. Every symphony, conductor, violinist was eager to be under Hurok's banner.

He died a man of means, and lived a full life. Who would have guessed that this Russian immigrant who worked for $3 a week in 1906 would rise so high and live on Park Avenue, in a palatial place, like a monarch? In his own way, the man was a genius.

Though Hurok concerts still exists, there will be no more Huroks. I would advise people against becoming impresarios. This is no time for people like us.

In 1948, as many as seventy independent managers, or impresarios, formed an organization to exchange information. We paid dues, had a bulletin. Today, I am one of a handful still operating on my own capital. There's a new manager in Milwaukee, and one in Boston. The Washington fellow would have gone under but he was smart—he went nonprofit. Then there's Columbia Artists Management Inc., but that's far removed from an individual like myself or Hurok. They have a chain of about 700 community concert bureaus around the country, and 70 or 80 competent people in the field.

Years ago, I used to do quite a bit of booking all over the Midwest, in places like Grand Rapids, Indianapolis, and South Bend. I would play towns where there were no agents, Now, most of these communities have their own managerial structures.

I think the tradition of the impresario died because artists' fees have become so outrageously high. Hurok was responsible for prolonging the life of the impresario. He presented *groups* of artists, not just soloists. That made money. But things have changed drastically. Though a few artists are devoted primarily to their art, the vast majority *talk* about making music, but are more interested in making money. In recent years, through the connivance of agents, a system has developed whereby almost everybody in the business trusts only in the dollar. And today's fees make it practically impossible for a local manager to operate on his own, without government, state, or community aid.

The few moneybag patrons get picked up by the Chicago Symphony and the Chicago Lyric Opera, who have fundraisers with a professional touch. Nevertheless, Allied Arts Corp. is still in good shape. I went in on my own. I'm 78 and I'm still on my own.

I'm not a modest man, but I'm not looking for monuments or orations either. My great pride is the organization, and I would like to leave it in the hands of people who can continue some of the things I started, like the series idea, with its opportunities for young artists, and the inexpensive ticket prices it permits.

I have children and grandchildren, but none who want to carry on the business.

Eventually, I hope to have somebody to perpetuate the organization. I would like to endow it as a legacy to an individual or a group, if need be, that has a good affiliation.

The new owners will have to manage Allied Arts carefully. You can't build up an audience pool of 100,000 people, as I did, overnight. It took me decades. And I couldn't have done it, and retained it, if I hadn't given people what they wanted. Over the past 40 years, some have wanted me to bring mainly quartets. I bring quartets, like the Juilliard, but not as my mainstay—they can't draw enough of an audience. Others wanted more avant-garde music, but I always hesitated about that. Most of my subscribers wouldn't like it, though in recent years, audiences have been more demanding of programs of this type. There is a more vociferous demand than ever before for newer music, twelve-tone pieces and the like.

I know that when you announce a Tchaikovsky program, you get a lot of takers. The same goes for big names. Arthur Fiedler has the largest following of any American conductor because he gives numbers of people music they want and understand. We just had him and the Boston Pops and sold out 4300 seats.

But I think the symphony orchestra has gained a much larger following over the years. Records helped. And so did men like Leonard Bernstein with his TV programs for youngsters. He speaks their language.

From another angle, not too much has changed over the 45 years I've been in the business. New York is still the capital of music. The major debuts take place there, and the world does reckon with a review in the *Times*.

As I've said, the only *big* difference in recent times is the artist's attitude, as reflected in higher fees. I remember during the Depression, when a good friend of mine, a famous violinist, charged $3000 a concert. He was only getting three concerts a year. Then he got an agent, who said he could get the musician many more engagements for a fee of $1000. The violinist agreed, and he played 85 concerts. But artists these days are very reluctant to lower their fees.

Looking back, I get a great deal of satisfaction from knowing that through me, many people over the years have attended concerts for the first time. I try hard to reach students and black people; how much I've succeeded is anybody's guess. Recently, I've worked through the Urban Gateways program. A while back, a young fellow who's since become the assistant manager of an eastern symphony called me just after he graduated as a music major from Roosevelt College. He wanted to organize a student league, and would I give him tickets at a reasonable rate? At first I thought I'd give him free tickets, but my experience has been that free tickets don't create a lasting audience; they just fill seats for one concert. So I let him have them for 50¢, for about a dozen attractions. He didn't do well at first, but then his operation grew. It was nice to see students coming to recitals with their violin cases. Nowadays, the only popular inexpensive deal is the piano series, for which the prices are still very low. You can get a seat for $2 to hear Serkin, Brendel, and others.

If I had it all to do over again, I don't think I would do much differently. Sure, I made some mistakes, and many events didn't sell—but both Hurok and I usually knew in advance when we would lose money. Therefore it never came as a shock. You have to have a feel for timing; I booked Arthur Schnabel on an Easter Sunday, and the place was jammed—they had to put seats on the stage.

Even with good instincts, you are always learning in the entertainment business. Even a seasoned impresario can sometimes be wrong—but not too often!

Rudolf Bing

I got to the Met in 1949, and spent my first few months observing Mr. Edward Johnson's last season while preparing my first, which opened in the fall of 1950. Those days provide an interesting contrast with the present. One could then plan and prepare a rather elaborate season, with excellent internationally known people, eight months ahead of time. Now one must plan two or three years ahead, which shows that the world's leading singers, of whom we have fewer and fewer, are in such incredible demand and are booking so far ahead.

I am partly to blame for this sorry state of affairs. Because I couldn't get one or two of the many good singers there used to be, I thought I'd better plan a year in advance. When the European houses discovered that I had booked their singers for the following year, this caused them to think *two* years ahead. That's how the rat race started. And has it gotten frenzied! Of course there was flying then, but not nearly as much as now. Today you have people singing on Monday in Hamburg, on Wednesday in Vienna, on Friday in London, and on the next Monday in New York, which is crazy. It ruins their voices. In the past, that madness was impossible. When I came to the Met I flew a lot too, but *commuting* between Europe and the States is a very recent development, which benefits neither the artists nor the public.

Artists do it because they love to hear different applause all the time. If they hear the applause of New York, they also want to hear the applause of Vienna—and they do not know how to say no. They're frightened that somebody else will get what they miss. They're greedy. Why? I don't understand it. The few singers who are in that sort of demand make enormous sums of money, and most of the time it goes for taxes anyway.

Why there isn't a goodly supply of exceptional new singers is an inexplicable phenomenon. There are certain periods in the history of music, or in the history of the world if you like, when great poets arise, and then there are lean periods. This also applies to singers. Then again, there *are* some great singers around today, although perhaps not as many as there were earlier in the century. A number ruin themselves prematurely, but quite a few are still in good voice and are a pleasure to listen to.

Rudolph Bing, former manager of the Metropolitan Opera, was interviewed in New York City in October, 1975.

Talent can't be cultivated artificially if it isn't there in the first place. A first-rate singer requires so many qualities. A great voice is really not enough any longer. You must also have general musicality and acting ability. Appearance counts too. If that rare combination occurs, a career usually cannot be stopped. I've seen such talent in my time—but of course, not too often. It's rare and probably always will be.

Before coming to America I held a variety of managerial jobs in Germany, Austria, and England. I moved to England in 1934 for a Mozart festival which soon turned into the world-renowned Glyndebourne Festival. Then came the war and when it ended I started the Edinburgh Festival in Scotland, at first to have another market for the Glyndebourne artists. All that differed deeply from the Met. To begin with, the Met seats 4000 and Glyndebourne, 800. Secondly, Glyndebourne was created by an extraordinary couple, a very strange and eccentric Englishman, John Christie, who was a near-genius of immense taste, and his wife. It was situated in a beautiful spot 160 miles out of London.

Mr. Christie had the wisdom to hire the great Fritz Busch as conductor and Carl Ebert as festival director. They contributed heavily to the highly cultivated artistic image of Glyndebourne. I was fortunate enough to be engaged as the general manager at the festival's inception. It became a very successful enterprise; indeed, it still is. During the war of course it stopped for a while and then we restarted it, with a different economic situation in effect. We tried to operate as economically as we could; the houses were plenty full; there was no chiseling; the union problem didn't exist. There simply is no comparison with the Met or with any other institution. All in all the situation can never be duplicated. Glyndebourne's a unique and lovely place. I had a very happy time there, particularly in collaboration with men like Busch. He became a very close friend of mine; he was supposed to come to the Met but he died suddenly in Enland. Carl Ebert, though, did do a couple of productions at the Met.

Of course, there were great singers at the Met long before I came—from Enrico Caruso to Kirsten Flagstad. What *I* tried to do, and with what success it is not for me to say, was to infuse more of a theatrical sense into operatic productions. I remember that when I put on my very first production, Verdi's *Don Carlos* as staged by Margaret Webster, it was a kind of revelation to the New York public. Even the critics recognized it as something special. From then on a strong emphasis on the theatrical aspects of opera as well as the musical became a matter of course at the Met. I had met Peter Brook, the outstanding director, in England and saw he was enormously talented and so I invited him to direct at the Met. He did a production of *Faust* and (if I remember right) one of *Eugene Onegin*. I got Alfred Lunt to direct *Cosi Fan Tutte* in my very early years. And as I said, Margaret Webster did my very first production; subsequently she did an *Aida*. Then I got Franco Zefirelli, another outstanding stage director, to do *Pagliacci*; Tyrone Guthrie did *Peter Grimes*; and there were quite a few others.

I always tried to get the most gifted directors, and I had very good luck. I also brought some great conductors to the Met—and naturally, a good conductor is vital to the success of an operatic production. Conductors set the style and tone and quality of the performance. I couldn't and wouldn't and don't want to pass judgement now on the relative merits of the conductors I hired, who ranged from Herbert van Karajan and Karl Böhm to Ernest Ansermet and Pierre Monteux. At present, James Levine, a young but first-rate opera conductor, is principal conductor at the Met. I was pleased to have brought him in before I left. Audiences are very responsive to him.

Although I think that the music in an opera comes first, I consider the drama crucial as well. On the other hand I see nothing wrong with concert versions of opera. Both singers and the public evidently enjoy them. It's clear that they cannot replace the real thing, with costumes and scenery, but some operas are simply too expensive to mount and it is better to hear them in concert form than not at all.

As for the character of the audience, I don't think it changed much during my time at the Met. In New York—and everywhere—listeners like what they know, namely, the nineteenth-century classics. Occasionally a twentieth century work clicks after some years and repeated performances, like Benjamin Britten's *Peter Grimes*; we did an outstandingly beautiful production of this work with Jon Vickers as Peter. Beyond such exceptions, though, audiences the world over love works like *Traviata* and *Bohème*, which is all right—*Traviata* and *Bohème* are great operas.

The fact that musical audiences seem much more interested in

nineteenth- than twentieth-century music is an interesting phenomenon in light of the fact that art lovers are quite responsive to twentieth-century art. My offhand reaction is that since visual art can be
displayed, perhaps it conveys a sort of snob chic to own modern
paintings, whether you like them or not. Contemporary music, on
the other hand, doesn't have the same kind of snob appeal.

Not much is happening today in the way of new operas. Composers are sensibly saying to themselves, "Why waste two years on
something that may never be performed?" The fact is, most opera
houses cannot afford to stage contemporary opera which, with a few
exceptions, isn't what the public wants to hear. I'm not criticizing
new works, I'm just stating a hard economic fact. Any manager in a
house like the Met, with its enormous expenses, must be extremely
reluctant to do contemporary works. The same applies to other
houses around the world, but less so in Germany where everything is
subsidized, and empty seats are paid for by the government. When
the money is available I believe you should produce a contemporary
opera—if it's good. Just as you don't engage somebody because he's
black but because he's good, so with new opera. And you continue to
perform it until the public catches on. Alban Berg's *Wozzeck* is a
good example of a first-rate modern opera, though now more than
fifty years old. *Wozzeck* is one of the greatest masterpieces of all time;
it doesn't sell like *Traviata*, to be sure, but it *is* accepted. And I commissioned, for example, Samuel Barber's *Anthony and Cleopatra* and
Martin David Levy's *Mourning Becomes Electra*, which was an interesting opera with a fascinating text in a brilliant production.

Porgy and Bess is a problem. The cast has to be black—but then
what do you do with your white cast while the opera runs? You can't
use black face, which is silly and condescending, and while there are
blacks at the Met, there aren't enough to fill a production. Opportunities have vastly increased for black singers, though. At the Met I
broke the color bar by hiring Marian Anderson. Even before Marian
Anderson, I had a black solo dancer in *Aida*. I never engaged people
because they were black, but I didn't not engage them because they
were black either. Leontyne Price obviously deserves to sing at the
Met. She is one of the great singers of our day.

During my tenure, the Met moved to Lincoln Center. I had no
regrets about leaving the old opera house. It was beautiful inside, but
impossible to run. Not much could be done with the stage. The new

acoustically excellent house is very good in every way, with all the up-to-date technical facilities. It's more expensive to operate, but what isn't these days? It's a part of a big cultural complex, and the upkeep of the central fountain is one of several added expenses. But I think it was well worth the move, and I am delighted that I was permitted to move into the new house and direct it during its first six years. In the old house we couldn't put on very good productions—despite great singing, a modern production was impossible there.

When I was at the Met a lot of young people attended operas, which was delightful; but nowadays, prices are so much higher—I have no idea what might have happened to youth attendance. I made no special financial provisions for young people, but we had standing room, which still exists, and we had a number of cheap seats. But now they're all high. We had special score desks in the old house as well as the new one, and a few students always would follow scores under the covered lights. I guess this practice still goes on.

Those were good years, all told, though if you run a huge enterprise, there are bound to be strains and frictions. When you deal with artists, you confront egos that may be a little bigger than average. So the strains and frictions increase. But on the whole, contrary to many reports, I think the Met was a very happy house, with no intrigue and no favoritism. We had differences and difficulties from time to time, but basically the atmosphere was friendly.

I was actively concerned with keeping morale high. How does one do that? One tries to be decent, one tries not to lie, one tries to keep people happy. Naturally, if somebody insists on doing such-and-such a part and you have to say, "I'm sorry, I don't think you can," he doesn't leave your office as a friend. But that's what management is all about. You have to have the courage of your convictions. Obviously, one makes mistakes, and there is not the slightest doubt that in nearly a quarter of a century I made mistakes. I made many. But some things must have gone well, because for the last nine or ten years of my tenure, we sold about 97 percent of capacity—and you can't do much better than that.

Then there were the unions. One just has to be realistic about them. They came into being for good reasons and are here to stay; one had better get on with them. In my time they were difficult and in some cases, outrageous—but sometimes so was management. I think that in spite of their power and importance, some labor unions have not entirely grown up. Too often, they're governed by the idea that they must fight. I mean, if the union representative came in and declared, "These are my terms," and management said, "Fine, granted," he would be dreadfully unhappy. Union leaders must appear to their members as great heroes who have fought bloody battles. But they do want the right things for their people. If they go overboard occasionally, so does management. Eventually, I hope both management and unions in the arts will come to realize that they are in the same boat.

I negotiated at the bargaining table from time to time. I now feel that I should have done more of that. At the time our lawyers said, "No, no, you keep out of it. Just come in at the end." Being relatively inexperienced, I naturally took the lawyers' advice. It would have been better for me to do more direct negotiating—but that's all past history.

I conceive of opera as one person's responsibility. I was attacked for not having a full-time music director. I would not have one because I felt that ultimately *one* man must be responsible for all decisions, that he must stand by those decisions or fall by them. Naturally I had advisors in every field, very good ones, both musically and artistically. I listened attentively to them—and then made up my own mind. In all my years at the Met I did more or less what I wanted. One of the last things was Mozart's *Magic Flute* with sets by Marc Chagall; another was a lovely production of *Otello* and in my last year, a beautiful *Tristan*.

I stayed too long at the Met. Nobody can remain for 23 years in such an important job and keep up his own standard. The house standard is something else. I'm conceited enough to feel that I did keep that up. But the press got bored with me—"My God, still Bing! Let's have somebody else."

After I left the Met, college teaching came along completely by accident. Mayor Lindsay was in my box shortly before I retired, and he said, "Now, you can't just sit at home. Why not teach at the City University?" I had never taught before. The idea terrified me. But I decided to try. At first I found it extremely difficult and strenuous, but eventually I enjoyed it, and the main thing is that the young people apparently enjoyed it too. At least they were not bored. You know, at the City University students rate their teachers once a year on anonymous forms. One kid wrote, "He's the best thing we've had since the Beatles." Now *that* was a compliment.

Instead of giving lectures, I encouraged dialogue. The course was supposed to be in operatic management. I don't suppose that any one of those students will be the next general manager of the Met, but they did get interested, they always came, and they asked intelligent questions. After teaching for three years, six semesters, I began to repeat myself. I felt it was enough and called it quits at the end of June 1976.

I am not a born teacher, but the fact that they kept me for three years seems to indicate that I was doing a reasonably good job. I didn't teach at all in the orthodox way. I didn't give tests. I just graded students when I had to according to the interest they showed and the intelligence of the questions they asked. It was purely personalized teaching. No doubt some kids came just because they had read my name in the papers—"This is the fellow who fired Maria Callas," and that sort of thing—but once they came they were interested and stayed for the term.

Now I work at Columbia Artists Management on various special projects. For instance, I'm doing a series of concerts at Carnegie Hall this year. So I've gone back to what I was doing fifty years ago in Vienna. I haven't been asked to the Met in three years—and I won't go without being asked.

Surveying the scene with a little perspective, I think it's rather a healthy time for American opera, which is springing up all over the country. Decentralization out of New York signifies an awakening to the importance of opera as an art, and to the existence of interesting music as well as of a vital public. The Met and the Met broadcasts have helped to foster this change. Deconcentration is a good thing. It gives many more opportunities to young singers. Before this regionalization took place, any young American singer who didn't start at the Met had to go to Europe to make a name. Even now we don't have full-fledged companies outside New York and those that exist have comparatively short seasons. However, there is the San Francisco Opera, which has a good long season, and The Chicago Lyric Opera with a pretty long one, and a variety of smaller companies, some of them very good.

The key question about all American opera companies including the Met is, "Can they survive economically?" In Europe every single opera house, with the exception of Glyndebourne—and even that one to some extent—is subsidized by the state or the city, or in cases like Milan by a combination of central and municipal government. There is no private opera except Glyndebourne, and the British Arts Council helps it. But in Vienna and Berlin, two leading musical centers, the houses are totally subsidized.

Singers were never my principal problem at the Met. Money was. It's the perennial problem. One never had enough money to set out a long-range general plan, something far beyond whether Miss X or Miss Y would sing next season. The lack of money interfered with new productions, which I think are the life-blood of any opera house. The Met has a deficit of $10 million or thereabouts! Such a sum cannot much longer be obtained by passing the hat. I've finally come to the conclusion that there has to be solid, substantial government assistance. Obviously we needn't look to the city at this point, and hardly to the state. Thus, without *federal* subsidy, opera in America cannot survive.

28: *John Edwards*

I've been an orchestra manager for 40 years, that is, almost all my working life except for early flirtations with the theater and with journalism. While in college, I decided that I wanted to be associated with an orchestra. When I went back home to St. Louis, I worked for a newspaper until I finally got a job with the St. Louis Symphony. Afterward I went to the National Symphony in Washington, back to St. Louis, to Los Angeles and the Hollywood Bowl, to the Pittsburgh Orchestra as associate manager, to the Baltimore Symphony as manager, back to Washington, back to Pittsburgh, and at last to the Chicago Symphony in 1967. So I've known a lot of orchestras and conductors in my time.

My family could hardly be called musical. They were active in civic affairs more than cultural ones. Father was an electrical engineer. I did have an aunt who taught piano, and she tried to teach me; but she gave up teaching and I gave up piano at about the same time. There was no professional performing in the family. I come from Welsh and German lineage. My German grandmother took me to concerts as soon as I was old enough to toddle around. So I listened to a lot of music. Of course, I found some of it boring and some entertaining. But all that music sort of lay there in the back of my mind. And then it came back when . . . I suddenly found that what I really wanted was some professional connection with music. Ultimately I got it, first by writing on music for the St. Louis *Globe-Democrat* starting in 1931.

I liked journalism very much. But eventually I got into the management business, though not always as the manager. At first, as an assistant, I did a lot of publicity, which meant I continued to do a lot of writing. I took voluminous notes. If I ever have the time, there are things I might write about. I remember best some of the people from those early years like Bruno Walter and Arturo Toscanini. There are only two very well-known conductors of our era with whom I've never worked—Koussevitzky and von Karajan. I've met von Karajan once or twice, but that's all.

Walter became a very good friend. At one point he asked me if I'd manage his affairs in the U.S. But I didn't see that as a career. I thought of Walter when I heard the Mahler ninth recently. In 1938, Walter conducted the Vienna Philharmonic in that piece, and re-

John Edwards, General Manager of the Chicago Symphony, was interviewed in Chicago in March 1975.

corded it. In those days, there were only 78 rpms, and the Mahler ninth took about 14 sides. On account of Anschluss, he was forced to leave Austria fast. They sent those records after him by boat. When Walter got to Washington, where he was guest conducting and where I was assistant manager, he told me that the records had just arrived and could I find a place for him to hear them? I made the arrangements. It's a notable performance, and it was the last time he conducted the piece. Walter had been very close to Mahler. So the performance, besides being marvelous and unique, is in many ways peculiarly authentic.

Walter was a wonderful man. As a young manager, I didn't have anything to offer him, but I was very receptive. And he was very generous. He imparted to me his enthusiasm and a lot of knowledge about Mahler, particularly the ninth symphony, and about *Cosi Fan Tutte* and Mozart. And *Don Carlos* and Verdi. All this happened on long afternoons in Washington, because in the beginning he wasn't very busy here. Just a few years later he clicked, so to speak.

Walter was world famous, just like von Karajan, who still doesn't really make it in the United States. Now von Karajan is a fantastic conductor, a most original man, but somehow American audiences have never really embraced him. Sir Thomas Beecham's case was a bit different. He was a great entertainer and a marvelous musician, but the professional musicians ganged up on him. They considered him an amateur. And because he had money, they felt that his good fortune was unfair, just as they felt that Koussevitzky's was unfair in a way, because his first wife was an heiress who paid for his "on the job training," you might say. Beecham was a fantastically witty man. His epigrams are legendary.

Such men had a tremendous effect on my whole outlook. With Beecham you felt joy, with Walter, reverence. Even when Walter made jokes, they were pregnant with meaning. For instance, when I was putting him on a train from Washington to Chicago called the "Liberty Limited," we had a whole business about "how can liberty be limited?" Beecham was just unbelievable, in a different way. At rehearsals he talked a lot. Orchestra musicians usually don't like a talking conductor. The famous story is told about a lot of orchestras and conductors and players, and fits almost anybody, about the conductor who talks too much, and the oboe player says, "Don't give us a big lecture on the philosophy of this composer; just tell us: Loud or

Soft?" But what Beecham said was fun and funny. He often made some very cutting remarks. Once, when I was with the St. Louis Symphony, he was doing the Sibelius Third. It's one of the lesser Sibelius works. We'd never done it. He said, in introducing the work, "Now don't be afraid of this, gentlemen. It's undeniably a first-class piece of second-rate music." Which made them smile. It was typical of him.

This is not to deny that he could be terribly insulting. I remember an incident in Los Angeles, a city where people have always evinced tremendous admiration or adulation of titled Englishmen. Beecham was asked to be the guest of honor at a luncheon in the Coconut Grove. For this sort of thing the symphony could draw a mob. They couldn't sell a thousand season tickets, but for a lunch with Sir Thomas B. they could turn out a thousand ladies. So there they were. Sir Thomas made his grand entrance, with a trio playing, of all things, the grand march from *Aida*. Naturally, it was offensive to him. The two ladies who escorted Beecham were heavy-set. When after lunch he finally got up on the dais, they asked him to speak, and he said, "The trouble with music in the United States is that it's dominated by fat-bottomed ladies." That's typical. When he was the conductor in Seattle, he said that Seattle was the intellectual dustbin of the United States—a widely quoted remark. Fortunately for him, the platitude that Americans like to be insulted is probably true.

Then there were others. Leopold Stokowski was an exciting and unpredictable person; and William Steinberg, my good friend, is a marvelous intellectual with tremendously wide culture, a great person, and great fun. To me the personal side of my work matters as much as the business side. I want to know everything about music and life—though I only have a chance to learn about 1 percent of what I want to know.

As for the business *per se*, I mostly taught that to myself—though there were some helping hands along the way. In St. Louis during my assistantship, the manager was a very distinguished, old-timer, once a C.P.A. with Price Waterhouse, who got interested in the symphony business about 1907, and became manager of the St. Louis Symphony in 1911 or 1912. For the rest of his life, he was kind of a Mississippi Valley manager. Quite a character. I learned a good deal from him.

In my office I have a photo of a group of managers of the thir-

ties. What a breed. Some of them were extraordinary. One is Pittsburgh's fabulous fund raiser. He taught me *his* specialty, someone
else about touring, Arthur Judson of New York taught me about artists in general. You learn something from everyone. But in putting it
all together, you create your own concept of the manager's role. I
never took any management courses.

A manager has two main functions. He has all the detailed work
of running a business—supervising a staff, taking care of the financial
operations, the banking and the investment, raising money, and he
has to negotiate contracts with the various unions—mainly, in our
case, the American Federation of Musicians. But of course, we have
our own building, so we have a separate contract with the stagehands
union. And that gets us into a whole new group of organized
painters, electricians, building maintenance people, elevator opera-
tors. For all this and much more, I am answerable to a board of
trustees which numbers 40. And there's an executive committee of
10, plus officers. Sometimes the board has been larger, sometimes
smaller. But this is the only place where I've managed a building,
and the only place I've had to deal with a professional chorus, as well
as an orchestra. The singers have an American Guild of Musical Artists (AGMA) contract. AGMA mainly takes care of the singers and
also instrumental soloists in their relationships with management.
Yehudi Menuhin started this organization in the thirties. Heifetz was
big in it. Originally, Judson was their target because of his famous
exploitation of a fantastically gifted young European violinist who became a *cause célèbre*. The violinist came over as a teenager. In those
days the Sunday Philharmonic broadcast in New York was *the* thing.
You listened to it religiously if for no other reason than that the
soloists and the conductors on it might be the stars of tomorrow. That
exposure meant a great deal. An unknown could come over here,
and they'd put him on the circuit and sell him, in those days, at a
rate of $500–$600 for a pair of concerts. But if he got on the Philharmonic broadcast and was a success, got a big audience response, his
fee could jump overnight to $2000 for a pair. This young violinist
didn't get that break. He was a marvelous player, but no one knew
him, and he didn't command a decent fee. His mother went everywhere with him; as a violinist he had to have an accompanist. So this
teenager's expenses were tremendous, and he lost money right away.
Then they put him on the Philharmonic show and he was a tremen-

dous hit. His fee went up, but the amount Judson paid him didn't change, a fact that emerged in the course of several suits and scandals. At that time Judson was so strong that he could banish a musician to oblivion. The violinist disappeared, *never to be heard of again* in this country or Europe. He just disappeared. In any event, out of this case came the American Guild of Musical Artists. Currently there are three orchestras that have AGMA contracts—ours, Los Angeles', and New York's. The L.A. and New York contracts provide for the use of outside choruses: in L.A., Roger Wagner's; in New York, two or three different choruses.

The hiring of musicians is now governed by auditions procedures that are stipulated in contracts. If there are grievances, I get involved in them and in other administrative matters like pension funds. I have to delegate a lot of the work.

The most time-consuming activity is dealing with volunteers. Besides the trustees, there is a governing board, which is a kind of general civic board: they're an additional 300 people. Then we have a women's association of 600; a junior governing board of 140. And those are all closely tied in to the operation of the Chicago Symphony on a volunteer basis. They're helpful in one way or another, mostly to raise money. Over and above all that we have a corporate group of about 30 men. They do a formidable job of fund raising. The symphonies are probably the most sophisticated of the not-for-profit groups. I'm constantly immersed in raising money, selling tickets, and organizing fund drives.

Then, I schedule concerts and work on programs with the music director. My relationship with Solti is fine. I think most managers have serious discussions with conductors about programming. In general, we try to tell them that such and such must be eliminated because it's too expensive. You have to think of balancing programs, playing avant-garde works as well as older ones. An article appeared in the New York *Times* a few weeks ago supplying a list of 11 orchestras that allegedly encouraged the works of living composers. And Chicago wasn't on it. So I went over everything performed since Solti got here, because I thought our record was pretty good. I found that in the several years he's been here, not including this year, we've done works by 64 living composers, of whom 38 were American. And these weren't short works. Sure, one may be Leonard Bernstein's *Candide* overture. But then there were pieces like Wilfred

Joseph's *Requiem,* which took a whole evening. This year, Roger Sessions will have half a program. We premiered Jacob Druckman's *Windows,* which won a Pulitzer Prize, and Leon Kirchner's *Music for Orchestra.* The audiences have been very tolerant, I'd say better than tolerant. If you want to contrast Chicago and New York, remember Boulez led kind of a double life. I think that was his problem. He had an official music director's role to play plus the role that he wanted to play as an innovator and advocate of new music.

Solti always has a new stack of tapes and scores to go through. He turns them over to Henry Mazer, the associate conductor, or Margaret Hillis, the director of the Chicago Symphony Chorus. I also go through them, make recommendations, giving each work plenty of time and thought. In general, we have to think of costs. We're fighting for our collective lives, like everybody else. We're just a little more dazzling at this level. Costs are immense. One doesn't really know what the answer is. You get a certain amount from ticket sales, and most orchestras don't get the maximum because they don't sell out. We're about 95 percent sold out. We would be completely sold out if it weren't for our policy, or the courtesy we extend, of having twenty concerts on Friday afternoons. We will continue to do that for the so-called "women's audience," which is by no means any longer made up just of women. Quite a few students come now. Altogether, the Friday afternoons give us a more lively audience response. But you have to raise the price a bit, and by so doing you lose some people.

Perhaps the worst frustration is that there's no time to sit down and simply think about our problems. That's one of the biggest headaches in management. You really need time to analyze a problem, or to *identify* it, and only then can you begin to work on a solution. But you've got to deal with a board, and every person on it considers himself *ipso facto* an expert. And there are also your subscribers. We get terrible, abusive letters from them. It's just amazing how violent their passions get, which in a way is very touching. It shows either that they're concerned, or that they are writing as a device for externalizing their psychiatric problems; and you're the unlucky recipient of their spleen. About 60 percent of the letters, and we answer every one, are complaints. They're addressed to every department and they all come to me. If I don't personally answer each one, I want to know what the answer is. Because very frequently after they get a card from someone else, they demand the top person. So I want to be sure that what's being said is something I can support. I don't want to have to reverse anybody working here.

We need to organize the community to produce more funds. Many managers won't touch this area at all. To them it's no more than begging. I've never looked at it that way—perhaps because my first job involved a fund-raising campaign. I've always felt it was a perfectly legitimate managerial task. I figure that it's selling, not begging.

Until I came here, I always seemed to work for the sixth best orchestra in the country. The big five have always been New York, Chicago, Cleveland, Philadelphia, and Boston. So the sixth has been St. Louis, Baltimore, the National, or Pittsburgh. When I came to Chicago they said to me, "We have a great orchestra and we want it to be the greatest." I said, "I think one should let other people make that kind of judgment." So our first slogan was *Second to None*. It was more becoming than *The World's Greatest*. Then we went to New York, where we were called the world's greatest. And we grabbed the accolade. Why not? You could now tie someone else's name to it. Now, a lady wrote me a four-page letter to this effect: "Where do you get your *chutzpah?* You claim you're the greatest when you can't prove a claim like that in the arts. Besides, who says it? You don't. You've invented the whole thing," and on and on in that vein. I sent her various clippings. And I wrote to her, "We obviously haven't persuaded you that we're the world's greatest, and from the tone of your letter, I don't think we've persuaded you that we're worth hearing at all. So it's hard to understand why you continue to be a season subscriber." I felt, well what's the use? You see, she'd buy the ticket in order to rail at us.

I kept her letter on file, and on the top of my mind because I thought whenever we are praised as the "world's greatest" in print I'd send her the clippings. Well, after the European tour, I had a regular cornucopia of stuff in different languages. I sent these to her, a little at a time. And now she doesn't write any more. But she's still a subscriber.

There's no end to public relations problems. The press is high on my list. Remember, it's a sphere where I've worked on both sides. The pretentiousness of our present-day critics doesn't fool me. I am troubled by their lack of basic reportorial skill. You see, in Chicago we really are living under the shadow of Claudia Cassidy who did music reviews for so long in the Chicago *Tribune*. Now, everyone says she is a marvelous writer. And I say, "Yes she is. It's like reading Edna Ferber. But it's not like reading Jane Austen. What she does has no relationship to real style or real command of the language." And given the fact that she knew little about music, and admitted her ignorance, it was absolutely incredible that she should have had so much power in our field! She had that power because the *Tribune* supported her. And the *Tribune* was God to a lot of people who have to do with running the Symphony. For a long time, no one would stand up to her until some of our subscribers did in the Jean Martinon era. But she had already annihilated him.

Today it's another matter. When critics write their opinions of a concert, they simply like it or they don't like it. They're gentlemen, and that's what they're paid to do. If you believe they enjoy a vast accumulation of wisdom through having heard a great many concerts, and if you can accept their views—fine. I find that I have never been overwhelmed by the authority of any critic, because they're all so vulnerable. No one can really know everything. Even a learned man like Winthrop Sargeant of *The New Yorker* is very vulnerable in many ways. It's not that he isn't a great critic. I think that he's rather entertaining to read. Very opinionated, but so are performers. Also rather conservative and resentful of anything that's too innovative. But the point is, he and all the others think they're legislators—that when they suggest something, we have to do it, simply because they say so.

Several years ago when Solti finished his second season, Bernard Jacobson, a critic who has left Chicago, wrote an article headlined, "218 Works Neglected by the Chicago Symphony." Two years later, he wrote another article at the end of the season, in which he said, regretfully, that we hadn't paid much attention to him. In all the time that had elapsed since he'd written his article, only 14 works on his list had been played. But Jacobson saw he couldn't claim credit for all of those, because by a process of deduction, he realized that at least five had been scheduled before his original article appeared. Goaded by all this, I went back to the old article. And he had indeed mentioned 218 pieces. Now what were they? There were 85 Haydn symphonies to begin with. There were about 30 Mozart symphonies. There were about 60 pieces by Vivaldi, and then there were a few Sibelius and Nielson symphonies, and most of Vaughan Williams.

(He had once got hysterical because on the Vaughan Williams anniversary we didn't play any Vaughan Williams. And I said to him, "Do you think the music sounds better in an anniversary year? Does that make it more palatable?" Actually I'm a great Vaughan Williams fan myself.)

Not that I was a gentle critic in my time. Actually, I could be a bastard. On the other hand, when *I* worked for a paper, it was not thought undignified to help the arts organizations by doing advance publicity for noteworthy events. If an artist came in early in the week for local concerts it was considered perfectly legitimate to do a feature article on him or her. To be sure, the artist wasn't killing anybody or starting a fire or running for office. But he or she was contributing something to the community. That was considered important enough in the St. Louis papers. But today's critics, nurtured by their various problems, have almost a *diktat* that nothing should be done to help sell tickets; it somehow implies an involvement that deprives you of the impartiality you need to differentiate among good, bad, or indifferent performances.

And the critics can be so irrational. The other day, we had a program that started with a string piece by Wolf-Ferrari. How did we pick it? Solti proposed it. I look through everything that's proposed by everybody—first to see when it was done most recently, because we try not to repeat all the time. This work had never been done. So that was a plus. Whether it was a good or bad piece is not something I consider. If the conductor has prepared it and he wants to do it, and if we think the conductor's good, we have a certain obligation to accept what he wants to do. On the same program, because we asked for a contemporary work, he did a piece by Zimmerman which happens to have been done by Boulez just recently in New York. Look, all of this week's avant-garde is déja-vu next week. Time passes so fast; if you take a piece that's ten years old, it's in many ways older than Beethoven. But if you haven't done it at all, it's worth doing; it fills a gap for the listener. However, one critic derided the program. He said the Wolf-Ferrari piece was trivial and banal and inexcusable. To devote the time of this great orchestra and the listeners to such fare is criminal. But, he said, it's the kind of piece that obviously the front-office management thinks is acceptable to its audience. Now after that he talks about the Zimmerman piece. He says, "Here's a piece that's not possible to judge on a first performance." And then he goes into a long excerpt from the program notes. And he winds up by declaring that it was good to hear. Now, the contradiction should be obvious, though many people who read it don't get it. The same front-office management that picked the Wolf-Ferrari also picked the Zimmerman.

The other day by chance, I happened to sit right across the aisle from this critic when we did the Nielson Sixth Symphony. He does a lot of sleeping at concerts, but this time he went to sleep as soon as the Nielson began. It was one of the fastest reactions I've ever seen. The Nielson is not an eventful piece in sonics; it hardly gets above a mezzo forte until the end, when there's a series of fanfares which does wake you up in case you've been sleeping. It's a powerful ending. So our man did come alive at the end, and he floundered around in his chair with a lot of turning from side to side. He looked over; I couldn't help smiling. And he saw me. I thought, "Now let's see what's in the paper tomorrow." The next morning he said he found the Nielson soporific. In spite of some charming moments, he was glad when the fanfares arrived. I call that honest reportage. Then again, if I had been two rows behind him, and he hadn't me, I wonder what he would have written. This would all be rather harmless except reviews often make a big difference. If there are two concerts of the same program, the second one can be hurt by a bad press. I don't mean to say that one should only have praise, because that would be as stultifying as the other is damaging. But there are ways to temper your remarks.

In spite of ups and downs in the press and in the economy the orchestra is doing fine. I started in management when the economy couldn't have been worse, and what happened? Why, a proliferation of orchestras. Costs are much higher now. Inflation has something to do with it. But we're also in a compensatory period as far as salaries go. After many years of getting less than living wages and having to supplement their incomes with all kinds of other jobs, often non-musical ones, the players suddenly insisted on a living wage. And they discovered their indispensability. Their importance in keeping the orchestra alive seemed to them to be much greater than that of the big givers. In a way, they're right. But that produced a brand-new perspective. Though the union is made up largely of non-orchestral musicians, it's gotten the symphony players' salary up to an average of $15,000—at least in the major orchestras.

Union officers generally come out of the pops field. In many cases they are guys who got too old to play. Within the union, there's a separate caucus for symphonic musicians, whom it once attempted to separate. However, the AFM has maintained control. It could deprive these men of getting outside work like jingles and other things that help them make a lot of money. Nevertheless ICSOM is a powerful voice within the union to secure better salaries and working conditions.

Management always reacted to orchestra musicians' demands with an outcry: "We can't afford it. We'll go bankrupt. We'll be out of business." But so far, nobody except Dallas and Miami, have gone out of business. Dallas has finally pulled itself together again, and is staggering forward. I don't know how they'll do. They're giving concerts, and so is Miami for that matter. How high can we go? No one really knows the answer to that. But in general, every time when salaries have been raised, the union pushed a little harder and the orchestra's raised a little more money, or increased its debt and borrowed more. I think the crucial question is: what happens in the five years after the Ford Foundation releases its grants and matching grants? About $85 million has been distributed to about 90 orchestras. If it lasts long enough, we will be lucky. What will happen is anybody's guess.

In our case, we have a budget of over $7 million. The total amount we ever got from the government, exclusive of two grants for our European tour in 1975—from the state and city—was less than $200,000. Government grants are nearly all project grants, except in New York State, where they have organized a portion of the money to go for operations. Now, the politicians, sensing the push for more money, and wishing to avoid the responsibility for allocating it—not necessarily appropriating it, but allocating it—have come up with a new nuisance, which may be tried in California—namely a voucher system. Vouchers are to be distributed to the population and used to purchase concert tickets. The recipient organizations exchange vouchers for state money. But if not enough vouchers come in, the arts institutions can't meet their budgets.

We don't know yet how the general economic malaise will affect orchestras in the long run. So far, there's been some decline in season-ticket and single-ticket sales, I've been told. And for the first time in many years, the first tickets to sell are the cheap seats. For at least 20 years, the expensive seats sold first, and it took longer to get rid of the other seats. This is not only true for symphonies, but also for large pops attractions and the theater as well. And that's a significant change. What it will do to us I don't know. Our fund-raising right now is just a few thousand dollars behind what it was this time last year, when we raised more than we ever raised before. This year we're trying for even more. You get over the tax hump and then you begin to see that probably you're not going out of business right away. Another year has been vouchsafed, and off you go.

I've had a hell of a good time. I have a reputation, they tell me, for enjoying adversity. The more things that happen, the more problems there are, the more I feel "with it." As a would-be playwright, I've been very much interested in the theater, and in Tennessee Williams in particular. Some Williams one-liners are marvelously useful. The great all-time one-liner of his comes at the end of *Streetcar*, when Blanche Dubois is being taken away by the hospital attendant. As she comes in to meet him, Blanche makes a deep curtsy, and says, "I've always been dependent on the kindness of strangers." And that's the symphony story.

29: *Paul Fromm*

Whitestone Photo

I am a wine merchant and a music lover. I have devoted my life to trying to build a living musical culture, one in which there is a sympathetic interaction among composers, performers, and audiences. I was struck very early by the isolation of contemporary composers from the rest of musical society and, indeed, from modern cultural life in general. For instance, consider a chic New York City apartment. You enter it, and on the wall is a Jackson Pollock painting, in the corner stands a Henry Moore sculpture, on the coffee table sits a book of poems by Robert Lowell. And on the phonograph? A recording of Vivaldi.

Now of course the preservation and perpetuation of older masterpieces is essential. Great art is great art and we cannot do without it. Also, before you can create something new, you must know your roots. As Picasso once put it, "We all had fathers." However, innovation, which is, after all, part of our cultural heritage, is just as crucial. In fact, what we consider today to be the grand tradition in music is nothing but the remains of successful rebellions. Machaut, Monteverdi, Beethoven, Wagner, and Schönberg were all lawbreakers. In order for musical life to grow and develop, rather than stagnate, we need people creating new works all the time. Listeners should be eager to hear the latest pieces. But somehow in this century, communication between composers and audiences has broken down more than ever before; the public for the most part barely tolerates, much less welcomes, new music.

This is indeed a sorry state of affairs. It is of course related to the current pattern of culture, which doesn't bode well for any serious creative endeavor. All the arts are subjected nowadays to strident commercialism; one sometimes wonders whether the serious artist is becoming an anachronism. (A funny story apropos of this: Toscanini was once asked by a reporter, "Maestro, you're the world's greatest conductor; why don't we ever see your name on the front page of the papers?" Toscanini replied, "In order to be considered hot news, I'd have to do more than conduct Beethoven. Maybe if I raped Grandma Moses . . .")

Then, music as a whole, not to speak of contemporary music, is up against greater odds than the other arts. Even people who are very highly educated in most aspects of modern civilization are poor

Paul Fromm, the patron of contemporary music, founder and director of the Fromm Music Foundation, lives in Chicago and was interviewed there and in Los Angeles in April 1975.

linguists when it comes to music. Ours is essentially a verbal-visual culture; our intelligentsia don't take music seriously enough. They consider it entertainment rather than serious art. Thus music is given a minor place in a child's education. Children learn math and science and even real literature from a very young age, to prepare them for more advanced study in these areas. How can they be expected to understand anything about any music with so little exposure to it?

On the basis of limited experience, audiences develop limited expectations. They become familiar with a few works of the past, but rarely those of the present, and then equate a narrow segment of musical literature with music in general. Most listeners continue to project expectations gained from the Brahms *Haydn Variations* onto Elliott Carter's *Variations for Orchestra* (1955) and other twentieth-century masterpieces. Naturally, if you expect one thing and get another, you're disappointed.

And no one can deny that much music of this century is difficult to understand under optimal conditions. I think it was Alban Berg who said that when many composers gave up tonality and the triad as the basis of their works, around 1910, an estrangement between the listener and the music of his time set in. Though unintentional, perhaps, there was a complete break in aural continuity between the music of Schönberg, Berg, and Webern (not to speak of the later Stravinsky), and that of their predecessors. Ever since, people have obviously been afraid to face the unknown. At the same time that composers began to diverge in major ways from the musical language of the past, listeners became less and less willing or able to assimilate new sounds. As the century progresses, fewer people seem to want to expend effort to understand something difficult. This has become a world of instant everything; records and TV hand you culture on a silver platter, without your lifting a finger. This is rather dangerous, because it's based on false premises. Ultimately, people can really be happy only if they're productive themselves; if you don't actually create, then satisfaction comes from getting your feet wet, taking the time and energy to wrestle with a work of art, to get to know it, to see what makes it unique. Audiences should be active participants, not passive receptors.

Then, the situation isn't much better for the composers themselves, who rarely choose isolation but rather have it thrust upon them. If the musical creator is out of touch with the world around him, he may become like the artist in Balzac's story, "The Unknown Masterwork," who felt his art would remain pure only if no one saw it. He withdrew from the world more and more to produce the Masterwork. Finally it was finished but he had gone crazy and his work was not art. To put it less poetically, if a composer works in a vacuum he tends to go more and more into himself and often replaces musical creativity with technical mathematical investigations which are meaningless as music. Being a hermit is not a very healthy condition for a composer.

I became aware of these issues gradually, as I was growing up in Germany, and continued to think about them after moving to the United States in 1938. I was born in 1906 in Kitzingen, a small Bavarian town where my father was a wine merchant. In those days, if you wanted to have an esthetic experience, you created it yourself. As a child I used to play four-hand piano transcriptions of symphonies by Beethoven, Brahms, Mahler, and Bruckner with my brother Herbert, who became a professional musician. In recent years I have become so critical that I cannot listen to my own playing any more, but I can still read music fluently. It's interesting—the scores I struggled with many years ago are still very much a part of me. When you actually play an instrument you are no longer a passive consumer of sound; you lose the so-called spectator relationship with the music and become an active participant in a creative experience. It's a glorious feeling.

Going to concerts was a big event for us. Two or three times a year we went to the next larger town, which had a little conservatory, and heard the school orchestra play a bad performance of Beethoven's Fifth or some such work. Nonetheless, we always looked forward to it.

My formal education was not much to brag about. At the age of fifteen I left school and began to earn my own living by working for a firm in Frankfurt. Culturally, Germany was thriving in the twenties. People were poor, but they needed and created a very special atmosphere. Frankfurt had two repertory theaters playing every night, two orchestras, and an opera house going ten months of the year. There was so much going on. I came into contact with a great variety of music, including many contemporary works. Then as today the gen-

eral public rejected modern music and occasionally protested vocifer-
ously against it. In those days, Bartók, Hindemith, Krenek, Milhaud,
Schönberg and Stravinsky were the young avant-garde composers. I
was as fascinated by their music at that time as I am today by the
music of such contemporary composers as Copland, Babbitt, Sessions, Shapey, Kirchner, Schuller, Foss, and all the rest.

The turning point which musically speaking made a twentieth-
century man of me came in 1927 in Frankfurt, when I heard for the
first time Stravinsky's *Rite of Spring* (which along with Debussy's *Jeux*
and Schönberg's *Pierrot Lunaire* I consider a musical landmark of
this century). It struck me with the suddenness of lightning. Here was
vital music that was far less characterized by academic purity than by
the range and depth of expression.

Ever since I arrived in the U.S. I have interested myself in the
music of my adopted country. Soon I became concerned about the
anomalous position the American composer occupies in our society.
His creativity is a major source of musical culture, but his status in
the musical world is uncertain. Because of the deepening rift between
artistic and commercial values he is excluded from influencing and
inspiring the direction of public taste. For years I pondered these
problems, and earned some money in the wine business; I had come
to America with only $1500. In 1952 I decided it was time to act on
some of my ideas, and the Fromm Music Foundation came into existence. My operating principle has always been, earn in the business, spend in the foundation. I'm probably one of the last surviving
independents; both my business and the Foundation are in good
shape.

The Fromm Foundation is a small one; our activities are not extensive. My aim all along has been to create some model activities
that could act as stimulants or examples. I derive my greatest satisfaction from being a catalyst on the contemporary music scene. When
the Foundation began, supporting the performance of new music was
still thought of as a philanthropic activity undertaken on principle
against all odds and not, as it should have been, as an act of faith in
the intrinsic quality of the music. It took about ten years for the
nucleus of a regular audience to emerge. Now we seem to have
reached the point where at least it is no longer necessary to insist on

the obvious—the contemporary composer must be given his rightful place at the center of musical life not because of moral imperatives but because of his achievements.

Over the years, the Foundation has initiated and supported a multiplicity of projects designed to help composers. Rather than subsidizing institutions or supporting other even more anonymous aspects of our culture, I have chosen to focus my programs on individual artists, individual works, and individual musical situations. Specifically, the Foundation has sought to influence the contemporary musical scene by commissioning young and relatively unknown composers as well as established composers; providing the best possible conditions for the performance of their pieces and other contemporary works; sponsoring, jointly with the Berkshire Music Center, the annual Tanglewood Festival of Contemporary Music, as part of a comprehensive program for the study and performance of recent music; subsidizing recordings and sponsoring special radio programs; sponsoring seminars for composers and critics; for many years supporting the magazine *Perspectives of New Music*. As of 1975, we had commissioned 112 composers to write a total of 120 works. I think that's quite a record.

For many years the Fromm Foundation was really an extension of myself. I never cared much for rigid organizational structure, so the Foundation bears little resemblance to most large institutions supporting the arts. We have always done things very informally; the foundation library consists of just a few file cabinets. I like this style of operating because we're small and don't want to become stale and lose our flexibility.

I moved the Foundation to Harvard in 1972. I felt I had invested a lifetime in the music of my time and wanted the work to continue after I'm gone. Of course I know there will be contemporary music as long as mankind survives. Art is part of the continuing process of life. I don't have grandiose ideas about posthumous glory. But I've been a good soldier, and I'd like what I've started to carry on.

My relationship with Harvard has developed into *une affaire de coeur*. It was my good fortune that Derek Bok, the president, comes from a musical home; his family founded the Curtis Institute in Philadelphia. I like Harvard because the administration seems to understand that musical and visual ideas are as valuable as verbal ones, that sounds and sights are just as essential to the formation of a civilized human being as philosophy and science. The Foundation maintains artistic autonomy; it is not an adjunct of the music department. Thus we can stay clear of department politics and rivalry. 25 percent of our budget goes to Harvard concerts of contemporary music; the rest is spent on activities outside of Harvard, as the three directors (myself, Gunther Schuller, and Elliott Forbes, chairman of the Harvard music department) see fit. The total budget in 1973 was $160,000.

How do we decide whom to commission? If you're a young composer it's unlikely you'd go to study with the village organist. Instead, you'd seek out a senior composer, probably at a major institution like Harvard, the New England Conservatory, Princeton, Columbia, Juilliard, the University of Illinois, Urbana, to name the most prominent. The Foundation is in contact with the composition departments of all these schools, plus senior composers who may not teach anywhere, and we solicit recommendations. When the occasional talented composer who doesn't study with anyone turns up, we still hear about him. We may overlook some, but not many.

I have always been interested in helping any gifted composer, whether or not his music appeals to me personally. Individualism is not a criterion for giving aid, nor is the composer's personality. After all, Beethoven wasn't the nicest man in the world; neither was Wagner. I'm glad I didn't live in Wagner's time because my reaction to him as a person probably would have impeded my ability to listen to his music.

What makes a new work good? There's no easy answer to that, no laboratory test. Sometimes there is a wide gap between the time of creation and the point at which a deserving work enters the mainstream of musical life. This is something you can't and shouldn't try to engineer. If you look for the so-called masterpiece, it will surely elude you.

Though it's hard to judge a new piece's ultimate value, there are certain criteria which can be applied to any work of art to determine its merits—craftsmanship, originality, and a very important dimension I call the humanistic component, which went largely neglected by many composers in the fifties and sixties. For a while, especially around Princeton, there was an almost obsessive interest in the theoretical, scientific, and mathematical aspects of music. Many composers were writing highly cerebral music for a very small audience. Their music is beautifully constructed; it must be a feat for scholars to *look* at those scores—much less to listen to them. But I have come to believe that music not meant to communicate some strong emotion is not viable and will not endure.

Psychologists often talk about art as an altered state of consciousness. If you penetrate below the level of logic and reason and reach the impulses and feelings that are below the conscious threshold, that's where musical imagination flourishes. Take Stravinsky's *The Rite of Spring*. That work is a primal elegy and exudes a kind of primitive joy which could only have been created because Stravinsky was able to go beyond logical thinking. He could not have constructed the *Rite* according to rigid preconceived rules. Or take Berg's *Wozzeck*, which has become *the* opera of our century. In it Berg dealt with the heartbreak of the human condition; it is a humanistic tour-de-force. Could a computer have been programmed to write it? I think not.

Of course, composers can't spend all their time in reveries; naturally they need a clear sense of how to translate their vision into a work of art. But too many composers in the recent past lost whatever audience they had because they concentrated too much on construction and too little on humanism. I'm afraid that the aridity of much of this music led to further alienation of listeners. People sat there in concert halls listening, sensing there was no crosscurrent that connected the new music with something more familiar; there was no emotion they could latch on to.

I think this trend may have been associated with the fact that these days it's almost necessary for a young composer to start his career on the faculty of a college or university; that's the only way he can earn a steady income. One of the most interesting phenomena of our day is that we have more composers now than ever before; without teaching jobs, they would have nowhere to turn.

I would advise the young composer, if he has a choice, to go to a small liberal arts college rather than a big established place like Harvard or Yale. At a smaller school he can have more influence over the college community; his musical activities take on more prominence. He will have the freedom to play the piano, conduct, or engage in whatever musical activities he chooses. He can have a lot of contact with students; he has a built-in audience for his music. In such a situation you can help to make the student body into contemporary people, artistically speaking.

And of course campuses tend to be lively, stimulating places; I've very much enjoyed living around the University of Chicago. But the danger for composers, especially at major institutions, is that they suddenly feel as if they have to compete with scholars in other fields on some mutually comprehensible terms. So your theory becomes the mode of discourse between you and philosophers and chemists. As you get increasingly accustomed to the milieu of the university, you might begin to think of yourself more as a scholar or a theorist than as a composer; if you are constantly among scholars and scientists you feel compelled to validate whatever music you write scientifically and critically. Artists shouldn't have to do this; they should just create. Then, since most performers and listeners won't have much to do with your music, you try to find some spirit of community in academia rather than in the musical community. This is perfectly understandable—but it can stifle artistic impulses.

Now, some young composers have rebelled; many seem to want desperately to get out of the universities. Take a man like David Del Tredici. He was an assistant professor at Harvard, just about to get tenure—and he felt he had to leave. Charles Wuorinen left Columbia. Somehow the atmosphere had a stultifying effect—it wasn't conducive to writing music.

They felt they had to get back into the mainstream of musical life somehow. But this isn't easy, and it's made worse by the increasing compartmentalization of musical life these days. Somehow people in different facets of music have little to do with each other. I find it very troubling that when I go to concerts of contemporary music in Chicago, I almost never see performers, musicologists, music teachers—and even other composers in the audience. Unless you play a composer's work, or a piece by one of his friends, he does not come to concerts of new music. I think this is very sad. It seems that among themselves, musicians have not created a community like those of painters, sculptors, poets, writers, and dancers; when one artist has a show, other painters go; when a playwright's first play is performed, other playwrights attend—not to accommodate a colleague, but to find out what's going on, to be stimulated. For years I have been appealing to composers to join together with each other and with other musicians, to recognize their interdependence, to encourage one another and further their professional interests. Composers themselves and then others in music must form the nucleus of an audience for contemporary music. Eventually they will be joined by other members of the arts community and a small but growing group of music lovers who share their belief that serious artistry need not be compromised, even in a society that confuses material success with real achievement.

Clearly composers need a sense of community; they can't and don't want to function in isolation. I had this strongly in mind when the Foundation got involved at Tanglewood. Originally Aaron Copland brought me there in 1955, with a small project which has blossomed into what I consider to be the core of the Foundation's work. We decided to try to build a real musical community, the kind that does not exist on campuses or in our urban centers, where the organized musical life is really controlled by commercial interests. Though large musical institutions are deficit-ridden, and I'm sorry about that, they still measure artistic success by the number of tickets sold. At Tanglewood we try to create a situation where commercial considerations are irrelevant. We bring together young performers and composers in an atmosphere of interdependence, where they have a chance to get inside each other's problems and learn from and stimulate each other. For a few weeks every summer they function as an organic community, not just as members of separate guilds who have no contact with each other. The experience is especially a revelation to performers, since it is perhaps the first time they get sustained exposure to the music of their time. Conservatories, though they're better in this respect than they used to be, tend to be steeped in the eighteenth and nineteenth centuries, and think the twentieth ended with Richard Strauss.

The high point of the summer's activities is the Contemporary Music Week. Gunther Schuller is in charge of putting together the programs for this festival; they include premieres and performances of older modern works, for soloists, chamber group, orchestra, and so on. The Festival has attracted a steady audience over the years. It doesn't bother me that this group of listeners doesn't grow enormously year by year, because the intrinsic musical value of the pieces played is transmitted not only to paying visitors but also to the several hundred students at the Berkshire Music Center, who will take the contemporary listening and playing experience home with them to all parts of the country.

As Stravinsky once put it, "I'm pleased but never satisfied" with how the festivals turn out. We're always learning how to improve. A recent lesson is that we have to be very careful about the older works we program, so that we include some of the classics of the century and thereby show audiences that there are twentieth-century pieces as vital and viable as the music of the past they know and love. Early on, the festival was more or less a musical trade fair, a place where you showed your new wares. Now we try to juxtapose "established" modern works with those which are new and untried. If you want to convince people that there is valuable twentieth-century music, you have to put your best foot forward.

Along with this awareness came a Foundation policy decision, in 1973. Right now, our credo is, don't *over*populate the musical world with new music. You shouldn't be the mother of children you can't raise. Other much larger foundations have commissioning programs these days—the NEA, Rockefeller, Koussevitzky; also, more and more performing organizations and successful performers commission works. We decided that if contemporary musical activity becomes a wholesale diffusion of new works, then no work will ever become familiar, so how can audiences get comfortable with it? How will it ever get integrated into the standard repertory? How many contemporary works can you recognize? So recently we have been putting more emphasis on repeat performances of already existing scores. Imagine how a composer must feel if his new piece is played once and then disappears into oblivion!

Bearing this in mind, we devised what I consider to have been a rather spectacular way of celebrating the Bicentennial, in conjunction with the Juilliard School and its director Peter Mennin, Pierre Boulez and the New York Philharmonic, and the National Endowment for the Arts. The reasoning went, if a performing institution is isolated from education, it becomes solely a vehicle for entertainment; on the other hand, if a musical educational institution is separated from the world of performances, it loses contact with live music. I proposed that the two join forces. For one week the New York Philharmonic suspended subscription concerts and Juilliard suspended its regular activities. The orchestra inserted a contemporary music week into its calendar. Musicians from Juilliard supplemented this with performances of works for chamber orchestra and smaller ensembles. All kinds of musically involved people from around the country—young conductors, community orchestra leaders, members of chamber groups, critics, attended rehearsals, public concerts, and workshops on the performance of new music. We hoped to send them home "indoctrinated," so to speak.

Two-thirds of the pieces played were important American works written in the last forty years; the other third were European.

I wanted the music integrated this way to show that American music of this century has finally achieved some independence and can stand on its own next to the best European compositions. I think the "Celebration of Contemporary Music," as it was called, was a high point of Fromm Foundation activities, and was also a particularly meaningful contribution to the Bicentennial.

We hope this celebration had wide repercussions. We can educate and encourage and devise model activities. But then it is up to enlightened conductors and performers to give new works sufficient exposure. I've thought a lot about the question of effective concert formats, and there's no easy answer. On the one hand, it is probably wise to integrate new works with the standard repertory; a ghetto existence is never healthy. On the other hand, many of our efforts to juxtapose contemporary music with masterworks of the past ended in frustration for everybody—the conservative audience didn't like having to hear a new work on the same program as, say, Beethoven's Seventh Symphony, and the composer didn't like being upstaged by Beethoven. Rather than throwing in the newest works with the greatest classics, it would probably be more effective if conductors would begin by introducing important music from the early part of this century, and from there lead gradually up to the music of the recent past and present. Now, it's unrealistic to expect the unprepared listener to grasp the forms, subtleties, and gestures of new music—or for that matter any music—in one hearing. But one hearing is often all the listener gets, if he gets that. Real understanding and appreciation can only come from a more systematic assimilation of musical styles and idioms; constant exposure to specific works is needed. Unless our planners of concerts integrate individual contemporary pieces that they themselves love into the repertory, our audiences will remain estranged from the music that should be closest to all of us—the music of our own time.

There has been so much agitation on behalf of contemporary music by now that no self-respecting conductor would openly oppose it. In the generation that preceded ours, people were not so tactful. When Walter Damrosch was asked, "What do you think of the new composers?" he retorted "I hate them." Our present-day conductor is more polite. He complains instead about his budget, the lack of rehearsal time, the conservative taste of the audience, or simply the dearth of really good contemporary scores.

We acknowledge his dilemma and suggest that so beleaguered a symphony conductor might do well to engage on a regular basis some guest conductors who have identified themselves with music of the recent past and present. They will be asked to devote half of the program to contemporary music and the other half to traditional music. Some managers and conductors will complain that audiences would boycott such concerts. On the contrary, I believe that people will be grateful for being shaken out of the rut of the concert-going routine and they will be honored by this evidence of trust in their intelligence and sense of adventure.

There *is* an extensive orchestral repertoire from the last forty years which can stand side by side with the Preclassical, Classical, and Romantic music now played by our orchestras. The music director who does not realize this is either inexperienced or uninterested.

If the performance of twentieth-century music is assigned to a conductor who would not have to learn the music during the orchestra rehearsals (as is so often the case) no or very little additional rehearsal time would be needed. The conductor's commitment might even inspire orchestra members to work out difficult passages at home. If the conductor believes in the music he is performing and is persistent, the audience will rise to the occasion. It is important that he be given the opportunity to bring works back the following seasons in order to establish them in the repertory.

The type of guest conductor I have in mind will travel about with a limited number of programs of contemporary music each season. The orchestras he conducts will perform the same music, perhaps in rotation if he is clever about it, and after a period of time, music audiences throughout the country will share a coherent experience of twentieth-century music. If there is an organized campaign to perform contemporary orchestral music, both existing music and new works will be equally in demand, and the composer will be encouraged to write for the orchestra. The real problem is not finding music but finding enough committed conductors. We do have outstanding conductors (some of them are noted composers) who are identified with twentieth-century music—Pierre Boulez, for one— and are equally experienced in the performance of the music of the past. Let's make more use of them!

Even with all the good intentions in the world, there is no question that if the the arts in general, not to speak of music, are to survive and flourish, the federal government is going to have to provide more funding. It's an old American bugaboo to try and keep the government out of everything, but this makes no sense any more. Look at the National Gallery in Washington or the Library of Congress or even some of our big state universities. All of these get federal help and none are less autonomous than private institutions; even if you itemize the funding of a private university you find that 60 percent comes from the federal level anyway.

But the prospects for enough federal aid are not very good right now. I myself am in a quandary over how I think government money should be spent. Though I think there's enough for both, if it comes down to a choice between funding the arts and rebuilding the cities, I suppose I favor dealing with social problems first. After all, people have to eat; then we can give them culture.

Meanwhile, there are state arts councils to help out. From 1965 [to 1977] I served on the Illinois Inter-Arts Council. Governor Kerner appointed a conservative judge as head of the council; he was a very decent chap and appointed me, saying the council needed a radical. I was music chairman for several years. Arts councils are effective in limited ways. They have most impact outside big cities, in places like Peoria or Rockford, where a few thousand extra dollars can make the difference between putting on low- or medium-level performances. I favor supporting neighborhood institutions and musical activities in the smaller towns, which are isolated from the mainstream of musical life and don't have another source of income, because whatever you give big establishment institutions is peanuts compared to what they need; for example, our whole budget is $1.3 million while that of the Chicago Lyric Opera is $5 million. It would be hard for us to help them out.

On the whole I enjoyed working on the arts council, but I would not want to be a trustee of the Chicago Symphony or any other huge outfit. The administrators of such institutions really want as trustees very wealthy people who are interested in the arts but know nothing about them, who will defer to the judgment of the manager. That's why those organizations get away with perpetuating a concept of the orchestra that is carried over from the nineteenth century. The format hasn't changed; everything is as it was. The first piece is a short curtain raiser, followed by a flashy concerto, and ending with a big piece by a Romantic composer—a symphony or a tone poem. I *am* on the governing board of the Chicago Symphony, and am an overseer of the Boston Symphony—though neither of these posts means much. When I was made overseer Erich Leinsdorf was still conducting in Boston. I asked him what my job was. "Oh that's easy," he aid. "I can explain it. An overseer is somebody who overlooks everything and oversees nothing." In all the years I have served, no one has asked me for my opinion, for better or for worse. I'm simply a name on a letterhead.

Looking over all my activities, I guess that patron would be the best title for me. I think of a patron as someone entirely different from a consumer. A consumer buys a concert ticket and munches down the concert in the same way he eats his breakfast cereal; it's a fast, pleasant experience with no particular consequences. Consumers of the arts generally don't invest too much in the esthetic experience. I ran into one such person at the Symphony. There to my right sat a society woman, one of those ugly "beautiful people," sumptuously dressed. After a Stravinsky work was performed, she turned to me and said, "You seem to be a little nervous." I said, "I'm not nervous. I listen to music and you don't." She had been three-quarters asleep and was fascinated by a certain intensity I showed. Imagine! Active participation in a musical experience is labeled nervousness. Are you supposed to sit in your seat in a kind of stupor and sleep the concert away, because afterward you might have a party where you want to be awake? I found the incident amusing, and sad; it says something about many of the people who have symphony subscriptions.

For consumers, art has become a status symbol. People collect pictures in the same way they collect vintage wines. I give a dinner party and take people down to my cellar and say, "You select the bottle." In other words, you really want your guests to see your collection of rare wines. The same thing goes for the pictures on the wall—and the concerts you attend. Leonard Bernstein once made a nice remark about all this: "Today a conductor or a performer is like a curator. He has to hang the music in the most favorable light."

I consider a patron to be someone who not only supports the arts and artists economically, but also nourishes the artistic spirit in society. In other words, he helps to evoke a musical milieu which is conducive to artistic and especially to creative activity. This is what all the Fromm Foundation projects have been designed to do.

I deplore competitive animosity among artists, so for the most part I have steered clear of conferring prizes. I did give a Fromm Prize in Los Angeles in 1975, against my better convictions, because of the peculiar nature of musical life in that city. My friends in L.A. told me that they needed an occasion that would focus attention on young composers. Just playing a new work doesn't get the same attention in L.A. as giving a prize. I would never do anything like that in Boston, New York, or Chicago, so the L.A. award may be the first and last Fromm Prize. There were four finalists, and all were honored by having their pieces played at a Monday Evening Concert at the Los Angeles County Museum. The Monday Evenings are the oldest contemporary music institution in the country. They were in existence long before similar groups were formed in other cities, and introduced the works of many young American composers, as well as by the masters like Schönberg and Stravinsky, both of whom lived in L.A. after they emigrated to this country.

I think the compliment I cherish most was paid to me by Stravinsky. In the spring of 1958 I received word from him that he wished to meet me in Chicago where he would stop over on his way from L.A. to New York. We sat together in the restaurant of Chicago Union Station. I ordered a cup of coffee and Stravinsky said, "Absolutely not. We must celebrate with champagne." He continued, "I want to know you because contemporary music has many friends, but very few lovers. *You* are one of the lovers." It was one of the nicest things anyone ever said to me. I'll never forget it.

Photo by Cornachio

or most of my life, I've put on concerts of one sort or another. My current title is Curator of Music at the Los Angeles County Museum of Art, which is somewhat misleading because we have no collection of music or instruments. When the new museum opened in 1965, they inaugurated a concert series which they asked me to run. I was happy to do so, since the widely known Monday Evening Concerts, which I directed, were transferred to the museum that year. For six years I ran both operations. I retired as director of the Monday Evenings in 1971 after being involved with them for over thirty years. Though it was a most rewarding experience I finally got tired of the rat race, especially the unending search for funds. But I'm still doing the museum series.

As a young man, I came to L.A. from Minnesota in 1939. Shortly after my arrival I got interested in the Evenings on the Roof, as the Monday Evenings were then called, which had just gotten underway; they were the only concerts around that did chamber music in a serious way and included much twentieth-century music in their programs. Soon I became a member of the board of directors and then concert coordinator. When Peter Yates, one of the founders, retired as director in 1954, I took his place. My job consisted of concocting the repertory, engaging the musicians, and the like.

As a youngster, I started out as a musician. How did I become a concert manager? It's the same old story: People who play an instrument but aren't good enough to meet the competition look for other musical things to do with their lives. Actually I began my professional musical "career" when I was seventeen. While studying music at the University of Minnesota I began playing the organ in silent movie theaters in Minneapolis. I did that until the time of talking pictures, when movie-house organists discovered that their jobs were not very stable. Then I did some church work and finally, when family responsibilities eased up, headed for Hollywood. It took me a long time to get situated, to find a niche. For a while I did some orchestrating for a few important film composers, and other odd jobs of that sort. My real interest lay elsewhere, in more serious music. The only advantage to film work was that if you did two or three or

Lawrence Morton, Curator of Music at the Los Angeles County Museum of Art and former director of the Monday Evening Concerts, was interviewed at his home in Los Angeles in April 1975.

maybe four pictures a year you made enough money so that for half a year or so you didn't have to earn anything. And the craft was sometimes interesting. I learned a great deal about instrumentation.

I wrote some music too. My compositions are all carefully tied up in a big box to be destroyed at my death. They're all very derivative. I had a few performances, but none of any significance. I've done a lot of writing for small magazines in this town, music columns for a quarterly and music library notes. And I wrote criticism for a little Beverly Hills paper. So I got around quite a bit.

Because I was a critic, I made friends with many composers and musicians. I soon came to respect the Roof concerts and wrote good things about them in my articles. I decided to get involved in the concerts in an active way. When Peter Yates retired I was asked to replace him. I was then 51. I guess I was the only fool around who would accept a job like that—all work and hardly any pay. (Don't mind my complaining. I enjoyed it.) I was able to make ends meet by doing writing and other things at the same time. As a single man, I was never interested in getting rich. A married man with responsibilities has to think more about his salary. I had had responsibilities when I was young; by middle age I could do as I pleased.

I live modestly, yet I consider myself one of the fortunate people in the world. Many of the young composers around town come to me and show me their scores. I'm delighted to talk, and analyze their music, with them. After Ingolf Dahl, the composer and teacher at USC, died, a couple of them asked me to teach them formally. But my knowledge—which I wouldn't call vast, but it's rather extended— is not organized in such a way as to allow me to give a coherent series of lectures. I said to these kids, "Keep bringing me your scores and I'll be glad to look at them. You won't have to pay me anything. I'm not a teacher, but I'll be your friend." Besides the composers, some young conductors consult with me, often over long-distance phone, about programs and repertory. I've been delighted by such close contact with creative people; I've been rather close friends with Aaron Copland, Pierre Boulez, and Igor Stravinsky, among others.

My friendship with Stravinsky came about through his interest in a Webern project I did at the concerts with Robert Craft. I got to know Stravinsky well and followed his musical development quite closely after he moved to California in 1941. By 1949 we were on intimate terms. I was with Stravinsky and his wife a great deal. They liked to come for dinner, perhaps partly because I'm very informal and they didn't have to dress up; also, I'm a good cook.

I can only remember a single occasion when he played me his music while he was still putting the finishing touches on it. Once, when Bob Craft was away, he called me rather excitedly. He had just finished a piece. Would I come to his house? Of course, I dropped everything and went up there. It was his Dylan Thomas piece (*In Memoriam Dylan Thomas* for tenor, string quartet, and four trombones, 1954). We both sat at the piano—I played the lower part—and we tried to read through it. He was not a good pianist; his fingers stuttered as he played. And I couldn't keep up with him, not knowing where the beat was half the time. I was not exactly frightened, but a little bit abashed at having been brought into so intimate a relationship with a newly created piece. I felt the need to say something. But what? I've been in that position with many of my composer friends. They bring new works to show me all the time and sometimes it's hard to react on the spot. But Stravinsky!

I don't really remember what I said to him that day. One was always very careful with Stravinsky. Who wouldn't stand in awe of such a person? I knew some people who called him by his first name; I never could. He told me once to call him by the name Igor in its patronymic form. I just couldn't bring myself to do that. I called him Maestro. If you read Bob Craft's books, you'll see that he always addressed him as Mr. Stravinsky.

The wonderful table talk reported in Bob's books reads very much like our conversations at lunch or dinner. The Stravinskys always had many reference books in the dining room because that's where questions of fact often arose during the wide-ranging discussions. Where is such and such a place? What's the altitude of that country? Temperature, rainfall, general climate? Actually, everything, not just geography and climatology, came up for discussion at the dinner table. Stravinsky was very witty. There's been a great deal of discussion about whether he really knew different languages fluently. Well he certainly had a working knowledge of several. He had a special dictionary with English, French, Russian, and German translations. If you looked up anything in English, you'd find the definitions in the other three languages. He was always concerned with the construction of language. Was a word like "scissors" singular or plural? Is there such a thing as a scissor? It also greatly interested him to see how the classical Russian works had been translated into English. I went to Europe with the Stravinskys in the mid-fifties and he was reading Turgenev simultaneously in English and Russian; he wanted to check the translation. I know he was deeply interested in the Nabokov translation of *Eugene Onegin*. He was skillful in all the languages he knew, though toward the end, as Craft tells us, he settled more or less into Russian, his native tongue.

I knew Arnold Schönberg only very casually. Our relations were distant but cordial. I was not in his inner circle as I was in Stravinsky's. A different group of people clustered around each master, although certain people like Robert Craft, Ingolf Dahl, and David Diamond went back and forth between them.

Schönberg taught at UCLA, and from that position exerted a big influence on music education in L.A. His textbooks focus on the classics; he never taught people twelve-tone technique. Stravinsky never taught. Somehow, there were no big activities centering around either composer, though each had a faithful following. But they certainly influenced the few of us who stood in awe of them and for whom contact with them was terribly important and exceedingly valuable. Usually, such innovation is applauded only by a very small segment of the population. Look what happened to musical life in Vienna, with its legacy of great composers. The core of the Western musical tradition was in the Viennese school. But Vienna itself had no part in it. Not one of Mahler's symphonies was premiered there. You can say great composers lived in Vienna in spite of itself. Johann Strauss, among all the possible choices, has become the "spirit of Vienna." Of course, there's the long, long tradition of anti-Semitism in that town which hurt Mahler and worked against Schönberg. But that's no excuse for slighting Mozart and Schubert.

On the whole our present situation is not encouraging in the sense that we have no successors to the great figures of an extraordinarily rich century—Stravinsky, Schönberg, Berg, Webern, Hindemith, Bartók, Mahler, not to speak of Ravel and Debussy. You look for a Schubert coming after Beethoven, a Brahms after Schumann, a Wagner after Berlioz and Liszt. I don't see the succession today. I suppose Boulez and Stockhausen come the closest, though it's hard to say, and I'm not too sympathetic to Stockhausen's recent musical trends; I guess they're related to an influx of Oriental culture which may be great, but is not for me. And of course there's Elliott Carter, who is, to be sure, a product of Stravinsky, plus mathematics, plus his own personality. That mixture yields complexity, but I don't always find much relationship between the complexity one looks at on the page and what one hears. I think Eliott is an extraordinarily talented man and a very good composer. Believe me, there's plenty of craft there. A real master is a real master. But the expressive side of his music seems to me to be lacking in some way, though it's hard to put one's finger on it.

There is no individual on the scene now for whom I would go all out and say, as Schumann did of Chopin, "Hats off, gentlemen, a genius!" This appears to be a transition period following a period of several great composers. Schönberg always said that he encouraged the second-rate: Theirs is the feeding ground from which something great might come. Techniques of composition and music making are in a state of flux right now. We don't have any great ideas that are establishing themselves as criteria. Don't get me wrong—I'm not pessimistic. I'm rather happy that we have such a quantity of new music, even if a lot of it is second-rate.

And there's reason to hope that the quantity will change into quality at some point soon. We've had whole eras in the history of music that were not terribly productive. Take the great eighteenth century, and all of Bach's contemporaries. There are people today trying hard to make something major out of Telemann. All the little baroque groups around town are discovering Telemann. Yes, he was a very competent composer—his music is no desert, but it's no flowering garden either. Then take the period between Bach and Mozart and Haydn. You've got the Mannheim school—historically very interesting, but hardly the kind of music that provides the greatest satisfaction.

This seems to be the great age for amateur composers. They have all that electronic equipment to play with, and many of them like to fuss around with pure sonority. These people have altered the art of composition beyond recognition. Peter Yates wrote me shortly after he'd gone to Buffalo that he'd found an interesting phenomenon—people composing pieces who couldn't read music, who didn't seem to need anything more than sheer sound to create "works of art."

The concepts of aleatoric music, taped music, composition by diagram instead of by note writing have all opened the way toward excessive amateurism. But that too will pass. I remember talking to Lukas Foss about the use of improvisation in contemporary composition. I told him that when I worked in the theater as a film organist, I improvised nine-tenths of what I was playing. One got sick of playing the Tchaikovsky *Romeo and Juliet* theme and the pop tunes that were necessarily part of the repertory. I had gone through all the old piano music I knew. So I just sat there and played around for hours at a time. It was very easy. When I was a kid, my older brother, who was a fiddler, and I used to make music every night after dinner. We'd go through reams of literature and then simply improvise. I can't do that anymore, certainly not with the same facility. So I said to Lukas, "Sure, improvisation is fine. But what do you end up with when you're through?" There's nothing to show for it, nothing on paper, nothing tangible. I think that joint improvisation was always a shortcoming of Lukas' improvisational group; it's so haphazard. But on the other hand, out of that experience came one of Lukas' best pieces. I daresay that a number of ideas in that piece occurred to Lukas in the course of listening to the players' improvisations in other pieces. But most people don't come up with anything substantial out of improvisation.

Judging recently composed music is always a tricky matter. Thus, selecting scores for performance at the Monday Evenings has never been easy. Intuition has a lot to do with the selection process. If a score comes in the mail and all of the several board members (who in the past included Ingolf Dahl and Leonard Stein) say, "Oh, that score is lousy," I would just set it aside. If they showed interest though, I'd examine it very carefully.

Recently we've started to get tapes as well as scores. They're made illegally—it's hard to make tapes in L.A. because the union's so strong. But they're made anyway. Of course, this saves time. I can listen once and know whether I'm interested or not. If so, I can listen again, study the score, and show it to others.

As for craftsmanship, our notions about it should come from pieces by great composers. If you know Stravinsky's music well, and if you know the greatest works of Webern, Schönberg, Hindemith, and Bartók, and their music is in the repertory of every decent musician, then these are the people who more or less set your standards. Stravinsky, Schönberg and Webern are certainly the three great influ-

ences of this century. When someone younger, like Stockhausen or
Boulez, comes along, you see or sense certain relationships with the
masters, you can't conceive of the two later composers in non-
Webern terms. That's crucial. There are certain other composers you
can't think of without Stravinsky. You get notions of craft and work-
manship from the great ones, so when you hear a new piece, you instantly make comparisons.

Influence is one thing, imitation another. Why do a derivative
piece if you have the work from which it's derived? I remember years
ago when the New York Philharmonic concerts were first broadcast
on the radio and Deems Taylor was the commentator. Generally I
thought he was too chatty and informal. But Taylor did make an important remark once to this effect: "Yes, composers can write music
in the style of Brahms, Bach, or Beethoven, but if they do so they're
exposing themselves to an awful lot of competition."

At the Monday Evenings, the percentage of old and new works
varies from season to season. The dividing line between "old" and
"new" is always shifting. It used to be 1900. Then it changed to
World War I, because you couldn't consider Debussy, for example,
new any more. Then Webern became the dividing line. By now,
some think even Boulez is passé. During my last year as director of
the concerts, I considered Webern the divider, although Schönberg,
Berg, and Stravinsky always remained in the "new" category. Really,
though, music of quality, whenever it was written, is timeless.

Once we select a program, we go about getting the musicians.
There is a pool of perhaps 100 or 125 people. Everyone in town
draws on them. Some play with Neville Marriner's chamber orchestra part of the year, others play ISCM concerts. It's always the same
group. Some have maintained their active interest in music despite
having to earn the bulk of their livelihood in other fields. Some are
youngsters out of the universities or the Young Musicians Foundation Debut Orchestra. They're all trying to find a place in the musical world for themselves. And they play very well. After a while we
know which musicians can do certain kinds of music and which
can't. We get to know their idiosyncrasies and their personal styles,
and whether they get along with other people or not. There's one
clarinet player I would never put with certain other players. He just
rubs them the wrong way all night. Having congenial musicians can
make a big difference to the performance.

I find that the quality of instrument playing among young people today is extraordinary. And I find them very sympathetic to new music. Many of them are not quite as tuned into Romantic music. Generally the ones who are good at playing contemporary music are also deeply interest in Medieval, Renaissance, and early Baroque music. I think there is some relationship between what they see in contemporary and very old music. The relationship might be what Bernard Berenson spoke of as the ineloquent in art, a quality that runs counter to the over-expressiveness of the nineteenth century. It's a cool music, rather than a hot and impassioned music.

It's also interesting to observe that many of the older listeners are most interested in the newest music. They don't seem to want to sit around and listen to the same old stuff any more. They're tired of it. Audience size has been fairly consistent over the years. I would say that in all of L.A. the audience for contemporary music is probably not more than a thousand people. You may find 400 of them at a Monday Evening, for an extraordinary event 600, which is capacity. I went last night to a contemporary chamber music recital at UCLA's Schoenberg Hall. There were roughly 300 people there. It seemed to me to be about the same audience that comes to the Monday Evenings. And from what I understand, the situation is more or less the same in New York.

But I rather suspect that we have more of a lay audience in this city for contemporary music than New York has. I think—though this may be hearsay—that New York has a largely professional audience for new music. I know that we get university people, scientists and, like New York, professional musicians interested in what's going on. Not so many performers as composers. I'm pleased that audience level has stayed fairly steady. After all, the concerts have been going on about forty years. Very few small musical organizations, especially ones with commitments to contemporary music, live that long. All too many survive for a year or two and then fade away. We have a loyal following, people who come to concerts year after year. There is one lady, a psychologist who taught at UCLA, who must be near eighty now, who's been around as long as I have. And in recent years, there's been a marked increase in student attendance.

We've tried to expand our audience with newspaper publicity, notices of concerts to a large mailing list, and letters that advertise the coming season and ask for financial support. Every year, with all that, we get 25 to 50 new people, and 25 to 50 drop out. Either they're weary of such concerts, or they decide, "Let's go to the Philharmonic this year." After a while, many return. Some don't come in ten years and all of a sudden they're back again. I can understand that. No one wants to go to the same kind of concert all the time. And because of the travelling distances in this town, you have to make choices. At Philharmonic concerts I see very few people I know. It's a completely different audience.

The Monday Evenings have done fine all these years—with no thanks to the newspapers. The press has been anything but helpful. The leading critics in my time have been enemies of music, not only new music, but all music. For instance Boulez came out here in 1956, I believe, for his first concerts in the U.S. apart from little theatrical things. At our concert he conducted a U.S. premiere of *Marteau sans Maître* and the press attacked it viciously. The performers got together and wrote a letter protesting the review. "The Battle of Boulez" went on for weeks and weeks. Then, when we first performed Luigi Nono there was a very harmful review entitled "The Right to Compose" suggesting that this right should be denied certain people, such as Nono. We convoked a sort of mass meeting of several hundred people to protest this position. See, if you censor the right to compose, you censor the right to perform and to listen. At the meeting we had three people representing the composer, the performer and the listener. We invited the critic to speak; he came, but uttered not a word.

Nor did he recant. Critics never take anything back. His attitude toward music was one you might expect in Hitler Germany or in the Soviet Union. How could a critic suggest that the *right* to compose should be abridged in any way?

Of course no critic is obliged to like everything. But what irritates me above all is bad reporting. For instance, we played a piece by Nono just before intermission and repeated it right after. Our man wrote that half the audience didn't come back to hear the repeat. Well, the plain fact was that half the audience *did* come back. Everything depends on how you slant your language. At the next concert I gave a little speech pointing this out. Such distortion is bad criticism. Neither of L.A.'s current principal critics reports very accurately. At least Martin Bernheimer of the Los Angeles *Times* knows his bias against recent music and doesn't come to Monday Evening Concerts too frequently. After the first concert of the season, he'll come to one or two others during the year and send his assistants to the rest.

What reviewers write doesn't matter much in any ultimate sense, but performers certainly are affected—their professional existence seems to depend largely on what sort of reviews they collect. For example, all the literature I get from New York impresarios about their artists is nothing but newspaper quotes. These don't mean anything to me—you can always extract a favorable comment from a review. I do know, though, some very good performers who refuse to play any more because they always got such bad reviews.

Many reviews of Monday Evenings were unfavorable, but I don't believe this affected our audience. On the other hand a positive review can help bring listeners in. I had at least one experience like that, in connection with a museum concert. We had an exhibition of art treasures from the Metropolitan Museum of Art and the Cloisters in New York. When I heard that some of the Cloisters collection was coming West, Noah Greenberg's Pro Musica ensemble came to mind. I invited them out. The group played first at one of the universities; the review of this concert was very positive, and our ticket sales boomed. We had sold-out houses. Noah Greenberg had already died; John Reeves White led and the performances were superb. Besides the music, the costumes were marvelous. I'm sure that very good review helped us a great deal.

The press can also do a lot to generate excitement for an important upcoming event. Like the premiere of a Boulez or Stockhausen piece. Some advance notice, more than an announcement, that a major event in the musical world is about to take place, always helps. You'd think a critic would have something to say about an important new work before it's premiered, not necessarily to bring business in, but to keep the community aware of what's going on. But somehow it doesn't work out that way. You don't get any such coverage in the L.A. press, though if the New York City Opera Company is coming, you get weeks of advance publicity, long stories about Beverly Sills and so on. Big financial investments, like Rudolf Serkin playing three concertos, usually get big personal stories. But for smaller events you get nothing beforehand and negative reviews afterwards.

I must add, however, that in the whole history of the Monday Evenings I think that only once has the *Times* neglected to run a review. I respect and appreciate that. At least we got our name in the newspapers. But I do think that it is also the critic's social obligation to create an atmosphere in the community for the acceptance of all kinds of music, principally new and difficult music.

Some assistant critics take more interest in recent music than their superiors. A critic who's now in New York comes to mind; he often covered my concerts when he worked in L.A. He'd call up the afternoon of a concert and ask, "Can I see a score of the work being premiered tonight?"

"Sure."

"I'll be there a little before curtain time, at 8:10, to look it over."

So I'd show him the score of a very difficult piece. Now, I'm an experienced professional musician. And I can't look at a difficult score and tell you anything about it in twenty minutes. I can't and he could?

Too often, critics are not musicians, or if they are they're failed musicians. Of course, there's Virgil Thomson, who's enormously talented and uses language superbly. Nevertheless, even he sometimes indulged in the most trivial sort of nitpicking. At his best, Thomson was the best critic we have had in this country since Paul Rosenfeld, who was writing about a slightly earlier period and wrote very differently from Thomson, at times indulging in a great deal of purple prose. But his enthusiasm for new music counted for a lot.

Basically, though, I don't like critics as a group, as a class, as an institution. I don't say they shouldn't exist. For example, reading the Viennese critic Edouard Hanslick is a pleasure. Of course his opinions about Wagner's music were wrong, but when he told you about *Tristan and Isolde* at Bayreuth you could at least count on his reporting. With most of our critics today, you can't even respect the journalism.

Much as I dislike them, critics are not the main enemy. Conductors of major symphonies, as Paul Fromm and others have pointed out, are as much to blame for not fostering a spirit of openness and acceptance of new music in the community. Like other orchestras in this country, the L.A. Philharmonic does very little contemporary music. Zubin Mehta, who [was] the music director for several years, is an extraordinarily talented person whose taste in music lies with the eighteenth- and nineteenth-century Viennese repertory. He'll give a great performance of Dvorak, for instance, but when he plays Stravinsky, it's really too bad. He's said publicly that he has no interest in Stravinsky's late music, but even when he plays the neoclassic pieces, it's clear he just doesn't "dig" them, as he doesn't "dig" Copland. He's just not too good at twentieth-century music. Every conductor has his limitations. It's just too bad that more leaders of important orchestras aren't too interested in the music of their own time.

The situation with the L.A. Philharmonic is not as bad as it could be; in fact, the change since Ernest Fleischmann took over as manager has been quite exciting. He's a real presence, a force for change. Fleischmann has made Mehta develop some kind of perception of and interest in newer music, which is certainly a positive development.

But even when Mehta is openminded, he has to deal with conservative audiences. During one season, for instance, he programmed five Schönberg works, beginning with *Verklärte Nacht* and working up to the *Orchestral Variations*. The subscribers hated every bit of it. Hundreds cancelled their subscriptions. And when the series of concerts was over, news about the unhappy patrons got into the press. I wrote a letter to Bernheimer, who printed part of it, about how strange it was that people interested in the arts, who are eager to see an exhibition of Klee or Kandinsky or many other painters contemporary with Schönberg, won't accept Schönberg's music. These people read James Joyce and Gertrude Stein and even Mallarmé. But somehow they can't and won't accept music of the same period.

I have one idea about why this is so: anything that appeals to the eye comes closer to the center of one's being than something one hears. I think the eye is closer to—shall I say—the consciousness of man? We close our eyes when we sleep; we don't shut off our ears. The eye, then, is, so to speak, the organ of consciousness. And so I think that a painting, a piece of sculpture, or even a book that you read are all eye experiences, and come more directly to the center of human consciousness than music does. So it takes longer to be able to accept new sounds than it does new sights. I don't know if this is so, but it's a decent speculation.

Also there's a point Stravinsky made very well. "People know what they like?" he asked. "No. People only like what they know."

Thus, when someone sends me a piece of new music, I have to work hard at it. One's early experiences with music establish habits that are hard to break, even if you're open to new experiences. I was brought up on music written long before the advent of serial and twelve-tone music, so I was tonally oriented. Because of the way I was educated, I felt uncomfortable at first with the music of Schönberg, for instance, as compared with the music of Brahms. At the age of ten I went to concerts in Minnesota to hear, say, Geraldine Farrar sing "Habanera" from *Carmen*. I grew up with that kind of music; most people do.

Around 1928 I moved to Chicago for a short time. Frederick Stock played some new music at his Chicago Symphony concerts. I first heard Hindemith and Stravinsky live in Chicago; Stravinsky passed through Chicago on tour in the thirties, when he was best known as a conductor. So gradually my ears got accustomed to the music of my time. But it took some extra effort, which many people don't take the trouble to make.

So the position of the composer in today's society remains a problematic one. We do all we can at the Monday Evenings, programming a lot of recent pieces and giving them decent performances. Our concert series has never commissioned works. We pay composers a rental or performance fee if the works are published. Composers also send us unpublished scores. From time to time we have paid a small fee for those—but only if the composer insisted. Mostly, they're so glad to get a performance that they don't even ask for it. It's a sorry situation—contemporary composers don't earn much money from their music, or get enough performances. Publishers don't help much; they usually won't bother with somebody who doesn't have a reputation. You can't gain a reputation without performances. You can't have performances without someone pushing your music. Composers do a great deal of this themselves, but sometimes they are not good salesmen. And sometimes they just don't have enough scores, which are quite costly to reproduce. Often when they've been used somewhere you don't get them back—they're thrown away. Certainly that's a miserable plight. Publishers who *do* print new pieces don't push them; when you rent recent scores they are in deplorable condition. When we gave a Varèse concert, the condition of the scores was so bad that parts of the bottom corners were torn off. The music was full of errors. I accused the publisher of sabotage. I said, "that's a fine way to treat a great composer." I marked 46 errors in two pages of music. *Forty-six mistakes in two pages!* I often find that we know more about the contemporary music in their catalogues than the publishers do.

We don't have much control over scores, but we do have more to say about rehearsal time. This varies from piece to piece, but generally we pride ourselves on our satisfactory preparation. Whenever a certain Times critic doesn't like a piece, he terms it under-rehearsed. But in most cases, with a new piece of music, a critic can't tell a good performance from a bad one. I never make judgments on a work's merits after one hearing. Even if I've had a chance to look at a score, how can I tell whether it's the work or the performance that's affecting me until I've heard it a few times?

Lately I've been very busy with the Museum concerts. There's always a big one for Christmas, usually consisting of broad, stately symphonic music. We have a jazz concert in the fall. Other concerts are usually arranged in conjunction with a special exhibition. For a show of Japanese art, I brought out a trio of Japanese musicians; for an American art exhibit I arranged for a concert of a wide spectrum of American music which started with Francis Hopkinson, who lived in the eighteenth century, and culminated in Charles Ives. I included a charming little piece, *Christopher Mockingbird*, with a flute off-stage. Of course, the Ives was the most interesting music on the program. Then, for Michelangelo's 500th birthday, I put together a concert around settings of Michelangelo's poetry and works inspired by him. Musically speaking, it was very uneven, but at least we had a musical celebration of a great artist's birthday. Only two of Michelangelo's contemporaries set his verse to music. I had three pieces of theirs for a small vocal group and instruments. Then I found two pieces by Liszt that were inspired by Michelangelo's works, like the statue of Lorenzo de' Medici in the Medici chapel in Florence. I found another piece called *In the Sistine Chapel*, a sort of fantasy. I did some Mozart, some songs by Britten and Wolff. We ended with a piece by Dallapiccola which, I discovered too late, used poetry not by Michelangelo but by his nephew. Rather a nice program, although it did not include a single masterpiece. Throughout the concert, I showed appropriate slides, the Sistine Chapel and such. I enjoyed it.

The Museum concerts are paid for by a woman trustee. I would say they cost around $25,000 to $30,000 a year. The Monday Evening budget is about the same. Funds for that come from various places—the California Arts Commission, the National Endowment for the Arts, the Martha Baird Rockefeller Foundation, and private individuals. Doctors have always given us a lot of money; music and medicine seem to be closely bound somehow. But we never have enough, though the budget problems could be solved overnight if government or business gave the arts a higher priority. Neither gives us as much money as it could.

The one thing I want to do before I die is to put on a whole concert without having to consider costs. Every other concert I've done has had the limitation—budget, budget, budget. I want to choose the best repertory and not have to worry about money—spend all I need for rehearsals, make no cuts or changes, just go ahead and spend.

I would love to do twentieth-century pieces that have not been done out here, like Boulez's *Pli Selon Pli* (1964). With respect to music of other ages, I've had a great many one-shot satisfactions which I'd repeat if I had the funds. One of my big achievements in L.A. was a performance of the Monteverdi *Vespers* in 1953, which would have been the U.S. premiere except someone in New York beat me by a few weeks. I'd like to do the *Vespers* again because no matter how often it's performed—and it isn't done much—you realize that the possibilities are infinite; no one knows exactly what to do about the instruments, since scores were not written out as fully as now in the late sixteenth and early seventeenth centuries. You have to work at the right antiphonal effects. I'd need the right chorus, the right solo voices—and a heap of money.

I have not been frustrated by anything much except the bloody budget. All the problems I've had could have been solved with money. Heaven knows, there's plenty of good repertory begging to be heard. We've made a sizable dent here in L.A., but there's a lot more yet to do.

Part Seven: Critics

Photo by Alice Snyder, Northwestern University

I certainly didn't plan to become a music critic. Like many of my colleagues, I got into the field more by chance than by design. An exception among us is Harold Schonberg of the New York *Times*, who maintains he knew by the age of eleven that he wanted to be a critic. As a young man, I was exclusively a musician—playing the organ, teaching voice, conducting choruses, composing; in high school I even toyed with becoming a doctor or an engineer. But a music critic? I didn't write a line of criticism until I was 29. Early in life, especially as I was growing up, it never occurred to me to be a writer.

I was born in the tiny town of Flat Rock Illinois, in 1928, into a non-musical family. My father taught several subjects at the local high school, and coached basketball. I heard some music at home on the radio, and we had a piano, though we did not own a phonograph until I was eleven.

But I first got excited by live music at our Methodist church. As a small boy, I sat by the organist, and drew occasional stops. And I loved to sing. Since mother thought I was a pretty good choir boy, I started studying the piano when I was seven.

I spent most of my time reading in the library, and never practiced piano. But being constantly unprepared for lessons made me a crackerjack keyboard sightreader. This skill proved invaluable. By high school I could accompany a local college chorus. And I put myself through college as an accompanist.

In my early teens, I thought I was destined for electrical engineering. During World War II nearly everyone, it seemed, wanted to be a radar technician or a submariner. Radar, a frontier phenomenon, intrigued me. I expected to learn to use it in officer training school. But the draft didn't catch up with me.

Meanwhile, a girl's ensemble I had trained performed in a state music contest. The judge turned out to be head of the voice department at the Northwestern University School of Music. He offered me a scholarship, and a job to supplement it.

So off I went to Northwestern, only to discover a music school with a strong music-education orientation. In fact, it was *the* Mid-

Thomas Willis, when interviewed at his home in Chicago in March 1975 was the music critic of the Chicago Tribune *and professor of music at Northwestern University. He has since resigned from the* Tribune, *is writing for* Chicago Magazine *and other publications, and is Concert Manager for Northwestern.*

western center for training music teachers—not exactly a hotbed of intellectual activity. So I took lots of courses at the School of Liberal Arts—semantics, intellectual history, German—which made Northwestern vastly more stimulating for me than if I'd just done music.

Soon I was in a play at the School of Speech; my role was that of Irish bartender in Synge's *Shadow and Substance*. Then, while doing the music for *Le Bourgeois Gentilhomme* by Molière, I met a director named Claudia Webster. She was a Bert Brecht fan who desperately wanted to revive *The Threepenny Opera*, with me as the music director. The project entirely absorbed me. From then on, I didn't think about much more than Brecht, Weill and Millie, my wife-to-be, and already a fine singer.

Besides my musical theater activities, I ran a weekly radio show for one year called "Your Campus Choir." And I did accompanying for some of the best voice teachers in Chicago, as well as for the music school, glee club, a cappella choir, downtown campus chorus, and the choral union.

I also took piano lessons all four years, from a fascinating man named Earl Bigelow, a student of Percy Grainger's. Earl was able to understand somebody like me with a wide and lively batch of interests, who couldn't practice all the time.

The years at Northwestern helped me make a career decision: I would be a choral conductor. To get the proper background, I'd do graduate work in musicology. I managed to get a scholarship to Yale. Millie and I got married, and took off for New Haven.

Yale was tough; I did not have the temperament of a round-the-clock Ivory Tower scholar. And Leo Schrade was a difficult man to study with. There were a few other faculty, but in effect, Schrade *was* the department. When he came over from Germany, he formed the music history program in the Yale Graduate School, separate from but equal to Hindemith's program in composition in the Music School.

Schrade was a brilliant scholar—a neo-Platonist—and a grand lecturer. But, with some reason, he was intolerant of American education, being very much the medieval instructor himself. His manner and demands were hard to handle.

By my third semester, I couldn't stand an exclusively academic existence. I had to do something as a performer. Park Barnard, director of the Yale Choral Society, asked me to be his accompanist and assistant conductor, maintaining that together we could shape a versatile chorus that would do unusual repertory. Naturally, I accepted his offer.

Early on at Yale, I also ran the audio lab. I had made records in loose partnership with a student at Northwestern named Martin Diller. We taped all the kids' recitals, using portable cutting lathes. On the basis of this experience, Quincy Porter gave me the job at Yale.

As you can see, it wasn't exactly a straight line scholar's career. Schrade soon saw that my heart was in choral conducting. He said that after I completed my Masters, he would try his best to get me a conducting job.

With my daughter Debbie on the way, we needed more money than my scholarship provided. For a while, Millie worked in a record store, and I was a fuel-oil truck dispatcher on the New Haven waterfront. The Korean War meant much defense industry. The summer after my second year, I worked for the Geometric Tool Company, as a thread grinder and a tool and die maker. My third year, I split my time between work and school, working in the factory from 7 to 10:45 A.M. and then dashing into Schrade's 11 A.M. class, just in time. I would change overalls in the men's room of Sterling Library. Schrade could not fathom this; it was totally outside his ken as a good German aristocratic scholar.

For a year I worked in Teaneck, New Jersey, as organist, choirmaster, and sexton of Grace Lutheran Church. From that moment to this I have never been without a church job.

After Teaneck, my good friend from Yale, Helen Boatwright, the singer, helped us relocate at Sweet Briar College. It seemed perfect: Millie would teach voice, and I'd lead the chapel choir, teach music history as an assistant professor, and give private organ and piano lessons. We went blissfully off to Amherst, Virginia. It turned out that the college was on an 800-acre plantation, north of Lynchburg. We had an absolutely glorious time. I was then 25.

It was 1954, and I found myself embroiled in a local integration battle; I conducted the first interdenominational, interracial All-Amherst County choral festival, with Negroes on one side of the church and whites on the other.

Apparently, my outside activities didn't sit too well with the Sweet Briar authorities—theirs was a sheltered school for white Protestant girls and they wanted no boats rocked. The whole music faculty tried hard to save my job, to no avail.

So I reapplied to Northwestern as a doctoral candidate, returning to my alma mater on a one-third teaching assistantship. I chose Monteverdi's *The Coronation of Poppea* as a thesis topic.

Extracurricular activity made life very busy. The lure of another Brecht play, *The Caucasian Chalk Circle*, was dangled before me, and I composed a score for it. The opportunity to use Bartók's researches in the Caucasus as the basis for a Brecht score was irresistible; in my book, Bartók is up there with Joyce and Brecht. I resolved that, from then on, my priorities would be doing music for plays, producing operas, and coaching kids in the musical theater. And incidentally, I would get my degree.

I formed a little chamber opera company, Cameo Operas. Our calling card was *Amahl and the Night Visitors*, which we performed with top soloists. A big old-line women's music club asked me to take charge of its Monday morning operas. I staged about two thirds of *Poppea*, long before anyone else. With that impetus, some money, and singers who had stayed in Chicago, I thought the time was ripe for a chamber opera company to do English and American works, and ultimately be attached to the Lyric Opera, Chicago's large professional organization. But this turned into a losing financial venture.

And then, out of the blue, Seymour Raven, the assistant music and theater critic of the Chicago *Tribune*, who was looking for a part-time music and drama reviewer, called me. Apparently the deans of the School of Music and the School of Speech at Northwestern had agreed that I was competent in both music and theater. Raven neither knew nor cared about my writing ability. He was after someone who'd accept on-the-job training.

I told Seymour I didn't want *another* part-time job. A little later, he offered me a full-time position. Again, my PhD studies would be delayed. I was interviewed by Claudia Cassidy, the *Tribune*'s highly controversial chief critic, and joined the staff on July 1, 1957. Less than a week later, I wrote my first review, of a Grant Park concert.

I was also in the midst of conducting and stage directing a performance of *The Mikado* at the Northwestern outdoor theatre. It broke all box-office records. But that was to be my swan song, my last fling: Seymour and Claudia insisted that I give up everything professional when I joined the *Tribune*. And I more or less did—for six months, anyway. I kept a nurses chorus and a church job, because the paper only paid $95 a week, and my son Chris had just been born.

I remember that first review. It was about a violinist, maybe Fritz Siegel, concertmaster of the Grant Park orchestra. The copy desk accepted all three paragraphs. The *Tribune* excelled in tiny notices as well as big reviews, and I was responsible for the mini-pieces. I had no time to agonize over them; little reviews had to be turned in very quickly. Never having written on deadline before, I came in and froze cold that first night, scared silly. The story had to be on the copy desk by 11 P.M., with only my initials on it: Claudia and Seymour were old-fashioned journalists who believed you got a byline only after you earned one. By mistake, the copy reader put on my byline. Seymour raised holy hell. For the next four months I wrote initialed reviews. At last my first review with an "earned" byline appeared.

My first stint as a critic proved short-lived. There just wasn't enough writing work for three people and I also functioned as departmental secretary, pasting up clipping scrapbooks. But I wasn't very neat, and Seymour and Claudia were afraid I still had too many friends in the music profession, like all these young singers from my opera company (even though I'd dissolved it). We had confidential material at the paper and they weren't sure I could keep my mouth shut. So my post was terminated after a six month "trial."

I found myself in a real bind. I had given up forty piano pupils, and the other part-time jobs. I was also hooked on the newspaper business. By this time I had made some lunchtime friends who could help me out—the editor of the *Tribune* Sunday magazine, and my future Sunday editor. When I told them I was "out," they said, "That's ridiculous. If you want to stay in and learn the business, you ought to be able to. We're not paying you so much—we can afford to keep you. Try the neighborhood news section."

So on January 1, 1958, I began work in the Trib's Neighborhood News section, where I surfaced as *the* specialist in school problems. I wrote about sewer bond issues, suburban teacher strikes, and board of education matters. I went on assignment with photographers for feature stories. And within a year, I picked up my chamber opera again. By the time a vacancy developed on the copy desk, my supervisor knew I knew the English language, and I became a copy reader. Shortly afterward I was promoted again—to night feature copy editor. This meant that, among other things, I handled Claudia's and Seymour's copy.

Seymour soon quit and became manager of the Chicago Symphony. He was tired of going out every night. Reviewing's hard for a family man, as anybody who does it, myself included, will attest. Seymour's replacement at the *Tribune* lasted six weeks before he was fired. Thereupon Claudia decided to do everything herself, and landed in the hospital. She recovered and came in one night for a long, heart-to-heart talk with me. That put me truly up against it. I had the opera company going again, and a good job; here was Claudia, asking me to go back with her. I settled my dilemma on the basis of power: I could have more influence with readers working for Claudia. Also, I figured I'd be happier writing about the arts, even though I already knew how hard it was to work for a perfectionist.

I had enormous respect for Claudia Cassidy as a newspaperwoman. I had not seen a professional anywhere on the *Tribune* (and by that time I knew them all) who could touch her. I always thought that my musical judgment was at least equal to hers. But in this business, experience is what you've got going for you, and hers far exceeded mine.

Before joining the *Tribune*, I hadn't read many critics. This changed when I became one. I read Virgil Thomson's columns with the greatest care. What a stylist! If at first I imitated anybody, it was Thomson. For past models, I dipped into George Bernard Shaw, Robert Schumann, and Hector Berlioz, probably the best music critics of all time. At Yale, criticism came up in my study of the Encyclopedists. Those early Frenchmen enchanted me; their period marked the beginning of a major critical tradition. I also knew the work of Edouard Hanslick, the Viennese critic who hated Wagner.

Each of the critics I have mentioned had his own conception of his role. At first, my job was defined *for* me: It was highly specialized work, which involved attending concerts and informing people about them, writing background profiles on the artists, and doing broader, often historical, Sunday pieces. Claudia had a lively interest in the history of music in Chicago; she made me do a lot of digging. I came to share her fascination.

Later on, I would formulate some different notions of the critic's role. Meanwhile, I enjoyed the concerts. Claudia wrote every press person in town that "Mr. Willis is to have his own set of tickets." As long as I was willing to work 95 to 100 hours a week, I could see everything in Chicago.

Officially we handled music and drama, but Claudia covered all the performing arts; so did I. We did nothing in the visual arts. Though I did not have a voice in setting policy, she never told me what to write. My feeling was, and remains to this day, that if I can describe an event well, and do it on solid conceptual grounds, I need not worry about my opinions. The newspaper management never tried to tell either of us what to say. We were basically autonomous. If we said that an article was important, scheduled space for it, wrote it well, assigned the pictures and asked for prominent display, our wishes were carried out. Nowadays, our department has less control over its copy.

Claudia held only one of my articles out, a review of Walter Hendl and Gary Graffman. It was the first and also the last intemperate piece I ever wrote. The next day she wrote me a note saying, "I asked that this be taken out—I'm sure you didn't mean it." I quickly learned to state chapter and verse when I was negative.

Those first years with Claudia were rough. She had a highly developed sense of formality, a glacial courtesy, and her own way of lacerating—always politely and delicately. But she did not always come out and say what she meant; I sometimes failed to realize that anything was wrong until her notes to the Sunday editor came tumbling back at me. Also, I never met her standards. It added up to a most instructive but painfully difficult period in my life. I'm not sure I would want to go through it again.

Finally, after eight years, came a turning point: In 1965, Claudia was retired, and I was named music critic. I had come to love the newspaper business. I liked having a sense of low-level professional competence. Being a tool and dye maker, an artisan, provided similar satisfaction. And I realized that somebody had to do the job. I knew few people who would do it better, and many who would do it worse.

Be that as it may, I get maybe three crank letters a week, five or six fairly well-reasoned disagreements, and two or three vituperative phone calls a month. Sometimes I'm hurt. And I've had to apologize, usually over factual mistakes, at times in print. I never get into a big fight about my opinions, possibly because I don't present them antagonistically. I try to say things as simply and as quickly as I can, to be strong but not to preach. Claudia taught me that passionless prose is meaningless. If you aren't committed to what you write, it shows. You need some conception of what's fueling you *and* the ability to convey it effectively. I've learned enough about newspapers by this time to know what looks intemperate in print. Also, when you stand on a soap-box, you have to watch your platform.

In 1966, an invitation to President Johnson's one-day Festival of the Arts started me thinking hard about my function. I was present as a guest, not a newspaperman. Claudia was invited, I wrote the White House that she'd retired, and they said, 'Why don't you come?' In consequence, two important things happened: I met Roger L. Stevens, the founder of the National Endowment for the Arts and Humanities, and I heard Dwight Macdonald speak, which caused me to ponder over my real role.

It was decisive for me to see that enormous assembly and take note of its political implications. As the Vietnam War raged, LBJ invited a lot of intellectuals to the White House; they raised hell about his policies. I got concerned about the relationship of government and art. Roger put me on his first music panel; our new Sunday editor helped make it possible for me to accept a presidential appointment to a government commission. Then and there I began seriously to contemplate, "Where am I? What am I actually doing?" Roger appointed Aaron Copland as head of the panel; Rudolf Serkin and Gunther Schuller were also members. That's when I began to encounter the power structure in American music. Before, I had dealt with press agents. Suddenly, I was out in the open.

At this point, I began significantly to diverge from Claudia's neo-Romantic idea about what critics do. When I took over, I made changes. The paper would now look at music as *I* understood it. Music for Claudia generally meant anything and everything performed by the very best artists in our highly paid cultural establishment. I felt this was not a viable position for a newspaper to take, conceptually or economically. By 1966, I thought it was time we covered rock music. My new Sunday editor agreed. Contemporary music was another area I opened up. Claudia showed hardly any interest in compositional activity outside the "establishment" forums. She would write intelligently about the occasional new opera at the

Lyric, or whatever came up at the Symphony, but university concerts, or performances of new works at art galleries, hardly got a line. Claudia had a really strong sense of legitimation. She did not consider herself a gate-keeper: She would not judge what new music should and shouldn't be played in big halls. She let others do the gate-keeping and wrote as a person on the receiving end, about whatever got a well-exposed performance.

I decided to go where I damn well pleased, inside or outside the large institutions, and write about what appeared to me to be newsworthy. Virgil Thomson led the way here; he had enormous guts on the New York scene, going off to a church, or wherever the spirit moved him. I still don't gad about as much as I'd like to, mainly because everything in Chicago happens on weekends, and it's hard to be in several places at one time.

We have a strange and difficult artistic community. Chicago is a city of baronies, dukedoms and oligarchies. It's a peculiar metropolis because of its size, its geography and its history. You can talk about musical life in American cities with reference to New York and Chicago, which in turn differ vastly. Most smaller cities and Los Angeles have very strong, highly unified arts power structures that are pretty easily deciphered. Everybody in L.A. music, for example, is responsible to "Buffy" (Dorothy) Chandler, who built the big Pavilion. Usually you find such an individual entrepreneur of the arts, be he or she philanthropist, impresario or professional musician. Seldom do you have a situation like Chicago's, where even minimal activity is accompanied by diversified power.

The power centers in Chicago are very clear: The Chicago Symphony, the Lyric Opera, the University of Chicago, Northwestern, Newberry Library, the Art Institute; often the directorates overlap. It's true we have a few struggling little dinner theaters, a few struggling composers who have a hell of a time getting their works performed and are attached to a few struggling conservatories, a music "establishment" on the north shore that wants to be the biggest little conservatory attached to a Big Ten university (Northwestern), and a liberal arts music department on the south side at the University of Chicago that resents its status within the college of liberal arts, and is constantly hamstrung. But then we have Olympian organizations that siphon off great gobs of the arts dollar to produce admittedly vital and interesting star-laden art. There's little in the middle that's reasonably priced and decent to listen to, no central situation where you could develop a larger constituency while giving newcomers a chance to perform.

The Lyric and the Symphony are fighting to maintain their size, even to expand their operations. That's not necessarily bad, but will divert funds from other smaller-scale arts activities. We need a public dialogue on artistic alternatives, though it may be impossible to restructure this situation while the big shots remain so big.

I write many columns on the city and the arts. One facet of Chicago's music history turned into my dissertation. I found to my great surprise that all past box office statements and programs in Orchestra Hall were still available in bound volumes. Being acquainted with data processing, I realized that a lot of fruitful cross-classifying could be done between these documents; I could look into correlations among all the elements in the programs vis-à-vis the box-office statements (they were even broken down into seat classifications). I had fifty years of this material! The thesis would simply be a presentation of the methodology, a "how-to" case study in the primary use of computers. That would be quick; interpretation of the data could follow. The *Tribune* did all my card punching, with a research grant from Northwestern.

The head of the university's computer department did the programming, and the director of the computer center was on my committee. He thought it a great thesis, and talked the musicologists into seeing its value. The idea came as a direct result of reading John Mueller's book on the American symphony orchestra. My topic zeroed in on one facet of Mueller's study. I demonstrated that if you extrapolated my method to his 28-orchestra sample and beyond, the computer could provide information that he missed. One practical computer spinoff could be to collect raw material from orchestras and assemble cumulative repertories, updated continuously, and then make these indexes available to each orchestra. The American Symphony Orchestra League expressed interest in this endeavor, but I suspect John Edwards, now manager of the Chicago Symphony, talked them out of it—though I never asked him—because too much confidential information would have come out. I still have those lovely computer programs. And I have printouts for use in my own work. I got the degree in June, 1966.

Soon after, I picked up a lectureship at Northwestern, and first off was asked to teach a course in twentieth-century music. From research for that class, I learned more about many areas, for instance, the conceptual musicians, who in many ways duplicated what the minimal and conceptual artists were doing.

Shortly I was able to use this knowledge in a practical way, for around this time I took charge of music at Christ the King Church in the Loop. It was an innovative parish, in which the two pastors were enthusiastic media people, one very talented in visual arts and photography, the other, in tape recorders and audio. We began to compose multi-media religious extravaganzas. You could say we expressed a *zeitgeist*—the social gospel does that. I undertook numerous big projects for the church that took place in hotel ballrooms and involved huge numbers of people and multiple projectors. I got excited about combining the "legitimate" performers' media, in which I had training, with photography and sound mixers. Though I had quit composing for awhile, here were real possibilities for creative activity that would keep me at least avocationally active as a performing composer. And that produced no conflict of interest. I could still be a detached critic while composing for church and in another context— experiments for my twentieth-century music class at Northwestern.

It would have been hard making it solely as a composer. Other countries do better by their composers; we in America have much less going for us. Even those who constitute the East Coast power base—the Gunther Schullers, Arthur Bergers, Eric Salzmans—get little "Establishment" help; the radio won't broadcast enough contemporary pieces to build a large audience; music publishers find it unfeasible to print new works; most record companies find it impossible to record them; the social elite can't find anything more than the not-very-powerful American Music Center to sponsor them. And surely all this is now so closely geared to the New York area that it's not much good for us out here.

As a critic, one of my aims is to establish greater credibility and a support base for contemporary music in my neck of the woods. I plan to talk to and write about more composers. If I can pique a reader's curiosity about a new work, perhaps he'll give it a try. You see, a newspaper is more than a mosaic of what's happened; articles report news but they can also *make* news. If, as I strongly believe, art is process, a newspaper's main function in relation to the arts is to catalyze. I may not speed things up as much as I'd like, but I leave my mark whether I discuss something or ignore it. What I leave out is as important as what I cover. Where I go matters not only because I'm there, but because I'm not somewhere else.

It's not easy to define my role as critic of the arts. There are basically three variables to consider: (1) the public, (2) the newspaper, (3) the arts institution; or, if you like, (1) the reader, (2) the critic, (3) the performing artist. I am always juggling these components. Therein lies the fascination. Your readership is so diversified; some are neither concert-goers nor musicians. Others are both. A few musically literate readers will have attended the concert you're reviewing; so did some who virtually need to be told where they were.

I distrusted didactic writing for a long time, and still think "teaching" in print must be very carefully conceived. The best education is frequently, though not always, unobtrusive. When our new editor came on strong about the newspaper as teacher, I wrote him a memo saying, "That is the last thing a newspaper ought to be." His response was, "*You're* a teacher. Why don't you think a newspaper should teach?" I answered, inform, yes, pontificate and spoon feed, no. I aim to educate readers as I do my students, provocatively but unpretentiously.

Classroom teaching helps my journalistic work, and vice versa. My role in the academy is vastly different because I sit there in print all the time. I often use articles to teach students; they, in turn, give me regular feedback on my columns. These daily reactions, from young people and faculty colleagues, are invaluable.

Being an active musician conditions both my writing and my teaching. I have a performer's reflexes. Readers should be aware of critics' inclinations; mine lean toward performers first, and then composers—in contrast, say, to Virgil Thomson, who naturally reacts to music primarily as a composer. In other words, within the critical profession, we each have a specialty. My experience gives me a feel for performance practice and problems, and how scores are interpreted; Virgil's hotline is hooked up to compositional processes and techniques, and how scores are constructed. Of course, our interests and knowledge extend beyond these territories. And other critics, like Harold Schonberg, have a still different bias. That's fine too. Harold's great—a true virtuoso newspaperman. He formulates a whole review in his head and then puts it down on paper—fast. Harold loves piano music, and plays it very well. And he has a capacious photographic memory. So does Claudia. She really sees things on a page in her mind.

Sure there's venality in my profession. Apropos of this, Peter Weiss made some striking remarks in a wonderful talk at Princeton a few years ago. He noted that it takes time to know *what you're being used for.* His comment really hit home, especially in the context of Brecht and Weiss's *Marat-Sade.* Weiss is *so* right. At one time, I bought Claudia's idea that complete detachment was possible. But now Weiss's warning is my touchstone. I usually know when I'm being used; there are even times when I allow it. But some critics operate this way most of the time. They get everything they can by trading power. I reject that. And I quite consciously part company with many segments of the critical fraternity on other grounds.

The younger ones tend to be record collectors. Most of what they hear and write is based on their perceptions of recorded sound. My aural experience is markedly different. Though a stereo set's important, once you've been enmeshed in *live* music, you can never react to music as a *product*, an object, something you can handle.

Then, there is a group among critics whom you might call "the taste makers," those who tell the public what's "right." I never cared to do that. I feel very strongly that we have to program constantly for *heterogeneity* in the arts. Really, we are in danger of being homogenized. Many supporters of hyper-intellectual music criticism reinforce and solidify the esthetic attitudes of the population they are serving. If I had to, I'd dispute the best of them on this, from Harold to Michael Steinberg to Martin Bernheimer in L.A. and Irving Lowens in D.C., all friends and good critics. Usually, though, I don't bother to argue, because I'm glad they're there too. I don't want to change them—I just think they're wrong. I learned early on that a good fight is a lot of fun and that conflict stimulates diversity.

My ideal critic? I have none. I don't think such a person should exist. A whole spectrum of viewpoints ought to be widely disseminated. The marketplace of ideas will take care of the weak ones.

There's something about the critic that causes many musicians and music lovers to get their hackles up. Why? For one thing, a critic has to come across as someone who knows more than his audience. There is just no way to get around this. We must be "informed"— one of those dreadful words—and many music lovers are not. Uninformed people don't like to be reminded of their ignorance. Tell them something they don't know, and they'll resent it—which won't stop them from appropriating the information to use at their next cocktail party.

In addition, *all* critics are assumed to be nay-sayers, because many are. People often ask me, "Don't you guys like *anything?*" As for intellectuals, not many respect journalism of any sort. It's hard to get them to take journalists seriously.

I will never give up journalism for pedagogy, but I'm realizing more and more how absorbing and complicated music education is. In this country, the profession of teaching music is not what it should be. Originally, the American music school sprang up mainly to instruct church organists and public school teachers. These places were often dominated by singing teachers, or descendants of singing teachers, from the old public schools or the old churches or the old singing societies. They had narrow ideas about what the study of music entailed.

Fortunately, after World War 1, the French conservatory influence crept into our schools, as gifted French teachers emigrated, and fine American composers, who had studied in Paris, returned with tales of the superior French institutions. The scope and methods of teaching performers improved immeasurably, but to this day most of our conservatories remain one-sided in their emphasis on performance. I've often written against this. Well-rounded musicians must do more than practice themselves silly; they need enough time for listening, reading history, studying theory, and composing. On the other hand, it's too often the case that musicology students get no opportunity to *make* music.

For all my grumbling, I greatly respect those who teach the craft of performance—I love artist-teachers. I am always learning something new from one craft-educator or another, whether a virtuoso piano teacher or a high school band director. Music lessons, in a group but especially private, can be most efficient and challenging ways to learn.

Teaching music outside music schools is another matter entirely. In this area we've made little headway; the way the system works, most people remain musically passive. One spinoff from populism suggested that we teach the "mass" audience about music. Fine. But that huge grouping is diversified. There are those who played instruments in high school and college ensembles, for fun, and went on to other careers. They don't need education in music so much as community bands or orchestras to play in, so they can continue to get active musical satisfaction.

And what of those who might like to play or sing but feel intimidated, fearing the musical language is outside their ken? The demystification of music is a top priority for music educators, but one which too few take seriously. One of my main goals as a teacher is to un-teach the attitude that American public schools engrain—that music is a magic world open only to youngsters who manifest "talent." What could be more arbitrarily defined, more elusive than "talent"? Not everyone can be a Caruso or a Heifetz, but anyone who wants to can make music and enjoy it.

I try to get this across in my classes. My main influences as an educator have been perception scientists like Jean Piaget and Jerome Bruner. I show kids how to teach music to themselves and their friends. My basic conviction is that we should encourage people to become composers, or at least to adopt the composers' outlook. I'm wary of an overused word like "creativity," but the best way to teach a kid to *listen* is to have him *compose*. It requires the integration of his sonic apparatus with concepts and people and environment.

When Northwestern gave me the big gut-level first-quarter music appreciation class, I decided not to teach kids what to listen for at concerts and what to discuss in the lobby. Instead, I began with awareness and perception. The students participate in projects. They divide themselves into groups, each of which is expected to come up with a performable composition. At first, they're lost. So for a few weeks you simply talk to them about, and have them bring in, interesting sounds. You try to recapitulate their early childhood experience of hearing for the first time. With each sound you discuss morphology and typology, emphasizing how you talk about sounds so as to differentiate, manipulate, and work with them.

Twice a week or so, we listen to a live performance, of a historically significant piece, to show how things were done "back then," or a more recent work that speaks to us about the instrumental bases that are integral to contemporary activity. The performers are music majors. One year my teaching assistants included a violinist, an oboist, and a pianist, all top notch. They did trios, playing a complete work and then rehearsing and dissecting it in front of the class.

One day the University Collegium came in and sang a Renaissance conductus, which gave us an entree into notation of the period, and led to the question of developing a notation so that one group could give its composition to another group.

The fundamental paradigm for the evolution of a group composition goes as follows: one student—or several—makes up a piece, learns to play it, figures out how to write it down, and hands the composition to a classmate who then has to play it. Afterward they engage in a dialogue about the new piece, which we usually record when performed.

You try to build value reactions into this feedback. For instance, the students have to think about what rehearsing really involves. Since most of them have record collections, they are used to hearing pieces complete and rehearsed, which means they frequently have trouble understanding how to use their own reflex processes to get a piece from the rough to the performable state. When a pianist brings in a piece and plays it, he is asked not only, "How long did it take you to learn this" but also, "Precisely *how* did you go about learning it?"

This helps students to find their innate musicality. While generating their own material, they find that they possess considerable musical resources. Their scores are based on "value loops" which *they* choose and which determine the "action" of their pieces. And *they* ultimately perform their creations, no matter how ill-equipped they started out. Going through all that two or three times a quarter causes them to grasp more about irreducible concepts of music than any other way I can think of.

To help them learn to react spontaneously—it's amazing how reticent they start out!—they keep a reactive journal of their musical experiences in and out of class. Also, they can talk their comments into a tape recorder. I encourage this; I like to get musical education as far away from print as I can. Musical language is not built on ABC's. With due respect for conventional teaching methods, I find unconventional ones work best, especially with nonprofessionals.

Naturally, my emphasis with pre-professionals is different. But I prefer having both types in the same class; they give each other perspective. I have the music students play for the nonmusicians, so they get some notion of what it's like to communicate with lay audiences. And amateurs and would-be pros alike should have some idea of what it's like outside the music school, so I invite managers, critics and successful performers to class to share their experiences.

I try diverse approaches because the rest of the music school doesn't. Sometime I want to teach a more conventional course on major trends in contemporary music. At present that's just not what's needed.

Someday I'd also like to write a textbook about mainstream music for those who are not music majors. Maybe it would suit the second quarter of my appreciation class. I'd write about the opera and the sonata and maybe a couple of other forms—but no more. I want to examine the principles of musical process in some detail and without being formalistic. I'd ground the works considered in an understanding of the composer's personal and cultural matrix. It wouldn't come out as merely "the sonata in terms of the classical tradition," but specifically, how Beethoven, say, used the sonata form.

I'm always looking for new approaches that emphasize process. A group of builders in Iowa have the right idea; they make educational packages in the do-it-yourself line that are better than most. With state money, they make up inexpensive boxes of materials to teach everything from plumbing to electricity. The photography package is excellent. I'd like to make one for guitar, and another for piano, with a miniature Steinway action—escapement and all—so that people can actually see all that happens when they push a key down.

I have a passion for musical instruments—how they work and how they sound. I hope my enthusiasm is infectious, and that my students come to realize how splendid instruments are when played properly.

Unfortunately, you often lack this appreciation when you're studying in a sheltered university environment. It's hard to avoid making your teachers into demigods, elevating intellectuality and denigrating performance. Under Claudia's influence I gained something I never had as a Yale student, namely, equal respect for great performers. Before my *Tribune* days, records, radio and an occasional recital were my only access to brilliant artists. At the paper I got to hear them alive. As a result, the Schnabels, Rubinsteins and Serkins became my heroes.

I came to appreciate not only their incomparable gifts, matchless discipline, and vast potential for providing pleasure, but also their tremendous value to our society. In short, I was and remain star-struck. Quite a few friends have tried to bring me down from the clouds, particularly composers, who maintain with some cause that the great performers don't give them a fair chance. But if music is to survive, we need outstanding performers to get us involved on the highest and most profound levels.

As I've said, my own reflexes remain those of a performer. For the last month I've said repeatedly to my wife, "I'm going to conduct more." If I had it to live over, teaching and writing would not take up as much of my time; I like to make music more than I like to make words.

Even so, being a full time listener has its gratifications. I've heard some knockout concerts. My singer is Lotte Lehmann, my conductor, Fritz Reiner, my opera, Reiner conducting *Don Giovanni*. I could go on and on. . . .

I strive to be as good a performer in my job as the best of these people are at theirs. I have no higher ideal than to be a virtuoso in my own context.

Two Reviews by Thomas Willis

A Blazing Evening of Song*

I heard consummate opera Thursday night in Orchestra Hall. Consummate in both senses, for it summed up my listening to date in one blazing evening of expressive song and at the same time completed my understanding of what vocal music can be and say. My ears, and I hope my heart, will never be the same for it.

Of course this is a personal, and therefore subjective statement. How else can one react to a performance that is as directly affecting as the grief of a loved one, as perfectly executed as the greatest works of our sculptors and painters, as human as a sigh, and as perfect as one's accumulated ideals can conceive it? As this is being written, my head is as filled with melody as my eyes were with tears during part of the performance.

* From the Chicago *Tribune*, October 14, 1972. Reprinted, courtesy of the Chicago *Tribune*.

Why does one weep at such an event? I have performed Rossini's *Stabat Mater*. I know those elemental accompaniments and the melodies which soar and float above them by heart. "Cujus animam" has strangled more than one tenor of my acquaintance with that high note midway in the first theme. Would-be dramatic sopranos in and out of church choirs have more or less negotiated the "Inflammatus" in my presence. The two a cappella choruses, one which shares its weeping with the bass soloist, the other speaking of paradise in gloriously simple chords, have been favorites for years.

And yet, there it was. A totally new work. Some scripture speaks of scales falling from the eyes, of deaf ears being unstopped. I now know something of what was meant. On the pages of this early 19th century masterwork, the notes arrange themselves in style patterns which later became clichés in the hands of progressive generations of mediocrity. Year after year, the sobs and slides and heart-on-sleeve effects parodied themselves a little more, until they have by now been fixed in our minds—and too many textbooks—as sentimental or corny or both.

But when everything comes together as it did Thursday night, the composer is once again recognized as the genius that he is and the music regains its power to affect us deeply, directly, and with an urgency that will not be denied. All of us in the hall are reborn a little. And what baby does not cry?

A night to forget facts? Not at all. The people involved should be proclaimed from the house tops, and two of their names are new. Of the four soloists, each with his or her special excellence, both Julia Hamari and Veriano Luchetti were facing an American symphony audience for the first time. She is a Hungarian-born mezzo who has been creating quite a stir in Europe and it is easy to see why. Nothing—except, perhaps, the pure Italian vowels and consonants of church Latin—seems impossible for her. Continually beautiful tone, breath to keep it steady or spin from an impassioned full voice to a whisper, and musicianship of an obviously high order combine.

Luchetti, who has sung opera in Baltimore and Cincinnati as well as his native Italy, has the true ring and soar of a major artist, the control to balance phases on the emotional blade, and a rarely heard sense of style and good taste.

Add to these the marvelous Heather Harper, equally able to keep a baroque trill from gargling and to cope with Rossini's passionate declamation, and Raffaele Arie, a bass of power, style and conviction. The Harper-Hamari team were as nearly a perfect match in the duet in Vivaldi's *Gloria*—an added plus earlier in the evening which also featured Ray Still's equally expressive oboe. And Mr. Arie made his dialogue with the "Stabat Mater's" inspired sopranos one of those almost unbelievable moments of totally unified communications in sound.

Of course, the success belonged to Carlo Maria Giulini, for it was he who put it together and made it happen. If I could, I would start all over and write about him, beginning with his quiet and stylish Vivaldi accompaniment for Willard Elliot's nocturnal bassoon.

But Giulini is a modest man who probably knows that there are other places besides church where the most honored in the procession comes last. For last night, he deserves our respect, admiration, and love, and I am sure he has it.

Musical Reflections Demystified, but Magic Lingers On*

It could have been planned but it wasn't. There I was in the Museum of Contemporary Art Monday morning discussing with the docent trainees the all-important human dimension in art education. And there I was Monday night watching it work out in practice.

In case you've forgotten your Latin and haven't done time in a German University recently, "docent" is another word for teacher. In museums, the term is used to describe the para-professionals or volunteers who guide groups thru exhibits and collections, explaining and discussing as they go along.

A good docent program is vital to museum education. Without it, a museum is an inanimate collection of art objects identified by an equally inanimate catalog and peopled by strangers. In the case of contemporary art, ideologies, concepts, and the objects themselves are often sealed by their creators in hyperintellectual hermetic compartments.

Docents can demystify the whole experience without destroying its magic-making capacity. If they have the right attitude.

What this attitude consists of was beautifully demonstrated by the evening concert of modern music by a New York group making its local debut. It goes by the name of "Speculum Musicae," which

* From the Chicago *Tribune*, November 7, 1973. Reprinted, courtesy of the Chicago *Tribune*.

means "Mirror of Music," but the performance was much more than that.

The young sextet—Paul Dunkel, Virgil Blackwell, Daniel Reed, Fred Sherry, Ursula Oppens, and Richard Fitz—negotiated a fiendishly difficult program with a relaxed, expressive manner which put the audience at ease from the beginning. Rare talents one and all, they had the intricate convolutions—and occasional clichés—of today's dense, complex musical vocabulary in their muscles as well as their minds.

Tho the audience clustered in front of the Matisses and Picassos was practically in the performers' laps there was never a trace of strain—only pleasure in their mutual undertaking and delight in the materials exposed.

The music was by four composers from the avant-garde of the 1960s: Charles Wuorinen, Harvey Sollberger, Mario Davidovsky, and Lukas Foss. The Foss piece was "Echoi," an elaborate four-part work which had its local premiere in 1964, when the Columbia University Group for New Music played in Mandel Hall. By illustrative coincidence, the other three composers shared that program as well.

"Echoi's" high point is a percussion cadenza which works it way from the battery into left field, starting with taps on the piano, proceeding across the neck of the cellos, and ending with a chuckle-raising tap on an oil drum lid lying on the floor. For all its obvious "echoes" it remains one of the more accessible "ear" pieces of its time.

Wuorinen's "Grand Union," having its world premiere, also depends on percussion, being scored for the unlikely—and not very successful—combination of cello and four drums. Freer in sound than some of his earlier work, it seems to exhaust its material long before it is over.

The two other pieces were more or less as expected. Sollberger's 1971 Divertimento for Flute, Cello, and Piano and the second of Davidovsky's apparently endless series of "Synchronisms" for tape and various instruments are powerfully organized, each to different ends. The Divertimento is just that, a deft, unpretentious occasional piece.

This was the first of the Contemporary Concerts, Inc., series. Next up, Feb. 18, is Stockhausen's "Stimmung," with the Collegium Vocale Cologne. Judging from the recording, it too, is a humanizing experience not to be missed.

32: Michael Steinberg

Photo by Photography, Inc.

I always suspected that somehow I'd be professionally connected with the world of music. By my early twenties, I knew I wasn't a composer, and that I lacked the diligence to be a pianist. I was fascinated with criticism; in fact, in some sense, I lusted to be a critic. But a full time writing job did not quickly come my way. I lived in Europe, met many composers, taught history to performers, and listened to a lot of music. All this helped shape my critical outlook.

I can't really say as much for my childhood. For most of it, I was a frustrated music-lover. Because my family moved around, I had few opportunities to hear concerts or study music seriously. I was born in Breslau, Germany, in 1928, left for England eleven years later, came to the U.S. in 1943, and have lived here ever since.

My father was a physician, my mother an art historian and art critic. We had art objects, a piano, and music at home. My mother played the piano fairly well. My father loved music very much but didn't play. As a child, I took piano lessons and practiced the stupid pieces selected by unimaginative teachers. I learned a good deal of the standard repertory by playing piano duets with my mother. I got to be pretty slick, a quick reader—adroit—but I never finished studying any pieces. I had that truncated sort of relationship with the instrument. In a way, I still do.

My interest in music was growing all the time. By the age of 12 or 13, music had become very important to me, but unfortunately, I was then in an English boarding school with little possibility of hearing any music. In Europe, I had no real musical guidance or outlet. My musical self didn't properly get going until I reached America, where there was much more access to music on the radio; also, for the first time, I could go to concerts.

They taught a minimal amount of music in my classy little St. Louis prep school. It was rather depressing and uninteresting—always at a low level. By high school I was interested in musical matters that went beyond anything taught in the beginning music appreciation courses.

My musical inclination and its fulfillment didn't come together until I got to Princeton. There I finally found other students who

Michael Steinberg, when interviewed in his home in Boston in October 1974 and September 1975, was music critic of the Boston Globe. *He has since resigned from the* Globe *and is now Director of Publications for the Boston Symphony.*

cared, professors who were willing and able to teach, and a huge library. At last I could start getting a real musical education, instead of just gobbling up bits and pieces over the world's dead body. Any college situation would to a certain extent have done the trick, but there were some specially good people in and around the Princeton music department.

Some of my courses were very useful, others were not. The teacher from whom I learned the most was Edward Cone. I hung around Cone constantly, throughout my undergraduate and graduate days. Though I only actually took one semester of harmony with him, I audited many of his courses, and got my first teaching experience as his assistant in a "Music 1" course.

Another person I learned a hell of a lot from was Charles Rosen, the pianist. I first knew him as an undergraduate on his way to becoming a professional musician. Rosen never took a single music course at Princeton. He knew from the age of 5 that he wanted to be a concert performer, and had studied theory as a little boy. By the time Rosen started college, he had had more harmony and counterpoint than you learn in undergraduate courses anyway. He was endowed with extraordinary intellectual as well as musical powers, and was interested in many things. So he majored in French and went all the way through to his PhD in French literature.

I gained so much from contact with Rosen—partly by talking, and partly by making music. We played four hands together. We read piles of orchestra stuff in improvised, four-hand arrangements, and went through all of the organ literature, three-handedly. For me, Rosen was a major source of musical enlightenment.

Though it opened my eyes in many ways, the Princeton department left a lot to be desired. As was so often the unfortunate case, the graduate program was sharply split into composers and musicologists. Among the faculty there was great jealousy about money and job allocations. My more mature reflections on this state of affairs are pretty much the same as my immature, on-the-spot thoughts in 1949 or 1950: It's a bunch of nonsense. I was a musicologist, but all my friends were composers. Rationally, both "camps" should support each other, but they didn't and don't. It struck me even then that composers were exclusively preoccupied with being composers; they didn't see the validity of anything else. Musicologists were beginning to change in my generation, but before that many people went into

the field out of history, not music. Often they did competent history
that was not very musical.

Nowdays, some first-rate scholars like Joshua Rifkin are also
composers and pianists and conductors—that is, practicing musicians. This was a dream 20 or 25 years ago. I think the musicologists
live rather blinkered, narrow lives. Even today, the first thing a musicology student takes is a proseminar in medieval notation; he spends
a whole year locked underground in front of a microfilm reader,
studying those dirty twelfth-century manuscripts, and everything
seems calculated to lock him off from the real musical world. Once,
I tried to suggest a remedy, when I was taking a Handel opera course.
None of us had ever heard the music we were studying at the time.
Much less was available on records. Wouldn't it be fun, I asked, to
perform a couple of scenes from a Handel opera? Instead of only talking about it in seminar rooms, why not actually come to grips with
problems of ornamentation, and continuo realization and all of that?
It was dismissed as a weird idea, although we did manage to set up an
evening, or even a couple of evenings, of readings.

Not only were two halves of the academic world cut off from
one another, but also both were cut off from the performing
world. And of course, that's still true. Over at Harvard, you will instantly raise hackles and itchiness of every kind if you ask, "What is
the place of a gifted performer in your music department?" Similarly,
the traditional hostility, or at best a certain standoffishness, between
critics and practicing musicians is a bad thing.

Though a music major, I was very unsure about what career I
wanted. In graduate school I assumed I would end up as a professor
teaching proseminars in medieval notation. Actually, I love teaching,
and most of the years I've been on the Boston *Globe,* perhaps seven
out of eleven, I've also taught in colleges and universities. I love history—historical thinking more than the *sitzfleish* details of historical
research. Among music critics, I'm probably considered very scholarly and musicological and academic in my inclinations. But I'm not
sorry that my career as a whole didn't go in that direction—it would
have been too stifling.

I gave my life as a graduate student artifical respiration by getting
a Fulbright Scholarship. I sort of stayed with musicology two extra
years in Rome, allegedly working on medieval music—an expansion

of extensive work for a seminar paper which my advisor thought could be parlayed into a doctoral thesis. I didn't choose to come to terms with what I secretly knew—that I wasn't really interested in pursuing the medieval scholar's route.

In Rome I looked at a lot, I learned Italian, and I got married to an American girl, also a Fulbright scholar—in art history. Musically, I experienced a consolidation of something that had started in my last Princeton years—a vital interest in contemporary music. Before I got there, Princeton had been a living center of new music, principally because Roger Sessions taught there. He left for Berkeley just before I arrived. For a few years, interest in the avant-garde died down. But in 1949, Elliott Forbes, now chairman of the Harvard music department, who was then teaching theory and conducting the glee club at Princeton, got polio, which put him out of action for nearly a year. Milton Babbitt took his place temporarily. Once he got his foot in the door, though, Milton never left Princeton. He brought in a great swirl of ideas about new music; he dropped names and ideas and concepts and sounds that none of us had ever heard before. He really turned our lives upside down. I was tremendously impressed and influenced and excited by all of the new music he introduced me to, the new ideas he caused me to consider.

In Italy, I had time to reflect on all that. Besides, I met all kinds of composers—Italians (like Dallapiccola in Florence and Petrassi in Rome), young Americans who were in Italy on Fulbrights, and some older Americans who were at the Academy in Rome. I met Elliott Carter there for the first time, and Alex Haif. What I got out of Italy professionally was a solid education in twentieth-century music and where it was going.

I also did my first newspaper writing in Italy. One evening before I left the U.S., I wrote a letter to Howard Taubman, who was then music editor of the New York *Times*. It said, in effect, "Look, you don't know me, but I'm on way to Italy for a year or two. I've done some writing for my college paper. Would you be interested in an occasional report about musical matters?" He agreed! An event soon presented itself—the revival of a rather rare opera (Bloch's *Macbeth*) in Rome. When I wrote asking, "How about this?" he replied with instructions on how long to make the piece, and where it should be sent. The next thing I knew, there was a check in the mail followed by a letter saying, "That was really nice; please send stuff along, any time." So duing the two years I lived in Italy, I did a piece a month for the *Times* Sunday music page.

When I returned, I taught in New York at the Manhattan School of Music for a while, but then got drafted during one of Mr. [John Foster] Dulles' scares, back in 1955, in the aftermath of Korea. Remember the alarm about those islands, Kemoy amd Matsu? I got swallowed up in one of the large draft quotas.

I had a bit of musical life in basic training. As the chaplain's assistant I played organ for both Protestant and Catholic Sunday services. I taught Methodist hymns to one group and Gregorian chants to the other. And I ran a choir. A little later I became an administrative type in the 7th Army Orchestra. The conductor when I got there was Kenny Schermerhorn, who now leads the Milwaukee Symphony. Afterward it was Henry Lewis, now with the New Jersey Symphony.

After wangling the job, I decided I really wanted to arrange for my wife Jane to come over; if I travelled all the time with the orchestra, that would be pointless. So instead I got an office job in Stuttgart in the 7th Army headquarters.

Returning to Germany in a U.S. Army uniform made the experience seem unreal; it was rather theatrical and strangely comic. Previously, I'd been most reluctant even to go through Germany. An Italian composer friend of mine, Luigi Nono, had encouraged me to go to the new music seminars at Darmstadt a few years earlier, but at that time I really couldn't cope with the idea of returning to Germany. Jane and I went back to America the first time through France, making a loop around Germany. But coming back in U.S. Army garb was so different that I found it entertaining and in some ways quite interesting. In Stuttgart there was plenty of music—a good opera company, good concerts, good theater. We lived in an apartment off-post, and from that point of view it wasn't so bad. None of this, however, had any great bearing on my musical persona.

After the army stint, I managed to recover my position at the Manhattan School. The place was seeking accreditation and they needed to beef up their history offerings. It was a propitious moment: Suddenly there was much for a historian to do; and I set up the whole program. It included a two-year undergraduate course, to which we eventually added graduate courses and mezzanine courses that were taken by senior undergraduates and graduate students.

Essentially, that was my work for six and a half years. But since it paid badly, I did writing on the side too. Before the Army, I'd been in touch with Irving Kolodin at the *Saturday Review,* who had not given me much writing to do, but had started me out as a proof reader. He needed somebody to catch his mistakes, the references to Beethoven's Requiem Mass and so forth. He'd given me one book review to do before I got drafted—Geiringer's study of the Bach family. I made contact with Kolodin again and this time he gave me occasional records reviews to do. I also wrote reviews for *High Fidelity*.

I did take one more stab at working up a doctoral dissertation. This time my topic was nineteenth-century opera. I didn't really get that one off the ground either.

Meanwhile I enjoyed teaching in New York. There was a certain missionary element about it. The students you get in a conservatory, the "future oboists of the world," are exceedingly skeptical about the value of learning anything but how to play their instruments. They resent history, theory, language requirements, whatever. In that situation it was fun to teach history, to see if I could present it in a lively fashion and yet stay musical enough to persuade them that maybe they weren't wasting their time. The challenge was intense, and I learned a lot myself. Having been brought up in the sheltered halls of Princeton, where one never *saw* an oboist, it was most interesting to live among all those blue-collar workers. I had a fair amount of success with the oboists, I must say.

It's pleasing to find former students in every major orchestra all over the country: I constantly run into them when I travel, and they say, "You know, the first time I ever heard this piece was in your class. Do you remember room 3C in Manhattan?"

In some little bit of a way, my teaching made them better musicians. Something about orchestra players had always worried me, though I didn't articulate what that was until recently. While teaching at the New England Conservatory concurrent with being at the *Globe,* I began to see clearly that the danger for orchestra musicians is that they will go crazy, and drive themselves to despair. Theirs is a very frustrating job. They are always under the spell of someone with a magic wand, who earns much more money, enjoys more applause,

gets more credit. In addition, there's something numbing about playing the same pieces over and over. For the wind players the situation's not so bad, but it's very hazardous for the string players. Flutists
start out hoping for good orchestra positions, but violinists dream
they will become another Heifetz or Oistrakh; it's a real blow when
they realize that rather than being celebrated soloists, they're likely to
end up playing fouth stand with the St. Louis Symphony. These people need support. The more talented they are, the more painful it
can be for them. You think of Dennis Brain, the great French horn
virtuoso, who at age 37, having felt he had done all he could as a
horn player, rammed his car into a tree. Other people turn to alco-
hol.

These are extreme cases, but I've seen enough of orchestra
players to know how bitter and unhappy they can become. Some *do*
stay grateful that even the dullest orchestral chores keep them in a
musical context, as opposed to a monotonous, non-artistic job. Many
survive because of an impassioned commitment to something completely different from performing, like religion or teaching.

This is a daily lesson I learned in New York from Gunther
Schuller, who was still playing principal horn at the Metropolitan
Opera and who of course had another whole life as a composer and a
jazz historian. He had learned a great deal from his father, who was
then assistant principal second violin in the New York Philharmonic.
The elder Schuller was enough of a musician so that the 198th time
through the Brahms First Symphony, he still found it an interesting
musical statement. When he retired in his middle sixties, he was just
as alive, just as uncrushed by the routine, as anybody could be. I
hoped to help music students, the future orchestra players, to be like
that—to get them to see what they did as part of a broader musical
experience, so that when they were in their sixties, they would be like
Arthur Schuller.

As a teacher, I didn't insist that my point of view was relevant to
my students' real interest. Apparently it was entertaining; attendance
averaged 99 percent. I wanted to let them discover my purpose on
their own. I wouldn't have dreamed of announcing to them, "This is
more relevant to you than you think." I did what had to be done,
quietly, simply. I only gave *listening* assignments. I'd play music and
ask them to comment on it. All they got was direct contact with
music. It was much less important that they know Bach's and Han-

del's dates than that they could tell who had composed a piece I played them, and had some sense of the different musical personalities.

I decided to leave the Manhattan School in 1963, only because it paid badly. Within a week of my resolving that the next academic year would be my last came an offer from the *Globe* and another from Queens College. The *Globe* looked more attractive.

No one was ever more surprised than myself at becoming a full-time critic. Some time before going to Boston, I had, with mixed feelings, given up any thought of ever doing criticism most of the time. For a moment in 1958 or 1959 it looked as though I would work for the *Herald-Tribune*. This fell through—a case of someone leaving who was not replaced. When that happened, it appeared that I simply wasn't destined to be a music critic. Then suddenly I got my chance. Tom Winship, then the managing editor of the *Globe*, had a system for the selection of a professional reviewer. His wife, a granddaughter of Elizabeth Sprague Coolidge, had various musical connections. He talked to her friends and produced a list of names, which apparently included me.

I didn't think my lifestyle would change much; it would be like doing a different routine in another town. Instead of spending X hours preparing and teaching a class, I would go to a concert, and afterward to the paper, to write about it. No one ever gave me an actual job description, and I had met scarcely any music critics. I knew I could write—quickly, if need be—and that I knew music.

Writing reviews for a daily paper would be a continuation of my work at the Manhattan School, I assumed, except that I would be at a typewriter instead of a classroom. My thinking hadn't changed; I still wanted to express the same ideas. I was the same person, hearing music the same way; I found the same things encouraging, and the same things distressing. I sensed a real continuity—a change of venue, but no change in my perceptions.

But I learned that there is a big difference between lecturing and reviewing. In a classroom, you can teach very effectively, without using a single technical term, because you can instantly illustrate everything. You can play the piano, dance, sing, shout, draw pictures. In a newspaper article, where you still want to avoid being technical, you can't dance and sing and play the piano. You have to invent metaphors for everything, with no space to do it at all adequately.

The result is a crazy tour de force, or, you might say, a crazy obstacle course, through which you maneuver as you write. You can't do what's most essential to the educational process—demonstrate.

I also had no notion that overnight I would be catapulted from a private citizen to a "public figure." Or that by expressing what I thought were commonplace views—they certainly wouldn't have dismayed my New York students and friends—that I would turn Boston on its head.

My first review provided an occasion for being particularly scandalous. I thought quite honestly that I was saying very ordinary things in a very ordinary way. That review provoked a barrage of 200 or so letters saying, "What is this?" "Who is this?"

It was on the first performance of Bernstein's *Kaddish*. [The review is reprinted at the end of this chapter.] Overnight, I was a source of scandal. That came as a real shock. The degree to which people get fired up, even now, by what I say continues to amaze me. Then there are peripheral ironies. When I began to think about leaving the Manhattan School it seemed difficult for me to get a good teaching job because I'd never finished that damn PhD. No sooner had I left Academia to be a newspaperman, then instantly the calls began coming in: Would I teach a course at Smith, at Brandeis, at the University of Massachusetts, at Harvard Summer School? They couldn't get enough of me. I was transformed from somebody who had lived a quiet private life into a public figure people pointed to at concerts. I was asked to lecture. And some people even wrote me obscene letters.

That, too, caught me unaware. By and by I learned that you never open letters with no return addresses on them, and that you read them all from the bottom up to see if they're signed.

The contents are fairly predictable; basically, "You're deaf and a fool. . . you don't know anything about music." Very unimaginative. Occasionally they get a little more piquant; sometimes they suggest venality or corruption.

At the end of my first year, I started another sort of storm, over the Haydn-Handel Society's annual Christmastime performance of the *Messiah*. I wrote about the problems of performance practice of eighteenth-century music. That produced a small barrage of anti-Semitic stuff, which occurred in a big way only once again—when Tom Winship asked me to write about the music at Robert Kennedy's funeral. I wandered onto the subject of John Kennedy's funeral and the music there—which got a lot of Catholics riled up and produced some nasty letters. I looked at that correspondence because the subject interested me so much. If they send me nasty letters because of what I write about the Metropolitan Opera, I don't care. But the issue of religious music, and specifically the music for JFK's funeral, was something else.

Very soon I began to wonder who my readership was. Think of the possible range. At one end there are specialists like Arthur Berger, and some fine professional musicians—among the most sophisticated in America. At the other end are those who have very little contact with the musical world but who read me because I'm a reasonably entertaining writer. In between, you find anybody tied to professional music in Boston, as performer *or* as listener.

I don't know to this day who really reads my stuff. I don't know what they want or what they like. I can never figure out what will raise their hackles. Three weeks go by without a single letter; then one piece which seems harmless to me will produce eight.

Anybody who makes public noises has the experience of being carelessly read and misunderstood. So many people read inefficiently. More than half of the complaining or angry letters I get are about things I never said. I'm not even talking about nuances; sometimes it's a total reversal.

Anything I write about singers is apt to elicit mail. Singers attract an impassioned following unlike that of other performing musicians. They have enraptured fans with a love for circumstantial detail concerning the lives and careers of their idols that you don't find among, say, admirers of pianists. Maybe that's because singing is the most direct musical manifestation. We can all sing—most of us badly—but for that reason we can all identify with the singer more easily than with the instrumentalist.

There's no machine between the singer and the listener. In a slightly abstract manner, it is probably the most sexual relationship that the listener can ever develop with a performer—it has the most sense of body heat, of physicality. The other *creature* is making sounds, as opposed to the creature who is skillful at causing wires or tubes to make sounds.

I don't mind being controversial; it's healthy for people to disagree. And for me, there is some sort of tickle to being noticed, especially after expecting to stay a private person for a whole lifetime. In a way, it's fun being someone else. But that's only a small percentage of the experience. And the trouble is, if you begin to see vanity as a factor, there is a greater vanity, according to which you not only want to be recognized, you want to be loved. Furthermore, you want to be recognized and loved for the right reasons.

I quickly realized that much of my small-scale celebrity derived from a misunderstanding of what I do and what I write. Not all of it, obviously, but just enough to make me uncomfortable about being a "controversialist." The responsibility turned out to be greater than I had anticipated.

But that's something you can't worry about too much, or it will drive you crazy. I have done my best to fulfill my intense commitment to music itself, a commitment that comes right from the center of me.

I think I manage to convey my sincerity to readers of all sorts. Persuading some of them of anything is another story; there are those with firmly entrenched opinions, though there are instances where I have influenced even them. At the other end of the spectrum you find readers who are far more malleable in an immediate sense. These are people who buy concert tickets or records on my recommendation, for whom an interesting critic functions as a consumer guide. Which is OK.

Among professionals and others who live with music, my role is not so much to tell them, "This is a really good recording of *Figaro* that you'll want to buy." Rather, we have ongoing discourse over the years that touches me just as it touches them. We teach each other. Dialogue matters. I'm at the opposite pole from my colleague Harold Schonberg at the New York *Times*, who believes that a critic should live in total isolation from the rest of the musical profession. I hang around with composers and performers and musicologists and would be starved and deprived and a much worse critic if I didn't.

No doubt there are limits to this, situations in which, either because of extreme closeness or extreme enmity, you ought to abstain from criticism. Friendship can be a problem, but it needn't imply wholesale endorsement of everything my friends do—or that I do. My friends are really more valuable to me if they say, "You know, that was a really lousy piece you wrote on Sunday." I might want to argue about it, and I might get angry, but that passes. If they were to say in a more general sense what a terrible critic Steinberg is, there probably would be no basis for the friendship anyway.

Critics like B. H. Haggin and Harold Schonberg live hermetic lives. They feel that it would be uncomfortable or unsafe to work in any other way. They don't want to face the consequences of having to write negatively about a close friend or a bitter enemy.

With my lifestyle, I've been able to straddle the various pitfalls. Since I came to music criticism so late in my career, I'd already accumulated many friends elsewhere in the musical profession. I wasn't about to give a farewell party and declare, "I'll never speak to you guys again." Of the friendships I've made since, almost every one started with a professional encounter, or an interview in which we discovered mutual sympathy. About none of my friends have I written only positively or favorably. There have been bad moments between us, but none, I hope, where I've been blinded, or rather deafened, by personal considerations.

In the critical "fraternity," I have one real friend in David Hamilton. I'm on good terms with a few others, like Tom Willis, but I don't see myself as part of a community. My standards and my modus operandi are very different from those espoused by my colleagues.

We have in common certain aspects of our professional lives. For example, we are constantly accused of not making "constructive criticism." I'm not at all sure what that means; I'd bet that 95 percent of the people who use the term only wish I would *like* more things. Recently, however, I have come to use the notion of "constructive criticism" as a point of departure in helping me to become a better critic. I now believe very firmly, and much more clearly than I did ten years ago, that to write positively is far more meaningful and much more difficult than to write negatively. Instead of writing that "so and so gave a junky recital," it's more valuable and a greater challenge to take a composer like Carter and explain why he's interesting, or tell why you find Alfred Brendel a wonderful pianist. Such positive criticism can be exceedingly useful. I now try to regulate my critical life according to this change of belief. At present, I'm much more apt to tell the story of why I think a piece is wonderful, or "X" is a good performer. I steer myself in that direction. Almost all my record reviews are favorable. I'd rather point out that somebody's done beautifully than that somebody else has made another dull recording of the Tchaikowsky fourth. This new tendency of mine has, as usual, been misread. Many of my detractors claim that I've turned soft over the years, or that I've been corrupted, or that I've tried but the paper has toned me down. Actually, this conceptual change was deliberate.

I *do* have frustrations within the newspaper bureaucracy. Space is one. It's constant. But beyond that, there are ideological problems. I have a feeling my employers really don't want me to write so much about music *per se*. Roger Greenspun recently did a marvelous piece on his getting fired as film critic at the New York *Times*. He felt that no one in charge was genuinely interested in a critic's confronting an art object itself; all that mattered to them was *news* about art—people buying or selling or, if possible, stealing things. My own extension of Greenspun's remarks is that editors want personality stories about artists, and concentration on performers rather than on composers. The moment I walk away from the center of music—if I do a nice personality piece like my interview with Bob Lurtsema of WGBH radio, or a story on a day in the musical life of an elementary school in Colrane, Massachusetts, or anything peripheral to music—I will certainly get a complimentary note from my editors, suggesting that I do more of the same. No one's threatened me, but the message is clear: I write about *music* only on suffrance.

This disagreement is a constant source of implicit or explicit friction. I find it somewhat ironical. I made a splash in Boston and brought some attention to the *Globe* not because I wrote amusing feature stories, but because of my musical thinking, and the writing that came out of it.

These workaday hassles are really minor. The rest, the triangle between music, writing, and myself, is very healthy and I love it. That's the important part. It keeps me going. I know much more about music than when I began ten years ago. If anything, I live even more intensely and fully with it. Also, I write better—still not well enough, but I'm learning.

For the first seven or eight years I followed the normal newspaperly procedure: I tapped out my article immediately after a performance. I often thought it would be nice to have more time, to sit and think about Monday's concert for Wednesday's paper. A couple of years ago, we put that practice into effect for technical reasons—it meant they didn't have to replate between the first and second editions. I used to come home after a concert, and get up in the morning, write, and hand my piece in at 10 or 11 A.M. I wrote without pressure, after a good night's sleep. At the beginning of this calendar year, we went back to the traditional method—and was I happy! What a wonderful feeling to be rid of the burden, to get home at 12:30 knowing it was done. As for the results, if I had to choose the twenty best or worst pieces I've written in ten years, I'd say some were written in a terrific hurry and others were written at my leisure. I've spent two days over Sunday pieces that were wonderful, and oceans more time over others that were wrong in every way. I've written reviews in three quarters of an hour that were scrambled and incoherent, and others that were neat and tight and full of life. To me, there is no correlation at all.

Is there an ideal critic? I suppose Berlioz and Shaw are somewhere in the backs of all our minds. Most professional musicians know Berlioz's *Evenings With the Orchestra*. Berlioz, Shaw, and Schumann were admirable, wonderful virtuoso writers of prose. Heine is often fascinating on music. Baudelaire offers a lot.

Among present-day critics, I find Andrew Porter of *The New Yorker* very stimulating. Likewise David Hamilton, who is an especially good model from the point of view of thoroughness.

All the people I've mentioned wrote or write for weeklies and monthlies. That requires a special skill, and these long essays on a regular basis are not my particular forte. It's the same as what I said about piano playing. If you give me unlimited time, I don't know if I could ever learn to play a Beethoven sonata as it's supposed to be played. Even if I had a whole week, I don't know that I would have the talent or the energy to produce a perfectly polished piece of chiseled classical Andrew Porter prose. If Andrew and I were in a competition to see who could write best for *The New Yorker*, he would win. And I would probably do it better for the *Globe*. They're different sorts of talent, each valuable in its own context.

I must say that most music criticism is uninformed, unperceptive, and sloppy. A lot of the writing is plain horrible. It's an ear sore. If critics are so tin-eared in the way they write English, how is anyone supposed to take seriously what they perceive through their ears about music? Also, a lot of critics are gratuitously nasty. [In the summer of 1974], when I was teaching a criticism class at the Ravinia Music Festival, we spent a morning with the pianist Alfred Brendel, who came around for a question period. Somebody asked him what he as a performing artist hoped for from criticism. Brendel thought about it, and the first thing he said was "good manners." Brendel's point was well taken. Unmannerliness is a problem. So is the glaring absence of professional qualifications. Too often reviewers simply don't know what they're talking about. They haven't done their homework, or they just have bad ears. This combination is painful and distasteful to most professional musicians. They find it contemptible, a word not stronger than the majority of performers and composers would use, at least off the record.

These usual objections to run-of-the-mill critics don't apply to people like Andrew or David or Tom; they are exceptions, though even they sometimes find themselves under attack. A famous performer recently objected to Porter on the basis of his intellectuality and his infusion of historical background into music criticism. She felt that Andrew talked down to her. That's a question of taste and style and critical approach.

Someone who had quite an effect on the way *I* look at things was B. H. Haggin. In my younger years, he was a great influence. I've moved away from almost every one of his ideas, but some of his approaches have stayed with me. I think Haggin, more than anybody else, represents criticism as a moral commitment. Also, he has a wonderful way of cutting through the crap and going to the heart of an issue.

Haggin wrote very generously about me when I first came to the *Globe*. He said my arrival was the most important event in American musical criticism since Virgil Thomson got started at the New York *Herald-Tribune* in 1940. He then went on to establish some differences between us. He classified Thomson as a super-stylish virtuoso writer, and me as a plain, clear, fluid, fluent, straight sort of writer. I am working on a book now, on Elliott Carter, and it will be clearly and decently written. But I will never be a virtuoso like Shaw, or one of the Sitwells or, speaking of today, Porter.

Virgil Thomson is the writer most frequently and correctly cited for his achievements in the daily newspaper world. Especially in his early years. Later, when he was becoming bored by them, Thomson fell asleep earlier and earlier at concerts, and his reviews had less and less substance. But the first five or six years of his criticism for the *Herald Tribune* were marvelous. He's opinionated, idiosyncratic, full of violent prejudices—and his was the best music writing ever done for a daily paper, probably the best in any language. I know nothing in a class with it. Thomson's someone I'd like to be as good as. If you go back over his first collection, from 1940 to 1946, you'll find one absolutely brilliant essay after another, all done on deadline.

True, even Thomson wearied of the standard repertoire. What keeps me going is that Boston has such a varied musical life. A few works do keep coming round and round. But there's plenty of opportunity for fresh stimulus and so much new music that, far from getting bored going to concerts, I have to keep myself from going to too many.

Fortunately, I think the fixation in the concert hall on eighteenth- and nineteenth-century German-Viennese music is beginning to break down a bit. To be interested in music on either side of that narrow segment no longer seems as eccentric as it did maybe 20 or 30 years ago.

Though there's plenty to keep me going in the journalistic sphere, I can see myself back in the academy on a steady basis some day. I still won't have a PhD, but I will have published a book or two. I think of writing a book as taking a longer breath. It's refreshing. I'm used to thinking of 1000 words, stop; to have the luxury of thinking 100,000 words, all on one topic, means using a different set of muscles, which is nice.

I started out as a teacher, and I can't ever quite let that go. Also, I would like to live in or around Boston for the rest of my professional life. I feel committed to this city's musical scene. I have a sense of citizenship here and value that very much. After my uprooted childhood and adolescence, it is pleasant to be anchored, to be told, "We want you here, you'll have a decent job, this is home."

Also on the plus side, I have enough latitude and freedom, and at least as much space as my colleagues on other newspapers. I can travel, and use stringers when necessary. Many of the conditions are excellent. I *would* like to have more material on music in the paper. The great space pinch, a sudden shortage of paper, makes expansion beyond reviews all the more difficult, but I can smuggle in pieces on Sundays and in slack seasons.

Lately, some bright new people have wandered into the critical profession. You can help them if they've already got the knack by giving lessons in music and English composition. But you cannot teach experience, and the ability to listen to concerts and bring your total personality to bear on what you hear.

Basically, critics are born. They need to have the critical temperament, which is a counterpart of the performer's temperament. To excel, the public performer and the critic need musicianship, dexterity, projection, and a certain kind of magic. If people have these qualities, you can help them. By far the best way I've seen was the old Rockefeller Foundation–University of Southern California set-up in the 1960s. People on two-year fellowships would spend the first year at USC, mainly attending lectures and classes. They spent the second year in an old-fashioned apprenticeship to an established newspaper critic, going to concerts and writing them up. When both people were right for each other—that has to be underscored—the method worked like nothing else.

Shorter workshops like those the Music Critics Association has been running are worthwhile as rescue wagons, or as first aid, or as a stimulus to sleepy critics. They can strengthen an isolated person, who is out of touch with the profession because he works in someplace like Moscow, Idaho. However, they fall down, just as the Rockefeller program did, on this score: They're no better than the people who teach them. The Rockefeller attempt had a bizarre irony built into it. It was conceived on the assumption that music criticism's catastrophic condition was due to the mediocrity of its practitioners on daily papers. Yet, the Foundation funded precisely those people to train a new generation of critics. It became a very expensive machine for the perpetuation of the status quo.

The workshop I ran at Tanglewood [in the summer of 1975] moved in a different direction from previous ones. There were next to no critics on the faculty. I had Edward Cone, my most influential teacher at Princeton, Robert Morgan, a composer, theorist, and non-journalist critic at Temple University, and David Hamilton for a brief visit. I had a non-musician, who is a superb writer and passionately interested in music: Ray Blount, the staff writer for *Sports Illustrated*. The trouble with many journalistically oriented critics is that they don't write as well as these last two, and they're not able to offer the kind of musical education Cone and Morgan can give.

As for my own new horizons, I would like to get into some literary and art criticism. Recently, I scratched where it itched a bit by writing a big article for *Atlantic* on Thomas Mann. I've also prepared a lecture on Thomas Mann and Music, which I have presented at Harvard, Smith, and 20 other campuses around the country.

With everything I do, I've found I'm a reactor, not a creator. I will react to anything, but from a blank slate I can go nowhere; I can't even start a conversation. When my kids were little, the stories I made up for them were variations on already existing stories.

In music, this makes me a closet fan. I'm really like all those people who adore opera singers—I'm in love with all the sopranos I know. Composers are my favorites. Rather than envy them I have great admiration for these people, and I love to be around them.

In my next life, I would like to be a tenor and sing the third act of *Tristan* beautifully. But I'm not jealous of those who can. I think of musicians as my allies and friends—people I can work with. Because really, we are all under one great musical umbrella.

Two Reviews by Michael Steinberg

There is something enviable about the utter lack of inhibition with which Leonard Bernstein carries on. His Symphony No. 3 (Kaddish) is a piece, in part, of such unashamed vulgarity, and it's so strongly derivative, that the hearing of it becomes as much as anything a strain on one's credulity. Can the narrator really have said "Do I have your attention, Majestic Father?" and did she declare to her God, "We are in this thing together, you and I?"

But yes, there it was, along with, at the end, the familiar figure of the composer himself, fetched from the wings by his wife (who had narrated), and bowing to the cheers and to the applause amid a veritable extravaganza of bear-hugs and kisses.

"Kaddish" was commissioned by the Boston Symphony and the Koussevitzky Foundation for the orchestra's 75th anniversary season, 1955–56. The composer responded with an ambitious work, laid out on a large scale. At its center stands the Hebrew Kaddish, the prayer of sanctification, traditionally used as a prayer for the dead, though its text speaks not of death but of the praise of God and the hope of peace. Bernstein has troped the liturgical words with an English text of his own, one in which the speaker fights her way, Job-like, from despair to faith.

The idea is splendidly imaginative, and it is tempting to think of what a poet like Auden might have made of it. But Bernstein as a writer of words has only fluency at his command, and that fluency produced a lava-flow of clichés wherein a few cozy intimacies (speaker to God, "We'll make it a sort of holiday") are contrasted against the tinny rhetoric of Norman Corwin's radio plays from the forties.

As a composer of music, Bernstein's bent is principally theatrical. He knows how to make an effect, and "Kaddish" is full of detail that really tells: the dense and anguished cadenza for chorus a cappella is an example, and so is the tremendous orchestral outburst, with trumpets shrilling on high C flat, that starts the finale. The last ten bars of Amen are quite wonderful, not only for the magic of their sonority, but for the precision and skill of their harmonic preparation as well.

At such a moment, Bernstein shows that he can compose, and I just wish he would. Mostly he seems to prefer the easier way of assembling a series of tricks. These tricks are mutually incompatible and they are generally irrelevant to the task at hand. The program note explains how atonal chromaticism is associated with despair and G flat major with faith, but no symbolism can justify the musical illogic of the transition. The idea of such a symbol is perhaps perfectly plausible, but Bernstein has just not managed to compose it out properly.

"Kaddish" was in the final stages of scoring last November when circumstances commanded its dedication "to the beloved memory of John F. Kennedy."

Charles Munch, during whose directorship "Kaddish" was commissioned, conducted this, its American premiere, and he led a spirited and exciting approximation. There were many ragged attacks and not quite comprehensible rhythms. I suspect that balances perhaps suffered because crowded conditions on stage necessitated the exile of a number of violinists. The principal chorus was that of the New England Conservatory, impeccably prepared by Lorna Cooke de Varon, and superb in every way. The Columbus Boychoir, Donald Bryant, director, had a substantial part as well: pitch and tone are amazing, rhythm less so, and there is no diction to speak of. The narration was by Felicia Monteleagre (Mrs. Bernstein), who for all of her intensity is not really an interesting performer, and who was made to sound metallically cold by the electronic amplification. Jennie Tourel sang the soprano solos, and she did so with utmost beauty and distinction.

The concert began with Handel's Concerto Grosso, Opus 6 no. 4, in a curious reading that demonstrated that it is possible to achieve a certain charm even with every imaginable feature of sonority, speed, articulation, and dynamics quite wrong. There followed Bizet's youthful Symphony in C, so attractive in its evocation of the 17-year-old boy's playing of Schubert duets. Mr. Munch slammed through it rather roughly, and I am afraid that both its performance and that of the Handel showed how much rehearsal the Bernstein symphony had required. I found it interesting that even Handel's and Bizet's relatively simple patterns of quarters and eighths came out pretty much all over the place, and I was the more braced, therefore, against the confusion caused by Bernstein's rather more complex metrical requirements.

Even in grief a musician cannot stop hearing with a musician's ears. At the [Robert] Kennedy funeral ceremonies in New York and Washington Saturday, music, chosen with imagination and tact, heightened the intensity of the experience.

It had been very different at the funeral of President John F. Kennedy in November 1963. Then the music—old-style Catholic liturgical music at its worst, and an embarrassing rendition of the Bach-Gounod "Ave Maria"—had been something to make one ashamed.

It was the one failure in a tragic ceremonial otherwise imagined and carried out with exemplary dignity, and it was one more reason particularly to appreciate, as a kind of musical redress, Erich Leinsdorf's performance of Mozart's Requiem at the commemorative Mass celebrated at Boston's Cathedral of the Holy Cross in January 1964.

Every note of music I heard on telecasts of the services for Senator Robert Kennedy was stirring, deeply moving, and absolutely right.

That it was possible was largely due to the liberalization following the second Vatican Council. It allowed the use of music whose associations are Protestant more than Catholic, the introduction of music with no liturgical associations at all, and it made possible the emphasis on the victory of life over death.

Kennedy the fighter was remembered in the Battle Hymn of the Republic, one of the great marching hymns. It was sung by Andy Williams at St. Patrick's Cathedral and picked up by crowds at various points later, most movingly at the Baltimore station just before the train passed through. It became the real theme music of the day.

One of the most beautiful moments was the brief halt of the funeral cortege at the Lincoln Memorial. There the Washington Choral Society sang Purcell's anthem, "Thou knowest, Lord, the secrets of our hearts," written for the funeral of Queen Mary II, wife of William III, on March 5, 1695, and used again at the 36-year old Purcell's own Westminster Abbey burial nine months later.

As the procession moved on, the chorus sang the hymn that ends Bach's St. John Passion, "Lord Jesu, thy dear angel send," a wonderfully strong tune that was about thirty years old when Bach used it, having given it one of the most miraculous of all his harmonizations.

But I think the most shattering moment of all, and the most unexpected for such an occasion, was the playing in St. Patrick's of the Adagietto from Mahler's Symphony No. 5 by members of the New York Philharmonic under Leonard Bernstein.

It was the one moment when music spoke of searing, nearly unbearable pain. It said things that needed to be said at some point during that day, but beyond that, Bernstein's choice of Mahler was a humanly sensitive gesture symbolizing Kennedy's rapport with youth. The Mahler boom of recent years has been particularly associated with young listeners, who hear in his utterances, with their paradoxes, their sincerity and boldness, their strange mixture of Angst and sweetness, something especially relevant and timely.

The Adagietto needs few instruments and it is short; that made it practical to play. It was perfectly judged as an expression of what was lost, before the Battle Hymn and Handel's "Hallelujah!" again reminded us that death shall have no dominion.

Index

Note: Page numbers containing full interviews with the subject are set in **boldface** type.

Academy of St. Martin-in-the-Fields Chamber Orchestra, 172-80 *passim*
Adler, Kurt, 334
Adler, Larry, 7, 9, **297-310**
Alea II, 73 (new music group)
Allen, Sanford, 18
Allied Arts Corporation (Chicago), 349-352
American Academy of Arts & Sciences, 57
American Federation of Musicians, 242, 253-60, 367, 374 (see also Musicians Unions)
American Music Center, 67
American Opera Society, 165
American Symphony Orchestra League, 421
Anderson, Marian, 308, 317, 357
Anti-Semitism, 201, 252-53, 397, 442
Antoniou, Theodore, 27-28, **71-78**, 233
  Events I, II, III, 74
  Protest I, II, 74
Armstrong, Louis, 299
Arnold, Malcolm, 305, 307
Arrau, Claudio, 8, 12, 16, 17, 21, **217-27**
Art and Music, 82, 102, 232, 357, 407, 431
Artymiw, Lydia, 8, **229-36**
Audiences:
  characteristics of, 210, 223, 249, 351, 356-57, 369, 391
  for contemporary music, 37, 59, 67-68, 76, 90, 223-24, 379, 401, 405
Auditions, orchestral, 246-47, 284-85

BBC (British Broadcasting Company) Orchestra, 182, 306
Babbitt, Milton, 8, 11, 20, 27-28, **39-59**, 63, 83, 85, 91, 132, 381, 437
  A Solo Requiem, 45
  Du (song cycle), 45
  Four Canons, 45
  Film score, 47
  Semi-Simple Variations, 132

  Three Compositions for Piano (1947), 47
  "Who Cares if You Listen?" 55
Bach, Johann Christian, 101, 102
Bach, Johann Sebastian, 76, 100-101, 120, 164, 165, 180, 198, 212, 220, 300-310, *passim*, 398, 400, 440
  authentic performance practice, 135-36, 173, 175, 199
  and Brahms and tonality, 132
  Mass in B Minor, 164, 165, 180, 199
  and teaching theory, 117, 141
  as transitional composer, 197
  Well-Tempered Clavier, 100, 135, 220
Baker, Julius, 243
Baltimore, 89, 298
Baltimore Symphony, 308, 364, 370
Bamburger, Carl, 130
Barber, Samuel, 329, 357
Barnard, Park, 413
Baroque Music revival, 145-47
Bartòk, Béla, 12, 16, 68, 75, 89, 119, 197, 329, 391, 397-399, 415
Bauer, Marion, 41, 42
Bayreuth, 97, 334
Bazelaire, Paul, 279, 280
Beardsley, Bethany, 51
Beecham, Sir Thomas, 365, 366
Beeson, Jack, 242
Beethoven, Ludwig von, 56, 58, 76, 77, 91, 101, 116, 150, 158, 191, 196, 208, 210, 211, 239, 286, 287, 345, 372, 378, 380, 383, 388, 400, 447
  artistic versus commercial aims, 197-98
  piano editions, 225
  tradition, 220-21
Benjamin, Arthur, 305-7
Berg, Alban, 16, 81, 86, 121, 379, 397, 400
  Wozzeck, 22, 292, 323, 337, 357, 384
Berger, Arthur, 54, 55, 422, 443
Berio, Luciano, 86, 89, 198

Berklee School of Music (Boston), 81
Berkowitz, Freida Pastor, 230
Berkshire Music Center, 38, 248-49, 382, 386;
  (*see also* Tanglewood)
Berlin, 12, 14, 17, 48, 72, 108, 113, 116-17,
  180, 199, 207, 212, 218-19, 221, 224,
  361
Berlin, Irving, 32, 189
Berlin Philharmonic, 207, 212
Berlin (East) Komische Oper, 334
Berlin Opera, 335
Berlioz, Hector, 73, 110, 112, 328, 329, 397,
  417, 447
Berman, Fred, 81
Bernard, Anthony, 172
Bernheimer, Martin, 122, 402, 424
Bernstein, Leonard, 36, 50, 91, 105, 118, 194,
  351-52, 368, 391, 442, 451
Bernstein, Martin, 62
Bigelow, Earl, 413
Bing, Sir Rudolf, 17, 20, 27, 283, 292, **354-61**
Black, Robert, 55
Blacklisting, 301
Blacks in music, 18-19, 169, 258-59, 283-88
  passim, 317, 329, 336-37, 357
  black Composers, 19, 286
Bloch, Ernest, 46, 63
Boalch, Donald, 148
Bok, Derek, 382
Boretz, Benjamin, 43
Boston:
  conservative musically, 191-93, 246
  dull musically, 81, 96
  as part of Eastern Establishment, 12
Boston *Globe*, 26, 434-41 *passim*, 446-47
Boston Symphony, xiii, 19, 36, 38, 54, 146, 182,
  191-93, 238, 246-50, 370, 451
Boulanger, Nadia, xii, 11, 33, 34, 63, 118,
  279-81
  and French system of music education, 141
Boulez, Pierre, 56, 76, 86, 88, 89, 91, 105,
  107, 122, 194, 261, 287, 369, 372, 387,
  390, 395, 397, 400
  Domaine Musicale, 91
  Marteau sans Maître, 402
  Pli Selon Pli, 408
Brahms, Johannes, 53, 57, 76, 77, 164, 176,
  191, 196, 223, 224, 233, 280, 379, 380,
  400, 406, 440
  authentic performance practice, 137, 281
  and Bach and tonality, 132
  as forerunner of Schönberg, 121

Brain, Dennis, 440
Brecht, Bertholdt, 65, 188, 413, 415, 424
Brendel, Alfred, 282, 352, 445, 447
Brico, Antonia, 163
British Arts Council, 361
Britten, Benjamin, 335, 356, 407
Broadcast Music, Inc., (BMI) 67
Brook, Barry S., xiii
Brook, Peter, 356
Brooklyn, 32, 34
Brooklyn College, 27, 67, 68
Brown, Earle, 7, 8, 11, 27, 28, 43, **79-91**
  Available Forms I, II, 88, 89, 91
  Folio, 85-88
  Perspectives, 86
  Music Before Revolution, 86
  Three Pieces for Piano, 83
  Twenty-five Pages, 83
  Time Spans, 88
Brown, James, 191, 192
Bruckner, Anton, 223, 380
Budapest String Quartet, 272
Buffalo, New York, 186, 193, 194
Buffalo Philharmonic, 17, 186
Buhlig, Richard, 14, 116
Busch, Fritz, 355

Cage, John, 81, 83, 84, 87, 91, 132, 173, 174,
  233
  *Four Minutes and Twenty-eight Seconds of
  Silence*, 132
  Interludes, 84
  Sonatas, 84
Calder, Alexander, 82
California, 14, 16, 208, 214, 243, 300-301,
  308, 332-38 passim
California Arts Commission, 408
California Institute of the Arts, Los Angeles,
  89, 116, 124-26
Callas, Maria, 360
Capone, Al, 299
Carmel Bach Music Festival, 244
Carter, Elliott, 122, 125-26, 224, 398, 437,
  445, 448
  Piano Concerto, 224
  Variations for Orchestra (1955), 22, 379
Caruso, Enrico, 347-48, 355
Casals, Pablo, 12, 16, 234, 264-75 passim,
  280, 304
  at Pradés Festival (1951), 12, 264
Cassidy, Claudia, 293, 302, 371, 415-20, 424,
  428

Cedar Bar, New York City, 84
Challis, John, 145
Chamber music, 212, 271-72
Chandler, Dorothy ("Buffy"), 336, 420
Chicago:
  Art Institute, 420
  Civic Orchestra, 168
  contemporary music scene, 25, 385
  Lyric Opera, 130, 351, 360, 390, 415, 420-21
  as Midwest cultural center, 238, 348-49, 420-21
  Museum of Contemporary Art, 431
  People's Symphony, 345-46
  second city syndrome, 16, 167, 370
  singers, 166
Chicago Symphony, 16, 19, 50, 118, 182, 238-39, 248, 259, 302, 308, 326-30, 346, 351, 364-71, 390, 391, 417, 420-21
  Chorus, 162-69 *passim*
  youth concerts, 326-30
Chicago, University of, 89, 385, 420
Chicago *Tribune*, 26, 301-2, 371, 415-17, 421, 428-30
Chickering Piano Company, 146
Chihara, Paul, 178
Chopin, Frederic, 24, 51, 233, 398
Cincinnati Symphony, 307
City College of New York, 66, 67
City University of New York, xiii, 27, 359-60
Cleveland Orchestra, 182, 253-61, *passim*, 370
Columbia Artists Management, Inc., 350, 360
Columbia Broadcasting System (CBS), 242-43, 267
  Chorus, 290
  Symphony, 243
Columbia Records, 147
Columbia University, 49, 89, 96, 241-42, 278, 383, 385
Commercialization of music and musical life, 195-200, 208-9, 245, 259-60, 266-67, 272-73, 282, 350-52, 381, 391-92
Competition/Prizes, 67, 211, 222, 392
Composers Forum, 42
Conductors (excluding interviews), role of, 181, 244-45, 257-58, 306, 318-19, 364-66, 404
Cone, Edward T., 63, 127, 435, 450
Contemporary Music (excluding interviews with composers)
  assessment, 90-91, 273, 383-84, 399-400

building audience for, 23-24, 77, 91, 178-79, 200, 224, 287, 323, 382, 387-90, 403, 422-23
electronic music, 48-50, 65, 398
performance problems, 49-54, 86, 406-7
resistance to, 20-22, 58, 76, 196-97, 233-34, 287, 323, 351, 357, 378-79, 405, 422, 449
Copland, Aaron, 7-13, 16, 27, **31-38**, 42, 43, 52-55, 85, 89, 105, 118, 381, 386, 395, 405, 419
  Appalachian Spring (1944), 36
  Billy the Kid (1938), 36
  Copland-Sessions concerts, 13, 35, 63
  Music for the Theatre, 43
  Piano Concerto (1927), 36
  Rodeo (1942), 36
  The Cat and the Mouse, 34
  "What To Listen for in Music" (course), 34
Cooley, Charles Horton, 8
Coolidge, Elizabeth Sprague, 441
Couperin, François, 148
Cowell, Henry, 88
Craft, Robert, 273, 395-97
Critics and Criticism, 26, 103-4, 122-23, 177-78, 225-26, 293, 317, 348, 372-73, 402-4, 417-20, 423-35, 441-51 *passim*
Crumb, George, 126, 138
Curtis Institute of Music, Philadelphia, 213-14, 230, 278, 382
Czerny, Karl, 16, 221, 226

Dahl, Ingolf, 189-90, 395, 399
Dalcroze School, New York City, 63
Dallapiccola, Luigi, 407, 437
Dallas Symphony, 253, 374
Damrosch, Walter, 7, 314, 389
Darmstadt, Germany, 75, 76, 88, 438 (*see also*, New Music)
Dart, Robert Thurston, 175
Davidov, Karl, 16, 206-7
Davidovsky, Mario, 432
Davies, Peter Maxwell, 125
Davison, Archibald, 100
Debussy, Claude, 33, 189, 223, 381, 397, 400
DeKooning, Willem, 23, 84
Del Tredici, David, 385
Denver, 62, 83, 84, 168
Depression, (1930s), 36, 42, 347, 352
Dett, R. Nathaniel, 314, 315
Diamond, David, 42, 54, 63
Dick, Marcel, 280

D'Indy, Vincent, 110
Dixon, Louise, 168
Dolmetsch, Arnold, 145, 146, 147
Donizetti, Gaetano, 292
Dowd, William, 145-46, 148
Downes, Edward, 27, **95-113**
Downes, Olin, 96
Draper, Paul, 301-4
Druckman, Jacob, 369
Dufaÿ, Guillaume, 101
Durkheim, Emile, 8
Dvořák, Antonin, 210, 233-34, 404
Dwyer, Doriot Anthony, 8, 14, 18, **237-50,**
    259

East Coast, 14, 15, 116, 123, 246
Eastman School of Music, 123, 239-42
Ebert, Carl, 242, 333-34, 355
Edinburgh Music Festival, 355
Edwards, John, 8, 326, **363-75,** 421
Elgin (Ill.) Symphony Orchestra, 162
Elgin (Ill.) Community College, 168
Ellington, Duke, 299, 310
Elman, Mischa, 347, 348
Enesco, Georges, 280, 281, 300
England, 12, 13, 136, 145, 172, 177-78, 223,
    355
Estrangement among composers, performers,
    theorists, historians
  Need for community among people in
    music, 23-25, 35, 127, 138-40, 194, 234,
    245-46, 274, 378-79, 386, 426-28
  Specialization within the music profession,
    24-25, 51-52, 126-27, 131-33, 136-37,
    274-75, 385-86, 435-36, 439
Europe and America, relationship between
  Cross-cultural influences, 11-16, 147, 168,
    179, 258, 425
  Europe in the twenties and thirties, 13,
    97-98, 117, 207, 218-19, 380-81
  European versus American: audiences, 86,
    223; critics, 124, 177-78; education, 97,
    117; music, 35, 388; musicians, 177, 182
  immigration to America, 12-15, 117, 147,
    179, 219, 380-81
  musical training in Europe, 33, 43, 72, 97,
    98, 117, 148, 156, 165, 182, 206-7, 218,
    258, 279-81, 334, 434-36
"Evenings on the Roof," *see* Monday Evening
    Concert Series
Ewen, Frederic, 65

Farrell, Eileen, 7, 8, 22, **289-96**
Fauré, Gabriel, 281
Faulkner, William, 44
Feldman, Morton, 43, 84, 91
Ficker, Rudolf von, 101, 102
Fiedler, Arthur, 351
Fine, Irving, 55, 56
Fine, Vivian, 63
"First Hearing" Radio Show, 105
Fitzgerald, Ella, 294
Flagstad, Kirsten, 355
Fleischmann, Ernest, 405
Flesch, Carl, 212
Fontainebleau, France, 34, 38
    School of Music, 33, 34
Fox, Felix, 62
Forbes, Elliott, 383, 437
Ford Foundation, 72, 374
Ford Symphony Hour, 306
Foss, Lukas, 381, 399, 432
France, 11, 12, 13, 34, 97, 118
Frankenstein, Alfred, 293
Frankfurt, Germany, 86
Free-lance musicians, 18, 269-70
Freud, Sigmund, 8
Friedberg, Karl, 130
Fromm, Paul, 21, 24, 25, 35, 287, **377-392,**
    404
Fromm Foundation, 72, 74, 287, 377-92
    passim
Fulbright Scholarship, 436, 437
Furtwängler, Wilhelm, 133, 210, 218, 221

Gallo, Fortunato, 348
George, Stefan, 98
German language, 65, 207, 253
Germany, 11-13, 17, 33, 43, 46, 78, 86, 88,
    97, 98, 125, 165, 180, 207-8, 218-223
    passim, 305, 310, 334-35, 348, 357, 380,
    434
  influence of, 76, 97, 98
  opera, 357
Gershwin, George, 32-34, 119, 189, 294, 300,
    304, 308, 357
  Concerto in F, 34
  Lullaby, 308
  Porgy and Bess, 294, 357
  Rhapsody in Blue, 304, 308
Gershwin, Ira, 308
Gideon, Henry, 62

Gideon, Miriam, 7, 9, 11, 16, 22, 27, **61-69**
   Cantata, 64
   Fantasy on Irish Folk Motifs, 66
   The Hound of Heaven, 65
   Nocturnes, 66
   Of Shadows Numberless, (piano suite), 66
   Psalms, 64
   Sacred Service I, II, 66
   Sinfonia Brevis, 66
   Songs of Youth and Madness, on poems of
     Friedrich Holderlin, 66
   Spiritual Madrigals, 64
Gieseking, Walter, 304, 305
Gigli, Beniamino, 347
Gilbert and Sullivan, 415
Gilman, Lawrence, 96
Giulini, Carlo Maria, 167, 221, 431
Glyndebourne Music Festival, 355, 361
Goldmark, Rubin, 32
Government support of the arts, 72, 78, 283,
   361, 374, 390, 408, 419
Graffman, Gary, 231-32, 418
Graham, Martha, 36, 96
Grainger, Percy, 413
Grayson, David, 234
Greece, 72-74, 77
Greenberg, Noah, 102, 103, 403
Griggs, John Cornelius, 10
Guggenheim Foundation, 34
Guthrie, Sir Tyrone, 356

Haggin, B. H., 445, 448
Haif, Alex, 437
Halèvy, Jacques F. 344
Hamilton, David, 445, 448, 450
Hampton Institute, 314-16
Handel, Georg Frideric, 175, 316-17, 436,
   441-42
Hanslick, Edouard, 404, 417
Harburg, "Yip," xii
Harlem School of the Arts, 6, 283, 314, 319-24
Harmonica, 297-310 passim
Harper, Heather, 430
Harpsichord-making, 26, 144-152
Harris, Roy, 14, 43, 54, 116
Harvard University, Cambridge, Mass., 27,
   99, 100-03, 117, 140, 145, 234, 382-85,
   436, 442, 451
Haydn, Franz Joseph, 107, 157, 177, 195-98
   passim, 212, 230, 328, 371, 398
Hayes, Ernest, 314, 318

Heifetz, Jascha, 17, 147, 212, 302, 208-9, 348,
   367, 440
Hellenic Group of Contemporary Music,
   Athens, 73
Helps, Robert, 51, 55
Henning, Roslyn Brogue, 81
Hentoff, Nat, 85
Hillis, Margaret, 8, 19, **161-69**, 369
Hilsberg, Ignace, 332
Hindemith, Paul, 53, 81, 89, 121, 162, 214,
   243, 308, 381, 397, 399, 406, 413
Hitler, Adolf, 12, 21, 57, 97, 147, 201, 208,
   252
Hoffman, E. T. A., 232
Hofmann, Josef, 162
Holiday, Billie, 310
Hollander, John, 45
Hollywood, 44, 123, 394
Horkheimer, Max, 86
Horowitz, Vladimir, 212
Howe, (Hubert) Tuck, 124, 125
Hubay, Jeno, 156
Hubbard, Frank, 12, 26, **143-52**
Human Rights Commission, 285
Humperdinck, Engelbert, 333
Hurok, Sol, 302, 349-52
Huxley, Aldous, 15, 189

Illinois State Arts Council, 168
I Musici (Virtuosi di Roma), 172
Indiana University, Bloomington, Indiana,
   162, 290-95 *passim*, 321
International Conference of Symphony and
   Opera Musicians, (ICSOM), 254, 255,
   374
International Society for Contemporary Music
   (ISCM), 55, 66, 125, 400
Italy, 12, 14, 40, 43, 88, 436-37
Ives, Charles, 9-11, 83, 91, 192, 198, 329
   Christopher Mockingbird, 407
   Concord Sonata, 80
   Over the Pavements, 192
   Three Places in New England, 91
   Variations on America, 329

Jackson, Mississippi, 11, 40, 47
Jacob, Gordon, 305
Janacek, Leos, 292
Jazz, 57, 80-82, 86, 126, 294
Jews and American Musical Life
   anti-Semitism, 46-47, 201, 208, 219

Jews and American Musical Life (*Cont.*)
  audiences, 179
  in Europe: Austria, 252; Germany, 201,
    218, 345; Poland, 344
  in New York, 12, 253
  musicians, 117, 168, 208, 218-19, 252-53,
    264, 299
  religious music, 7, 32, 62, 66, 188, 348
  as scholars and teachers, 147, 168
  Yiddish culture: influence, 188; music, 7,
    188-89; theater, 185-87
Jewish National Alliance, 345
Jewish Theological Seminary, 64, 67
Josephs, Wilfred, 368-69
Josquin des Prés, 139
Journal of Philosophy, 44
Joyce, James, 20, 34, 44, 415
Judson, Arthur, 367-68
Juilliard School of Music, 25, 27, 51, 52, 162,
    164, 253, 266, 278, 321, 332, 351, 383,
    387
Juilliard Quartet, 150, 273
Julius, Ruth, 20

Kabuki theater, 135
Kaminska, Ida, 344
Kaminska, Rachel, 344
Kennedy, John F., 443, 453-54
Kennedy, Robert, 443, 453
Kern, Jerome, 189, 300
Khatchaturian, Aram, 310
Kinkeldey, Otto, 100
Kirchner, Leon, 63, 117, 369, 381
Klemperer, Otto, 218, 318
Klengel, Julius, 207
Klomroth, Wilfrid, 315
Kodaly, Zoltán, 156
Kohn, Karl, 56
Kolodin, Irving, 439
Kostelanetz, André, 307
Koussevitzky, Serge, 27, 37, 38, 54, 118, 191,
    315, 364-65, 387
Koussevitzky Foundation, 50, 451
Krause, Martin, 220, 221
Kreisler, Fritz, 213, 252, 258, 300, 347
Krips, Sir Joseph, 257

Landowska, Wanda, 146, 147
Landrum-Griffin Act, *1959*, 254
League of American Composers, 13, 35, 63,
    66

Lee, Ella, 334
Lehmann, Lotte, 429
Leibowitz, René, 279, 280
Leinsdorf, Erich, 191, 245-46, 391, 453
Leipzig, Germany, 207
Leoncavallo, Ruggiero, 356
Leonhardt, Gustav, 150
Leschetizky, Theodor, 14
Les Six, 33
Levee, Sara, 130
Levine, James, 56, 356
Levine, Julius, 7, 11, 12, 16, **263-75**
Levy, Martin David, 357
Lewis, Henry, 438
Ligeti, György, 76, 89
Limonick, Natalie, 11, 15, 16, **332-39**
Lincoln Center, *see* New York
Liszt, Franz, 16, 191, 196, 220-21, 239, 345,
    397
Little Orchestra Society, 165
Loebel, Kurt, 12, 18, **251-61**
Loesser, Frank, 308
London, 17, 125, 148, 172, 175, 180, 189,
    199, 214, 282, 298-310 *passim*, 355, 357
  British Museum, 148
  Covent Garden, 306
  Grotian Hall, 300
  Royal College of Music, 175
  Royal Festival Hall, 180
London Chamber Orchestra, 172
London Philharmonic, 182
(London) Royal Philharmonic, 357
London Symphony Orchestra, 175, 182
Los Angeles
  Chamber Orchestra, 172, 176-77
  Coconut Grove, 366
  critics, 122, 402-4
  cultural climate, 116, 123-25, 179, 245-46,
    392, 401, 420
  Hollywood Bowl, 244-45, 308, 364, 368
  Museum of Contemporary Art, 431
  musicians, 123, 176-77, 400
  compared with New York, 116, 123-24, 401
  opera in, 333-39 *passim*
  Pomona College, 248
  Schönberg in, 14-16, 63, 116-21, 332, 397
  Stravinsky in, 14-16, 121, 189, 395-97
Los Angeles County Museum, 15, 392-94, 407
  school, 186
Los Angeles Philharmonic 14, 16, 19, 124,
    243-46, 308, 402-5

Los Angeles *Times*, 122, 402, 407
Lowens, Irving, 424
Luening, Otto, 48
Lunenburg, Massachusetts, 80
Lunt, Alfred, 356
Lurtsema, Bob, 446

McBride, Charles, 278
McCarthy, Sen. Joseph, 301
Macdonald, Dwight, 419
MacDonald, Jeannette, 347
MacDowell, Edward, 33
Machaut, Guillaume, 82, 101, 378
Maderna, Bruno, 88, 91
Mahler, Gustav, 127, 158, 223, 252, 364-65, 380, 397
Manhattan School of Music, 97, 100, 438
Mann, Robert, 271
Mann, Thomas, 98, 308, 450-51
    Dr. Faustus, 44
Mannes College of Music, 24, 130, 138-39, 141, 270
Marlboro Music Festival, Marlboro, Vermont, 226, 233, 235, 269
Marriner, Neville, 8, **171-83**, 400
Martino, Donald, 57
Martinon, Jean, 371
Mason, Elizabeth B., x
Massine, Leonide, 243
Matisse, Henri, 323
Maynor, Dorothy, 6, 7, 21, 283, **314-24**
Mazer, Henry, 7, **326-30**, 369
Mead, George Herbert, 8
Mehta, Zubin, 16, 215, 404
Melos, 124
Mendelssohn, Felix, 132, 196, 198, 250, 281
Mennin, Peter, 387
Menotti, Gian Carlo, 214, 329-30, 336, 415
    Amahl and the Night Visitors, 336
Menuhin, Yehudi, 300, 367
Meredith, George, 45
Messaien, Olivier, 50, 73
Metropolitan Museum of Art (New York), 102, 135, 403
    The Cloisters, 103, 403
Metropolitan Opera (New York), 11, 17, 27, 53, 96, 104, 105, 165, 283, 291-92, 317, 333, 348, 354-61 *passim*, 443
    Saturday matinee broadcasts, 7, 104-5, 165
Metzger, Heinz Klaus, 86, 87

Michelangelo, 407
Milhaud, Darius, 33, 214, 303, 305, 307, 381
Miller, Robert, 51
Milstein, Nathan, 86, 212, 309
Mimesis, 3
Minneapolis, Minnesota, 394
Minneapolis Symphony Orchestra, 108, 169, 172
Minnevitch, Borrah, 298
Mitropoulos, Dmitri, 22, 53, 292
Mobility,
    Horizontal (geographical), 16-18, 179-80, 189-200, 206-8, 214-16, 218, 222-23, 226-27, 238-39, 243, 279, 281, 295-96, 299, 316-17, 334, 354
    Vertical (social), 18-19, 183, 210-13, 245, 247, 253-54, 260-66, 284-85, 288, 303
Monday Evening Concert Series ("Evenings on the Roof"), 14, 15, 120, 189-90, 245, 392-95, 400-403, 407
Monteux, Pierre, 319, 326, 356
Monteverdi, Claudio, 190, 281, 378, 403, 415
Moore, Dorothy Rudd, 283, 287
    Dirge and Deliverance, 287
Moore, Douglas, 242
Moore, Henry, 82
Moore, Kermit, 18, **277-87**
Morgan, Robert, 450
Morowitz, Oscar, 323
Morton, Lawrence, 7, 15, 20, 24, 189-90, **393-408**
Moscow, 206
Moscow Conservatory of Music, 206, 207
Mozart, Wolfgang Amadeus, x, 53, 57, 76, 91, 106-10, 132, 163-64, 167-69, 177, 190, 191, 196-99, 208, 211, 212, 245, 268-69, 316, 317, 327, 356, 359, 365, 371, 397, 398, 407, 453
    artistic versus commercial aims, 197
    authentic performance practice, 152, 157, 173, 181
    Don Giovanni, 53, 108, 109, 429
    Letters, ix
    A Musical Joke, K 522, 108-110
Münch, Charles, 191, 221, 246-47, 452-53
Munich, 48, 72, 86, 91, 97-99, 101, 106
    Schwabing, 97
Musical Leader, 42
Music Critics Association, 450
Musicians Union—see Unions
Muzak, 18, 57, 78, 177

National Broadcasting Company (NBC), 98
Symphony, 7, 246, 256, 282, 298
National Conservatory of Music, Athens, 72, 73
National Endowment for the Arts, 125, 322, 387, 408, 419
National Institute of Arts and Letters, 57
National Symphony Orchestra, Washington, D.C., 240, 241, 364-65, 370
Nazism, 11, 46, 201, 208, 219, 305
Neel, Boyd, 172, 175
New England Conservatory of Music, 248, 439
New Haven, Connecticut, 10, 413
New Jersey, 34
New Jersey Symphony, 438
New music, 378, 379, 383, 388, 392, 401-7, 419, 422, 438
New School for Social Research, 27, 34, 35, 88
New York City, 11-23 passim, 32-35, 40, 47, 49, 55, 59, 62-64, 76, 96-99, 102-3, 110-13, 119, 123-25, 130, 164, 166, 179, 186, 199, 223, 241-43, 252, 264-66, 272, 278-82, 287-88, 290, 298-310 *passim*, 332, 408
as music center, 116, 119, 241, 352, 360, 401, 420, 422, 439
Carnegie Hall, 19, 62, 96, 223, 303-4, 314, 348, 360
Carnegie Recital Hall, 126, 249
City Center, 301
Contemporary Music Ensemble, 125
Lincoln Center, 357; Alice Tully Hall, 126, 323
Pro Musica Ensemble, 102, 103
The New Yorker, 303, 371, 447
New York *Herald-Tribune*, 96, 441, 448
New York Philharmonic, 7, 16, 18, 25, 50-53, 80, 91, 104-8, 147, 182, 241, 243, 247-48, 259, 266, 286, 307-8, 314, 367-70, 387, 420, 422, 438, 440, 453
New York State, 374
New York State Council on the Arts, 323
New York *Times*, 19, 54, 96, 103-4, 107, 352, 368, 412, 437, 444, 446, 448
New York University, 44, 62, 278;
Contemporary Newsletter, 124
Town Hall, 164-65, 223, 302, 316
Washington Square College, 41, 43
Nielson, Carl, 371, 373
Nixon, Marni, 123

Nono, Luigi, 89, 91, 402, 438
Northwestern University, 25, 80, 162, 412, 420-21
School of Music, 412, 415, 426
Numus West (music magazine), 124

Opera in America, 165, 242, 283, 291-92, 317, 333-39 *passim*, 360-61
Ormandy, Eugene, 22, **155-59**, 215, 306

Paderewski, Ignace, 162, 348
Palestrina, Giovanni Pierluigi de, 120
Pan-American Society, 63
Paracelsus, 111
Paris, France, 11, 17, 32-35, 41, 86, 111, 113, 148, 172, 180, 199, 223, 206, 208, 210, 214, 279, 281-82
Bibliothèque Nationale, 148
Conservatoire de Musique, 148, 151
Left Bank, 34
Theatre de Champs Élyseès, 180
Parker, Horatio, 10
Patchen, Kenneth, 81
Pavarotti, Luciano, 293
Peekskill, New York, 32
Penderecki, Krzystof, 124
The Performing Tree, 339
Perle, George, 47, 55
Perlis, Vivian, x, 10
Perotin, 82, 91, 101
Perspectives of New Music, 382
Peters, Gordon, 168
Peters Music Publishers, 225, 226
Petrillo, James, 256, 303, 346-47
Philadelphia, 41, 72, 73, 156, 213-14, 230-31
College of Art, 232
College of Performing Arts, 231-33
Musical Academy, 73, 113, 231
Philadelphia Orchestra, 113, 156, 182, 230-31, 255, 259, 307, 318, 370
Piaget, Jean, 8, 426
Pianism, 135, 220-21, 225, 231-32
Piatigorsky, Gregor, 9, 12, 16, 17, 156, 191, **205-16**, 239
Picasso, Pablo, 304, 378
Piscator, Erwin, 218, 219
Piston, Walter, 100-101, 140, 249
Pittsburgh Symphony, 326-30, 364, 366, 370
Plato, 3
Pleyel Mfg. Co. (pianos), 150
Political Activism, 301-03, 304, 307, 336, 414

Pollock, Jackson, 23, 82, 84
Ponchielli, Amilcare, 292
Popper, Dr. Jan, 333, 336-38
Porter, Andrew, 300, 447, 448
Poulenc, Francis, 33
Prades, France, 12, 264, 267, 280; *see also* Casals
Prague, Czechoslovakia, 210, 335
Price, Leontyne, 357
Princeton University, 25, 27, 42, 46-49, 52, 57, 58, 89, 315, 383, 424, 434-35, 439, 450
Prodigies, 219
Project for the Oral History of Music in America (POHMA), x, xii, xiii
Prokofiev, Serge, 214
Puccini, Giacomo, 335, 356
Puerto Rico, 269

Queens College, New York, 24, 96, 104, 130, 139, 141, 270, 441

RCA (Radio Corporation of America), 48, 49, 98, 357
Rachmaninoff, Sergei, 213, 233, 239, 300, 309
Radio, 7, 8, 80, 104-5, 238, 256, 314, 412
Radio City, New York, 98
Rahn, John, 43
Ran, Shulamit, 73, 89
Rauschenberg, Robert, 84
Ravel, Maurice, 33, 214, 300, 308, 397
Raven, Seymour, 415-17
Ravinia Music Festival, 447
Records, 51, 86-87, 175-76, 179, 195, 200, 224-25, 256-57, 292-93, 318-19, 378, 424
Reiner, Fritz, 53, 165-66, 257, 326, 429
Religious Music
  Christian, 7, 180, 290, 314, 394, 412, 453-54
  Jewish, 7, 32, 62, 66, 188, 348
Reynolds, Roger, 125
Rifkin, Joshua, 436
Rochberg, George, 233
Rochester, New York, 239
Rockefeller Foundation, 49, 387, 408, 450
Rock Music, 126, 419
Rodgers, Richard and Lorenzo Hart, 189
Rodzinski, Arthur, 244, 318
Roisman, Joseph, 272

Rooks, Shelby, 319
Roosevelt, Willard, 323
Rosen, Charles, 127, 435
Rosenberg, Harold, 82
Rosenfeld, Paul, 404
Rossini, Gioacchino, 430
Rothko, Mark, 84
Royal Philharmonic, *see* London
Rubinstein, Arthur, 212, 231, 308, 428
Rudin, Andrew, 233
Ruggles, Carl, 198, 200
Russia, 206, 213, 310

St. James Presbyterian Church, Harlem, 319
St. Louis, 372
St. Louis *Globe Democrat*, 364
St. Louis Symphony, 17, 214, 239, 364, 366, 370
Saint-Saens, Camille, 244, 281
Salmond, Felix, 278
Salt Lake City, Utah, 75
Salzer, Felix, 28, 130
Saminsky, Lazare, 11, 62-63
San Francisco, 293, 336
San Francisco Opera, 334, 360
San Francisco Symphony, 259
Sargeant, Winthrop, 371
Sarnoff, Gen. Robert, 48
Saturday Review, 439
Scott, Cyril, 300
Schachter, Carl, 24-28, **129-141**
Schaffer, Lois, 248
Schenker, Heinrich, 28, 130-31, 133, 138, 140
Schermerhorn, Kenneth, 438
Schillinger System, 81, 83
Schnabel, Artur, 14, 116, 117, 134, 212, 223, 226, 352, 428
Schneider, Alexander, 269
Schönberg, Arnold, 41-42, 44, 64, 75, 81, 86, 123, 127, 189, 197, 212, 224, 243, 279, 280, 308, 323, 380, 381, 392, 398, 399, 400, 405, 406
  evaluation by Leonard Stein, 116-23
  as innovator, 74, 378, 379
  isolated from American mainstream, 118, 119
  Moses and Aaron, 167
  musical complexity of his works, 20, 118, 121, 122, 167, 397
  performance problems, 52-53, 120

Schönberg, Arnold (*Continued*)
 Pierrot Lunaire, 81, 212, 224, 246, 381
 still not in standard repertory, 56-58
 as teacher at UCLA, 14-16, 119, 120,
  332-33
 writings: *Preliminary Exercises in Counter-
  point*, 117; "Self-Analysis," 118, "My
  Evolution," 121
Schonberg, Harold C., 412, 423-24, 442-43
Schrade, Leo, 413
Schubert, Franz, 158, 223, 233, 273, 397
Schuller, Arthur, 440
Schuller, Gunther, 50, 51, 56, 72, 125, 335,
  381, 383, 386, 419, 422, 440
 The Visitation, 335
Schumann, Robert, 24, 158, 223, 232, 233,
  417, 447
 Kreisleriana, 232
Schuman, William, 54, 106, 196, 398
Seeger, Ruth Crawford, 116
Serkin, Rudolf, 226, 234, 349, 352, 403, 419,
  428
Sessions, Roger, x, 13, 22, 27, 35, 42-43, 46,
  50, 54-55, 59, 63, 369, 381, 437
 The Black Maskers, 42, 63
 Violin Concerto, 54
Shakespeare, William, 45, 134-35, 140, 145,
  220
 The Tempest, 220
Shapey, Ralph, 381
Shaw, George Bernard, 417, 447-48
Shaw, Robert, 162, 164
Sherman, Thomas, 317
Shifrin, Seymour, 55
Shostakovitch, Dmitri, 76
Sibelius, Jan, 41, 223, 366, 371
Sipser, Philip, 254
Skrowaczewski, Stanislaw, 169
Smit, Leo, 36
Smith, Adam, xiii
Smith College, 442, 451
Sollberger, Harry, 432
 Divertimento (1971), 432
Solti, Sir Georg, 221, 326, 368, 369, 371-72
Sousa, John Philip, 315
South America, 38, 222-23, 316-17
Speculum Musicae, 273, 431
Standard Oil Symphony Hour, 245
Stanford University, 72, 73
Starr, Louis M., viii
Stein, Gertrude, 34, 90

Stein, Leonard, 14, 16, **115-27**, 332, 399
Steinberg, Michael, xi, 8, 22, 24, 26, 326,
  366, 424, **433-54**
Steinberg, William, 245
Stern, Isaac, 176
Stevens, Roger L., 419
Stock, Frederick, 118, 166, 406
Stockhausen, Karl Heinz, 89, 125, 127, 224,
  397, 400
 Stimmung, 432
Stokowski, Leopold, 96, 113, 156, 257, 285,
  366
Strauss, Richard, 121, 158, 214, 305, 335, 386
 Don Juan, 158
Stravinsky, Igor, 16, 20, 41, 42, 77, 87, 107,
  110, 112, 113, 121, 165, 189, 197, 214,
  224, 273, 308, 309, 323, 333, 379, 381,
  386, 391, 392, 397, 398, 399, 400, 404-6
 and Nadia Boulanger, 11, 33
 in California, 14, 15, 395-97
 Chanson Russe, 309
 The Firebird, 113
 In Memoriam, Dylan Thomas (1954), 356
 Laurence Morton's description, 395-97
 Les Noces, 169
 performance problems, 53
 Petrushka, 113
 Piano Concerto, 41
 The Rake's Progress, 53
 The Rite of Spring, 96, 110, 113, 121, 381,
  384
 writings: *Poetics of Music*, 87
Strelitzer, Hugo, 333-34
Suzuki Method, 6, 169, 321
Symphony of the New World, 284-86
Szell, George, 182, 253, 255, 257-61

Tanglewood Festival of Contemporary Music,
  382, 386
Tanglewood Music Festival, Lenox, Mass.,
  25, 27, 32, 38, 55, 72, 73, 80, 246, 248,
  249, 281, 316, 450
Taubman, Howard, 103, 437
Taylor, Deems, 400
Tchaikowsky, Peter Ilyitch, 16, 91, 106, 157,
  206, 233, 245, 281, 287, 351, 356, 397,
  399
Tcherepnin, Alexander, 305
Telemann, Georg Philip, 398
Television, 22, 23, 282, 290-91, 379
Text setting, 45, 46, 64, 65

Theory
  Boulanger (French system), 33, 140-41, 279-80
  Importance, 26, 63, 100-101, 130-41 *passim*, 232
  Schenker, 28, 130-31, 133, 138, 140
  Schillinger, 81, 83
  Schönberg, 15, 63, 117, 120, 132, 332
Thomas, Michael Tilson, xiii, 7, 8, 14, 15, 17, 21, **185-202**
Thomas, Norman, 302
Thomashevsky, Boris, 187
Thomson, Virgil, 34, 242, 293, 404, 420, 423, 448
  The Mother of Us All, 242
Three Centuries of Harpsichord Making, 148
Tokyo, Japan, 282
Tomas, Rudolf, 278
Toscanini, Arturo, 7, 97, 158, 176, 241, 256-57, 318-19, 364, 378
Tovey, Donald, 107
Tucker, Richard, 348
Tudor, David, 84

Ukrainian Music Institute, 230
Unions, 243, 252-60 *passim*, 283, 303, 346-47, 358-59, 367-68, 373, 399
Union Theological Seminary, 165, 166
University of Buffalo, 194
University of California at Los Angeles (UCLA), 14, 15, 116, 118, 119, 203, 401
University of Hartford, 274, 279
University of Illinois, Urbana, 383
University of Minnesota, 103, 394
University of Pennsylvania, 41
University of Southern California (USC), 14, 15, 17, 116-18, 189, 194, 214, 243, 244, 332-38, 395
United States Air Force, 81
United States Army, 98, 253, 265-66, 438
United States Navy, 98, 162, 240
Urban Gateways Program, 352
Ussachevsky, Vladimir, 48

Vallee, Rudy, 298
Varèse, Edgard, xii, 81, 83, 110-13, 189, 198, 406
  Arcana, 110-13
Varèse, Mrs. Louise, 111, 112
Vaughan Williams, Ralph, 305-7, 371-72
Vengerova, Isabelle, 130

Venice, 88, 110; Opera House, 197
Verdi, Giuseppi, 130, 292, 333-35, 356-57, 359, 366
Vickers, Jon, 356
Vienna, 13, 17, 43, 86, 101, 120-21, 214, 252, 360, 361, 365, 397
Vienna Philharmonic, 252, 364
The Village Gate, 302
Vincent, Edgar, 293
Vivaldi, Antonio, 91, 200, 431
Von Glehn, Alfred, 206
Von Karajan, Herbert, 305, 356, 364

Wagner, Richard, 118, 121, 127, 139, 157, 158, 333-34, 378, 383, 397
  Tristan und Isolde, 296, 359, 404, 454
Wagner, Roger, 368
Wallenstein, Alfred, 244
Walter, Bruno, 105, 118, 123, 165, 218, 221, 252, 319, 364-65
Washington, D.C., 47, 98, 240, 390, 424, 453
  Kennedy Center for the Performing Arts, 233
  Library of Congress, 165, 272, 273, 390
  National Gallery, 390
Weber, Ben, 55
Webern, Anton, 50, 81, 82, 86, 91, 118, 121, 279, 395, 397, 399, 400
  Six Pieces for Orchestra, 91
Webster, Margaret, 355-56
Weill, Kurt, 218, 219, 413
Weimar, Germany, 17, 207
Weisberg, Arthur, 119
  Contemporary Chamber Ensemble, 119
Weisgall, Hugo, 63, 64
Weiss, Peter, 424
Weissenberg, Alexis, 194
Welch, Roy Dickinson, 46
West Coast, 14, 15, 124
Westminister College Choir, 315
White, John Reeves, 403
Wieniawski, Henri, 131, 344
Williamson, John Finley, 315
Willis, Thomas, x, 7, 25, 26, 124, **411-32**, 445, 448
Wolff, Christian, 84
Wolf-Ferrari, 372
Wolpe, Stefan, x, 91, 119
Women in music, 19, 68-69, 162-67, 234-35, 239-40, 242, 247-50, 258-59, 285, 287, 296

Women in music (*Continued*)
  composers, 19, 68-69, 163, 249-50
  performers, 18-19, 162-63, 247, 249, 259
Wood, Elizabeth, 20
Woodworth, Wallace, 100
Works Progress Administration, (WPA), 42
World War II, 47, 81, 98, 108, 118, 147, 162,
    230, 253, 256, 412
Wuorinen, Charles, 385, 432
  Grand Union, 432

Yale University, 10, 162, 242, 384, 413, 417,
    428

Choral Society, 413
  Graduate School, 413, 428
Yates, Peter, 14, 119, 394-95, 398
Young Musicians Foundation (L.A.), 191, 400

Zefirelli, Franco, 356
Zelzer, Harry, 20, 22, **344-52**
Ziegler, Dorothy, 239
Zimbalist, Efrem, 213, 349
Zimmerman, Fred, 266, 372
Zuckerman, Wallace, 150
  Modern Harpsichords, 150
Zukofsky, Paul, 51, 54
Zweig, Fritz, 335

DATE DUE

MAY 1 3 '82			
GAYLORD			PRINTED IN U.S.A.